ADAPTING INTERNATIONAL CRIMINAL JUSTICE IN SOUTHEAST ASIA

How is international criminal law adapted across time and space? Which actors are involved and how do those actors seek to prosecute atrocity crimes? States in Southeast Asia exhibit a range of adapted approaches towards prosecuting international crimes. By examining engagement with international criminal justice especially in Cambodia, the Philippines, Indonesia, and Myanmar, this book offers a fresh and comprehensive approach to the study of international criminal law in the region. It nuances categories of the 'global' and 'local' and demonstrates how norms can be adapted in multiple spatial and temporal directions beyond the International Criminal Court. Further, it proposes a shift in the focus of those interested in international criminal justice towards recognising the opportunities and expertise presented by existing adaptive responses to international crimes. This book will appeal to scholars, practitioners, and advocates interested in international criminal law, international relations, transitional justice, civil society, and law in Southeast Asia.

EMMA PALMER is Lecturer at Griffith Law School, Griffith University, Australia. Palmer was awarded her PhD from University of New South Wales (UNSW) Law, Sydney, where she was a Research Assistant for two Australian Research Council (ARC) Discovery Projects focused on international criminal law. She has worked as a lawyer and analyst.

T0382281

ADAPTING INTERNATIONAL CRIMINAL JUSTICE IN SOUTHEAST ASIA

Beyond the International Criminal Court

EMMA PALMER

Griffith University

CAMBRIDGE
UNIVERSITY PRESS

CAMBRIDGE
UNIVERSITY PRESS

University Printing House, Cambridge CB2 8BS, United Kingdom

One Liberty Plaza, 20th Floor, New York, NY 10006, USA

477 Williamstown Road, Port Melbourne, VIC 3207, Australia

314-321, 3rd Floor, Plot 3, Splendor Forum, Jasola District Centre, New Delhi - 110025, India

103 Penang Road, #05-06/07, Visioncrest Commercial, Singapore 238467

Cambridge University Press is part of the University of Cambridge.

It furthers the University's mission by disseminating knowledge in the pursuit of education, learning and research at the highest international levels of excellence.

www.cambridge.org
Information on this title: www.cambridge.org/9781009305853
DOI: 10.1017/9781108669450

First published 2020
First paperback edition 2022

A catalogue record for this publication is available from the British Library

Library of Congress Cataloging in Publication data
Names: Palmer, Emma (Writer on law), author.
Title: Adapting international criminal justice in Southeast Asia: beyond the International Criminal
Court / Emma Palmer, Griffith University, Queensland.
Description: Cambridge, United Kingdom; New York, NY: Cambridge University Press, 2020. |
Based on author's thesis (doctoral – University of New South Wales, 2017) issued under title:
International criminal law in Southeast Asia: beyond the International Criminal Court. |
Includes bibliographical references and index.
Identifiers: LCCN 2019057479 (print) | LCCN 2019057480 (ebook) | ISBN 9781108483971
(hardback) | ISBN 9781108669450 (epub)
Subjects: LCSH: International crimes–Law and legislation–Southeast Asia. | International
criminal law–Southeast Asia. | Criminal justice, Administration of–Southeast Asia. |
Complementarity (International law)
Classification: LCC KNC982.I57 .P35 2020 (print) | LCC KNC982.I57 (ebook) | DDC 345.59–dc23
LC record available at https://lccn.loc.gov/2019057479
LC ebook record available at https://lccn.loc.gov/2019057480

ISBN 978-1-108-48397-1 Hardback
ISBN 978-1-009-30585-3 Paperback

For Hudson

CONTENTS

TABLES

ACKNOWLEDGEMENTS

The survivors and victims of violence must be heard first. The faces, voices, and experiences of individuals far more qualified to write this book infuse this work and I am filled with emotion, respect, humility, and gratitude.

I acknowledge the Traditional Custodians of the lands on which this book was written and pay my respect to the Elders, past and present, and extend that respect to all Aboriginal and Torres Strait Islander people.

I could not be more grateful for the support and encouraging atmosphere provided by Griffith University and UNSW Law throughout this research. My particular thanks are due to Sarah Williams and Andrew Byrnes, to whom I am greatly indebted. Many members of the UNSW Law Faculty also provided extensive and often crucial advice and revisions. In particular, I thank Fleur Johns, Lisa Toohey, Melissa Crouch, Daniel Joyce, Gabrielle Simm, and Ben Golder. I also thank Jenny Jarrett and Theunis Roux and acknowledge the financial assistance provided by the UNSW Faculty for this research, including from the HDR Fieldwork Support Fund, alongside the Australian Government's Postgraduate Award. I also received support from the Australian Human Rights Centre, especially from Louise Chappell, Andrea Durbach, and Diane Macdonald. Thanks also to my former UNSW colleagues Emily Waller, Bhatara Ibnu Reza, Rosemary Grey, Souheir Edelbi, Holly Blackmore, Aline Jaeckel, Jarra Hicks, Bernhard Ruben 'Fritz' Sumigar, Natalie Hodgson, Anna Huggins, Scarlet Wilcock, Gabriela Cuadrado, Shipra Chordia, Peter Blanchard, Lauren Butterly, Zsofia Korosy, Josh Pallas, and Sara Dehm. At Griffith Law School, thank you Susan Harris-Rimmer, Therese Wilson, Mary Keyes, Edwin Bikundo, Samuli Haataja, Pene Mathew, Don Anton, Olivera Simic, Kate van Doore, Kylie Burns, and everyone else for their encouragement and feedback. I also acknowledge the financial support of the Law Futures Centre and thank Melanie Davies. Thank you to Sara Davies, Caitlin Mollica, and the wider Griffith community – especially the Gender Equality Research network – for your support.

Too many individuals supported my research and fieldwork to be mentioned here. Those listed represent a broader range of individuals who invited me into their homes and businesses, provided information and contacts, and shared often deeply personal stories; I can never fully repay their time and trust. Thank you Zainal Abidin, Zaw Naing Wynn, Indri Saptaningrum, Nursyahbani Katjasungkana, Greg Heesom, Christoph Sperfeldt, Melanie Hyde, Debbie Stothard, Nick Cheesman, Kyaw Min San, Eugene Quah, Rebecca Lozado, Amielle del Rosario, Imelda Deinla, and Bill Pace. I am deeply grateful to all those who provided anonymous formal interviews, as well as the countless others who offered off-the-record comments, advice, meals, and stories, despite possible security risks and their incredibly busy lives involving much more important commitments.

Countless academics have provided inspiration throughout this thesis, many of whom are cited in this work. My deep thanks to Suzannah Linton and Robert Cryer first of all. I especially thank Gerry Simpson for organising the inaugural Australian International Criminal Law Workshop in 2013. Comments and suggestions provided by Gerry, John Tobin, Kiran Grewel, and Kevin Jon Heller during that workshop stimulated this research. In various forums many others including Hannah Woolaver, Yuyun Wahyuningrum, Tim McCormack, Frédéric Mégret, Holly Cullen, Philipp Kastner, Sean Richmond, Michelle Burgis-Kasthala, Jacqui True, Nicole George, Phil Orchard, Laura Shepherd, Kirsten Ainley, Sophie Rigney, Simon Chesterman, Rebecca Gidley, Maria Elander, Rachel Hughes, and Monique Cormier have provided feedback, encouragement, or even casual comments that nevertheless deeply influenced this book. Special thanks to Renée Jeffery, Priya Pillai, Christoph Sperfeldt, and Nicole Williams for their comments and to Clare Morrison, Michelle Simpkins and Joshua Saunders for their referencing support. I am grateful for the enthusiastic support and guidance of Joe Ng and Gemma Smith, editing by Catherine Rae, and the whole Cambridge University Press production team.

All errors of course are completely my own.

My parents Joanne and Jeremy deserve special gratitude for their constant support and encouragement (and childcare), as well as my siblings Georgina, Rohan, Sean and Lucy. Thank you also to Jess, Sonja, Claudia, Miriam, Ruby, Emily, Kirsty, India, and Laetitia.

Jesse: thank you for your patience; for putting up with my absence; and for constantly stabilising, uplifting, prioritising, and feeding us. Thank you for your unique perceptions and for embodying what matters and why.

Thank you to Hudson who grew with the book and lightened it all – and to all his wonderful carers who made it possible.

CASES, LAWS, AND TREATIES

Cases

Laws

Treaties

ABBREVIATIONS

ADHOC	Cambodian Human Rights and Development Association (*Association pour les droits de l'Homme et le développement au Cambodge*)
AICHR	ASEAN Intergovernmental Commission on Human Rights
AJAR	Asia Justice and Rights
ASEAN	Association of Southeast Asian Nations
ASP	Assembly of States Parties to the International Criminal Court
BIA	Bilateral Immunity Agreement
CARHRIHL	Comprehensive Agreement on Respect for Human Rights and International Humanitarian Law
CAVR	Commission for Reception, Truth, and Reconciliation
CHRAC	Cambodian Human Rights Action Committee
CICC	Coalition for the International Criminal Court
CNRP	Cambodia National Rescue Party
CoPP	Communist Party of the Philippines
CPP	Cambodian People's Party
CRC	Convention on the Rights of the Child
CRP	Community Reconciliation Process
CTF	Indonesia - East Timor Commission of Truth and Friendship
DC-Cam	Documentation Center of Cambodia
DK	The Democratic Kampuchea regime
DND	Department of National Defense, the Philippines
DPR	People's Representative Council/House of Representatives, Indonesia (*Dewan Perwakilan Rakyat Republik Indonesia*)
ECCC	Extraordinary Chambers in the Courts of Cambodia
ECCC Agreement	Agreement between the United Nations and the Royal Government of Cambodia concerning the Prosecution under Cambodian Law of Crimes Committed during the Period of Democratic Kampuchea, 6 June 2003
ECCC Law	Law on the Establishment of the Extraordinary Chambers in the Courts of Cambodia for the Prosecution of Crimes Committed during the Period of Democratic Kampuchea, 27 October 2004

ELSAM	Institute for Policy Research and Advocacy (*Lembagi Studi dan Advokasi Masyarakat*)
EPJUST I and II	European Union–Philippines Justice Support Programmes I and II
EU	European Union
FIDH	International Federation for Human Rights (*Fédération internationale des ligues des droits de l'homme*)
FUNCINPEC	National United Front for an Independent, Neutral, Peaceful, and Cooperative Cambodia (*Front uni national pour un Cambodge indépendant, neutre, pacifique et coopératif*)
GONGO	Government Organized Non-Government Organisation
ICC	International Criminal Court
ICRC	International Committee of the Red Cross
ICSCICC	Indonesian Civil Society Coalition for the ICC
ICTJ	International Center for Transitional Justice
ICTR	International Criminal Tribunal for Rwanda
ICTY	International Criminal Tribunal for the former Yugoslavia
IHL Act	An Act Defining and Penalizing Crimes against International Humanitarian Law, Genocide and Other Crimes against Humanity, Organizing Jurisdiction, Designating Special Courts, and for Related Purposes, Republic of the Philippines Act No. 9851
IKOHI	Indonesian Association of Families of the Disappeared (*Ikatan Keluarga Orang Hilang Indonesia*)
ILC	International Law Commission
IMTFE	International Military Tribunal for the Far East
IPT	International People's Tribunal for 1965
JSMP	Justice System Monitoring Programme
KKPK	Coalition for Justice and Truth Seeking (*Koalisis Keadilan dan Pengungkapan Kebenaran*)
Komnas Perempuan	National Commission on Violence Against Women (*Komisi Nasional Anti Kekerasan Terhadap Perempuan*)
Komnas-HAM	National Commission on Human Rights, Indonesia (*Komisi Nasional Hak Asasi Manusia Republik Indonesia*)
KontraS	Commission for Disappearances and Victims of Violence (*Komisi untuk Orang Hilang dan Korban Tindak Kekerasan*)
KPN	National Commission of Inquiry (*Komisi Penyelidik Nasional*)
KPP-HAM	Commission on the Human Rights Violations in East Timor
KPTKA	Independent Commission for the Investigation of Violence in Aceh (*Komisi Independen Pengusutan Tindak Kekerasan di Aceh*)
KUHAP	Criminal Procedures Code, Indonesia (*Kitab Undang-Undang Hukum Acara Pidana*)

KUHDT	Military Disciplinary Law, Indonesia (*Kitab Undang-Undang Hukum Disiplin Tentara*)
KUHP	Criminal Law Code, Indonesia (*Kitab Undang-Undang Hukum Pidana*)
KUHPM	Military Criminal Law Code, Indonesia (*Kitab Undang-Undang Hukum Pidana Militer*)
Lao PDR	Lao People's Democratic Republic
LICADHO	Cambodian League for the Promotion and Defense of Human Rights (*La Ligue Cambodgienne pour la Promotion et la Défense des Droits de l'Homme*)
LPSK	Institute for the Protection of Witnesses and Victims (*Lembaga Perlindungan Saksi dan Korban*)
MILF	Moro Islamic Liberation Front
MNHRC	Myanmar National Human Rights Commission
MNLF	Moro National Liberation Front
MPR	People's Consultative Assembly, Indonesia (*Majelis Permusyawaratan Rakyat Republik Indonesia*)
ND-Burma	Network for Human Right Documentation – Burma
NDF	National Democratic Front
NGO	non-governmental organisation
NHRI	National Human Rights Institution
NLD	National League for Democracy
NPA	New People's Army
PAHRA	Philippine Alliance of Human Rights Advocates
PCICC	Philippine Coalition for the International Criminal Court
PGA	Parliamentarians for Global Action
PKI	Communist Party of Indonesia (*Partai Komunis Indonesia*)
PRK	People's Republic of Kampuchea
PRT	People's Revolutionary Tribunal
SELDA	Association of Ex-Detainees against Detention and Arrest (*Samahan ng Ex-detainees Laban sa Detensyon at Aresto*)
Special Panels	Special Panels in the District Court in Dili
TNI	Indonesian National Army (*Tentara Nasional Indonesia*)
TRC	Truth and Reconciliation Commission
TWAIL	Third World Approaches to International Law
UN	United Nations
UNFFM	United Nations Independent International Fact-Finding Mission on Myanmar
UNTAC	United Nations Transitional Authority in Cambodia
UNTAET	United Nations Transitional Administration in East Timor
UPR	Universal Periodic Review

USDP	Union Solidarity and Development Party
US	United States
VOC	United [Dutch] East India Company (*Vereenigde Oost-Indische Compagnie*)
YLBHI	Indonesian Legal Aid Foundation (*Yayasan Lembaga Bantuan Hukum Indonesia*)

1

Localising International Criminal Justice in Southeast Asia

After all, *international justice should not be regarded as a concept foreign to this part of the world* ... All Asian countries, without exception, are states parties to the four Geneva Conventions, and have thereby agreed to criminalise the grave breaches defined in those treaties, which form a major part of the war crimes contained in the Rome Statute, and to prosecute the perpetrators ... However, some persistent obstacles remain, often due to misunderstandings ... Clarifying these matters is crucial for *progress* to occur[1]

...we can't continue with this ... one *dimensional* kind of: bring it to court and what justice means is legal justice. Justice ... can be achieved only ... through a combination of different interventions and measures[2]

...we talk about all these things and then we ask people to also remember that there is no set *chronology or order* for how things should happen'[3]

...Rome was not built in one day. True indeed. But it can also be said that Rome began its decay when it failed to be cognizant of the changing needs of the times[4]

1.1   International Criminal Justice in Southeast Asia

Legal responses to atrocity crimes do not only result from international norms being transmitted to receptive 'locals'.[5] Instead, they are initiated and modified by a range of actors who adapt arguments and persist with

---

[1] (Song, 2016: 8)
[2] Interview I14, emphasis added. See Appendix B for a list of interviewees, who have been kept anonymous to protect those who did not wish to be identified.
[3] Interview M1, emphasis added.
[4] (Republic of the Philippines, 2013: 2).
[5] 'Local' represents a subjective viewpoint and is used in this book as shorthand for a cluster of possible such perspectives (recognising that homogeneous localities rarely, if ever, exist in communities of intersecting identities), but normally refers to individuals acting within states (see Section 1.3.2, this chapter; Chapter 7; Shaw & Waldorf, 2010).

advocacy efforts over time, across different spaces, and within changing circumstances. This has been the case in some states in Southeast Asia,[6] where serious violations of human rights that are alleged to amount to international crimes continue to be perpetrated, often with impunity, but also alongside the development of laws and mechanisms for prosecuting such violence.

From 2016, President Rodrigo Duterte's government was implicated in the deaths of thousands of alleged drug users and dealers within the Philippines, which forms the subject of a preliminary examination by the International Criminal Court (ICC) (ICC Office of the Prosecutor, 2018). Since 2000, hundreds of thousands have been forcibly evicted from their lands in Cambodia (Global Diligence, 2014) and elsewhere in the region (GRAIN, 2015). Between August 2017 and 2018, reports indicated that 'over 725,000' Rohingya men, women, and children, fled violence in Myanmar (Independent International Fact-Finding Mission on Myanmar, 2018: 751). In Indonesia, the government continues to fail to live up to promises to respond to serious human rights abuses, including the killings of possibly a million individuals in 1965 (Cribb, 2009; Komnas-HAM, 2012).

How can perpetrators of such shocking violence be brought to justice? International criminal justice is concerned with prosecuting international crimes, including genocide, crimes against humanity, and war crimes, usually based on laws replicating the Rome Statute of the International Criminal Court[7] and generally with some international involvement. One possibility is therefore to pursue prosecutions for such crimes before the ICC, which is located in The Hague in the Netherlands. However, among other jurisdictional and admissibility barriers, just two of the eleven states in Southeast Asia – Cambodia and Timor-Leste – are parties to the Rome Statute of the ICC, which would provide one source for ICC jurisdiction over such crimes. This is despite the Rome Statute's wide acceptance by 123 state parties worldwide at the end of 2019. The Philippines was a party from 2011, but withdrew from the Rome Statute in 2018, effective from March 2019, while Malaysia acceded in the same month, but then withdrew its accession.

---

[6] While 'Southeast Asia' can be considered a constructed concept, for the purposes of this book it includes the eleven nations falling within the United Nations (UN) category of South-Eastern Asia: Brunei Darussalam, Cambodia, Indonesia, The People's Democratic Republic of Laos (Lao PDR), Malaysia, Myanmar, the Philippines, Singapore, Thailand, Timor-Leste, and Vietnam (the ASEAN members plus Timor-Leste).

[7] Adopted 17 July 1998, entered into force 1 July 2002.

Scholars have identified some reasons why states in the region have not joined the ICC. These include a fear of 'harassment suits' from opponents, international (United States) pressure, insufficient domestic infrastructure or legislative support (Toon, 2004), the presence of ongoing conflicts, and a preference for addressing human rights abuses within domestic jurisdictions (Freeland, 2013). This under-representation of the region within the ICC system led to concerns that Asia was 'seriously lagging behind in international criminal law' (Song, 2011: 2).

International criminal law scholars have recognised that a version of 'international criminal justice', involving the use of 'international' or 'internationalised' institutions to prosecute individuals for international crimes might be considered 'normalised' (Mégret, 2005; Epstein, 2014). The Rome Statute and ICC represent an important legal institutional component of this idea. In particular, ratifying the Rome Statute is a significant measure for states to give effect to the 'norms' – or intersubjective beliefs about what is 'appropriate' behaviour (Finnemore & Sikkink, 1998) – promoted by international criminal law. As a result, some have argued that the 'nations of Asia must ratify the Rome Statute and become full members in the international pursuit of justice against war criminals' (Goldstone, 2011: 19). Others argue that '[e]xpanding the role of Asian countries [in the ICC] is highly important to building a truly international system of criminal justice' (Kim, 2017: 271).

From that perspective, by not joining the ICC, the states in Southeast Asia appear to have rejected a '*norm of international criminal justice*' that – while contested – promotes securing individual criminal accountability via prosecuting international crimes, perhaps with international involvement, including through ratifying the Rome Statute and incorporating its provisions into domestic law (Clarke, 2009; Sikkink & Kim, 2013; Mégret, 2014; Kim, 2017). While international criminal justice arguably comprises a collection of norms, 'norm' is used here to capture this relatively narrow, but contested, definition and focus for international criminal justice. Although international law recognises individual criminal responsibility for other serious crimes, such as terrorism or significant drug or environmental offences (Ratner et al., 2009: 10), the Rome Statute provides the ICC with jurisdiction over crimes against humanity, war crimes, genocide, and the crime of aggression. The developing norm favouring individual prosecutions before international tribunals has focused upon the first of these three crimes in particular

(Sikkink 2011b: 16).[8] This book considers the mechanisms involved in prosecuting these 'international crimes' in four states in Southeast Asia: Cambodia, Indonesia, the Philippines, and Myanmar. It is important to note that the reference to Southeast Asia in the title of the book is not meant to indicate that these countries somehow are representative of that region. Rather, they have been selected to demonstrate varied approaches to international criminal justice *within* Southeast Asia (see Section 1.4). The book draws on a range of theoretical approaches that supplement what has been (arguably problematically) termed a 'mainstream' (Weber, 2014; see d'Aspremont, 2016: 627–8) or 'first wave' (Acharya, 2014: 185) constructivist suggestion: states might internalise international norms through interaction between *spatially* differentiated (international and local) actors and ideas (see Riles, 1995; Hughes, 2008; Buckley-Zistel, 2016) over *time* (Craven et al., 2007; Koskenniemi, 2012; Simpson, 2014; Zimmermann, 2016), which should encourage the 'external' idea (once it has emerged) to flow in the *direction* of receiving 'locals' (Acharya, 2004) – who ideally implement it in law and practice. That sort of understanding implies a linear path where, with the socialising influence of 'civil society'[9] and other states, governments might progress towards accepting a norm of international criminal justice, including by ratification and implementation of the Rome Statute or (at least) the adoption of domestic laws and practices that closely replicate the international model. The withdrawal of the Philippines and in/out approach of Malaysia in 2019 already confound that story, but there is more to tell.

States in Southeast Asia have had significant engagement with the concept of international criminal law. Most Southeast Asian countries

---

[8] The ICC has jurisdiction over aggression only after 17 July 2018, though 'crimes against peace' were prosecuted in the region following World War II. This book therefore focuses on crimes against humanity, genocide, and war crimes, though there is domestic legislation that might apply to aggression, such as 'crimes against peace' in Article 421 of Vietnam's Criminal Code, No. 100/2015/QH13, 27 November 2015, amended and supplemented by Law No. 12/2017/QH14 or via other criminal code provisions concerning aggression against the state. Southeast Asian states strongly supported including the crime of aggression during the negotiations concerning the Rome Statute.

[9] 'Civil society' refers to professional associations, community groups, women's organisations, trade unions, 'humanitarian aid organizations, associations of survivors and family members of victims, human rights and development NGOs, lawyers, academic, mental health and medical associations, and religious organizations' (Roht-Arriaza, 2002: 98). It does not typically refer to political groups, though there may be close relationships between political organisations, the government, religious groups, and various civil society actors, all of whom may work closely with particular media platforms (Jeffery, Kent, & Wallis, 2017).

that have experienced conflict in recent decades have held related trials (Payne & Sikkink, 2014). There have also been historic international crime trials, particularly after World War II (Sellars, 2015). All eleven Southeast Asian states are parties to the Geneva Conventions,[10] although only seven have ratified the Genocide Convention,[11] six Additional Protocol I, and five Additional Protocol II (see Appendix A).[12] As of June 2019, just two states remained Rome Statute parties (Cambodia and Timor-Leste), but six had legislation criminalising two or more of the crimes of genocide, crimes against humanity, and war crimes.[13] With two exceptions,[14] all Southeast Asian states sent delegations to the 1998 Diplomatic Conference that finalised the ICC's Rome Statute. The participating states supported an independent court that respected the primacy of national jurisdictions,[15] but mostly argued that the Court should have jurisdiction over aggression or other crimes beyond those eventually included.[16] Singapore, in particular, played a significant role in the negotiations (Struett, 2008: 128). Brunei Darussalam, Indonesia, The People's Democratic Republic of Laos (Lao PDR), the Philippines, and Thailand then all contributed to the Preparatory Commission for the ICC held in early 1999, which developed the Court's Rules of Procedure and Evidence and Elements of Crimes. There was therefore some regional engagement with the process of establishing the ICC, although states did not necessarily have their core concerns reflected in the final version of the Statute.

Since the Rome negotiations, the region has experienced a spectrum of approaches to international criminal justice, including the establishment of international(ised) criminal institutions such as the Extraordinary

---

[10] Geneva Conventions I–IV, adopted 12 August 1949, entered into force 21 October 1950.

[11] Convention on the Prevention and Punishment of the Crime of Genocide, adopted 9 December 1948, entered into force 12 January 1951 (Genocide Convention).

[12] Protocol Additional to the Geneva Conventions of 12 August 1949, and relating to the protection of victims of international armed conflicts, adopted 8 June 1977, entered into force 7 December 1978 (Additional Protocol I); Protocol Additional to the Geneva Conventions of 12 August 1949, and relating to the protection of victims of non-international armed conflicts, adopted 8 June 1977, entered into force 7 December 1978 (Additional Protocol II).

[13] Cambodia, the Philippines, Timor-Leste (all have been Rome Statute parties), as well as Vietnam, Indonesia, and Singapore.

[14] Cambodia, which faced resource constraints, and Myanmar, which was relatively isolated at the time (see Chapter 5).

[15] (United Nations, 1998): 73, 200 (Indonesia), 109 (Malaysia), 106, 194 (Thailand), 111 (Vietnam), 82 (The Philippines).

[16] Ibid.: 124 (Singapore regarding chemical weapons), 165 (Indonesia), 176, 291 (Thailand), 178, 287 (Vietnam), 292, 340 (The Philippines).

Chambers in the Courts of Cambodia (ECCC) and Special Panels in the District Court in Dili (Special Panels); Rome Statute ratifications; and the adoption of domestic legislation addressing international crimes – as well as other transitional justice procedures. This suggests that regional approaches to international criminal justice may be more complex than the low (and fluctuating) level the Rome Statute ratification suggests. It also presents a different question than has been the focus of literature addressing international criminal law in Southeast Asia to date. Rather than analysing specific legal mechanisms (such as the ECCC), or asking *why* states have *not* ratified with the Rome Statute, this book asks: *how* have actors in Southeast Asia engaged with 'international criminal justice' by adopting laws and establishing institutions to prosecute international crimes, including beyond the Rome Statute framework? This specific issue is yet to be addressed,[17] despite its importance for those interested in how to respond to atrocities in the region.

This book has several objectives. It analyses how four states in Southeast Asia have developed laws and institutions for prosecuting international crimes. It seeks to shift discussions about international criminal justice beyond debates about the ICC, by emphasising the complex ways in which actors adapt conceptions of international criminal justice. It therefore assesses how actors in states, international organisations, and civil society have interacted and adapted ideas about international criminal justice. Using the case studies of Cambodia, the Philippines, Indonesia, and Myanmar, it demonstrates how the mechanisms for prosecuting international crimes across these states challenge assumptions about how norms are diffused over time, spatial designations between 'local' and 'international' ideas and actors, and the direction in which ideas and influences evolve across the world. The potential influence of a range of actors located in diverse and shifting spaces must be taken into account when analysing international criminal justice. This argument presents several practical implications for those interested in responding to international crimes in Southeast Asia and beyond.

1.2 The Norm of International Criminal Justice

The idea that individuals should be prosecuted for committing international crimes before international criminal tribunals has gained

---

[17] For an overview of transitional justice approaches in certain states across the wider Asia-Pacific region, see (Jeffery and Kim, 2014; Linton, 2010).

increasing popularity in recent decades (Struett, 2008). Still, the idea of placing limits upon violent conduct, even in war, has ancient and diverse roots, including from within Asia. From an ancient law against cannibalism in the Shun Period, to the Methods of the Sima and the Wei Liaozi military commentary of the fourth century BCE, and the writings of Sun Tzu, Chinese thinkers placed constraints upon waging war (Daqun, 2012: 351). The Laws of Manu in India also 'laid down some of the earliest foundations of humanitarian rules for armed conflict' (Song, 2013: 211).

Following World War II, trials in Nuremberg, Tokyo, and elsewhere in the world (including in the Asia-Pacific region) developed important principles of international criminal law. International criminal law shifted the historic emphasis of international law on state responsibility towards a focus upon holding individuals accountable for their crimes, often with international involvement and in post-conflict settings. The approach of prosecuting crimes before tribunals that were in some way separated from domestic courts gathered momentum alongside the establishment of International Criminal Tribunals for the former Yugoslavia and Rwanda, and tribunals to address crimes in Sierra Leone and Lebanon, among other places. This trend, or 'norm cascade', has been described as now being 'embodied' in the establishment of the ICC, its principle of complementarity, and the ratification of the Rome Statute by states across the world (Schiff, 2008: 3, 257; Struett, 2008: 24). It is also said to have contributed to a 'justice cascade' leading to further domestic prosecutions for human rights violations (Sikkink, 2011b).

An extensive field of 'transitional justice' has developed alongside international criminal laws and institutions. Like 'international criminal justice', transitional justice is a contested concept. Generally speaking, transitional justice 'can be defined as the conception of justice associated with periods of political change, characterized by legal responses to confront the wrongdoings of repressive predecessor regimes' (Teitel, 2003: 69). Transitional justice may be offered as a 'toolkit' for responding to mass atrocities – one tool being international criminal law prosecutions (Harris-Rimmer, 2010a: 19; Shaw & Waldorf, 2010: 3). Arguably, the 'ICC is seen as the key enforcement mechanism' for transitional justice (Campbell, 2014: 55). However, truth commissions, amnesties, civil society forums such as peoples' tribunals, lustration, security sector reform, and other community reconciliation and memorial projects are all transitional justice mechanisms (Jeffery & Kim, 2014 :1). Therefore, international criminal law forms one aspect of a broader set of transitional justice approaches.

By contrast, terms such as 'international criminal justice', 'international criminal law', or 'international criminal accountability' often refer to substantive legal principles, such as specific crimes, modes of responsibility, or trial procedures. They also encompass various ideas about the need to 'end impunity' for atrocity crimes, normally through criminal procedures – possibly delivered by the ICC, or with international involvement (Boas, 2012). This version of international criminal justice, or *'the norm of international criminal justice'*, promotes the investigation and prosecution of (and potential convictions for) international crimes with reference to international institutions and laws.

One way that states can demonstrate that they embrace international criminal justice is by ratifying the Rome Statute (Simmons & Danner, 2010; Goodliffe et al., 2012). However, international criminal law extends beyond the Rome Statute and has overlapping and shifting boundaries drawing on domestic and various areas of international law (Ratner et al., 2009: 10). Indeed, its intersections with different legal fields arguably 'constitute a rather uncomfortable combination of inherently different types of law' (van Sliedregt, 2012: 8).

The content of any international criminal justice 'norm' has also been contested.[18] Third World Approaches to International Law (TWAIL) scholars have drawn attention to the importance of colonial and post-colonial experiences, including those of individuals throughout the broader 'Third World' (rather than just states), in understanding and evaluating international law (Anghie & Chimni, 2003; Burgis-Kasthala, 2016). Critical international criminal law literature has also challenged progressive narratives of the history of international criminal law, with 'wariness in regard to absolute moral sentiments which emanate from [international criminal law's] centre, The Hague' (Schwöbel, 2014: 11).

Others have argued that the norm of international criminal justice has particular content, for example, the requirement of prosecutions (or at least genuine investigations that might lead to them) and an emphasis upon the Rome Statute text, which might constrain the possibility of developing alternative approaches to international crimes beyond the ICC framework (de Vos, 2015; Steer, 2014). Indeed, there has been a growing focus on the relationship between international criminal law and domestic legal systems (Roht-Arriaza, 2013; Woolaver, 2019), including through the lens of 'pluralism' (Stahn & van den Herik, 2012; van

---

[18] Contestation is used in a general way in this book to suggest the action of disputing, opposing, or arguing.

Sliedregt & Vasiliev, 2014). A pluralist perspective suggests that international and domestic approaches to international criminal law are not inherently conflicting, but are dynamic and able to 'co-exist as part of the fabric of a single, coherent system' (Steer, 2014: 56). This same period has also seen the proliferation of theoretical 'approaches'[19] to international criminal law including (despite early divisions between the two 'fields': Koh, 1997: 2615–16; Bederman, 2000), with reference to constructivist international relations scholarship (Slaughter et al., 1998; Bederman, 2000).

1.3 The Socialisation and Localisation of the International Criminal Justice Norm

A constructivist approach is concerned with identities and the role of social norms – such as the importance of ending impunity for international crimes – including legal norms such as substantive case law and treaties, in transforming state behaviour (Ruggie, 1998; Wendt, 1999; Finnemore, 2000; Kratochwil, 2001). A facet of the broad array of constructivist perspectives identifies relationships between widely held intersubjective ideas (norms), international law, and legal compliance. One prominent branch includes *socialisation* and process-oriented frameworks for explaining why states might 'obey' laws and change their practices. Generally speaking, socialisation approaches aim to explain how states might be persuaded to adopt and internalise particular norms through communication and engagement, including through negotiating, ratifying, and implementing treaties. Such frameworks, for instance those proffered by Koh (1997) and Goodman and Jinks (2013), may focus upon or promote the adoption of particular norms, such as encouraging states to comply with international human rights laws. As a result, some constructivist approaches are oriented towards 'moral goals' and specific policy recommendations, for example, that states implement certain norms promoted by treaties and international law-making practices in domestic law or policies (see Price, 2008).

Other scholars also draw on constructivist approaches, but emphasise power relationships and may take a Marxist, feminist, or 'Third World' perspective, or distance themselves from 'constructivist' terminology

---

[19] 'Approach', 'framework', 'perspective', and 'theory' are used interchangeably in this book to describe different theoretical structures and methods for understanding phenomena, including the diffusion and reconstruction of norms.

altogether (Price & Reus-Smit, 1998; Anghie & Chimni, 2003; Epstein, 2014). For example, post-colonial scholars critique such 'mainstream' or 'first wave' constructivist literature by pointing to the 'norm diffusion' embodied by colonialism, which 'bore all the trappings of "appropriate-ness"' (Finnemore & Sikkink, 1998; Epstein, 2014: 301), as well as the ways that both liberalism and constructivism favour universalisms (Epstein, 2014: 298). Some have emphasised the 'value-laden quality of criminal law' and the significance of power relationships in exercising justice (Abbott, 1999: 375).

In the human rights realm, constructivist transnational advocacy scholars have developed multilayered theoretical frameworks for under-standing legal obligation. Margaret E. Keck and Kathryn Sikkink (1998) used a 'boomerang' model to explain how transnational advocacy net-works of NGOs, states, and intergovernmental organisations work to encourage states to protect human rights. Thomas Risse and Sikkink (1999) proffered a 'spiral' framework to explain how such networks influence the integration of human rights norms through stages of adaptation, moral discourse, and institutionalisation. These sophisticated frameworks have been further contributed to by an array of literature suggesting that norms can be 'vernacularized' (Levitt & Merry, 2009), contested (Wiener, 2014), translated (Zimmermann, 2017), 'localized' (Acharya, 2004, 2014), and developed through processes such as 'circulation' (Acharya, 2013: 469). Rather than focusing upon how norms might be accepted by particular 'local' actors through socialisation, the *localisation* framework (explained further shortly) considers how ideas might themselves be restructured by 'local' actors (Acharya, 2004: 251): 'In constructivist perspectives on socialization, norm diffusion is viewed as the result of adaptive behavior in which local practices are made consistent with an external idea. Localization, by contrast, describes a process in which external ideas are simultaneously adapted to meet local practices.'

Thus, 'constructivism' is diverse and difficult to define. However, in general, constructivism 'rejects a simple law/power dichotomy, arguing instead that legal rules and norms operate by changing interests and thus reshaping the purposes for which power is exercised' (Slaughter et al., 1998: 381). While 'the field of international criminal justice has been largely insulated from constructivist analysis of justice processes' (Ullrich, 2016: 567), socialisation approaches would tend to suggest that states can be encouraged to internalise particular understandings of norms such as 'international criminal justice' through communication and engagement, including via joining treaties like the Rome Statute. Alternatively, they would suggest that states reject norms where they conflict with local practices, or might adopt them only for symbolic or rhetorical purposes, with little intention of implementing them – perhaps reflecting an 'action-identity' gap [Davies, 2013], 'institutionalization-implementation' gap [Betts & Orchard, 2014], 'decoupling' [Goodman & Jinks, 2008], or a form of 'ritualism' [Charlesworth & Larking, 2015]. These types of constructivist frameworks are useful for analysing states' approaches towards prosecuting international crimes. However, scholars, including other constructivists, have increasingly drawn attention to and critiqued certain assumptions about how norms are adopted over time, the location of ideas and actors (space), and the direction of influence (directionality).

1.3.1   Time

Those seeking to explain why the spread of international criminal justice might have stalled in the Asia region have been led to ask, 'What are the main factors inhibiting the other Southeast Asian states from accepting the [ICC]?' (Toon, 2004: 219) or to discuss 'possible reasons for this reluctance on the part of Asia-Pacific countries to embrace the Court' (Freeland, 2013: 1031) – and to then address such concerns Kapur, 2013; (Findlay, 2014; Schuldt, 2015; Takemura, 2018). That is, to consider how these states could progress from rejecting international criminal justice towards accepting it over time.

Scholars have identified various aspects of time that are relevant for analysing international criminal law. For instance, the norm of international criminal justice might be presented as arising from an accumulation of events progressing from certain spaces and times. It is common to describe international criminal law as evolving from the Treaty of Versailles (or trial of von Hagenbach, or earlier – as in Section 1.2), to Nuremberg and Tokyo from 1945 to 1948, the ICTY's establishment, and Rome in 1998, as if this involves an evolution.[20] A second temporal aspect is suggested by Alexander Hinton's argument that 'implicit within transitional justice time is a highly normative concept of past and present' (Hinton, 2013: 87), that

---

[20] Whereas the 'history of war crimes law can be comprehended as a series of undulations between recourse to the administration of local justice and grand gestures towards the international rule of law' (Simpson, 2007: 33).

'suggests a teleology of movement from a contaminated pre-state' of violence 'to a purified post-state of a modern liberal democratic order', with a transitional justice mechanism 'serving as the mechanism of change' (Hinton, 2013: 94). This perspective accentuates flawed assumptions about the effects of transnational justice, including prosecutions, upon societies and the institution of democracy (Gidley, 2019).

A third aspect concerns the evolution of the international criminal justice norm. Some scholars have argued that (particularly 'mainstream' socialisation) constructivist approaches can seem to imply that states' adoption of international legal obligations proceeds along 'a linear scale from resistance to norm adoption' (Zimmermann, 2016: 102), beginning with discourse, followed by the adoption of a global international legal regime, and ending with the internalisation of the relevant principles. This has also been described as an 'institutionalization "line" that exists on a spectrum, from signing and ratifying international treaties at one end, to the adoption of domestic legislation, policies, and even standard operating procedures, at the other end' (Betts & Orchard, 2014: 5). A related perspective is evident in one narrative of international criminal law that presents the ICC as 'not simply a high point of international criminal law but something of an end-point, too (the domestic finally ceding to the international)' (Simpson, 2007: 34).

However, it is important to note that constructivists *do* recognise that socialisation is not a simple process and even that 'the spread of norms based on persuasion by good arguments is a highly improbable occurrence', as it takes place within diverse structural contexts (Deitelhoff & Zimmermann, 2014: 20). In reality, states' public positions of support for a norm may differ from actual actions within that state – for instance, states may ratify international law treaties without enforcing their provisions domestically. International relations approaches suggest that this might occur because states lack capacity to implement the international norm (Goodman & Jinks, 2008); enforcement is not in states' interests and the ratification was purely instrumental (Risse & Sikkink, 1999: 12); or there is a lack of 'norm entrepreneurs' able to 'vernacularise' or translate the norms in a manner that renders them acceptable to local audiences (Finnemore & Sikkink, 1998; Levitt & Merry, 2009). Moreover, it has been recognised that treaty ratification alone is insufficient to lead to state compliance with the treaty norms, such as the protection and promotion of human rights (Risse, 2017: 137).

Still, depending on the normative perspective of the author, the hope and expectation of 'mainstream' constructivist scholarship in particular was that some form of socialisation will lead states to change their practices for the better. Thus, Risse and Sikkink 'do not assume evolutionary progress toward norm implementation' (1999: 34), but, more subtly, argue that even 'instrumental adoption of human rights norms, if it leads to domestic structural change such as redemocratization, sets into motion a process of identity transformation so that norms initially adopted for instrumental reasons, are later maintained for reasons of belief and identity' (Risse & Sikkink, 1999: 10). If this process towards acceptance does not occur, it may be due to a range of factors, such as the type of government 'regime' and the social vulnerability of its leaders (Risse, 2017). As Lisbeth Zimmermann (2016: 103) observes, '[w]hen viewed through the norm socialization lens, the outcomes of norm diffusion [other than acceptance] can only ever be described as deficient, never as different'. In a similar way, international criminal law obligation may be cast as ideally evolving through socialisation towards legal adoption via ratification of the Rome Statute, the implementation of international criminal laws, and internalisation of these norms within domestic contexts (de Vos, 2015; Zimmermann, 2016: 103).

This book concentrates on this third aspect of time and international criminal law: the hope and anticipation of linear progress from rejection towards acceptance of the norm of international criminal justice over time, unless a state rejects or stalls in its 'progress'. To do so, it draws on some more recent constructivist arguments that norms can be adapted, translated, vernacularised, or, to use the terminology explored shortly, 'localised'. For instance, a chronological account told today of Cambodia's progression from ratifying the Rome Statute, to adopting domestic international crimes legislation, to prosecuting international crimes at the ECCC replicates a familiar, linear plot promoted since, arguably, the 1998 Rome Conference. However, this perspective limits the opportunity to explore how states (including Cambodia) might take alternative routes towards enforcing international criminal law, or why state and non-state actors might prioritise other goals. The case studies in this book challenge notions of temporal progress. They also suggest that historic experiences persistently shape contemporary laws and legal enforcement in important and dynamic ways.

1.3.2   Space

Analysing the spread of international criminal justice, especially through Rome Statute ratification across the world, requires a *spatial* awareness.

On one hand, related advocacy often appears non-grounded, taking place through online press releases, petitions, and social media campaigns. The Rome Statute also arguably promotes a vision of international criminal justice that defies spatial boundaries. It addresses crimes which are 'of concern to the international community as a whole' – and of which, in a sense, we are all presented as victims (Kendall & Nouwen, 2013). On the other hand, there is increasing recognition that international criminal justice, or at least international law, comprises aspects of locality, perspective, or geography (Riles, 1995; Mahmud, 2007; Hughes, 2015; Buckley-Zistel, 2016). Crimes are perpetrated, documented and prosecuted by courts in specific locations with geographic jurisdictions; court rooms physically divide participants from observers (Buckley-Zistel, 2016: 19); perpetrators and survivors of international crimes (and those who are both) reside in particular countries; national laws are made in capital cities; and protests take place in carefully selected locations. Colonial histories may also have enduring effects on legal systems, national identities, and economic contexts (Mahmud, 2007). Further, the Rome Statute's principle of complementarity rests upon a distinction between domestic territorial jurisdictions and the ICC, to be resolved via the operation of that legal principle.

Legal geographers have argued that law shares a relationship with notions of space, including via the legal designation of boundaries, such as between the 'public' and 'private', as well as through the ways in which 'legal spaces are embedded in broader social and political claims' (Blomley, 1994: xi; Bennett & Layard, 2015). 'Space',[21] from this perspective, not only suggests a physical area or expanse (including particular places), but is also constructed within, and can constrain, social and power structures (Ruggie, 1998; see Bennett & Layard, 2015). A spatial awareness recognises that 'even the initial characterization of [an] issue must take place from the situated viewpoint of one system or another' (Riles, 1995; Knop et al., 2012: 634). Different actors may take different positions as to whether a given matter pertains to international criminal justice (or, for instance, human rights, development, or conflict resolution) depending on their background, training, and location. For example, this author's background influenced the focus of this research upon international criminal justice, the choice to approach this topic with reference to

---

[21] This book does not engage with the relationships and differences between 'space', 'place', and 'scale', but recognises that 'place' is often understood as a 'space' with a particular subjective meaning.

particular international relations frameworks, and its analysis (Burgis-Kasthala, 2016). Spatial considerations are important for this book as it explores responses to international criminal justice within certain places – states in Southeast Asia – and tests a theoretical approach that explores interactions between 'local' and 'international' norms and actors.

Scholars often identify different 'levels' (Goodale, 2006; Björkdahl et al., 2016) of engagement with norms such as international criminal justice, including 'international', 'regional', and 'local' ideas and actors. Constructivist scholarship has demonstrated the important role of domestic and transnational advocacy networks and 'norm entrepreneurs' in diffusing norms (Keck & Sikkink, 1998). International relations scholar Amitav Acharya (2012a: 1) has drawn attention to the especially important role of 'credible local actors' and 'the divide between transnational actors who operate across continents and time zones and local actors ... who are situated within single time zones and marginalized locations'. These divisions between local and international actors highlight the importance of perspective and may foreground colonial experiences (Mahmud, 2007; Epstein, 2014). Some scholars have also promoted the potential benefits of customary or traditional ('local') justice measures (Shaw & Waldorf, 2010: 4; Jeffrey & Kim, 2014: 17). In particular, postcolonial, 'anti-liberal' (Buckley-Zistel, 2016) and anthropology scholars have demonstrated how international criminal justice mechanisms can fail to integrate local concerns and even cause harm (e.g. Clarke, 2009; Drexler, 2010; contributions in Shaw et al., 2010). In contrast, customary approaches to dispute resolution and reconciliation may offer advantages, including flexibility and legitimacy, and still provide some accountability for perpetrators (Shaw & Waldorf, 2010).

However, this 'local turn' has been criticised for 'romanticising the local' (Björkdahl et al., 2016: 11; Kochanski, 2018), risking the marginalisation of some groups (Shaw & Waldorf, 2010: 16), such as young people or women and failing to recognise how the global and local spheres are 'intertwined' (Björkdahl et al., 2016: 10; Buckley-Zistel, 2016: 18). Even beginning to analyse issues in terms of their 'global' or 'local' aspects arguably requires taking a particular perspective and adopting an assumed sense of 'scale' (Riles, 1995), as if there were '"authentic" local values that could be rediscovered and then strengthened only through careful listening' (Deitelhoff & Zimmermann, 2014: 23). Any such artificially distant point of view rests upon contestable assumptions and subjectivities, including for this author. It could arguably 'reify the "global" or "local" as self-evident categories for making sense of the

ICC's relationship with affected communities' (Ullrich, 2016: 549). These classifications can represent processes of exclusion and inclusion that establish 'an implicit dichotomy between good global/universal norms and bad regional/local norms' (Acharya, 2014: 185), which are expected to 'clash' (Shaw & Waldorf, 2010: 5).

In response, some scholars have pointed out that, in practice, the boundaries between actors and norms blur and shift rather than being 'fenced off by some form of boundary' (Buckley-Zistel, 2016: 22). Indeed, 'the things we call "global" are often circulating locals' (Merry, 2006: 40; Björkdahl et al., 2016: 4), while 'if the local is constructed over space and time, so is the global' (Buckley-Zistel, 2016: 24). For instance, some consider the concepts of transitional justice and international criminal justice to have derived from practices in Nuremberg and Tokyo, subsequently reproduced to represent 'pervasive global norm[s]' (Buckley-Zistel, 2016: 24).

Further, actors and ideas labelled state, non-state, local, or global, can engage and intersect, rather than clash, even if this interaction involves some friction (Tsing, 2005; Shaw & Waldorf, 2010). Homogeneous localities rarely, if ever, exist in communities of intersecting ethnic, socio-economic, gender, racial, and other identities. There may be as many local meanings of 'international criminal justice' as there are identities within one location, ethnic grouping, or individual (Levitt & Merry, 2009; Campbell, 2014: 57; Deitelhoff & Zimmermann, 2014: 23; Anderl, 2016). This suggests that spatial designations, such as local or global, may be better understood as dynamic and mutually reinforcing social constructions than firm categories.

The terms 'local' (generally meaning domestic), 'international', and 'global' are therefore used in this book with these qualifications in mind, including to explore how apparently 'local' or 'international' ideas about international criminal justice might relate to the mechanisms for prosecuting international crimes in Southeast Asia. This provides an opportunity to examine the accuracy and helpfulness of such geographic characterisations for discussing international criminal justice in the region.

1.3.3   Directionality

Constructivists have long recognised that domestic actors play an important role in helping norms to 'emerge' and as norm entrepreneurs (Finnemore & Sikkink, 1998; Sikkink, 2011b). However, investigations into how certain 'international' norms become popular can betray assumptions about the movement of ideas across both time and space, or *directionality* – especially that 'global' influence flows *towards* the 'local' (Deitelhoff & Zimmermann, 2010: 22) – or 'a norm travels from A to B' (Anderl, 2016: 199). After all, we are talking about an *'international criminal justice'* norm being adapted 'by' or within states in Southeast Asia. This aspect is not the same as the temporal concern mentioned previously, which addressed the assumption (or hope) that states progress towards accepting international norms over time. Nor is it confined to the division between different 'spaces'. Rather, directionality concerns the trajectory of ideas across and between constructed spaces. In particular, it addresses the notion that certain norms flow *from* the international *to* the local. Despite promising research concerning how 'local' actors and concepts, especially in developing states, contribute towards norm-making processes (Merry, 2006; Levitt & Merry, 2009; Acharya, 2011; Zimmermann, 2016, 2017), that approach remains relatively less common, particularly in relation to international criminal law (deGuzman, 2018).

The concept of directionality indicates that 'questions about norm diffusion in world politics are not simply about whether and how ideas matter, but also which and whose ideas matter' (Acharya, 2004: 239). For some, the dissemination of international norms, or even their adaptation to some extent, is considered 'a good thing' (Zimmermann, 2017: 210). For instance, scholars and civil society actors consider how international organisations and states can best disseminate the international norms represented by the Rome Statute to recipient states and communities, albeit potentially with the assistance of credible local mediators – such as national members of the Coalition for the International Criminal Court (CICC) (Schroeder & Tiemessen, 2014). The influence of international actors and legal regimes, including via ICC outreach and broad notions of complementarity (Moffett, 2015), may be emphasised over the agency and alternative approaches of 'others'.[22] This could manifest in a preference for domestic international crimes legislation to be modelled as closely upon the Rome Statute as possible (see Stahn, 2015), or in advocacy for *international* criminal justice responses to the commission of international crimes, such as via the ICC or internationalised tribunals.

Some scholars have tackled this issue of direction by emphasising the *agency* of 'local' actors in adapting norms, including by considering 'top

---

[22] The word 'others' without capitalisation is not used here to depict a particular Lacanian meaning and encompasses the symbolic 'Other' of subjectively shared meanings and values.

down' and 'bottom up' norm construction (see Sikkink, 2011a, 2011b) and via a concept of 'localisation' developed with reference to 'Southeast Asian histiographical concepts' (Acharya, 2014: 186). Localisation seeks to move away from an external/good, internal/bad dichotomy by explaining how 'credible local actors', including from civil society, adjust concepts using their awareness of local conditions. To do so, actors reshape both the norm itself (the international idea) and local practices (Acharya, 2004). Thus, the process is one of mutual *adaptation* rather than one-sided *adoption*. This 'localisation' approach has been applied in relation to a variety of geographic areas and norm types (Capie, 2008; Williams, 2009; Imai, 2011; Arndt, 2013; Collins, 2013; Cloward, 2016) and could now be considered, alongside socialisation, to represent the second of the 'two major approaches to norm diffusion' (Zimmermann, 2017: 3).

For localisation, adaptation involves 'external norms' being 'reconstructed to fit with local beliefs and practices even as local beliefs and practices may be adjusted in accordance with the external norm' (Acharya, 2004: 251). That is, ideas are reconstructed both from the 'outside-in' and the 'inside-out', especially through the agency of local actors who both work within, and seek to challenge and change, social structures (Sikkink, 2011a). Acharya argues that localisation is likely where credible local actors see an opportunity to incorporate useful ideas that improve, rather than undermine, existing institutions. In this way, local '[b]orrowing supplements, rather than supplant[s] an existing norm hierarchy' (Acharya, 2004: 251). Local civil society might decide to *adapt*, rather than adopt, an international concept where, for example: it seems removed from local priorities; is difficult to explain; could be adjusted to become more practically useful; represents double standards or primarily serves others' interests (including donors'); or could be managed differently so as to maintain or improve relationships with domestic authorities (Acharya, 2012a: 4).

By emphasising *local* influence upon norm creation, the localisation approach challenges any 'directional' (external-to-local) emphasis. Indeed, it may seem to take almost the reverse approach by favouring the adaptation of international norms – suggesting that adapted norms might be more stable or lead to internalisation of the 'full' norm over time – and downplaying the influence of actors from other states or international organisations such as the UN (Zimmermann, 2017). Yet, localisation remains focused upon how 'external' norms are received and adapted 'internally'. This means that it is still directed towards understanding how international ideas flow towards 'locals': for example, how the norm of *international* criminal justice might be adapted. There have therefore been attempts to even further reverse the focus on 'international' norms. For instance, a theory of norm 'circulation' conceptualises the 'creation and diffusion' of norms as a 'two-way process' in which global norms are contested and adapted (localised), but 'local feedback is [also] repatriated back to the wider global context along with other locally constructed norms' (subsidiarity) (Acharya, 2013: 469). This perspective recognises that 'locals' can modify, create, and export new norms. It also contests a temporal understanding of norms being diffused over time, since this repatriation is an ongoing process.

Zimmermann has challenged some of the assumptions and normative precursors that underpin both the socialisation and localisation approaches in her analysis of rule of law norms in Guatemala (2017). She argues that external norm promotion activities interact with the domestic 'translation' of norms through dynamic 'feedback loops' (Zimmermann, 2017: 61). This is not a bargaining process or necessarily a deliberate strategy, but local contestation leads to changes both in the ways in which interactions occur, as well as 'the final form into which global norms are translated' (Zimmermann, 2017: 5). This focus upon how debates about responding to historic violence actually occur – that is, upon the interactions themselves – helps to illuminate how ideas clash but also intersect, within often highly charged, shifting, political contexts.

The case studies in this book draw on these concepts by analysing the adaptation of a particular international norm – international criminal justice – across several states in Southeast Asia and assessing how this takes place over time, across certain spaces, and in certain directions. The subsequent chapters are concerned with how actors have responded to and adapted a *norm of international criminal justice* that, for example, promotes individual criminal accountability and ratification of the Rome Statute. This book therefore does not escape having a directional approach. However, the case studies and conclusions illuminate some of the problematic aspects of focusing on how 'international' norms are transformed and present responses to this challenge.

In summary, analysis of the spread of norms like international criminal justice has sometimes anticipated that states should progress – potentially with the engagement of norm entrepreneurs – from a beginning point (impunity) towards an end: the acceptance of international norms (international criminal justice). If states do not appear to be implementing such principles by adopting and enforcing the necessary laws, this seems to indicate the rejection of the international norm, or that internalisation or localisation is stalled or still in process. This view suggests that the goals of international criminal justice are achieved over *time* through interaction between *spatially* differentiated actors and ideas, which encourages the external idea to flow in the *direction* of receiving locals. All three aspects suggest a linear path where, with the possible influence of civil society actors, outsider states move from rejecting the Rome Statute towards inclusion within the ICC framework, represented by ratification or (at least) the adoption of domestic laws that closely replicate the international model.

More recent constructivist scholarship, including the localisation framework introduced, challenge these assumptions, including that external norms and actors are the predominant influences upon local action. Paying attention to local agency can even foreground post-colonial histories and power structures, as actors engage in circulatory 'feedback loops' in debates about norms.

This book uses a simplified localisation framework to help structure its analysis. It considers: first, the historic context for norm adaptation; second, how different actors might use 'local initiative' to 'frame'[23] and more extensively 'adapt'[24] external norms to create some value for local audiences; and finally, how new laws and institutions are developed in which local influences remain highly visible, or are even 'amplified' (Acharya, 2004: 251). Each of the case study chapters takes this approach.

However, localisation also has limitations. It still anticipates a process of norm adaptation that anticipates long-term positive change: it 'is an evolutionary or "everyday" form of progressive norm diffusion' (Acharya, 2004: 252). Further, almost by definition, localisation maintains a spatial distinction between 'local' and 'international' actors. Finally, it retains a focus on international 'norms' and much of the mainstream constructivist vocabulary – and is thus open to criticisms that it 'does not go far enough' in challenging mainstream instrumentality (Zarakol, 2014: 328). A number of examples in this book help to illustrate and further develop these issues, including the concepts of time, space, and direction.

---

[23] 'Framing' describes the processes by which actors attempt to 'call attention to issues or even "create" issues by using language that names, interprets, and dramatizes them' in different ways to 'create alternative perceptions of both appropriateness and interest' (Finnemore & Sikkink, 1998: 897).

[24] 'Adaptation' involves 'external norms' being 'reconstructed to fit with local beliefs and practices even as local beliefs and practices may be adjusted in accordance with the external norm' (Acharya, 2004: 251).

1.4   Research Design

This book does not escape the limitations of the socialisation and localisation approaches. Instead, it explores and highlights them by examining how some states in Southeast Asia have developed mechanisms for prosecuting international crimes since World War II. In doing so, it tests the usefulness of a localisation framework for analysing states' approaches towards the international criminal justice norm. It reveals the complex ways that aspects of time, space and direction relate to states' laws and institutions for prosecuting international crimes.

Legal researchers have increasingly been called upon to support their claims using cross-disciplinary methods, perhaps especially where the field of law concerned is more closely or overtly directed towards questions of social policy (Roux, 2014: 178). This is arguably the case for international criminal law, given its relationship to policy questions about responding to social disruption. By addressing 'international law' as a social construct (see Wendt, 1999: 2, 280–1; Focarelli, 2012), this book responds to a central issue for international criminal *law* – analysis of national international criminal justice laws and mechanisms, and their adoption – with reference to social sciences approaches, especially from the international relations field. In doing so, it draws on a tradition that cements the use of social sciences methodologies within the legal field (Halliday & Schmidt, 2009), just as such methods are gaining traction within international criminal law scholarship (Nouwen, 2014; Burgis-Kasthala, 2016). Rather than suggesting a particular way to perform research, a constructivist approach makes contingent claims and 'opens up a set of issues' (Finnemore & Sikkink, 2001: 396). Despite this, since Jeffrey T. Checkel (1998) bemoaned the lack of empirical support for constructivist claims, scholars have taken up that challenge and called for more attention to be devoted to how ideas spread (Risse et al., 1999; Finnemore & Sikkink, 2001). Similarly, this book applies qualitative methods to analyse international criminal justice in four states in Southeast Asia, including drawing on interviews and a thematic analysis of legal, government, media, and non-governmental organisation (NGO) documents. That said, given the breadth of its subject matter, it also draws upon country studies produced by international law, transitional justice, and political science scholars.

This process was necessarily selective because not all documentary material could possibly be analysed, nor potential interviewees accessed. Further, each document, including legal texts and official statements made before international institutions, reflects the particular preferences and contexts of its authors (see Smith, 1993; Orford, 2013) and were subjectively interpreted. While 'what states *do* should matter a lot more than what they *say*' (Bederman, 2000: 494) – and official statements do often differ from actual policy – practice must often be established from reports and other communications. Similar considerations apply to non-state organisations. This is one reason to supplement and triangulate documentary materials with interviews, but interviews do not entirely supplant these concerns and include their own limitations, as discussed shortly. In particular, the data collection and analysis process was restricted by timeframe, access, selectivity, reliability, and bias issues. Thus, this research is not comprehensive and its examples and statements are best used to test and illustrate ideas, rather than claiming to represent accurate accounts of events.

Southeast Asia – here meaning the ASEAN member states plus Timor-Leste – provides an opportunity to analyse states' approaches to international criminal justice within a geographic grouping that comprises some overlapping priorities and historical features, but also different economic, political, and cultural contexts and varied civil society engagement in legal processes. Regional states represent a diverse range of attitudes towards international criminal law, as well as the Rome Statute, from apparently somewhat supportive to – perhaps in the majority of cases (see Toon, 2004; Freeland, 2013) – oppositional. Further, examining the reception of international criminal justice in Southeast Asia may very slightly redress the imbalance of international criminal law and transitional justice scholarship, which has mostly focused on Africa, Latin America, and Europe (Jeffrey & Kim, 2014: 2).

This research employs narrative country-based case studies: Cambodia, the Philippines, Indonesia, and Myanmar. This book does not argue that law in all or other states exhibits the adaptation of the international criminal justice norm, or that no other theories can explain approaches to prosecuting international crimes. It is primarily concerned with investigating international criminal law with in Southeast Asia and draws on international relations theories to structure the analysis – while noting issues that arose from this approach. There is 'always the danger' that case selection will be subjective (George & Bennett, 2005: 51), but an attempt was made to select the cases based on specific criteria. Arguably, since constructivist research has now established the significance of norms, fruitful studies ought to provide more detailed claims through 'carefully paired comparisons or a larger set of cases', ideally based upon 'least likely' or 'easy' scenarios (Bennett & Elman, 2007; Klotz, 2008: 53).

The case studies for this book were selected in 2014 on that basis, after identifying the existing laws and institutions addressing international crimes in Southeast Asia (see Table 1.1, Appendix C).

First, to analyse a 'least likely' case for exhibiting *either* the socialisation or adaptation of international criminal justice, a case study was sought where, despite serious allegations of international crimes having been committed in recent decades, the (lack of) laws, policies, or actions in response strongly suggested the rejection of ideas about international criminal justice. Myanmar was a 'least likely' country since despite the alleged commission of international crimes, it lacked any laws for prosecuting international crimes as such and therefore appeared, without closer analysis, to have rejected the norm of international criminal justice (noting that this selection process occurred prior to the ICC's more recent attention toward Myanmar). Although other states lack specific international crimes legislation, such as Brunei Darussalam and Lao PDR, the extent and recency of the violence in Myanmar, by comparison, warranted its selection (as *least* likely). Thailand has also not ratified the Rome Statute or passed legislation specifically making international crimes domestic offences. Yet there had been some engagement with international criminal justice, including an attempt to provide amnesties to those involved in the 'Red Shirt protests' in 2010, a civil society–led request for the ICC to review that period, as well as internal investigations into violence in 2013–14. Thailand therefore did not appear to reflect the 'least likely' case at the time.

Second, this book uses a case that seemed 'most likely' to indicate the *acceptance* of the norm of international criminal justice, but unlikely to show much adaptation: a state that has also experienced allegations of international crimes, but has ratified the Rome Statute, adopted international crimes legislation, and prosecuted cases. Initially, the most likely case appeared to be either Cambodia – which had prosecuted international crimes before an internationalised tribunal (the ECCC), ratified the Rome Statute, and had international crimes legislation – or Timor-Leste, which is also a Rome Statute party where international crimes were prosecuted within an internationalised tribunal (the Special Panels) and international crimes were included in its 2009 Penal Code. Cambodia was selected for the reasons explained shortly.

Third, the concept of 'localisation' suggests that, rather than states adopting laws reflecting the international norm, laws or institutions will incorporate adaptations reflective of local context. In order to select a 'most likely' case for the localisation of international criminal justice, it

Table 1.1 *Overview of Southeast Asian countries*[a]

State	Rome Statute Ratification	International Crimes Explicit in Domestic Legislation[b]	Specially Established ICL Mechanism
Brunei Darussalam	No	Geneva Conventions Order, No. S40, 30 May 2005 (grave breaches)	No
Cambodia	11 April 2002	Articles 183–194 Criminal Code of the Kingdom of Cambodia 2010; and ECCC Law (crimes against humanity, war crimes, genocide)	ECCC
Indonesia	No	Law 26/2000 (crimes against humanity and genocide)	Law 26/2000 Human Rights Courts
Lao PDR	No	No	No
Malaysia	4 March 2019 (rescinded)	Geneva Conventions Act 1962 (grave breaches)	No
Myanmar	No	No	No
The Philippines	30 August 2011 (withdrawal effective 19 March 2019)	Republic Act No. 9851, 2009 (IHL Act) (crimes against humanity, war crimes, genocide)	No
Singapore	No	Geneva Conventions Act, Ordinance 15 of 1973, Revised 1985 (grave breaches); Section 130D of the Singapore Penal Code (genocide)	No
Thailand	No	No	No
Timor-Leste	6 September 2002	Penal Code, Decree-Law No. 19/2009 (book II, chapters I-II) (crimes against humanity, war crimes, genocide)	Special Panels
Vietnam	No	Criminal Code, No. 100/2015/QH13 (chapter XXVI) (aggression, crimes against humanity, war crimes)	No

[a] Selected case study countries are in shaded rows.

[b] War crimes, crimes against humanity, genocide, or aggression, rather than underlying crimes such as 'torture'. 'Ordinary' crimes that could be used to prosecute underlying conduct of international crimes such as murder, rape, torture, and other crimes, including under military legislation, have not been included here.

was therefore necessary to review the domestic laws concerning international crimes in Southeast Asia. Apart from Cambodia and Timor-
Leste, the Philippines, Indonesia, Singapore and Vietnam all have specific
legislation to allow more than one offence of genocide, crimes against
humanity, or war crimes to be prosecuted nationally, while Malaysia and
Brunei Darussalam also have laws addressing the grave breaches in the
Geneva Conventions (see Table 1.1). For most of these states, a relatively
peaceful history in recent decades seemed to provide less opportunity to
explore how the norm of international criminal justice has been adapted,
since it might be easier for some to explain a lack of laws or policies as
resulting from a lack of alleged crimes. The Philippines and Indonesia
were exceptions, since – as the chapters discuss – both had experienced
allegations of serious violations. Both had also developed laws and institutions for responding to international crimes: in the Philippines prior to
and after becoming a Rome Statute party and in Indonesia through
domestic legislation. Both appeared to be strong cases for localisation,
but through establishing different mechanisms. The Philippines had not
established a tribunal or special chambers to prosecute international
crimes as in Indonesia and – unlike Indonesia – was a Rome Statute
party with comprehensive international crimes laws. As a result, this
book considers both Indonesia and the Philippines as 'most likely' cases
for the adaptation of international criminal justice.

Finally, in order to consider an internationalised structure which
operated in a very different context to the only *domestic* special chambers
in the region (under Law 26/2000 in Indonesia), it was decided that
Cambodia, rather than Timor-Leste, would provide a more diverse
'likely' case study for acceptance, although it is conceded that Timor-
Leste would also have contributed useful insights and comparisons
between the Special Panels and Law 26/2000.

Turning to the analysis of these cases, this book adopts the position
that identities, norms, and interests are mutually constituted and that
states or regions may be considered 'socially constructed' (Acharya,
2012b: 23). This suggests that there is no real question of what states
'think', but only of what their representatives say or do – and what
individuals perceive to be the state 'position' (Epstein, 2011). Yet, as
indicated, practice must often be established from reports and other
communications. Similar considerations apply to non-state organisations, including NGOs.

This book relies upon a wide variety of documents, including academic
literature, NGO reports, legislation and case law, government foreign

affairs statements (including before treaty bodies), UN Security Council and General Assembly and Human Rights Council Resolutions and documents, and records from the negotiations of the Rome Statute, as well as relevant news reports. This material was examined to ascertain how international crimes might be prosecuted under national laws and to identify related arguments about prosecuting such conduct (using basic thematic coding). Prominent identified themes are drawn upon in the following four chapters to show how foreign states and international organisations, authorities, and civil society actors debate international criminal justice by drawing on – and contesting – certain themes, which might relate to the localisation concept of 'local initiative'. As already mentioned, this process was selective and limited, since documents, including legal texts and official statements made before international institutions, reflect the particular preferences and contexts of their authors and are subjectively interpreted, while 'real' positions may not be reflected in official statements.

A number of interviews were also held with representatives of local and international civil society and (more rarely) official institutions who may have engaged in debates about international criminal justice in the case study states (see Appendix B).[25] These were undertaken predominantly to supplement the document analysis by helping to further reveal general themes and arguments about international crimes, and are also drawn upon in the following chapters. The number of formal interviews (thirty-three recorded semi-structured interviews) was too small and selective to be generalisable and the quotes from them should only be considered illustrative, though many other informal discussions were held. The themes identified from documents and interviews are then considered as background for the legal analysis of specific provisions of the laws and institutions established to respond to international crimes (in the fourth section of the following chapters). The book does not seek to prove that particular arguments, people, or events caused laws to be written in a particular way and so does not adopt (for instance) the language of process tracing. Instead, it analyses these laws and institutions against an international criminal justice 'norm', drawing on the localisation approach, to reveal and explore diverse understandings of international criminal law.

---

[25] Held in accordance with UNSW HREAP B: Arts, Humanities & Law, No. 14084 and at Griffith University, Research Ethics Reference No. 2018/910.

On top of these issues, it is arguably not possible to assess legal phenomena across different legal systems because of the inherent subjectivities of the observer. Potentially only deep immersion into each of the foreign legal 'cultures' provides sufficient knowledge to undertake any such analysis.[26] All researchers who claim to interpret legal phenomena – perhaps particularly those from outside post-colonial states – can replicate 'a much older distribution of power, steeped in colonial, paternalist relations, between those who have the power/knowledge to speak, and those who are, once again, spoken about or for' (Epstein, 2014: 305). Both observers and participants in legal systems might conceive of 'culture' and its relationship to law in different ways. Yet this need not inhibit either immersed or 'external' researchers from contributing valuable analysis of laws or legal institutions. Indeed, 'once the futile hope to grasp any holistic "essence" of culture is given up, a functionalist outsider's account need not be inferior to a culturalist insider's account; it just highlights a different perspective' – that is, 'an observer's perspective [provides] an alternative to, not a substitute for, the participant's perspective' (Michaels, 2006: 365).

Still, inevitably this Australian author's lack of specialised knowledge of all Southeast Asian states' legal structures, languages, or histories cannot substitute for a participant's in-depth knowledge and does not attempt to. Instead, it aims to provide a complementary assessment – albeit still a subjective and limited one. This reality is difficult to escape but has been front of mind throughout the research process, which attempted to maintain a 'reflexive' approach. To be clear about its normative aims, this book openly draws attention to approaches to international criminal justice 'beyond the ICC' – not necessarily to *promote* the prosecution of international crimes by other means, but to generate space for listening and discussion about alternative possibilities for responding to serious acts of violence.

1.5   Conclusion

International criminal justice is concerned with the prosecution of core international crimes (genocide, crimes against humanity, war crimes, and aggression), usually based on the Rome Statute of the ICC or closely replicating laws, and with international involvement. States in Southeast Asia have been depicted as rejecting this norm, including because most

---

[26] On the problematic nature of dealing with 'culture', see (Michaels, 2006: 362, 379); and regarding comparative legal cultures see (Picker, 2013).

have not ratified the Rome Statute. This aligns with a socialisation approach towards the diffusion of norms, which anticipates that states can be persuaded to adopt international norms through engagement over time, including via developing, ratifying, and implementing treaties. Yet the significant activity concerning responses to alleged international crimes in Southeast Asia suggests that states may not have entirely rejected the norm of international criminal justice, even if they have not wholly accepted it. Localisation suggests that local actors can, instead, *adapt* international norms. However, this approach minimises the influence of international actors. It also still anticipates that adaptation will help states to eventually adopt the international norm (as a step on the linear path), or at least might lead to *some* implementation and a more favourable result than insisting upon full acceptance.

The subsequent four case study chapters each explore these issues using a similar structure that slices engagement with international criminal justice over three axes. They begin by recalling the historic context of international criminal law in that state, in a generally chronological manner, illustrating how that engagement changes over time. The chapters then take a different perspective of these developments by explaining (in turn) how different conventionally grouped sets of actors – foreign states and organisations, government and security authorities, and civil society – have engaged with the norm of international criminal justice. The next sections demonstrate how these processes of adaptation are visible in the laws and mechanisms for prosecuting international crimes in each country. Finally, the case studies end with some reflections upon whether the norm of international criminal justice has been 'socialised' or 'localised' in that state – and consider what questions remain.

The final chapter argues that the laws and mechanisms for prosecuting international crimes in Southeast Asia reflect the adaptation of the international criminal justice norm by diverse state and other actors in various locations. It notes that a localisation framework is helpful for exploring these processes. However, it also identifies some limitations of that approach and proposes some possible ways forward. This book challenges assumptions about how ideas are adapted over time, across different spaces (local/global), and in certain directions (outside-in/ inside-out). Finally, it identifies implications for those advocating for international criminal justice in Southeast Asia, both for past and ongoing atrocities.

Engaging with International Criminal Law alongside an Internationalised Tribunal

Cambodia

2.1 Introduction

Cambodia has faced both internal and external conflict, including for a period of more than thirty years extending into the late 1990s. This time frame encompassed the Second Indochina (Vietnam) War and internal conflict both before and after the period of 'the Democratic Kampuchea regime' (DK), from 1975 until Vietnam gained control of Cambodia in 1979. During DK, up to a quarter of Cambodia's population died as a result of killings, torture, forced transfers, starvation, and forced labour (Kiernan, 2003: 586–7; Chandler, 2008a). In the 1990s, as the International Criminal Tribunals for the former Yugoslavia and Rwanda (ICTY, ICTR) were beginning their operations, international attention turned towards securing accountability for DK-era crimes, including the possible establishment of international criminal mechanisms.

An internationalised criminal tribunal, the ECCC, was established under Cambodian law in 2004,[1] but also operates pursuant to an agreement with the UN (ECCC Agreement).[2] It prosecutes DK's 'senior leaders ... and those who were most responsible' for international crimes and other violations of international and domestic law.[3] As at June 2019, the ECCC had convicted three defendants for charges including genocide, crimes against humanity, and grave breaches of the Geneva Conventions. This may appear to indicate that Cambodia's

---

[1] Law on the Establishment of the Extraordinary Chambers in the Courts of Cambodia for the Prosecution of Crimes Committed during the Period of Democratic Kampuchea, amended 27 October 2004, NS/RKM/1004/006 (ECCC Law).

[2] Agreement between the United Nations and the Royal Government of Cambodia concerning the prosecution under Cambodian law of crimes committed during the period of Democratic Kampuchea, 6 June 2003 (ECCC Agreement).

[3] Article 2 new, ECCC Law.

leaders have accepted the norm of international criminal justice, at least for historic crimes. Yet the reality is more complex. When measured against the norm of international criminal justice (see Chapter 1), the ECCC's 'shortcomings and weaknesses continue to hamper its effectiveness' (Ryan, 2015). Key actors within the government have sometimes displayed opposition to the ECCC and sought to block its prosecutions (Kent, 2013). It is also a court with selective jurisdiction – being focused on a small group of senior leaders and the historical period of DK.

In relation to contemporary or prospective crimes, Cambodia has ratified the Rome Statute[4] and incorporated international crimes into its Criminal Code, using text modelled closely upon the Rome Statute, though with some variations.[5] However, the Cambodian government has been accused of significant human rights violations, including the alleged commission of crimes potentially within the jurisdiction of the ICC (Global Diligence, 2014). No significant action has been taken by national (or international) authorities to prosecute this conduct.

This chapter analyses the mechanisms for prosecuting historic, as well as contemporary, allegations of international crimes. It considers engagement with international criminal justice as Cambodia ratified the Rome Statute, when it incorporated international crimes laws into domestic legislation, and as judicial mechanisms in Cambodia prosecute international crimes (or decide not to). Section 2.2 examines the history of international crimes trials in Cambodia. It shows that Cambodia does not provide an example of progression towards acceptance of the norm of international criminal justice, but neither is there only stalling or complete rejection of this norm. Section 2.3 demonstrates how international and Cambodian government actors and civil society have sought to influence Cambodia's laws and institutions for investigating and prosecuting international crimes. Section 2.4 then examines the key features of these mechanisms. Section 2.5 argues that Cambodia's interaction with international criminal justice disturbs any assumption that international law norms are diffused over time and from certain locations outside Cambodia (spaces) to within the country (direction).

---

[4] On 11 April 2002.
[5] Criminal Code of the Kingdom of Cambodia 2010, translation by Bunleng Cheung (Criminal Code).

2.2   Historic Engagement with International Criminal Law

There are two main reasons why it is important for this book to review the historic development of international criminal justice mechanisms in Cambodia. First, as discussed in Chapter 1, 'mainstream' constructivist approaches suggested that international norms may be diffused through socialisation activities including the ratification of multilateral treaties, implementation of international law into national legislation, and the enforcement of those laws. This implies a relatively linear progression from rejection towards the acceptance of international norms, although some researchers have pointed out that this process can stall or involve contestation. Typically, 'the outcomes of norm diffusion are described either in dichotomous terms or as points on a linear scale ranging from rejection to full adoption' (Zimmermann, 2017: 37).

It is impossible to comprehensively discuss the complex historical and political situation in Cambodia. Rather, this section proceeds in a loosely chronological manner to consider whether Cambodia's approach to prosecuting international crimes has progressed from a position of resistance towards acceptance of the norm of international criminal justice.

Second, it identifies certain themes arising from these events that have resurfaced in debates about implementing international criminal justice: concerns with sovereignty; protecting Cambodia's peace, stability, and hierarchical social and power structures; selective and politicised responses to alleged crimes; and development.

2.2.1   Sovereignty, Security, and Selectivity: Occupation and the People's Revolutionary Tribunal

The territory of modern-day Cambodia has been the site of external interference, often associated with armed conflict and violence, such as during the French colonial period and Cambodian *Issarak* movement.[6] During World War II the Japanese abolished the French protectorate, following which French administrators arrested Buddhist nationalist leader Son Ngoc Thanh as a 'war criminal' in one of relatively few post–World War II trials held in Indochina (Heder, 1999; Schoepfel-Aboukrat, 2014). These trials were selective and faced administrative and

---

[6] For one overview of Cambodia's history, see *Prosecutor v. Nuon Chea and Khieu Samphan*, Case No. 002/19-09-2007/ECCC/TC, Trial Chamber, Case 002/01 Judgment, 7 August 2014 (Case 002/01 Judgment), paras. 79–167.

political challenges, including those arising from 'the perceived collaboration of the French Indochinese government with Japan until March
1945' (Schoepfel-Aboukrat, 2014: 128). Cambodia's independence was
formally recognised in 1953, within a period of conflict involving both
internal and international actors that continued until the Khmer Rouge
established DK in 1975. Democratic Kampuchea, and the international
crimes associated with it, persisted until Vietnam took control of Cambodia in 1979 (Becker, 1998). Yet, conflict between the Vietnam-backed
People's Republic of Kampuchea (PRK) government – succeeded by the
State of Cambodia – and Khmer Rouge forces continued into the 1980s
and 1990s.

These events were central to Cold War geopolitics and involved
significant external intrusion, including US bombing of Cambodian
territory in the early 1970s. Some Cambodian leaders sought out external
assistance to support Cambodia's geopolitical position, such as Norodom
Sihanouk, who fostered relations with China, the Soviet Union, and
ASEAN and Western states over the course of decades (Peou, 1995: 12;
Cheunboran, 2018: 235). However, these events also encouraged a 'perception of [Cambodia's] vulnerability to both foreign interference and
domestic conflict' (Peou, 1995: 1).

In 1979 the PRK established the People's Revolutionary Tribunal
(PRT) without any pre-existing legal infrastructure – it is estimated that
only six to ten lawyers survived DK and the judicial system had been
dismantled (Donovan, 1993: 445). The PRT convicted former DK leaders
Pol Pot and Ieng Sary for the crime of genocide,[7] but would have
contributed to any view held by Cambodia's leaders that international
criminal justice can be political. In the West the proceedings were largely
rejected as a 'show trial' in the midst of Cold War opposition to the PRK
(Group of Experts for Cambodia, 1999; Linton, 2010; Hughes, 2015).
While some concerns may have stemmed from unfamiliarity with civil
law procedures (Fawthorp & Jarvis, 2005; 47), the defendants were also
tried *in absentia* with inadequate procedural protections (Selbmann,
2016). Recent criticisms of the ECCC – and international criminal law
more generally – echo earlier criticisms that the PRT was politicised,
involved selective temporal and personal jurisdiction, and presented due
process concerns (Human Rights Watch, 2014). Still, the PRT gathered
evidence, was one of the first tribunals to prosecute the crime of

---

[7] *People's Revolutionary Tribunal Held in Phnom Penh for the Trial of the Genocide Crime of
the Pol Pot – Ieng Sary Clique*, Judgment, 19 August 1979, 29–30.

'genocide' under the Genocide Convention,[8] and was the first international crimes prosecution in Southeast Asia to involve the significant influence of another Southeast Asian state. It therefore represented a point of engagement with international criminal justice.

The PRT convictions helped to justify Vietnam's occupation of Cambodia as the PRK established the 'dominant narrative of the Khmer Rouge era, with a handful of absent, demonic perpetrators and millions of innocent victims' (Chandler, 2000: 73). Though the PRK appears to have detained some lower-ranking Khmer Rouge cadres (Huy, 2002, Linton, 2010: 49), the focus of the PRT upon the highest leadership (the 'Pol Pot – Ieng Sary clique')[9] was further maintained in Cambodia's education system (Hinton, 2008: 70) and criminal laws during the PRK period, which linked opposition to the Vietnamese regime with Pol Pot (Gottesman, 2003: 241).

Meanwhile, due to Cold War divisions concerning Vietnam and the PRK, a Khmer Rouge coalition retained Cambodia's seat at the United Nations (UN) until 1991. Indeed, the 'United Nations and Western powers did little in response to mounting evidence of [DK] atrocities ... China did worse, emerging as the Pol Pot regime's main external sponsor' (Ciociari & Heindel, 2014: 15; Mertha, 2014). These dynamics illustrated the potential for politicisation and the selectivity of international attitudes towards the commission of international crimes.

2.2.2 Stability, Peace, and Development: UNTAC and Elections

In contrast to the PRK's emphasis on having ended DK, the period following Vietnam's withdrawal from Cambodia in 1989 and the establishment of the United Nations Transitional Authority in Cambodia (UNTAC) in 1992 involved a policy of 'collective amnesia' as the Khmer Rouge period was removed from public discourse and educational programs (Chandler, 2008b: 355). Elections in 1993 resulted in a power-sharing agreement between Hun Sen's Cambodian People's Party (CPP) and FUNCINPEC,[10] led by one of Norodom Sihanouk's sons, Norodom Ranariddh. Both parties competed for the support of Khmer Rouge

---

[8] See (Schabas, 2000) regarding earlier genocide cases. The PRT definition of genocide differed from that in the Genocide Convention, see (Schabas, 2001: 289); and as to whether this may have been a translation issue, (Gutman, 2015: 180).

[9] Decree Law No. 1, Establishment of People's Revolutionary Tribunal at Phnom Penh to Try the Pol Pot – Ieng Sary Clique for the Crime of Genocide, 15 July 1979.

[10] National United Front for an Independent, Neutral, Peaceful, and Cooperative Cambodia in English, commonly known as FUNCINPEC.

members (Brown & Zasloff, 1998: 251) and the government granted amnesties to Khmer Rouge defectors in 1994.[11]

The emphasis on reintegration was not just propounded by the Cambodian government. During the preceding years of the Paris Peace negotiations, 'no Western states' had supported prosecuting DK crimes (Ainley, 2014: 145) and proposals to refer to 'genocide' in the peace agreement were rejected (Fawthrop & Jarvis, 2005: 100). China, which re-emerged as one of Cambodia's largest providers of aid and foreign investment, and some other states, continued to oppose trials during the negotiations between the Cambodian government and the UN to establish the ECCC (see Section 2.3.1) (Etcheson, 2004: 193). Meanwhile, the continued presence of Khmer Rouge forces in border areas presented a challenge for Cambodia's peace, albeit one of declining importance following a pardon granted to Ieng Sary in 1996. Thus, Cambodian approaches to international criminal justice were formulated in an atmosphere of military insecurity (Peou, 2009: 122).

By the late 1990s, Cambodia had experienced decades of conflict during which international aid had been politically and practically complicated to deploy (Fawthrop & Jarvis, 2005: 65–6). However, a significant amount of assistance was provided to Cambodia following the establishment of UNTAC, including for rule of law and judicial development, though much was diverted as the result of corruption and inefficiencies (Malena & Chhim, 2009). In June 1997, apparently with international encouragement, Cambodia's Prime Ministers requested the UN's assistance to prosecute international crimes committed during DK (United Nations, 1997; Hammarberg, 2001; Heder, 2011). In July 1997, Hun Sen's CPP ousted Ranariddh and the FUNCINPEC party. China offered some 'political and economic breathing space while Phnom Penh was condemned and isolated again from the region and the world' and some international aid was suspended (Cheunboran, 2018: 237). In the context of this recent instability, the CPP sought to secure Cambodia's (and the government's) security and redevelopment. International crimes trials provided one potential route towards securing both goals (Etcheson, 2004: 202).

2.2.3   Independence and Engagement: ECCC Negotiations

In 1998, the UN General Assembly asked the Secretary-General to appoint a Group of Experts to 'evaluate the existing evidence [of DK

---

[11] Law to Outlaw the Democratic Kampuchea Group, 14 July 1994.

crimes] and propose further measures' (United Nations General Assembly, 1998: para. 6). Several months later, Pol Pot died. There is insufficient scope to detail the history of the negotiations to establish the ECCC that followed the Experts' report, as many others have done (e.g. Hammarberg, 2001; Fawthrop & Jarvis, 2005; Scheffer, 2008, 2012; Heder, 2011; Gidley, 2019),[12] though some relevant arguments are drawn upon in Section 2.3. The discussions were complex: they dealt with Cambodian and international law and occurred during the extensive upheaval and aftermath of the CPP taking power (with ongoing concerns about how to manage remaining Khmer Rouge forces and defectors), alongside disagreements between UN actors and representatives of various states about the discussions and proposed outcomes. They were also acrimonious, with 'stalemates' contributed to by both the UN and Cambodian negotiators (Hammarberg, 2001: Scheffer, 2012).

However, alongside these challenging discussions, after 2001 the government and judiciary undertook a number of actions that appeared to indicate an interest in prosecuting international crimes. In 2002, Cambodia became the first country in Southeast Asia to ratify the Rome Statute. Cambodia's Supreme Court also upheld the conviction of a Khmer Rouge General, Nuon Paet, for a 1994 attack on a train that killed 'at least 13 Cambodians' and in which 'three western tourists and some Cambodians [were] taken hostage' (Fawthrop & Jarvis, 2005: 166). Soon after, Khmer Rouge Colonel Chhouk Rin was convicted for his role in the incident. These developments – which took place during the ECCC negotiations – may have been directed towards an international audience (Linton, 2010: 48). Yet the trials arguably also 'appeared to indicate a willingness by the authorities to get serious about Khmer Rouge prosecutions, albeit belatedly and following sustained pressure from the foreign embassies and families of the victims' (Fawthrop & Jarvis, 2005: 194). Ung Choeun (known as Ta Mok) and the leader of the S-21 security centre, Kaing Ghek Iev (Duch), were later captured and indicted 'for crimes against domestic security with the intention of serving the policies of the Democratic Kampuchea group' and genocide (Royal Government of Cambodia, 2004). It seemed as if there was increasing engagement with international criminal law in Cambodia, but this was alongside challenging negotiations for a tribunal.

---

[12] For links to detailed chronologies, see Cambodia Tribunal Monitor. Chronology & Negotiating History, www.cambodiatribunal.org/history/tribunal-background/chronology-negotiating-history.

After further discussions and the adoption of the ECCC Agreement in 2003, a Law on the Establishment of the Extraordinary Chambers in the Courts of Cambodia for the Prosecution of Crimes Committed during the Period of Democratic Kampuchea (ECCC Law) was amended in 2004. The ECCC was established as an 'internationalised' tribunal with national and international co-prosecutors, co-investigating judges, and investigating trial and appeals judges (there are now also international and national civil party lead co-lawyers). As discussed in Section 2.4.2, the ECCC has jurisdiction only over crimes committed during DK and is therefore limited to prosecuting historic incidents.

2.2.4   Social and Power Structures: Power, Buddhism, and the Military

Cambodia adopted laws that would allow forward-looking prosecutions by amending, with French assistance, its Criminal Procedures Code and Criminal Code to incorporate international crimes in 2007[13] and 2009, respectively. The ECCC has convicted perpetrators and judicial and 'non-judicial' reparations projects have been implemented. However, the Cambodian government resisted the ECCC's investigations of the former Commander of the Democratic Kampuchea Navy and several other mid-level commanders (in Cases 003 and 004).[14] There are also ongoing concerns about human rights and judicial independence in Cambodia (International Bar Association's Human Rights Institute, 2015). In 2007, scholar and NGO worker Urs argued that 'donors continue to spend tens of millions of dollars a year on rule of law promotion efforts in Cambodia and yet fail to disrupt the power structure that prevents fair trials' (Urs, 2007: 64). Little has changed since then. Power relationships in Cambodia, including within the CPP, are 'characterized by extreme levels of executive control' (Urs, 2007: 63). The possibility that judges have viewed their role as 'subordinates of the Executive' has also been offered as a potential barrier to judicial reform in Cambodia (Urs, 2007: 64). These cultural and social dynamics have therefore provided an important – but complicated – context for prosecuting international crimes in Cambodia.

These hierarchies within the government and society persist (in varying forms) alongside the enduring impact of religious and historic

[13] Criminal Procedure Code of Kingdom of Cambodia 2007, translation by Bunleng Cheung.
[14] Hun Sen quoted in Brinkley (2013).

Khmer teachings. The issue of seeking justice for DK crimes 'touches the hearts of each and every person in Cambodia' (Etcheson, 2004: 181) and is therefore affected by intersecting individual, social and, cultural backgrounds. For example, for many in Cambodia, where officially 98 per cent of the population are Buddhists (Central Intelligence Agency, 2019), understandings of international criminal justice may be influenced by Buddhist teachings. Thus, some scholars have suggested that international crimes prosecutions might conflict with 'non-legalistic traditions that offer alternatives to the pursuit of peace' (Peou, 2009: 121) or a Buddhist 'mindful understanding of the past' (Hinton, 2008: 79). Others have indicated that prosecuting only the most senior leaders of DK might be consistent with traditional patron-client relationships (Urs, 2007: 83; Malena & Chhim, 2009: 4–5), a 'stay in your place' mentality (Urs, 2007: 82), or of Buddhist 'Karmic justice' in the next life (Ear, 2010: Gray, 2012). It has also been suggested that survivors are more interested in learning the truth about DK and understanding its crimes ('Why did Khmer kill Khmer?'), than in securing retribution (Urs, 2007: 74).

Still, the relationship between Buddhism and passivity or submission is contested (Haynes, 2014: 207). The disruption of colonial control and DK, which outlawed religion, also complicates the identification of traditional values, power hierarchies, and identities in Cambodia and in diaspora communities (Vickery, 1984: 177). Further, there were not always clear boundaries between 'victims' and 'perpetrators' (Bernath, 2015). Many Cambodians (including Hun Sen) were DK cadres or, like Sihanouk and his family, were otherwise implicated in the regime. Cambodia's history of insecurity may also have promoted the significance of the military for some officials and members of the public. In summary, applying clear identities or categories to individual actors remains a difficult (and arguably inappropriate) task.

In the midst of these complex debates, elections in 2013 and 2018 were surrounded by violence and repression (Human Rights Watch, 2013), and opposition leaders and activists were exiled, arrested, and even assassinated. There have been accusations that the current administration and security forces are involved in the commission of international crimes, including forcible transfers associated with land grabbing, estimated to have affected up to 770,000 Cambodians (Global Diligence, 2016; Hunt, 2016). These incidents involved the use of Cambodia's courts to prosecute political opponents and critics of the CPP, at the same time as the ECCC prosecuted DK crimes.

2.2.5   Summary: History

Cambodia's government was eventually willing to allow the prosecution of DK crimes through establishing a past-oriented internationalised mechanism focused on a small number of perpetrators. It also adopted laws that could allow for prosecutions of crimes committed in future. However, '[r]ather than its leaders feeling vulnerable to prosecution or being socialised into observing human rights and democracy norms, Cambodia seems to be regressing in its human rights record' (Ainley, 2014: 154). In terms of international criminal justice, the focus here, the government has reportedly obstructed some ECCC prosecutions and is alleged to have facilitated the commission of international crimes without promoting prosecutions. At various points, different actors have drawn on or discussed the importance of prosecuting international crimes. However, to say that a process of norm socialisation has occurred successfully in Cambodia, or has stalled or been rejected, does not capture the contestation evident in discussions about international criminal law. The next section demonstrates how ideas about sovereignty, selective justice, stability, development, and the social structures just discussed have been drawn upon and debated by a variety of actors seeking to shape international criminal justice in Cambodia.

2.3   Local Initiatives and Adaptation

Norm entrepreneurs can attempt to 'spread transnational norms' and the localisation framework suggests that approaches 'that accommodate local sensitivity', especially where international proponents 'act through local agents', are more likely to lead to institutional change (Acharya, 2004: 249). This involves more than attempts to persuade state actors to adopt international norms through socialisation. Instead, localisation involves actors identifying international norms that might assist their own various goals and, using local initiative, reframing them for their particular purposes and contexts. 'Local' actors may also alter (adapt) the foreign idea by picking out the elements considered desirable for their context and discarding other aspects. A thematic analysis of public statements (from the time of the ECCC negotiations until 2017)[15] reveals how international states and NGOs, Cambodia's government leaders,

---

[15] Supplemented by interviews where indicated.

and civil society actors have used international norms and local initiative to influence perceptions of international criminal justice in Cambodia.

2.3.1 International States and Organisations

Despite an initial lack of interest on the part of some international actors in pursuing accountability for DK crimes, once engaged, many argued that international criminal justice in Cambodia must take place in an 'impartial' or 'independent' manner. This did not mean independent from international influence, but, on the contrary, that external personnel and governance would be crucial. The US originally sought a tribunal established by the UN Security Council (Scheffer, 2012: 364) and the Group of Experts recommended establishing a 'United Nations tribunal' similar to the ICTY and ICTR, located in the Asia Pacific, but not in Cambodia (Group of Experts for Cambodia, 1999: paras. 171, 179). For various reasons, this option was not popular (Hammarberg, 2001; Scheffer, 2012: 367), but the UN remained concerned about potential political interference in and the corruption of Cambodia's judicial system. The UN pulled out of negotiations in 2002, stating that any court must demonstrate 'independence, impartiality and objectivity' (United Nations, 2002).[16] UN and some international actors considered international criminal justice to require external control.[17]

Yet some states, including Russia, Brazil, and other Latin American states, initially opposed establishing an international criminal tribunal without Cambodia's consent (Scheffer, 2012: 370). China's UN delegates 'pursued an aggressive lobbying strategy, attempting to kill the tribunal before it [was] born' (Etcheson, 2004: 194). Other actors adjusted their position as to how international criminal justice should be pursued in relation to Cambodia. Human Rights Watch argued that in the same week of the ICC's inauguration in 2003, other ICC 'member states such as France, Japan, the US, Australia and India have supported the Cambodian government's position and consistently pressured the United Nations to make unprincipled concessions' (Human Rights Watch, 2003: 2). There was no generalisable 'international' position concerning the prosecution of international crimes in Cambodia.

The concerns of the Group of Experts and the UN Secretariat were partly vindicated. Various actors – especially international NGOs – have

---

[16] See also (United Nations Secretary-General, 2003: 7, 11).
[17] E.g. (Amnesty International, 2003; Human Rights Watch, 2003).

consistently criticised the Cambodian government for interfering with ECCC proceedings.[18] On the other hand, in 2013 the US State Department concluded that 'there was no evidence' that 'public comments by government leaders on matters related to the ECCC's jurisdictional mandate' had 'inhibited the work of the court' (United States Department of State, 2013: 18). Thus, international actors have debated whether 'independent' international criminal justice can be delivered in a localised manner in Cambodia.

When the UN General Assembly, with Cambodian support (Fawthrop & Jarvis, 2005: 195), asked the Secretary-General to resume negotiations to establish a Cambodian tribunal in 2003, he was requested to ensure the ECCC would operate with 'justice, fairness and due process of law' and in an 'efficient and cost-effective' manner (United Nations General Assembly, 2003). The ECCC Agreement requires that unless there is ambiguity, the ECCC procedures 'shall be in accordance with Cambodian procedural law', but also requires the ECCC to exercise 'jurisdiction in accordance with international standards of justice, fairness and due process of law'.[19] The ECCC has struggled to secure sufficient funding at times, both from international actors and the Cambodian government (Ciociari & Heindel, 2014: 99, ECCC, 2014). It has undergone extensive restructuring in an attempt to improve efficiency (White, 2014), but debates about the ECCC's procedural fairness, expense and duration continue (Cohen et al., 2015: Open Society Justice Initiative, 2016).

Some international (and Cambodian) actors hoped that the ECCC would support Cambodia's reconciliation, peace, and judicial reform, including by having a '"ripple" effect on the administration of criminal justice in Cambodia' (Leuprecht, 2003: para. 19). In 2003, the UN General Assembly recognised 'the legitimate concern of the Government and the people of Cambodia in the pursuit of justice and national reconciliation, stability, peace and security' (United Nations General Assembly, 2003).[20] According to the Japanese ambassador, international crimes trials would 'play an important role as a catalyst for strengthening Cambodia's general judicial system, providing a good model in legal proceedings based on due process, efficient administration and support systems'.[21]

---

[18] See also (Cambodian Human Rights Action Committee (CHRAC), 2015); e.g. (UN Human Rights Council, 2010) in para. 29 (Belgium), para. 44 (The Netherlands).
[19] Article 12, ECCC Agreement.
[20] See also Preamble to the ECCC Agreement.
[21] Quoted in (Barton 2006); see (European Union, 2014b: 11).

This wider impact upon the judicial system was also expected to take place through training and via Cambodian lawyers and judges working at the ECCC. French and Japanese lawyers assisted with revising Cambodia's domestic laws, with French assistance in particular to amend the Criminal Code, which came to include international crimes. The UN Office of the High Commissioner for Human Rights has assisted with legal and judicial reform, including via ECCC 'legacy' programmes (United Nations, 2013). Such activities attempt to enhance the ECCC's positive impact on the judiciary in Cambodia (McCarthy & Un, 2015). Moreover, as a Deputy Co-Prosecutor of the ECCC put it in 2017, there has been a hope that the 'principles and values in these decisions and judgments will assist those involved in the democratic process to lead the country and its institutions in the right direction' – the success of which is debateable (Hughes, et al., 2018: 312; Gidley, 2019).

Thus, some international actors have pressured for 'independent', fair and efficient international crimes trials and provided critical financial and other assistance to support the ECCC's operations and broader impact in Cambodia. However, there are multiple perspectives of what 'international criminal justice' might involve in Cambodia. These are further exposed in the following analysis of Cambodian government statements.

2.3.2   Cambodian Authorities

Members of the Cambodian government probably held different individual opinions, but the majority of CPP members appear to have supported establishing a Khmer Rouge tribunal with at least some international elements (Etcheson, 2004: 184) – although Party decision-making responsibility rested in few hands (Fawthorp & Jarvis, 2005: 187). In comparison to the emphasis of many international actors on prosecuting DK crimes with international management and due process, the CPP-led government promoted 'win-win' and 'triangle' strategies. These responded to the country's violent past and current situation by promoting development through ensuring peace and stability, Cambodia's international reintegration, and protecting Cambodia's legitimacy as a sovereign state (Hun Sen, 2002). Later, a 'rectangular strategy' focused on ensuring 'good governance' (including legal and judicial reform) in an environment of 'peace, stability and social order'; development partnerships; economic growth; and Cambodia's integration 'into the region and the world' (Hun Sen 2004, 2013). These principles have also been invoked in government statements regarding international criminal justice.

When Hun Sen requested the UN's assistance to prosecute DK-era crimes, he noted that 'Cambodia does not have the resources or expertise to conduct this very important procedure' (United Nations, 1997). Establishing a tribunal may have been viewed as one, though not necessarily the only, way to access additional international funding for these purposes and to foster Cambodia's development. This was particularly likely following Hun Sen's coup, when states such as the United States needed to demonstrate to domestic constituents that Cambodia was a valid aid recipient.

However, Cambodia received assistance from states both opposed to and in favour of an international tribunal. It is not clear whether Cambodia's leaders' greater financial incentives were to accept a tribunal established by the UN Security Council or to accept aid from China and others that opposed international crimes trials (Etcheson, 2004: 202). Cambodia has now experienced consistent economic growth for many years and receives significant foreign investment, especially from China (World Bank, 2019a, 2019b). Development challenges persist, especially concerns about neo-patrimonial governance and corruption (Malena & Chhim, 2009; Global Witness, 2016), but in general there may be declining material motivations for pursuing international criminal justice.

Cambodia's leaders have also presented economic prosperity, institutional development, and 'justice' as being interrelated with securing Cambodia's stable peace.[22] In 1999, Hun Sen stated that '[n]ational reconciliation and peace are indispensable requirement[s] of the Cambodian nation and people' (Hun Sen, 1999: 2). In Tokyo in 2001, Hen Sen claimed 'peace cannot last without justice. Therefore, Cambodia is determined to close the darkest chapter of its own history and look forward toward progress, prosperity and democracy' (Hun Sen, 2001: 2).

'Peace' has encompassed the government's own legitimacy and political stability. Hun Sen's preference was to prosecute only the top Khmer leaders, given the widespread involvement of the population in the criminal conduct (Ciorciari & Heindel, 2014: 30) or, at least, with some association to DK. This included members of the current government, including Hun Sen himself who had defected from DK. On the other hand, the 1979 PRT had already identified and labelled a 'clique' of

---

[22] E.g. 'Peace, stability and national reconciliation are *sine qua non* conditions for economic development and poverty alleviation for the Cambodian people' (Kingdom of Cambodia, 1999: 2).

responsible senior leaders (Pol Pot and Ieng Sary), providing a narrative that could support peace as well as the government's stability. A tribunal would potentially mean the 'government is now allowed to say, "Look, we're not the Khmer Rouge"'[23] and also 'use [a tribunal] as a gun to threaten the Khmer Rouge'.[24]

A version of international criminal justice was deployed that involved pursuing peace and stability, particularly by focusing on the responsibility of a select group of individuals. The government argued that now that Cambodia's conflict was over, further trials (beyond the ECCC's first two cases) should not be pursued. Minister of Information Khieu Kanharith reportedly explained in 2010 that the 'purpose of forming the court was to seek justice for victims and guarantee peace and stability in society' and '[i]f the court walks farther than that, it will fall' (Sokha & O'Toole, 2010; Brinkley, 2013). Thus, peace, reconciliation, and stability have been important elements of the Cambodian government's statements about international criminal justice.

Government statements during the ECCC negotiation also emphasised Cambodia's desire to re-join the international community as a human rights–respecting democratic state. International criminal justice has been associated with Cambodia having 'turned a corner of history, putting firmly behind the darkness of its recent past history and emerging into a new dawn of its future' (Hun Sen, 2002). Cambodia's reports to international treaty bodies have mentioned the ECCC,[25] suggesting that Cambodia's leaders expect that establishing an international criminal tribunal buttresses its democratic credentials. As Hun Sen told the UN General Assembly in relation to the draft ECCC Agreement: 'We are back on the international scene and have become a proud member of ASEAN' (Hun Sen, 2000: 1). Thus, international crimes trials offered opportunities to contribute to all three arms of the 'triangle strategy': apart from providing one avenue for material benefits (aid) and hopefully development, accountability could help peacefully distance the government from DK and provide 'a way for Cambodia to become a fully accepted member of the international community' (Etcheson, 2005: 144).[26]

---

[23] Interview C2.
[24] Interview C4.
[25] E.g. albeit in response to questions about the ECCC, (Committee against Torture, 2010).
[26] An NGO representative opined that Cambodia joined the ICC because 'Cambodia always want[s] ... to be first to have their name in the world. They also join everything ... World Trade Organisation, ASEAN, OPEC: ratif[y] it', Interview C1.

Perhaps unsurprisingly given historic experiences of intervention, the Cambodian government tried to navigate the tension between inviting international criminal justice approaches and avoiding interference by emphasising Cambodia's sovereignty.[27] As stability returned to Cambodia, Hun Sen promoted the use of Cambodian, rather than international, courts to prosecute former DK leaders (Hun Sen, 1999: 3). Cambodian leaders also drew attention to the double standards involved when international actors argued that foreign control of Cambodia's international crimes trials would ensure impartiality. Hun Sen argued: 'If foreigners have the right to lack confidence in Cambodian courts ... we have the right to lack confidence in an international court' (McCarthy, 1999).[28] The same argument was deployed to counter the plans for additional Case 003 and 004 indictments at the ECCC. Hun Sen warned: 'The UN and the countries that supported Pol Pot to occupy Cambodia's seat at the UN from 1979 to 1991 should be tried first. They should be sentenced more heavily than Pol Pot' (Brinkley, 2013: 45). When Cambodia ratified the Rome Statute, Hun Sen suggested that Cambodia expected support from other states to nominate a Cambodian judge to the ICC (Falby, 2002). In this manner, government statements about international criminal justice directed attention towards politicisation, selectivity, and the importance of protecting Cambodia's sovereignty.

The themes invoked by the Cambodian government in debates about international criminal justice were summarised in Deputy Prime Minister Sok An's speech to Cambodia's National Assembly when Cambodia eventually ratified the ECCC Agreement. He pointed out that: 'even before [seeking UN assistance], our Government has held to the following principles as its guiding lights'. These were: first, 'to provide justice' to victims; second 'to maintain peace, political stability and national unification', and third, 'respect for our national sovereignty' (Sok An, 2004: 1–2). In this way, Cambodian government actors proffered a perspective of international criminal justice that would embrace the principles of justice, stability, reintegration, and sovereignty. On the other hand, Cambodia has rarely availed itself of opportunities to contribute to international dialogues about the ICC at the regular Assembly of States Parties meetings

---

[27] E.g. Hun Sen claimed that '[f]ollowing the 1998 elections ... we conducted a "win-win" policy leading to reach genuine national reconciliation *without external influences*' (Hun Sen, 2002, emphasis added); see also (Hun Sen, 2001).

[28] During the ECCC negotiations, Foreign Minister Hor Namhong asked, 'But what has the international community been doing vis-à-vis the Khmer Rouge lately?', quoted in Hammarberg (2001).

held in The Hague. More recently, however, the Cambodian government has also professed its respect for 'the due process of law and the independence of the judiciary' at the ECCC,[29] though questions about its commitment to international criminal justice persist. Debates about prosecuting international crimes are therefore ongoing. They also involve contributions from a range of non-state actors.

2.3.3   Civil Society

A thriving network of Cambodian NGOs emerged in the 1990s, many of which were beneficiaries of foreign funding alongside UNTAC (Sperfeldt, 2012a: 150). Yet a history of repression also resulted in relatively 'low levels of associational activity' and some reluctance to challenge authorities (Malena & Chhim, 2009: 4, 8). Although civil society actors offered to assist with drafting legislation and provided 'moral support to the UN' during the ECCC negotiations (Sokheng, 2002; Peou, 2009: 114), there were few opportunities to act as norm entrepreneur 'mediators' until the Court was being established. Cambodian-based civil society actors have pursued international criminal justice through documenting crimes, monitoring, promoting, and assisting the ECCC. Many of them work with international partners and some have also submitted communications to the ICC.

In the late 1990s, some NGOs in Cambodia that received international funding pursued strategies that would appear 'objective' in an attempt to establish their credibility.[30] For example, the Documentation Center of Cambodia (DC-Cam), which was established by Yale University's Genocide Program but became an independent NGO in 1997, began organising the substantial archives of DK. This made it difficult to ignore the scale of the crimes and contributed to the impetus for an accountability mechanism (Etcheson, 2004: 201). As one former NGO worker explained, 'You cannot first come in and say we want to try this person, that's not going to work. You start with collecting documents. That is the first step in any situation'.[31] This experience has been exported through DC-Cam collaboration with the Network for Human Rights Documentation-Burma (ND-Burma) (International Center for Transitional Justice, 2013). Documented crimes began to be publicised, contributing to calls for prosecutions.

---

[29] E.g. (Cambodia, 2013: 10).
[30] Interview C4.
[31] Interview C4.

Organisations like Asian International Justice Initiative's KRT Trial Monitor, Youth for Peace, Cambodian Human Rights and Development Association (ADHOC), and the Cambodian Defenders Project also monitored and critiqued ECCC proceedings (CHRAC, 2011). Some, though especially international, NGOs and actors criticised the ECCC's cost, delays, and alleged corruption and political interference. Having been established thirty years after its period of temporal jurisdiction and then taking many years to reach verdicts, the ECCC has sometimes been associated with the idea that 'justice delayed is justice denied', though that view is also contested (Menzel, 2007; Hughes et al., 2018) (international criminal tribunals notoriously take long periods to reach verdicts and are expensive) (Ciociari & Heindel, 2014: 93).

The ECCC's victim (civil party) participation and judicial and non-judicial reparations mandate was developed with NGO assistance (Sperfeldt, 2012b). Civil parties, including from diaspora communities in France and the United States, have participated in trials and proposed reparations projects. The lawyers for civil parties are Cambodian and international. With their assistance, civil parties propelled the inclusion of additional gender-based violence charges at the ECCC, for example (Studzinsky, 2011: 100). Cambodia-based NGOs were also integral to the consultation, design, and implementation of the ECCC's civil party participation and reparations processes, including by providing community contacts, implementing reparations projects, and facilitating meetings (Sperfeldt, 2012a, 2012b).[32]

Court outreach services drew on local knowledge to publicise the ECCC's activities in a community-relevant manner, including by engaging with Buddhist monks to use their 'standing in this society … to complement the Court proceedings' (ECCC, 2011; Sperfeldt, 2012a; Stegmiller, 2014). The ECCC's nationally administered Victims' Support Service has brought more than 300,000 Cambodians to observe court proceedings (ECCC, 2015: 9). NGOs have developed television, radio, and other community education formats that explain and promote ECCC proceedings to the Cambodian public (Sperfeldt, 2014). Civil society activities included at least some attempt by ADHOC to discuss the ICC and the international crimes in Cambodia's Criminal Code, although 'participants seem[ed] more interested in the Khmer Rouge past than in a distant institution in The Hague' (Raab & Poluda, 2010: 3).

---

[32] Case 002/01 Judgment, paras. 1113, 1127–40.

Various actors have used local initiatives to contextualise the norm of international criminal justice – predominantly with reference to a domestic and past-focused mechanism, the ECCC – and have transported these experiences to promote justice in other contexts.

A former NGO actor has argued that to be successful in promoting DK trials, Cambodian NGOs needed 'a very good team' but 'not only from the local but from international. Without the support from the international ... it's very difficult to operate in this environment because the opposition and the government may play against you easily'.[33] Cambodian civil society is sometimes described as being 'donor-driven' and 'Phnom Penh centred' rather than having evolved from an activist social base (Malena & Chhim, 2009: 8). Few, if any, of the transitional justice projects discussed in this chapter could have been undertaken without any international finance or seconded international staff (Dosch, 2012; Sperfeldt, 2012a). However, this does not detract from the crucial role of local actors in initiating community projects, seeking out funding, and contributing to NGO activities (Dosch, 2012: 1085). Indeed it is difficult to draw clear boundaries between 'local' and 'international' norm entrepreneurship in Cambodia.

Cambodian and international actors have collaborated in initiatives aimed at addressing atrocities committed subsequent to DK, including possible prosecutions before the ICC. For example, Forum-Asia credited Cambodian organisations ADHOC and the Cambodian League for the Promotion and Defense of Human Rights (LICADHO), as well as the European Union, Norwegian Embassy, and others for having 'paved the way' for Cambodia's ratification of the Rome Statute in 2002 (Forum-Asia, 2001). In 2005, with the support of the European Union, the International Federation for Human Rights (FIDH) held a roundtable event with local members of FIDH, ADHOC, and LICADHO, to discuss the implementation of the Rome Statute (FIDH, 2006a: 5) as part of a project linking this topic to the establishment of the ECCC. ADHOC maintained some focus on the ICC, including by holding a subsequent related workshop in 2012 (ADHOC, 2012). In these cases, local NGOs in Cambodia worked with international partners to encourage support for new international crimes laws. International criminal law has also been used to advocate for contemporary accountability, so that both the ECCC's past-focused prosecutions and the ICC may have a future

---

[33] Interview C4.

impact.[34] A former NGO representative thought that the indirect influence of prosecuting the former regimes is 'invisible but it's very powerful. People know that if you do something wrong, something's going to happen to you, no matter how long after the event [it is]'.[35] This was also a reason for implementing the Rome Statute, which could send 'a strong signal to future perpetrators of the most heinous crimes that impunity will no longer be tolerated' (FIDH, 2006b).

In recent years, local and international groups have submitted communications to the ICC Prosecutor under Article 15 of the Rome Statute, alleging that members of Cambodia's political elite are guilty of international crimes.[36] For example, in 2014, the political opposition, Cambodia National Rescue Party (CNRP), announced a complaint to the ICC concerning land confiscations (Sokchea, 2014). A communication was eventually filed formally on behalf of victims by the international law partnership Global Diligence, represented by Richard Rogers, a former Head of Defence Support Section at the ECCC (Global Diligence, 2014). In September 2016, Rogers argued that the ICC Prosecutor's stated prioritisation of land related crimes should encourage her to focus upon the Cambodia allegations (Global Diligence, 2016). As at June 2019, the outcome of these communications remained unknown. The Cambodian government had deflected the communications as a political and potentially 'defaming' (Yun & Lipes, 2013) 'joke' (Ponniah, 2014; see Soumy, 2016). Officials do not appear to have taken further action to investigate the relevant conduct – for instance, under Cambodia's domestic international crimes legislation.

Some civil society actors retain concerns about double standards and the selective application of international criminal justice. One NGO representative explained that 'we hope the Prosecutor and ICC [can] somehow ensure equality before the law. [So that it] doesn't matter whether this is in [the] African continent' or there are 'financial constraint[s]', the ICC would provide even treatment to all States Parties.[37] This may be linked to historic experience, since the slowness of the international response to Khmer Rouge crimes suggests to some that

---

[34] In relation to post-election violence in early 2014, one NGO representative suggested considering 'whether or not [the] ICC can remind [the authorities] "you need to strengthen the rule of law"', Interview C6.

[35] Interview C4.

[36] E.g. by Khmer National Liberation Front (KNLF), (Yun and Lipes, 2013); and World Organization for Human Rights, (Crothers, 2014).

[37] See also (ICC, 2003). Interview C6.

the ICC would also be slow to pursue prosecutions.[38] Another inter-viewee also observed that the 'ICC is not as strong as domestic court[s], because it doesn't have the police'.[39]

If the ICC does not decide to investigate crimes in Cambodia, there may also be fears that Cambodian authorities will use this as an excuse *not* to respond to complaints within the domestic legal system, which have faced significant challenges, including to the security of activists (Global Witness, 2012). One NGO representative suggested that 'if you relodge [your complaint] at the national court system they will say "refer to the ICC, the ICC said there is no problem". So ... It's a shelter somehow to those kinds of criminals'.[40] He argued that the ICC would not deter contemporary crimes unless it could address the 'gap', where although international crimes have been committed (for political, gravity or evidentiary reasons) the ICC seems 'too high' or 'too far'.[41] Otherwise, 'you create a lot of expectations and then nothing happens'.[42]

Thus at least some local NGO actors challenge the ICC's selectivity and ask it to do more. Just as Hun Sen once argued that the UN 'should play a crucial role in preventing conflicts' (Hun Sen, 2000), an NGO actor asked: 'we know ICC is an international criminal law court, it is a permanent court, it is a court. But can they do more than a court? For example, on prevention issues, can they do it?'[43] The argument that the ICC could do more in Cambodia promotes the importance of international criminal institutions. The documentation, monitoring, and victims and outreach activities mentioned support the prosecution of international crimes in trials before the ECCC. In these ways, actors have used local initiative to promote the 'norm' of international criminal justice in Cambodia.

2.3.4   Local Adaptation

The previous section explained how international states and organisations, Cambodian authorities, and Cambodia-based NGOs have

---

[38] 'Even [the] ICC ... Relating [its situation] to [the] Khmer Rouge as example ... The leader[s] during [the time of Khmer Rouge] power, nobody accepted [a court] then. But when they have no power, they'll arrest [them] ... And that's the challenge you see?', Interview C1.
[39] Interview C1.
[40] Interview C6.
[41] Interview C6.
[42] Interview C6. See also Interview C1.
[43] Interview C6.

attempted to influence Cambodia's approach to prosecuting inter-national crimes. This section explores how some actors have also aimed to move beyond translating the international norm for domestic adop-tion by further reconstructing, or adapting, understandings of inter-national criminal justice in Cambodia – selecting and discarding aspects of the norm to offer new interpretations.

To begin with an example, apart from the Article 15 communications mentioned, it seems that Cambodia-based NGOs attempt to address concerns about 'land grabbing' with a human rights, development, or domestic property law, rather than international criminal law, focus. There may be doubts that much of the violence associated with land issues would technically constitute international crimes, but more per-tinent is the immediate need to defend and protect land activists who are themselves subject to domestic prosecutions (e.g. see Anstis, 2012; Keo, 2016). NGOs rarely publicly link the ECCC's conviction of DK leaders for forcible transfers in Case 002/01[44] to contemporary accusations of forced evictions in Cambodia in their advocacy, despite acknowledg-ments that contemporary land disputes partly derive from historic events (Anstis, 2012).[45] To directly compare the current government to pros-ecutions associated with the Khmer Rouge period is not necessarily helpful in the present environment, compared to alignment with devel-opment and domestic law norms. Rather, circumstances require and encourage 'local' actors to respond to alleged international crimes using adapted, though still judicial, approaches that interpret international criminal justice as having a more historic role.

However, the concept that prosecuting international crimes might be associated with improving judicial institutions is an interpretation that could be useful for activists. Cambodia's domestic international crimes laws are arguably relatively complete (see Section 2.4), so that one NGO representative speculated that some civil society actors 'may say that "I've done my job because genocide, war crimes, crimes against humanity has been codified in the Penal Code already, Cambodia has already signed, ratified the ICC, that's all."'[46] Instead, it may be broader issues of judicial independence that present the remaining barriers to international

---

[44] *Prosecutor v. Nuon Chea and Khieu Samphan*, Case No. 002/19-09-2007/ECCC/TC, Supreme Court Chamber, Appeal Judgment, 23 November 2016 (Case 002/01 Appeal Judgment).

[45] Interview C1.

[46] Interview C6.

criminal justice and other reforms. As one actor put it, '[w]e have good law but enforcement'[47] is the problem. Thus, rather than only advocating for the government to 'end impunity', or working only with the ECCC, many NGOs prioritise judicial capacity building or provide legal aid and community education.[48] Much of this training might be considered legal development work and – rather than focusing on the prosecution of international crimes – covers a variety of related justice and human rights areas, such as access to justice, resolving land disputes, children and women's rights, and issues such as torture and forced confessions.[49]

The norm of international criminal justice, which normally involves prosecutions, has been interpreted in Cambodia as attracting expertise and funding that could also change individual behaviours through education, and thereby have longer-term societal impacts. Law students are a particular focus. An educator who has worked at international crimes tribunals and now teaches in Cambodia believes that encouraging students to think 'critically' 'will have a far greater impact than working at the ECCC, [it's] not even close'.[50] Another NGO representative agreed that 'the only hope may be the younger generation' and school curriculum changes, which have been promoted by the ECCC reparations process, 'the only entry point where international criminal law can be more referred to or can be more researched' in Cambodia beyond the ECCC.[51] Thus, particularly as Cambodia has a high proportion of younger people, long-term strategies aimed at the youth and judiciary are a focus for activities that employ the norm of international criminal justice for broader, educational purposes (Westoby, 2013).

The ECCC has also been accompanied by broader transitional justice projects that adopt some aspects of the idea of prosecuting international crimes. The Group of Experts found little Cambodian interest in establishing a truth commission and heard that any 'commission could not be a substitute for trials' (Group of Experts, 1999: para. 202). However, there have been extensive local memorial and other transitional justice activities in Cambodia (Westoby, 2013). DC-Cam has worked to document and exhibit the history of atrocities, including by promoting the

---

[47] Interview C1.
[48] Interview C5.
[49] As one NGO representative explained, 'the high profile issue[s] in Cambodia ... the children, land and women', Interview C1.
[50] Interview C2.
[51] Interview C6.

construction of a large 'Institute'. The Cambodian Defenders Project organised a series of Women's Hearings where survivors and witnesses publicly shared accounts of gender-based violence committed during DK (Ye, 2014). The Hearings and related projects arguably demonstrated that 'many small and localized initiatives can ... be equally important to more grandiose undertakings such as the establishment of an inter-nationalized criminal tribunal' (Ye, 2014; Tek & Sperfeldt, 2016: 135). Alongside wide-ranging recommendations for governments, civil society, and international organisations, expert panels at the Hearings also suggested that the ECCC investigate and prosecute sexual violence crimes.[52] Thus, these forums did not represent a substitute for international crimes prosecutions, but adapted some of their features, including through the use of witness testimony and documentation.

NGO advocacy often refers to the ECCC and the ICC as the venues for international criminal justice and the Rome Statute as a model for legislation (FIDH, 2006a). However, some responses to international crimes have been adjusted to incorporate 'local' Buddhist or cultural views. Across the transitional justice field, following the UNTAC period, 'non-governmental organizations proliferated in Cambodia and dis-courses of reconciliation, human rights, and justice were localized, often in Buddhist terms, in another reworking of the genocidal past' (Hinton, 2008: 66). This may partly have arisen from a perception expressed by one international actor based in Cambodia that:

> In [the Cambodian public's] mind [the ECCC accused] were already guilty. And a lot of that stems from a sort of different sense of justice that we have in the West. And there's no concept of trials so they're like, why are these people getting treated so well when the common criminal who steals a chicken or a moto is tortured, beaten and thrown in terrible prisons for years and these people get to live in nice cushy digs, air conditioning, things like that.[53]

There are indications of a shift towards international NGOs preferring to support community-derived ('bottom-up') initiatives that encourage dialogue about past crimes, rather than focusing only upon prosecutions (Malena & Chhim, 2009: 8; Westoby, 2013: 46), even if still linked to the ECCC. Regardless of the reason, the norm of international criminal justice is integrated with community-led responses to the atrocities.

---

[52] E.g. (Cambodian Defenders Project, 2013: 5).
[53] Interview C2.

This tilt towards local engagement being an aspect of international criminal justice has extended to the way that international criminal law reparations are designed at the ECCC. The ECCC Chambers have approved reparation projects including memorials and public exhibitions, as well as initiatives that claim to be 'culturally adapted', including community self-help groups, testimonial therapies,[54] educational programmes and apps, exhibitions, and theatre.[55] Many local and international actors have supported creative projects not directly linked to the ECCC, but sometimes stimulated by – including – as a reaction to, the Court's existence and shortcomings, such as an annual 'peace walk', pagodas, theatre, exhibitions, oral history, and radio programs (Westoby, 2013; Herman, 2018). One NGO has trained Buddhist monks 'to be more effective in their ability to encourage people to talk and share' and thereby equip them to contribute to community stability and reconciliation (Westoby, 2013: 174). Another project adapted television programs about the ECCC proceedings to 'create environments favourable for longer-term reconciliatory processes *beyond the ECCC*' (Sperfeldt, 2014; Sperfeldt et al. 2016: 7 emphasis added). Scholars have observed that '[d]ialogue, between individuals and across communities as a whole, is considered crucial in creating a *space* in which reconciliation can occur' (Westoby, 2013: 48 emphasis added). Similarly, for an international actor, 'I view [related debates] and other people do too as a battle over space between the government and civil society'.[56] The ECCC has contributed to securing such 'space' through facilitating an influx of funding, ideas, and debate about prosecuting international crimes, but the situation continues to be challenging, especially since the Cambodian government has tightened restrictions on NGO activities (Human Rights Watch, 2016b). Still, artistic developments including theatre, dance, art exhibitions, and numerous films about life during and pre-DK have proliferated alongside the ECCC.[57]

It seems that for all its weaknesses, international attention and the establishment of the ECCC has attracted expertise and funding towards prosecuting international crimes in Cambodia. Individuals within

---

[54] See (TPO Cambodia, 2015); Case 002/01 Judgment, para. 1131.
[55] *Prosecutor v. Nuon Chea and Khieu Samphan*, Case No. 002/19-09-2007/ECCC/TC, Trial Chamber, Case 002/02 Judgment, 16 November 2018 (Case 002/02 Judgment).
[56] Interview C2.
[57] Director Rithy Panh reflects on the relationship of film (and its ability to depict physical presence) to justice in this interview (Cruvellier, 2018).

Cambodia have initiated and capitalised on this 'space', taking up opportunities for education and dialogue about justice, history, and personal experiences, in order to promote an understanding of international criminal justice that encompasses and amplifies these activities. Actors within Cambodia have engaged in diverse initiatives beyond the ECCC that adapt understandings of international criminal justice, including to promote broader contemporary institutional reforms and intracommunity dialogue.

2.3.5 Summary: Local Initiative and Adaptation

International and government actors have discussed international criminal justice in Cambodia with reference to independence, due process and efficiency, sovereignty, selectivity, reconciliation, peace and stability, reintegration, and development issues. Civil society actors from around the world have advocated for prosecuting international crimes and have assisted the ECCC through documentation, monitoring, working with civil parties, and community outreach. To do so, Cambodians have engaged international partners and organisations, including by submitting communications to the ICC.

Thus, both international and Cambodia-based actors have been engaged in debates about prosecuting international crimes that occurred in the past, as well as in relation to contemporary or future violations. However, some have also taken up advocacy in other priority areas or have turned their attention towards educating future generations, judicial reform, and broader reconciliation initiatives. Through such legal and community engagement, a variety of actors have adapted international, state, and community notions of international criminal justice. These processes of adaptation are evident in Cambodia's mechanisms for prosecuting international crimes.

2.4 Mechanisms for Prosecuting International Crimes in Cambodia

Cambodia has a civil law legal system partly derived from the French protectorate period, although colonial and DK upheavals have contributed to obscure the exact content of Cambodian law (Adams, 2005; FIDH, 2006a).[58] There are several avenues for responding to

---

[58] A modified version of the French criminal code, the 1956 Criminal Law, was adopted post-independence. A 1954 Code of Military Justice included some offences against

international crimes committed in Cambodia. First, there are international mechanisms. Cambodia has ratified most international human rights and humanitarian law treaties, including the Rome Statute. Second, Cambodia passed the ECCC Law in 2004. Third, international crimes are included in Cambodia's Criminal Code. Finally, amnesties and pardons have been provided in the past and may still be available, including for international crimes.

2.4.1 International Mechanisms

A new internationalised tribunal or other states' universal jurisdiction might be deployed to prosecute international crimes committed in Cambodia in future. The ICC may also have jurisdiction over such crimes committed after 1 July 2002. However, Cambodia has not adopted specific legislation for cooperating with the ICC or ratified the Agreement on Privileges and Immunities of the ICC, which may complicate its cooperation with any ICC investigation – for example, that results from the Article 15 communications discussed.

Cambodia has ratified the four Geneva Conventions and a number of other relevant international humanitarian law and human rights treaties, including Additional Protocols I and II (see Appendix A). In 2007, Cambodia's Constitutional Council drew on Article 31 of the Constitution to suggest that 'law' in Cambodia includes international human rights treaties to which it is a party,[59] though Article 31 also says that the 'exercise of such rights and freedom shall be in accordance with the [Cambodian] law'. Still, the situation for humanitarian law treaties is unclear, as is the question of which laws take precedence where domestic legislation is inconsistent with international treaty obligations.[60] In

---

wounded or dead soldiers. The 1980 PRK Decree Law 2 remained the only criminal 'law' until UNTAC adopted 'Provisions relating to the Judicial and Criminal Law and Procedure Applicable in Cambodia during the Transitional Period of 1992'.

[59] *Kingdom of Cambodia Constitutional Council Decision 092/003/2007*, Case No. 131/003/2007, 26 June 2007, see Article 31 of the Constitution of the Kingdom of Cambodia 1993; this interpretation was suggested in (Committee on the Elimination of Discrimination against Women, 2011: para. 23) regarding a ratified treaty. Cambodia's government has suggested that the Constitution 'recognizes and respects human rights' in accordance with the terms of Article 31, see e.g. (Cambodia, 2013: para. 86).

[60] See (Teilee, 2010). In *Prosecutor v. Kaing Guek Eav alias Duch*, Case No. 001/18-07-2007/ECCC/TC, Trial Chamber, Decision on the Defence Preliminary Objection concerning the Statute of Limitations of Domestic Crimes, 26 July 2010 (Statutory Limitations Decision), para. 39 the Trial Chamber found that Article 15 of the International Covenant

practice Cambodia has adopted domestic legislation to implement its obligations under international treaties.[61] The localisation framework suggests that as norms are reshaped in Southeast Asia, they may lead to new or modified institutions and practices 'in which local influences remain highly visible' (Acharya, 2004: 251). The next section reviews the Cambodian legislation that has been passed in order to address international criminal law.

2.4.2   The ECCC Law

The ECCC in many ways demonstrates an idea suggested by the 'localisation' framework: that institutions can represent a convergence between 'local' concerns and selected aspects of 'normalised' international criminal justice. The ECCC Law is a Cambodian law providing for 'Extraordinary Chambers' to be established within Cambodia's court structure. However, as discussed, the ECCC is an 'internationalised' tribunal, formed by agreement between the Cambodian government and the UN (the ECCC Agreement) and Cambodian law (the ECCC Law). It involved an adaptation of the norm of international criminal justice in its structure, procedures, the time period it focuses on, and the people and crimes it prosecutes (see Palmer, 2016).

Cambodian and international aspirations that the ECCC might build domestic capacity and support Cambodia's sovereignty were reflected in the Court's internationalised structure, which draws on Cambodian and international law and employs national and international staff. The inclusion of national and international roles, including national/international co-prosecutors and judges, might have been hoped to encourage knowledge transfer between the different groups, but also led to divisions within court operations along these spatial lines (Ciorciari & Heindel, 2014; Christensen & Kjeldgaard-Pedersen, 2018).

Article 12 of the ECCC Agreement provides that ECCC procedures 'shall be in accordance with Cambodian law', but reflecting the arguments of some international actors (see Section 2.3.1), the ECCC Law also requires that ECCC trials be conducted 'in accordance with existing procedures in force' with reference to international procedures if there is

---

on Civil and Political Rights, adopted 16 December 1966, entered into force 23 March 1976 (ICCPR), was applicable to the ECCC because of Article 33 new, ECCC Law.

[61] E.g. Law on the Prohibition of Chemical, Nuclear, Biological and Radiological Weapons, 3 December 2009; Law on the Protection of Cultural Heritage, 25 January 1996.

uncertainty and 'international standards of justice, fairness and due process of law'.[62] The ECCC allows for limited victim participation and reparations, though these were not explicitly included in the initial ECCC Law. Both processes came to be an integral (if controversial) part of the ECCC's activities. They are formalised in the ECCC's internal rules of procedure and evidence, which drew on Cambodian criminal procedure (influenced by French civil law tradition) as well as the processes of other international criminal tribunals (including the ICC).

Adaptation is also evident in the ECCC's narrow jurisdiction to prosecute the 'senior leaders of Democratic Kampuchea and those who were most responsible for the crimes and serious violations of Cambodian laws related to crimes, international humanitarian law, and international conventions recognized by Cambodia' committed between 17 April 1975 and 6 January 1979.[63] The Cambodian government might have been open to wider temporal jurisdiction,[64] but this restricted scope was acceptable to them and more comfortable for the foreign governments implicated in the Cambodian conflicts before and after DK, including the United States (Ciorciari & Heindel, 2014: 29). While the UN had sought a broader personal jurisdiction, the narrow approach was important for the Cambodian government's 'narrative of rescue' (Ainley, 2014: 149) and thereby its own future stability. For all parties, this jurisdiction could reflect one tenet of the norm of international criminal justice, 'the idea that certain individuals are *particularly* to blame' (Mégret, 2015: 84).

Focusing on this period presented other temporal issues, however. In contrast to notions of international criminal law as progressive (see Chapter 1), the ECCC must apply its jurisdiction using historically recognised crimes, rather than more recent developments in international criminal law jurisprudence. The ECCC has jurisdiction to prosecute most international crimes, but also includes other crimes under Cambodian and international law. The ECCC may prosecute the crimes of genocide,[65] crimes against humanity,[66] grave breaches of the Geneva

---

[62] Article 33 new, ECCC Law.

[63] Article 2 new, ECCC Law.

[64] Linton (2005: 5) observes that 'the RGC did attempt to widen the temporal jurisdiction to 1970–1998 which would have brought in acts that would meet the General Assembly's 1974 definition of aggression, but it seems that this was simply a negotiating tactic' partly because 'it [would] have brought the wrath of the USA, China and Vietnam down on the government'.

[65] Article 4 ECCC Law.

[66] Article 5 ibid.

Conventions,[67] the destruction of cultural property during armed conflict,[68] and 'crimes against internationally protected persons pursuant to the Vienna Convention of 1961 on Diplomatic Relations',[69] though not the crime of aggression (see Linton, 2005). The definition of genocide is adopted from the Genocide Convention.[70] While Cambodia had ratified the Rome Statute by the time the amended Law was adopted in 2004, the Law largely replicates the crimes against humanity provisions from the earlier ICTY and ICTR Statutes.[71] These appeared a more appropriate starting point for determining the content of international criminal law in the late 1970s than the more recent Rome Statute.[72] Thus, the Law does not include the additional definitions included in Article 7(2) of the Rome Statute about crimes against humanity, nor, for example, its range of sexual and gender-based violence crimes (Williams & Palmer, 2015). It also omits the war crimes included in the Rome Statute or Additional Protocols beyond the grave breaches,[73] including those committed in a non-international armed conflict that arguably had less certain status in customary international law during the relevant period. International lawyer Suzannah Linton observes that this omission could have been explained if the DK period was considered an international conflict. However, this was 'not consistent with the aims and objects of the drafters' who did not want the full period of Cambodia's war from 1970 or earlier, when international actors were implicated in the conflict, 'opened up to scrutiny' (Linton, 2005: 47).

The ECCC Law also incorporates select aspects of domestic Cambodian law. For instance, it provides the Court with jurisdiction to try crimes of homicide, torture, and religious persecution included in the

---

[67] Article 6 ibid.
[68] Article 7 ibid.
[69] Article 8 ibid.
[70] Ratified by Cambodia 14 October 1950 before entry into force, 12 January 1951.
[71] E.g. the ECCC Law has no requirement for crimes against humanity to occur during an armed conflict, as in Article 5 of the Statute for the International Criminal Tribunal for the former Yugoslavia (ICTY Statute), but does require that crimes against humanity involve an 'attack directed against any civilian population, on national, political, ethnical, racial or religious grounds', as does Article 3 of the Statute for the International Criminal Tribunal for Rwanda (ICTR Statute), but not the ICTY Statute.
[72] The UN Secretary-General suggested that crimes in the ICTY Statute were all recognised in customary international law (United Nations Secretary General, 1993).
[73] Cambodia became a party to the first two Protocols in 1998. See Appendix A.

1956 Penal Code,[74] but not other Cambodian national crimes, including, for example, sexual violence crimes. Cambodia's Constitutional Council suggested that the ECCC's jurisdiction and removal of statutory limitation periods did not breach provisions in the 1956 Penal Code concerning the non-retroactive application of criminal law.[75] However, the ECCC Trial Chamber was unable to agree that it could apply the 1956 law, partly due to a dispute as to when Cambodia's devastated judicial system became capable of prosecuting international crimes.[76] This demonstrated how attempts to infuse international criminal justice with domestic laws can require international criminal tribunals to assess and adjust to apparently local laws, contexts and events.

The ECCC Law does not address modes of liability, though the Chambers have drawn on ICTY and ICTR jurisprudence to justify reliance upon the first two forms of 'joint criminal enterprise' (but not the third).[77] Like the ICTY and ICTR Statutes, no defences are included and Article 29(4) of the ECCC Law confirms there is no defence of superior orders. Thus, the Chambers refer to the relevant domestic laws for the period under examination, including the defences in the 1956 Penal Code as well as jurisprudence from other international tribunals (Linton, 2005: 36).[78]

The ECCC Law therefore involved the establishment of a new institution for prosecuting past international crimes in Cambodia. However, it was adapted in various ways, including in its temporal, personal, and subject-matter jurisdiction. While international norm entrepreneurs can attempt to 'spread transnational norms', the localisation framework suggests that approaches 'that accommodate local sensitivity', especially where international proponents 'act through local agents', are more likely to lead to institutional change (Acharya, 2004: 249). This approach helps to explain the contribution of various actors to Cambodia's internationalised criminal justice mechanism. Some, but not all, foreign states and international NGOs demanded international criminal justice for DK crimes and opposed a Cambodian-managed tribunal. However,

---

[74] Article 3 ECCC Law.
[75] *Kingdom of Cambodia Constitutional Council Decision 040/002/2001*, Case No. 038/001/2001, 12 February 2001; Statutory Limitations Decision, para. 6.
[76] Statutory Limitations Decision. Cases 003 and 004 charges included violations of the 1956 Code.
[77] Case 002/01 Appeal Judgment, paras. 768–810.
[78] E.g. *Prosecutor v. Kaing Guek Eav alias Duch*, Case No. 001/18-07-2007/ECCC/TC, Trial Chamber, Judgment, 26 July 2010 (Case 001 Judgment), para. 553–4 regarding duress.

Cambodian NGOs lacked access to the ECCC negotiations. Cambodia-based efforts to document international crimes were important and involved individuals from Cambodia and elsewhere – including Helen Jarvis, a Cambodian citizen from Australia who worked with the Cambodian government. Yet the mediation of local civil society norm entrepreneurs was less significant in establishing the ECCC than the term 'localisation' might suggest. There was a relative lack of avenues for Cambodia NGOs to 'localize a normative order . . . by building congruence with outside ideas' (Acharya, 2004: 249), especially within socio-cultural power hierarchies (Malena & Chhim, 2009: 7). The ECCC structure therefore largely did not reflect their priorities, nor was the Law progressive. Later opportunities to shape the ECCC's operations were taken up, however, by developing and supporting the outreach, civil party participation, and reparations procedures.

On the other hand, the Cambodian *state* actors who developed the ECCC draft agreement restructured notions of international criminal justice by incorporating elements that supported their priorities of sovereignty, stability, and development. For example, the aspects of international criminal justice involving some international involvement, due process rights, and limited jurisdiction over senior leaders were accepted. However, Cambodia's leaders rejected the idea that international crimes trials would be entirely internationally managed and the ECCC has drawn its procedures from both international and Cambodian sources. Thus, consistent with both constructivist theories that emphasise domestic input and the localisation framework (see Chapter 1), 'local' actors also influenced Cambodia's approach to international criminal justice.

The ECCC has been heavily criticised, but it operates largely within fair trial standards and has secured convictions.[79] The ECCC prosecutions might suggest that the government at least supported pursuing past-focused trials. However, the adapted nature of the ECCC's legal framework and the government's opposition towards prosecuting more than the initial small group of ECCC accused do not indicate that Cambodia's leaders were willing to fully adopt, or have internalised, 'normalised' understandings of international criminal justice, even for earlier crimes. Instead, the ECCC represents a set of instruments that borrowed from notions of international criminal justice, but 'in which local influences remain highly visible', as well as historic experiences – that is, a 'localised' institution (Acharya, 2004: 251; Palmer, 2016).

---

[79] See Case 002/01 Appeal Judgment, paras. 109–239.

2.4.3   Domestic Criminal Legislation

In relation to contemporary or future crimes, Cambodia's development of domestic international crimes legislation and practice also does not clearly represent the rejection, or acceptance, of the norm of international criminal justice. Cambodia's 2010 Criminal Code includes crimes that could encompass similar conduct to international crimes, including murder, torture and 'barbarous' acts, violence, rape and sexual assault, illegal arrest or detention, and discrimination. Cambodia's legal Commission of the National Assembly drafted international crimes provisions for this Code and the 2007 Criminal Procedures Code, with the assistance of French lawyers (FIDH, 2006a: 50). The Code includes crimes against humanity, genocide, and war crimes and provides jurisdiction where there is a link to Cambodian territory, victims, or perpetrators, though it does not confer universal jurisdiction.[80] Article 7 clarifies that the Code is to be interpreted in light of its provisions, 'subject to international treaties' (such as the Rome Statute) and Article 8 suggests that the Code should not prevent survivors of international humanitarian law violations from pursuing prosecutions under other relevant laws – for example, the ECCC Law.

The Code draws on the Rome Statute crimes provisions with minor variations (Meisenberg, 2015).[81] Notably, it extends liability for international crimes to 'legal entities' (but not the state).[82] Like the ECCC Law, the Code does not include the definitions contained in Article 7(2) of the Rome Statute regarding crimes against humanity, leaving scope for courts to interpret terms such as 'deportation or forcible transfer of population' in context. The crime against humanity of persecution does not extend to grounds other than 'political, racial, national, ethnic, cultural, religious or gender',[83] though this is more expansive than the ECCC Law, which only referred to 'political, racial, and religious grounds'.

---

[80] Articles 19–20, 22, Criminal Code, although it extends to crimes committed by Cambodians overseas or by a foreigner against Cambodian victims, 'against the security of' Cambodia, or where the offence was committed against a Cambodian diplomatic or consular agent or premises or related to counterfeiting (Article 22).

[81] For example, the definition of genocide in Article 183(4), Criminal Code, includes 'imposing *forceful* measures *or voluntary means* intended to prevent births'.

[82] Articles 187, 192, 198, Criminal Code.

[83] I.e. excluding 'or other grounds that are universally recognized as impermissible under international law' as in Article 7(1)(h) of the Rome Statute. Article 188(8), ibid.

The war crimes provision in Article 193 of the Code is adopted in similar form to Article 8(2)(a) of the Rome Statute, which also addresses grave breaches, although – as in the ECCC Law – Article 193(5)-(8)[84] protects 'civilians'. This could exclude such crimes committed against medical and religious personnel and the unlawful deportation, transfer, or confinement of non-civilians (Meisenberg, 2015: 129–31).[85] The ECCC Law only included these grave breaches, whereas Article 194 of the Code merges Article 8(2)(b) and (c) of the Rome Statute in prohibiting a list of war crimes in both international and non-international conflicts, reflecting a conception of international criminal responsibility for war crimes that has broadened over time. It omits some of the Rome Statute violations, such as enlisting or conscripting children under the age of 15, the use of prohibited weapons other than poison, sexual violence war crimes, and declaring that no quarter will be given (Meisenberg, 2015: 134), which suggests some adaptation. Finally, providing a foreign state with 'the means of undertaking hostilities or aggressions' is punishable under the Code,[86] though it includes neither aggression nor crimes against peace.

The Code incorporates criminal responsibility provisions that are as expansive as those in the Rome Statute (Meisenberg, 2015: 135). For example, co-perpetrators are those who 'by mutual agreement, commit the relevant criminally prohibited act', or 'attempt to commit a felony',[87] which, by focusing on the agreement, rather than taking a 'substantial step', arguably reflects a lower culpability threshold for attempt than Article 25 of the Rome Statute. Moreover, the Code criminalises planning to commit genocide or crimes against humanity, including participating in a group or organisation to do so.[88] It also includes the 'incitement … to discriminate, to be malicious or violent against a person or a group of persons because of their membership or nonmembership of a particular ethnicity, nationality, race or religion'.[89] This provision suggests incitement to commit genocide,[90] but appears broader. On the other hand, the Code does not include an explicit superior responsibility provision.

---

[84] Equivalent to Article 8(2)(a)(v)–(viii), Rome Statute.
[85] However, the chapeau of Article 193, Criminal Code, refers to acts committed against 'persons or properties protected by Geneva Convention[s]', which could protect a broader range of victims.
[86] Article 444, Criminal Code.
[87] Article 26, Criminal Code.
[88] Articles 185 and 190, Criminal Code.
[89] Article 496, Criminal Code.
[90] Article 25(3)(e), Rome Statute.

The Code includes various defences, such as in relation to mental disorders[91] and self-defence.[92] As to superior orders, Article 32 says that perpetrators of genocide, crimes against humanity *or war crimes* 'shall not, under any circumstances' be exempted from responsibility because the act was authorised or not prohibited by law or performed subject to an order, which goes beyond Article 33 of the Rome Statute and Article 17 of the 1997 military law,[93] but reflects Article 29(4) of the ECCC Law[94] and the position in customary international law (Gaeta, 1999).

Cambodia has not ratified the 1968 Convention on the Non-Applicability of Statutory Limitations to War Crimes and Crimes Against Humanity,[95] but the Code[96] and Criminal Procedures Code[97] provide that the limitations periods do not apply for genocide, war crimes, or crimes against humanity.[98] However, the Code does not establish any special chambers or mechanism for investigating and prosecuting international crimes and Cambodia's Criminal Procedures Code does not include specific procedures for prosecuting international crimes.[99] This means that there is a lack of clarity as to how these provisions would actually be enforced to promote the norm of international criminal justice domestically.

Cambodia's Criminal Code – with prospective jurisdiction – was therefore closely modelled on the Rome Statute. While its extension of liability to legal entities (corporations), as well as the exclusion of particular definitions and war crimes, included an element of international (especially French) engagement alongside the ECCC (FIDH, 2006a), it also partly resulted from the domestic drafting process and was acceptable to Cambodian authorities and NGO actors. The new offences came alongside other amendments to the Code that were condemned as

---

[91] Article 31, Criminal Code.

[92] Article 33, Criminal Code.

[93] The Law on General Statutes for the Military Personnel of the Royal Cambodian Armed Forces, CS/RKM/1197/005, 6 November 1997.

[94] See Case 001 Judgment, para. 552.

[95] Adopted 26 November 1968, entered into force 11 November 1970. The provisions of this Convention may not reflect customary international law and are unlikely to apply where states have inconsistent legislation (Ratner et al., 2009: 160).

[96] Article 143, Criminal Code.

[97] Article 9, Criminal Procedure Code.

[98] See Statutory Limitations Decision.

[99] Other than in relation to provisional detention in Articles 210 and 608, possibly influenced by ECCC decisions, e.g. *Prosecutor v. Kaing Guek Eav alias Duch*, Case No. 001/18-07-2007/ECCC/TC, Trial Chamber, Decision on Request for Release, 15 June 2009.

infringing on human rights, particularly freedom of speech (e.g. LICADHO, 2010). The comparative success of including international crimes provisions was 'widely seen as a result of ADHOC advocacy [as part of the project with FIDH], described by international partners as the most consistent and best heard voice defending the Rome Statute in Cambodia' (Raab & Palouda, 2010: 2). The Code's (albeit minor) deviations from the Rome Statute could make it difficult for national proceedings to provide a barrier for ICC prosecutions based on the principle of complementarity (Meisenberg, 2015), making it hard to understand the legislation as purely a 'performance' for the ICC (de Vos, 2015: 405) or internalisation of the norm of international criminal justice. However, in general, the adoption of these laws could be considered consistent with one aspect of the norm of international criminal justice: allowing for domestic international crimes prosecutions. In other words, as a step towards accepting the norm, with minor adaptations. Still, Cambodian law retains avenues to exclude perpetrators of international crimes from criminal sanction.

2.4.4   Amnesties and Immunities

There are multiple possible reactions to the commission of international crimes, ranging from no response, to the use of amnesties, to the establishment of international criminal tribunals. Each of these responses, including amnesties, is found in both international practice and transitional justice approaches (Teitel, 2000), although the provision of amnesties for international crimes has a problematic relationship to the norm of international criminal justice (Pensky, 2008; Jeffery, 2018). Amnesties and pardons have been employed by Cambodia in the past, including for DK defectors in the Law to Outlaw Democratic Kampuchea Group in 1994 and a Royal Amnesty issued for Ieng Sary in 1996. This was reflected in Article 40 new of the ECCC Law, which allowed the ECCC to determine the scope of any previous pardons or amnesties. In a decision demonstrating the potential for friction between Cambodian laws and the international criminal justice norm, the ECCC Pre-Trial Chamber found that Ieng Sary's prior conviction before the PRT, the Royal Amnesty granted in 1996, and the amnesty law of 1994 did not prevent his prosecution.[100]

[100] *Prosecutor v. Ieng Sary*, Case No. 002/19-09-2007-ECCC/OCIJ (PTC75), Pre-Trial Chamber, Decision on Ieng Sary's appeal against the closing order D427/1/30, 11 April 2011.

The position within domestic courts for future prosecutions under the Criminal Code is unclear. Article 90 new (4) of the Constitution allows the National Assembly to adopt a general amnesty and the Code confirms that this encompasses expunging convictions, but does not prevent survivors from seeking compensation for the damage they have suffered.[101] Similarly, Article 27 of the Constitution allows the King to grant partial or complete amnesty. While the Rome Statute provides that it applies to Heads of State and other officials,[102] within Cambodia the King is considered inviolable under Article 7 of the Constitution, although the monarch's role today is predominantly formal. The question of the compatibility of Article 7 with Article 27 of the Rome Statute does not appear to have been addressed when Cambodia ratified the Rome Statute or amended the Code, possibly because the pre-eminence of the Constitutional position was considered 'clear' to parliamentarians (FIDH, 2006a: p. 7 (fn. 4)). Articles 80 and 104 of the Constitution also provide members of the National Assembly and senators with parliamentary immunity.[103] Thus – reflecting concerns about Cambodia's stability and potentially concerning royalty, social hierarchies and Buddhist conceptions of forgiveness – amnesties, pardons, and limited immunities may still operate with respect to prosecuting international crimes in Cambodian Courts.

2.4.5 Enforcement

Cambodia has been the site of international crimes trials at the PRT and at the ECCC, the latter of which has now convicted three individuals and – with intermittent opposition of the Cambodian national judicial officers at the ECCC and the Cambodian government – investigated a further five.[104] In doing so, due to the requirements of the ECCC Agreement and ECCC Law, the ECCC has made use of Cambodian

---

[101] Articles 149–151, Criminal Code.

[102] Article 27, Rome Statute and on the position more generally, see e.g. (Ratner et al., 2009: 156; Akande and Shah, 2010); and at the International Court of Justice, *Arrest Warrant of 11 April 2000 (Democratic Republic of the Congo v. Belgium)*, Judgment of 14 February 2002, ICJ, 14 February 2002.

[103] However, Article 126 of the Constitution provides that government members are not immune for crimes committed in the course of their duties. Note that parliamentary immunities are not necessarily respected, see (Human Rights Watch, 2016). Though see Article 51, Common Statute on Civil Servants 1994.

[104] Ao An, Im Chaem, Meas Muth, Sou Met, and Yim Tith.

domestic law.[105] The relationship between Cambodian and international legal principles has sometimes presented complexities, as in relation to amnesties[106] and the detention of the ECCC accused by the Cambodian Military Court until their transfer to the ECCC in 2007.[107] In Case 001, the ECCC Trial Chamber found that the 'ECCC Law not only authorizes the ECCC to apply domestic criminal procedure, but also obligates it to interpret these rules and determine their conformity with international standards'.[108] International human rights and criminal laws have therefore been enforced by the ECCC, though with reference to domestic laws and procedures. Other actors, including from civil society, have then engaged with these laws since the ECCC commenced operations, including in relation to victim participation and reparations, as well as prosecuting sexual and gender-based violence, and in stimulating diverse community activities (Sperfeldt, 2012a). Thus, rather than an international norm being accepted through the entrepreneurship of civil society, a variety of actors have influenced Cambodia's approach to prosecuting past international crimes at the ECCC on an ongoing basis, in ways that emphasise or seek to alter different aspects of international criminal justice. Moreover, the ECCC has produced jurisprudence that has been drawn upon by other international criminal tribunals, demonstrating how approaches towards international criminal justice can be drawn from localised sources.[109]

There have been a number of other trials in Cambodia that relate to human rights violations that might be considered international crimes,[110] including: the Nuon Paet trial referred to in Section 2.2.3, the 2006 conviction of military and police personnel for sixty-two extrajudicial killings, another case in 2006 in which six police officers were found guilty of torture and, since the new Code was promulgated, a 2010 case involving police, military police, and soldiers charged with arbitrary killings, as well

---

[105] See e.g. (Shany, 2013) regarding the use of domestic criminal law in relation to the joint criminal enterprise doctrine.

[106] *Prosecutor v. Ieng Sary*, Decision on Ieng Sary's appeal against the closing order D427/1/30, 11 April 2011.

[107] E.g. *Prosecutor v. Duch*, Decision on Request for Release, 15 June 2009.

[108] Ibid., para. 15.

[109] E.g. *Prosecutor v. Dominic Ongwen*, ICC Case No. ICC-02/04-01/15, Pre-Trial Chamber II, Decision on the confirmation of charges against Dominic Ongwen, 23 March 2016, paras. 90–2.

[110] It is beyond the scope of this book to undertake a detailed analysis of whether such acts would constitute international crimes, but they do provide examples of conduct that, on its face, could be investigated as such.

as a range of other prosecutions for offences such as physical assault and forced confessions.[111] In 2013, a town governor, Chhouk Bandith, was convicted of causing bodily harm under the Code for shooting garment workers in Svay Rieng Special Economic Zone during protests in 2012. His co-defendant, a police chief, was found guilty of the lesser charge of 'illegal use of a weapon'. Both convictions were upheld on appeal and Chhouk Bandith turned himself in to authorities in 2015 (Titthara, 2015), though arguably with a relatively short sentence of eighteen months. Such cases have not involved Cambodia's international crimes legislation, but suggest that domestic courts may, on occasion, hear cases brought for serious harms perpetrated by officials. Then again, these trials are the exception and criticisms of their fairness, selectivity, and political interference continue to be directed towards the Cambodian judiciary, as well as at the ECCC (McCarthy & Un, 2015).

The practice of the ECCC and the more recent allegations of international crimes being committed in Cambodia, despite the Criminal Code's international crimes laws without accountability, suggest that attitudes towards the norm of international criminal justice might differ for different events over different time periods. This is consistent with Zimmermann's suggestion that resistance, adaptation, or adoption of norms reoccurs differently over time, as successive laws are proposed, passed, and implemented (or repealed) (Zimmermann, 2017). Cambodia's innovative, but imperfect, international criminal laws and institutions have not evolved from rejection of accepting normalised ideas of international criminal justice, via the influence of international actors or norm entrepreneurs upon receptive 'locals'. Instead, Cambodia's leaders and civil society actors continue to engage with this norm in a locally adapted manner.

To summarise, Cambodia's legislation for prosecuting international crimes was closely modelled upon the Rome Statute. Some deviations, particularly in the ECCC Law, might be explained by legal doctrines such as the non-retroactive application of criminal laws, or as reflecting customary international law and Cambodia's treaty obligations. Other adaptations – including the restrictive approach to war crimes (more pronounced in the ECCC Law), the narrow jurisdiction in the ECCC Law, inclusion of corporate liability for international crimes in the Criminal Code, and the retention of pardons and immunities – might

---

[111] For a list of relevant prosecutions, see Transitional Justice Research Collaborative. Cambodia, https://transitionaljusticedata.com/browse/index/Browse.countryid:19.

more helpfully be explained by reflecting on Cambodia's historic experiences and the engagement of international and Cambodian state and non-state actors in the law-making process.

2.5 Conclusions

The application of the localisation framework in this chapter highlights how interactions between different perspectives did not result in Cambodia's authorities simply adopting the UN preference for an internationally controlled tribunal (or others' preference for no tribunal) to respond to DK crimes. Nor, while Cambodia has ratified the Rome Statute and adopted domestic international crimes legislation, is there an indication that other international crimes will be prosecuted in Cambodian courts. On the other hand, it is not accurate to characterise Cambodia as having rejected all aspects of the norm of international criminal justice. Instead, local actors transformed an international concept for local use, while some international actors changed their perception of what form of international criminal justice might be appropriate, as a localised structure became more popular at the ECCC, and legislation was drafted for prospective crimes. This case therefore supports more recent constructivist frameworks such as 'localisation', that emphasise norm contestation and adaptation, rather than expectations about how 'socialisation' might lead to the internalisation of norms.

Internationalised tribunals such as the ECCC have been discussed as possible models for other regional contexts, such as in Sri Lanka, demonstrating how local adaptations may influence global norms (UN Human Rights Council, 2015). Cambodia's leaders also adjusted their conceptions of sovereignty and peace, which came to be understood as goals that could be supported by international criminal justice, and passed comprehensive legislation for prosecuting future international crimes, despite continuing to show mixed support for the ECCC. The localisation framework not only emphasises local agency in this process, but also highlights how local actors can reshape the set of possible outcomes – in this case, resulting in the novel internationalised structure of the ECCC (the operations of which extend beyond rhetoric, as it does act as a prosecuting institution), alongside new Cambodian international crimes laws in the Criminal Code.

However, the localisation framework has limitations. First, this chapter identified security and development as important factors in this process and it might be argued that Cambodia's government primarily acted so as to maximise its material wealth. Yet, during the period of most direct international engagement with Cambodia's government functions after UNTAC was established, Cambodia's leaders initially followed a strategy of reintegration and amnesty (rather than the international criminal justice norm of prosecutions). The Cambodian government's decision to later pursue the establishment of an international criminal tribunal and to ratify and implement the Rome Statute was not the only available choice to attract aid or investment (Etcheson, 2004). However, it provided an opportunity to appear to protect Cambodia's peace, political stability, and – with negotiation – sovereignty, as well as potentially investment. It is more helpful, for the purposes of understanding Cambodia's international crimes laws, to interpret Cambodia's material and security situations as providing contexts within which its leaders viewed pursuing international criminal justice as the most appropriate course of action, consistent with constructivist theory.

Looking forward, an international civil society actor has argued that Cambodia's attitude towards international criminal justice 'comes down to the donors and money ... it would be very interesting to see what would happen if the government was indicted and formally investigated by the ICC. Right, would they cooperate? Probably not'.[112] From this perspective, an ICC investigation could create a clash between material needs and the norm of international criminal justice. A similar tension may have already arisen with the faltering Case 003 and 004 investigations (Karnavas, 2016). However, Cambodia's leaders have historically interpreted such apparent conflicts as opportunities for adaptation in light of varied normative and material priorities.

This presents a second issue: Cambodia's engagement with international criminal justice challenges any expectations of *temporal* progress or normative models of a 'transitional justice time', in which international criminal justice leads to a 'purified' ending (Hinton, 2013). In Cambodia's case, this expectation is depicted in ECCC outreach pamphlets illustrated with images of a liberal democratic future consisting of factories and electricity, as well as the ECCC's early slogan of 'Moving Forward through Justice' (Hinton, 2013: 94) or the idea that 'I've done my job'. Instead, Cambodia's approach to investigating or prosecuting serious violence does not suggest progression towards accepting the norm of international criminal justice (or simple rejection).

---

[112] Interview C2.

A third implication relates to *space*. If 'localisation' is given 'special normative value', this may simplify notions of what 'local' means, when identities are in reality complex (Zimmermann, 2016: 105). For instance, Buddhist norms influence the discourse surrounding international criminal justice in Cambodia (Urs, 2007; Ear, 2010; Gray, 2012), but it is important not to overgeneralise about the impact of cultural or religious practices. The perception of some that Cambodians prefer forgiveness and reconciliation or – paradoxically – have 'a different sense of justice' in which ECCC prosecution appears 'cushy', demonstrates this danger (see Section 2.3.4, this chapter).[113] In particular, the intersecting accounts of DK survivors and younger generations are highly complex, especially given the lack of clear divisions between victims and perpetrators and the occurrence of intergenerational trauma (Westoby, 2013: 188; de Langis, et al. 2014; Bernath, 2015).[114] Focusing on local actors could also obscure the possible criminal responsibility of international perpetrators (Drexler, 2010: 50). This situation supports the body of literature that suggests that global/local distinctions can be artificial or at least subjective, and may be insufficient to explain normative change in a given context (see Chapter 6).

Finally, the localisation framework suggests that local actors seek to appear neutral and not influenced by 'outside forces', in order to ensure their credibility with state actors and facilitate the spread of norms (Acharya, 2004: 251). In contrast, Cambodian officials and NGOs utilise treaty body reporting processes and frequently work with international partners (see Section 2.3.3, this chapter). It seems that 'local' influence has in part come from the ability to deploy international funding and draw on international expertise. Cambodian ECCC personnel, witnesses, and civil parties influence international criminal law through their daily work. Yet international expatriates working with the ECCC, government, and Cambodian NGOs, the substantial Cambodian diaspora, and Cambodians who have been educated overseas, all contribute to debates about international criminal justice. This complexity confirms that norms are not diffused in an external-to-local *direction*. Ideas come from many places – a testimonial therapy reparations project is rooted in Buddhist practice, but was informed by international programs. The adoption of

---

[113] Interview C2.

[114] E.g. consider the multiple perspectives of male and female survivors of forced marriage (many of whom remain married) and their children.

national laws modelled on the Rome Statute, though with some adaptations, may have restrained the scope to develop more creative legislative approaches, but NGO representatives have still used their own initiative and draw on cultural and religious practices to explore community-based reconciliation processes. While local/global divisions can help to reveal the input and agency of particular actors categorised as 'local', and challenge any assumption that norms flow towards accepting (or rejecting) locals, the reverse assumption of local norm construction should not be taken at face value. Instead, it may be the ongoing combination and contestation of various actors and ideas that stimulates normative change.

These temporal, spatial, and directional aspects are related. For instance, the ECCC's narrow temporal and personal jurisdiction arguably demonstrates that a 'danger of localizing transitional justice ... is that these mechanisms may inadvertently create a narrative that localizes the origins and dynamics of a conflict and thereby ignores the larger context in which it emerged' – a danger for all international crimes trials with defined remits (Hinton, 2010: 10). In Cambodia's case, focusing on DK may sideline atrocities and 'every day' harm experienced in the surrounding conflicts and today, in various places. Therefore, neither assumptions about socialising norms over time, nor the localisation framework's anticipated, albeit long-term, trajectory from resistance towards the adaptation of institutions and its emphasis upon the 'local', should obscure the complex relationships between different ideas and actors. This argument is returned to in Chapter 7.

Cambodia continues to face challenges in securing international criminal justice. This does not indicate that processes of socialisation or localisation are incomplete, but that adaptation is always occurring. Further, even though Cambodia is a Rome Statute party, most of this engagement with international criminal law has taken place beyond the ICC. The next chapter turns to another state that has been a Rome Statute party, the Philippines, to explore how actors engage with international criminal law in a different context, where international criminal law has been incorporated into domestic legislation, but there is no international tribunal.

Implementing International Criminal Justice

The Philippines

3.1 Introduction

The Philippines signed the Rome Statute on 28 December 2000, adopted legislation to incorporate international crimes into domestic law in 2009, ratified the Rome Statute in 2011, and withdrew in 2018 (effective in March 2019). Although the Philippines has not established an international crimes mechanism comparable to the ECCC, institutional developments and public statements by the Philippines' leaders in the past have indicated support for the norm of international criminal justice. However, the lack of enforcement of the Philippines' international crimes legislation and events since President Rodrigo Duterte took office suggest that the government of the Philippines has certainly not accepted the norm of international criminal justice. Rather, debate continues.

Section 3.2 outlines the ongoing saga of international criminal justice in the Philippines. Section 3.3 explores how actors have used their experiences and initiative to debate the laws and institutions for investigating and prosecuting alleged international crimes in the Philippines. Section 3.4 examines the key features of these mechanisms, which continue to be discussed and developed. Section 3.5 then shows how approaches to international criminal justice in the Philippines have involved dynamic interactions and adaptation.

3.2 Historic Engagement with International Criminal Law

Several themes emerge from the history of international criminal justice in the Philippines, including the importance of national independence, peace, and human rights, as well as engagement with international law – including through prosecuting international crimes. However, different groups also contest the importance and meaning of these ideas and principles. Moving from colonial occupation towards 2019, this section shows that events in the Philippines have not proceeded on a 'linear scale from resistance' to international criminal justice, towards 'norm adoption' (Zimmermann, 2016: 102).

3.2.1 Sovereignty and Independence: Colonialism and World War II

Spain ceded the Philippines to the United States in 1898, the same year that Philippine revolutionary forces declared independence. After the Philippine-American War of 1899–1902 and an unstable political period of US control, elections were held in 1935 (making the Philippines arguably 'the oldest democracy in the region') and a new Constitution with a 'Bill of Rights' was approved (Jetschke, 1999: 136). Yet, the Philippines remained a US colony when Japan invaded in 1942. As a result, although the Philippines' 'mixed' legal system has a 'civil law' emphasis upon codification from the Spanish colonial period, it has also been influenced by US common law, as well as local conditions. The latter elements include *Katarungan Pambarangay* ('*barangay*', village or district), Islamic and Indigenous customary legal systems.

Japanese forces occupied the Philippines until February 1945, though Japanese authorities granted notional independence in 1943. The occupying forces perpetrated crimes including sexual violence and torture (Röling & Rüter, 1977: 398; Ileto, 2007: 75).[1] Philippine resistance movements fought alongside American forces to overcome Japanese occupation, which strengthened Philippine-US ties, but also arguably contributed to nationalism and a shift towards a greater 'identification with Asian states and peoples' (Ileto, 2007: 75).

The World War II period also led to the evolution of international criminal law. The Philippines was the only Southeast Asian state with a national appointed as a judge at the International Military Tribunal for the Far East (the Tokyo Tribunal or IMTFE), probably because the United States retained authority there (Boister & Cryer, 2008: 43). Eighty-seven war crimes trials were carried out in the Philippines before and parallel to the IMTFE, based on a US law allowing for such trials to be authorised by military command (Totani, 2014: 21). In one such trial,

---

[1] See e.g. *Isabelita C Vinuya et al. v. The Honorable Executive Secretary Alberto G Romulo et al.*, G.R. No. 162230, Supreme Court, Republic of the Philippines, 28 April 2010 (*Vinuya*).

General Yamashita Tomoyuki, a commander of the Japanese 14th Army that invaded and occupied the Philippines, was prosecuted for unlawfully disregarding and failing to discharge his duty as a commander and sentenced to death. The trial, before a US military commission, was criticised on procedural grounds (Prévost, 1992)[2] and Yamashita (unsuccessfully) petitioned for writs of habeas corpus and prohibition before the Philippines[3] and US Supreme Courts.[4] The application of command responsibility in the *Yamashita* decision influenced proceedings at Nuremberg, the IMTFE, and subsequent trials in the Philippines and beyond (Hart, 1980; Cassese, 2008: 237–43).[5]

After the United States recognised the Philippines' independence in 1946, Philippine courts conducted another seventy-two World War II–related trials for crimes committed against Americans and Filipinos under Executive Order No. 68 of 1947 (Totani, 2014: 22). These included the trial of General Kuroda Shigenori, another commander of the Japanese 14th Army. In that case, the Philippines Supreme Court found that the 1907 Hague Convention and Geneva Conventions formed 'part of the law of our nation even if the Philippines was not a signatory to the conventions'.[6] Domestic politics and evolving geopolitical relations with Japan may have influenced Kuroda's trial, which seems to have benefited from the Filipino participants' desire to exhibit the fair operation of the newly independent country's justice system (Totani, 2014: 54). Kuroda's hearing took approximately three times as long as that of Yamashita and raised fewer concerns about fairness than the earlier US-administered proceedings (Totani, 2014: 55).

Yamashita's and Kuroda's different trials illustrate that internationally implemented accountability will not necessarily produce fairer trials than locally managed mechanisms, though both were affected by political concerns. In summary, the Philippines has fought for independence multiple times, has a mixed legal system that historically included a Bill

---

[2] The dissenting opinions of Justices Murphy and Rutledge, *In re Yamashita*, US Supreme Court, 4 February 1946 (*In re Yamashita*).
[3] *Yamashita v. Styer*, G.R. No. L-129, Supreme Court, Republic of the Philippines, 19 December 1945 (*Yamashita*).
[4] *In re Yamashita*.
[5] Command responsibility was incorporated into the Rome Statute and Statutes for the ICTY and ICTR.
[6] *Kuroda v. Rafael Jalandoni*, G.R. No. L-2662, Supreme Court, Republic of the Philippines, 26 March 1949 (*Kuroda*), as well as arising from the US and Japan's obligations.

of Rights, and has prosecuted international crimes before both US
military commissions and post-independence Philippines courts.

3.2.2 Peace and Justice: Marcos and Civil Society

Following independence in 1946, the Philippines drew upon its 1935
Constitution to build democratic institutions.[7] However, there were
tensions between the goals of peace and justice. The Philippines experienced non-international armed conflict between government forces and
separatist groups, including the Moro National Liberation Front (MNLF)
and a breakaway group, the Moro Islamic Liberation Front (MILF). This
conflict has very old roots stemming from Spanish efforts to secure
control over Islamic sultanates in Maguindanao in the fifteenth and
sixteenth centuries – and is not entirely resolved,[8] intermingling with
inter-clan (rido) rivalries and other factors (Jeffery, 2018). During the
Cold War, the Philippines was implicated in 'a U.S.-led anticommunist
struggle' (Bryant, 2005: 62) against the New People's Army (NPA, the
armed wing of the Communist Party of the Philippines, CoPP), National
Democratic Front (NDF) and aligned groups (Leary et al., 1984: 12),
some of which still claim to fight a 'people's war against US imperialism'
(National Democratic Front of the Philippines, 2016).

Ferdinand Marcos became president in 1965 and imposed martial law
in 1972. During this time, corruption and a range of government measures compromised the independence of the judiciary (Leary et al., 1984).[9]
Under Marcos' government, the Philippines experienced economic crisis
alongside serious human rights violations such as extrajudicial killings.
These abuses were concentrated in some of the poorest regions, where
the NPA/CoPP/NDF (Alston, 2008) and MNLF and MILF were most
active (Leary et al., 1984). Indeed, human rights violations were often
linked to development concerns, including through the arrest and intimi-
dation of trade union activists (Leary et al., 1984).

---

[7] As amended on 18 June 1940 and 11 March 1947 (superseding the 1943 Constitution as
approved by the Preparatory Committee on Philippine Independence, 4 September
1943 during Japanese occupation).

[8] The related 'Bangsamoro' peace process, leading to the 'Bangsamoro Organic Law'
(Republic Act No. 11054, passed by Congress in July 2018) continued to be implemented
in 2019.

[9] In particular, the Executive's ability to replace Supreme Court judges and to demand and
hold letters of resignation from lower court judges.

Many states and other actors were initially slow to criticise Marcos. However, in the late 1970s the International Commission of Jurists and Amnesty International reported significant violations of human rights law including 'torture, abductions and killings of dissidents by military units' (Amnesty International, 1979: 109), while the Permanent Peoples' Tribunal heard a case brought by the NDF and MNLF against Marcos in 1980. The US Carter administration contributed some pressure towards the regime to cease human rights violations and the Reagan administration, while more supportive of Marcos, also recommended reforms, including that elections be held (Jetschke, 2011). Despite the challenging environment, NGOs such as Task Force Detainees of the Philippines were founded during the Marcos regime, as trust in the state declined and organisations and church groups carried out important community functions (Angeles, 1994: 52; Bryant, 2005: 63), as well as forging links with diaspora and international civil society (Jetschke, 2011).

While Marcos announced some amnesties for political detainees in the late 1970s (Amnesty International, 1979: 108), the ending of martial law in 1981 secured neither accountability for human rights violations nor the independence of the judiciary, while the economic situation failed to improve. The public assassination of opposition figure Senator Benigno Aquino in 1983 (which was widely attributed to the government, but officially blamed on communists) further stimulated Philippine civil society, as international support for Marcos waned (Linton, 2010: 193; Jetschke, 2011: 124).[10] After widespread public protests known as the 'People Power' or 'EDSA' Revolution, Marcos accepted a US offer for asylum in 1986. As civil society and popular opposition to Marcos escalated in this period, Philippine and international actors had criticised the regime with reference to human rights standards (Jetschke, 2011).

3.2.3   Democracy and Human Rights after Marcos

The election of Senator Benigno Aquino's widow, Corazón Aquino, as President in 1986 enhanced the formal importance of human rights for the Philippine state. The government released political prisoners and ratified international human rights and humanitarian law instruments

---

[10] Marcos established investigative commissions. The second, the Agrava Board, attributed the assassination to the military, but did not accord individual responsibility. A trial during Corazón Aquino's administration found sixteen soldiers (including a General) guilty for their role in the plot.

(Angeles, 1994; Appendix A). The 1987 Constitution 'adheres to the policy of peace, equality, justice, freedom, cooperation, and amity with all nations'.[11] It also protects a range of human rights in Articles III and XIII, forbids torture,[12] and established an Ombudsman to investigate complaints against public officials.[13] A Presidential Committee on Human Rights investigated crimes perpetrated during Marcos' regime and the Commission on Human Rights was established as a constitutionally 'independent office' – a National Human Rights Institution.[14] In 1991, a 'Joint Circular on Adherence to IHL and Human Rights' suggested that 'human rights-related incidents allegedly committed by' the armed forces or police should be investigated or prosecuted (ICRC, 2016a).

Aquino's presidency thus 'started with great expectations for social change' (Bryant, 2005: 64). However, the Presidential Committee investigations did not lead to prosecutions for international crimes that may have occurred during Marcos' regime. Moreover, political violence did not cease. One reason was that much of the military had been trained under and had supported the Marcos regime. After its collapse, the 'military structure, its mentality, culture and problems, remain[ed] intact' (Angeles, 1994: 109). Aquino's administration initially denied responsibility for disappearances and killings by vigilante groups, but these 'civilian self-defense' organisations were later endorsed as protecting communities from communism. The government also 'discredited' critical local human rights NGOs by claiming they were aligned with communist groups (Jetschke, 2011: 271).

Nonetheless, coalitions and networks such as the Philippine Alliance of Human Rights Advocates (PAHRA) built ties between local and international civil society actors and secured increased funding (Jetschke, 2011: 192). NGOs and the Commission on Human Rights documented ongoing human rights violations and abuses including enforced disappearances, killings, and torture – and the lack of corresponding

---

[11] Article II(2), The Constitution of the Republic of the Philippines 1987 (Philippines Constitution).

[12] Article III(12), ibid.

[13] Article XI(5–14), ibid., see also Republic Act No. 6770, An Act Providing for the Functional and Structural Organization of the Office of the Ombudsman, and for Other Purposes, 17 November 1989.

[14] The Commission was created by Article XIII(17), Constitution, but formally established on 5 May 1987 by Executive Order No. 163, Declaring the Effectivity of the Creation of the Commission on Human Rights as Provided for in the 1987 Constitution.

accountability – including for crimes committed by non-state actors (Human Rights Watch, 1991: 312; Angeles, 1994: 22–5). Thus, civil society highlighted the gap between the Philippines' embrace of international legal instruments concerning human rights and international humanitarian law and the reality of continuing violence.

Fidel Ramos became president in 1992 and 'made human rights reforms an important pillar of his reform program' (Jetschke, 2011: 195). Many NGOs adopted a strategy of 'critical engagement: a process whereby an NGO works simultaneously with and against state agencies' (Bryant, 2005: 66). This included providing education about international humanitarian law as these principles were incorporated into official policies (Santos Jr, 2003: 571; Lozada et al., 2013: 30–3). In 1996, the NDF made a 'Declaration of Undertaking' to apply international humanitarian law (following a declaration regarding common Article 3 of the Geneva Conventions and Additional Protocol II in 1991), stating that the NDF had gained the status of belligerency, which has been a contentious issue (ICRC, 2012). The government secured a Comprehensive Agreement on Respect for Human Rights and International Humanitarian Law (CARHRIHL) with the NDF in 1998 and an agreement to respect international humanitarian law with MILF in 2001,[15] though debates about MILF's 'belligerent' status persisted.[16] In 1998 an 'ICC Task Force' was established to undertake studies and provide recommendations about the ICC.[17] Despite these agreements, extrajudicial killings and torture perpetrated by state and non-state actors continued, while corruption in the judiciary remained (Bureau of Democracy, Human Rights and Labor, 1998) and amnesties were awarded (see Section 3.4.3). Private claims for reparation launched in this period were also met with challenges.[18] While a class action on behalf of approximately 10,000 Philippine nationals in the US courts

---

[15] Agreement on peace between the government of the Republic of the Philippines and the Moro Islamic Liberation Front, signed 22 June 2001 and see the Implementing Guidelines on the Humanitarian, Rehabilitation and Development Aspects of the GRP-MILF Tripoli Agreement on Peace of 2001, signed 7 May 2002.

[16] E.g. *The Province of North Cotabato v. The Government of the Republic of the Philippines Peace Panel on Ancestral Domain*, G.R. Nos. 183591, 183572, 183893, and 183951, Supreme Court, Republic of the Philippines, 14 October 2008, Separate Concurring Opinion, Puno CJ.

[17] Administrative Order No. 387, Providing for the Creation of a Task Force on the Proposed Establishment of the International Criminal Court, 24 March 1998.

[18] E.g. *Rogelio Aberca et al. v. Maj. Gen. Fabian Ver et al.*, G.R. No. 166216, Supreme Court, Republic of the Philippines, Decision, 14 March 2012.

secured an award for damages under the US 'Alien Tort Claims Act' in 1992,[19] Philippine courts did not enforce the judgment.[20]

Further, the uneven impact of economic development meant that communist and socialist groups retained supporters. The conflict between the military and MILF escalated during Joseph Estrada's presidency (1998–2001) and intensified after Gloria Macapagal-Arroyo (Arroyo) became president in 2001, as the 'War on Terror' attracted greater US military support during a military operation named 'Oplan Bantay Laya'. There were allegations that both state and non-state actors violated international humanitarian law in this period (Bureau of Democracy, Human Rights and Labor, 2004; Ibon Foundation, 2010). Thus, human rights and international humanitarian law formed a crucial part of Philippine domestic political discourse. However, ongoing conflict led to compromises in ensuring accountability where these principles were violated.

3.2.4 Implementation, but Not Enforcement: Arroyo and New Legislation

The Philippines passed domestic international crimes legislation towards the end of Arroyo's Presidency (2001–10). Inter-agency consultations on an international humanitarian law bill had commenced in 2001. The Philippine Red Cross National IHL Committee directed the drafting process in consultation with Philippines and international civil society and government stakeholders, with some assistance from the International Committee of the Red Cross (ICRC).[21] On 12 August 2003, International Humanitarian Law Day, Representative Lozada announced the introduction of an 'Omnibus IHL Bill' addressing international crimes (Santos Jr, 2003: 577).

However, these initiatives stalled. The Philippines had signed a 'Non-Surrender Agreement' with the United States in May 2003 under which

---

[19] E.g. *In re Estate of Ferdinand E Marcos Human Rights Litigation: Agapita Trajano; Archimedes Trajano v. Ferdinand E Marcos and Imee Marcos-Manotoc*, Case No. 91-15891, 978 F.2d 493, US Court of Appeals, Ninth Circuit, 21 October 1992; *Maximo Hilao v. Estate of Ferdinand Marcos*, Case No. 95-15779, 103 F.3d 767, US Court of Appeals, Ninth Circuit, 17 December 1996.

[20] *Priscilla C Mijares et al. v. Hon. Santiago Javier Ranada et al.*, G.R. No. 139325, Supreme Court, Republic of the Philippines, 12 April 2005.

[21] The Philippines Thirteenth Congress, Draft Explanatory Note (for a 'Philippine Statute on Crimes against International Humanitarian Law', undated copy on file with author), (Draft Explanatory Note).

each party agreed not to hand over nationals to an international tribunal without consent.[22] The Philippines government emphasised that this did 'not in any way prevent us from becoming a state party to the ICC Statute' (Santos Jr, 2003: 570), but the US negotiations appear to have contributed to the delayed ratification of the Rome Statute (Conde, 2002). In July, a civil society group filed a petition for *mandamus* to compel the transmission of the signed Rome Statute to the Philippines Senate for ratification (Santos Jr, 2003: 577), but the Supreme Court determined that it had no jurisdiction to make such an order.[23]

The government favoured preserving independence and internal stability in its approach towards international criminal justice. During time on the Security Council in 2004, the Philippines advised that justice for perpetrators of crimes in Timor-Leste should be carried out 'bearing in mind the views, sensitivities and cooperation of the parties concerned' (United Nations Security Council, 2004). In 2005, the Philippines 'lauded' the efforts of the ICTY and ICTR to refer cases to national courts and confirmed that the Philippines understood these courts as being 'designed to promote peace' and 'foster national reconciliation' (United Nations Security Council, 2005).

At home, support for international criminal justice remained fragmented. The Arroyo administration established a police investigative body, 'Task Force Usig' in 2006, and the 'Melo Commission' investigated the killing of journalists and activists. The Commission concluded that while evidence suggested that certain individuals were responsible for some crimes, there was no 'official or sanctioned' military policy to illegally 'liquidate' activists (Melo et al., 2007). Indeed, Human Rights Watch reported that it 'could not identify a single successful prosecution for any of the political killings ... cited by local civil society and human rights groups' (Human Rights Watch, 2007: 48). In 2007 the Armed Forces of the Philippines and Philippines National Police established human rights offices. However, in 2008, the Special Rapporteur on Extrajudicial, Summary or Arbitrary Executions, Philip Alston, produced an influential report detailing the 'extrajudicial executions of leftist activists in the Philippines' (Alston, 2008: 2). It noted that the 'many measures that have been promulgated by the Government ... are encouraging' but

---

[22] See *Bayan Muna v. Alberto Romulo and Bias F Ople, Supreme Court*, G.R. No. 159618, Supreme Court, Republic of the Philippines, 1 February 2011.

[23] *Sen. Aquilino Pimentel, Jr et al. v. Office of the Executive Secretary et al.*, G.R. No. 158088, Supreme Court, Republic of the Philippines, Decision, 6 July 2005.

had 'yet to succeed' and made a number of institutional recommendations (Alston, 2008: 3).

These initiatives focused on human rights, extrajudicial killings, and enforced disappearances, which were generally not labelled as international crimes.[24] Yet international and national civil society actors continued to draft 'international humanitarian law' bills (see Section 3.3.3). Eventually, Congress passed international criminal law legislation in December 2009, the 'IHL Act' (see Section 3.4.2). Despite these developments, the Arroyo administration's political will to secure justice for either contemporary or historic international crimes remained ambiguous.

Fifty-eight people were murdered, including thirty-two journalists, in the 'Maguindanao massacre'[25] of 23 November 2009, reportedly 'the largest number of journalists murdered in a single incident worldwide' (Article 2, 2012). The killings were attributed to the Ampatuan family, 'one of the most powerful and abusive state-backed militias in the Philippines' (Human Rights Watch, 2010: 4). Prosecution efforts proceeded slowly and the trials of more than ninety individuals continued in 2019.

In relation to historic crimes, in the *Vinuya* case of 2010, the Supreme Court held there was no valid remedy in Philippine law for the 'comfort women' who had experienced sexual violence during the Japanese occupation in World War II, since the Court could only 'urge and exhort the Executive Department to take up the petitioner's cause' with Japan, which the Department had not done.

Alongside these challenges, at least since the Philippine Coalition for the International Criminal Court (PCICC) was established in September 2000, local NGOs and other actors had unsuccessfully sought ratification of the Rome Statute. Despite some investigations and legislative developments, there was a failure to prosecute either historic or more recent alleged international crimes.

3.2.5 Ratification and Engagement with the ICC – Then Withdrawal

A new opportunity was presented by the election of Benigno Aquino III (Corazón's son, 'Noynoy') in June 2010 (Human Rights Watch, 2011: 4).

---

[24] Though Alston noted that the CPP/NPA/NDF use of 'people's courts' may constitute a war crime and encouraged the prosecution of extrajudicial executions.

[25] Also known as the 'Ampatuan massacre'.

In his first State of the Nation address, Benigno Aquino observed that 'the attainment of true justice does not end in the filing of cases, but in the conviction of criminals' (Aquino III, 2011). Various stakeholders agreed to work towards forming a national monitoring mechanism on extralegal killings and enforced disappearances,[26] and the government ratified the Rome Statute on 30 August 2011. Administrative Order No. 35 in 2012 created an 'Inter-Agency Committee on Extra-Legal Killings, Enforced Disappearances, Torture and Other Grave Violations of the Right to Life, Liberty and Security of Persons' to combat the 'impression of a culture of impunity' by investigating unresolved historic and contemporary cases.[27] In 2014, the government and MILF secured the Comprehensive Agreement on the Bangsamoro, a framework peace agreement in which 'the Parties acknowledge[d] their responsibilities to uphold the principles of justice'.[28] An annex to the Agreement provided for the establishment of a Transitional Justice and Reconciliation Commission to, inter alia, 'promote healing and reconciliation' and address 'historical injustices, human rights violations and . . . land dispossession' (Transitional Justice and Reconciliation Commission, 2016: 119).

Despite this apparent progress towards embracing justice and accountability norms, there were accusations of further human rights violations. The deaths of state officers, separatist fighters, and civilians during an anti-terrorism operation in Mamasapano in 2015 highlighted the potential domestic relevance of international criminal law. Then, after Rodrigo Duterte took office in June 2016, thousands of alleged drug users and criminals were killed without trial in a 'war on drugs', including through police operations supported by the President (Human Rights Watch, 2017). This was promoted as a response to insecurity related to the use of drugs, particularly in urban areas (Curato, 2016; Tusalem, 2019).

Possibly in response to NGOs and the Commission for Human Rights raising the prospect of an ICC investigation (Antiporda, 2016), in October 2016, the ICC Prosecutor noted that 'any person in the Philippines who incites or engages in acts of mass violence . . . is potentially liable to prosecution before the Court' (ICC Office of the Prosecutor, 2016).

---

[26] See (Republic of the Philippines, 2012: paras. 49–51).
[27] Administrative Order No. 35, Creating an Inter-Agency Committee on Extra-Legal Killings, Enforced Disappearances, Torture and Other Grave Violations of the Right to Life, Liberty and Security of Persons, 22 November 2012.
[28] Comprehensive Agreement on the Bangsamoro, 27 March 2014.

At the 2016 ICC Assembly of States Parties (ASP), the Philippines' delegate was 'very concerned about the decision of some States Parties to withdraw from the Rome Statute', but argued that 'legitimate police operations against drug offenders' do not qualify as an international crime and reminded the ASP that the Philippines is 'willing and able to prosecute' Rome Statute crimes (Republic of the Philippines, 2016). In 2017, two groups publicly lodged communications with the ICC Prosecutor requesting her to investigate alleged international crimes in the Philippines (Biron, 2017; Gavilan, 2017) reportedly alongside other confidential communications (Cabico, 2018). By February 2018, the Prosecutor opened a preliminary examination analysing crimes 'allegedly committed … since at least 1 July 2016, in the context of the "war on drugs" campaign', including 'extra-judicial killings in the course of police anti-drug operations' (ICC Office of the Prosecutor, 2018).

This prompted the Philippines government to lodge its withdrawal from the Rome Statute in March 2018 – a reversal from its earlier support for the Court.[29] The Supreme Court of the Philippines heard arguments concerning petitions by six senators, the PCICC, and others opposing the domestic legality of the withdrawal in September 2018.[30] However, the Supreme Court did not publicise any decision before the withdrawal became effective in March 2019 (after the twelve-month delay prescribed by the Statute). These developments demonstrate that while debates about international criminal justice continue within the Philippines, including politically and via the Commission on Human Rights and courts, state institutions have not recently supported the ICC. While the Philippines has adopted international crimes legislation and ratified the Rome Statute, the impact of these laws and other mechanisms upon practice and future enforcement is evolving.

3.2.6 Summary: History

The norm of international criminal justice has not been accepted in the Philippines over time through ratifying and implementing international

---

[29] See (United Nations Treaties, 2018). This likely removes any obligation for the Philippines to cooperate with an ICC investigation since a Pre-Trial Chamber had not approved one before 17 March 2019, see Article 127, Rome Statute (see Palmer, 2019a).

[30] *Pangilinan, et al. v. Cayetano, et al.* [2018], G.R. No. 238875, 16 May 2018 and *Philippine Coalition for the International Criminal Court [PCICC], et al. v. Office of the Executive Secretary* [2018], G.R. No. 239483, 8 June 2018 (*SC Petitions*).

treaties. Rather, there are at least two approaches towards international criminal justice that continue to lie in tension. The first advances the Philippine's global reputation as a democratic state with an influential civil society and favourably recalls the country's history of developing international criminal law and resisting governments that fail to respect human rights. The second emphasises that the Philippines is a post-colonial country that has experienced internal unrest and insecurity, in which securing stability could conflict with ideals of justice. International and national state and non-state actors have attempted to influence these dual characterisations in various ways.

3.3   Local Initiatives and Adaptation

The Asian Human Rights Commission (an NGO) has suggested that the Philippines demonstrates how the 'strengthening of a legal framework fails to displace, if not restructure, flaws in the process of investigation, prosecution and adjudication of cases' (Asian Human Rights Commission, 2013: 2). Implementing the norm of international criminal justice requires officials to accept ideas about how judicial processes 'should' work, including to overcome gaps between laws and practice. This section considers how international, official, and civil society actors have attempted to influence international criminal justice in the Philippines, including by advancing new laws and working towards their enforcement, as well as undertaking more adaptive approaches.

3.3.1   International States and Organisations

International state and non-state actors have influenced the Philippines' engagement with international criminal law since the World War II trials. The technical assistance provided by the ICRC during the drafting of the IHL Act has been mentioned. A civil society representative attributed a number of initiatives taken by the government, such as establishing an armed forces human rights office, to 'the strength of the social movements',[31] but another noted the influence of Alston's 'controversial report, which embarrassed the Philippines' (see Alston, 2009).[32]

Yet international positions towards international criminal justice in the Philippines have been inconsistent. The United States retains

---

[31] Interview P5.
[32] Interview P4.

significant influence and a strong military presence in the Philippines extended by the 2014 Enhanced Defense Cooperation Agreement.[33] As mentioned, the United States probably discouraged the Philippines from ratifying the Rome Statute in the early 2000s. Some projects funded by various countries' overseas development assistance pursue international criminal justice goals, but are framed as supporting national initiatives.[34] Other states have attempted to influence the Philippines' domestic approach to international criminal justice more overtly. For example, following the 'Maguindanao massacre' mentioned in Section 3.2.4, Australia called for the Philippines to 'ensure alleged perpetrators of serious human rights violations are brought to justice' (Australia Permanent Mission Geneva, 2012; though see New Matilda, 2008), while a Malaysia-led group investigated the Mamasapano incident and recommended that 'combatants found to have committed crimes, should be prosecuted accordingly and penalized' (International Monitoring Team, 2015). A Special Envoy of the Swiss Federal Department of Foreign Affairs has also chaired the Transitional Justice and Reconciliation Commission related to the Bangsamoro peace process involving the conflict with MILF (Office of the Presidential Advisor on the Peace Process, 2014). Interestingly, the ICC was not mentioned in the 2008 Working Group report for the Philippines' first Universal Periodic Review (UPR) (UN Human Rights Council, 2008b). Still, foreign states – alongside NGOs – sponsored several local forums to discuss ratifying the Rome Statute and in the second UPR 'cycle' in 2012 many states commended the Philippines' 2011 ratification of the Rome Statute (UN Human Rights Council, 2012b).

International reactions toward the 'war on drugs' in the Philippines have also been mixed. During the third (2017) UPR cycle, Iceland and thirty-seven other states – including Australia, the United Kingdom, and the United States – signed a statement urging the Philippines

---

[33] Agreement between the Government of the Republic of the Philippines and the Government of the United States of America on Enhanced Defense Cooperation, 29 April 2014, upheld in *Rene A. V. Saguisag et al. v. Executive Secretary Paquito N. Ochoa, Jr, et al./ Bagong Alyansang Makabayan (Bayan), et al. v. Department of National Defense Secretary Voltaire Gazmin et al.*, G.R. No. 212426 & G.R. No. 212444, Supreme Court, Republic of the Philippines, 12 January 2016.

[34] E.g. European Union–Philippines Justice Support Programmes (EPJUST I and II), aimed at improving access to justice, 'fighting impunity' – especially for extrajudicial killings and enforced disappearances, and enhancing transparency, including via the national monitoring mechanism.

government to 'take all necessary measures to bring killings associated with the campaign against illegal drugs to an end and cooperate with the international community to investigate all related deaths and hold perpetrators accountable' (Permanent Mission of Iceland in Geneva, 2015). Yet some other states commended the Philippines on its contributions to protecting human rights. For example, 'China expressed support for the campaign against illegal drugs', Myanmar stated that 'the response to the threat posed by illegal drug use should be left to the Government' and Romania 'commended the Philippines for its human rights-based campaign to eliminate the drug menace' (UN Human Rights Council, 2017b, paras. 36, 86 and 98). In 2018, the President of the ICC's ASP, which consists of representatives of the states that are party to the Rome Statute, responded to news of the Philippines withdrawal with 'regret', noting that this could 'negatively impact our collective efforts towards fighting impunity', and noting the Philippines' historic and recently reaffirmed support for the ICC (ICC Assembly of States Parties, 2018b). A group of 'UN human rights experts' has called for an independent investigation of human rights violations in the Philippines and condemned the ICC withdrawal (UN Office of the High Commissioner of Human Rights, 2019). Yet, in general in 2019, foreign embassies in the Philippines appeared less vocal about past or ongoing human rights violations in the 'war on drugs', or the withdrawal, at least publicly. Thus, international actors have taken varied approaches towards international criminal justice in the Philippines, although many have focused on institutional reform and, to an extent, monitoring alleged international crimes.

3.3.2   The Philippines Authorities

The Philippines government has propounded its support for international criminal justice and 'fighting impunity' (Republic of the Philippines, 2014). Reflecting the themes identified in Section 3.1, official statements, especially since Benigno Aquino's administration, emphasised the Philippines' human rights achievements and the importance of civil society, as well as its development needs and the tensions between peace and justice (and drug-related insecurity since Duterte's election).

Government statements have stressed that the Philippines has secured significant progress in protecting international human rights and humanitarian law (e.g. Republic of the Philippines, 2011). The Philippines' statement at the 2010 Kampala Review Conference for the ICC recalled that World War II trials in the Philippines 'established the principle of command responsibility for war crimes' and that its support for the ICC was 'anchored on the policy enshrined in the Philippine Constitution ... guaranteeing full respect for human rights' (Republic of the Philippines, 2010: 3, 1). In 2015, the Philippines government success-fully nominated Raul Pangalangan[35] to replace the late Philippines sen-ator Miriam Defensor Santiago as an ICC judge, affirming 'its continuing support' for the ICC (ICC Assembly of States Parties, 2015: 10). The Philippines' statements at the ASP consistently called for other states, especially in the Asia-Pacific, to ratify the Rome Statute (e.g. Republic of the Philippines, 2015).

The government also acknowledged the role of civil society's inter-national criminal justice advocacy. At the Kampala Review Conference, the Philippines statement mentioned trainings undertaken 'in partner-ship with civil society groups' (Republic of the Philippines, 2010) and at the first ASP the Philippines attended as a state party, its representative gave 'special thanks' to the Coalition for the International Criminal Court (CICC), including in the Asia Pacific, and PCICC, observing that '[t]hey were with us through the entire process of ratification' (Republic of the Philippines, 2011). The Department of Justice, Department of National Defense (DND), Department of Foreign Affairs, and Office of the Solicitor General were all represented in a working group alongside civil society that developed draft ICC implementation and cooperation legislation filed in 2016 (see Section 3.4.2).[36] Thus, at least during Benigno Aquino's administration, the Philippines supported the ICC as a global and civil society initiative to end impunity of which it was part.

On the other hand, the Philippines consistently mentioned development and peace and stability-related concerns in its statements about international criminal justice. While government statements had perhaps not emphasised the principle of sovereignty to the same degree

---

[35] A former dean of the law school at the University of Philippines, PCICC co-chair, and Philippines delegate at the Rome Conference.

[36] House Bill No. 2835, An Act in Compliance by the Republic of the Philippines with Its Obligations under the Rome Statute of the International Criminal Court and for Other Purposes, filed 10 August 2016 (ICC Cooperation Bill); House Bill No. 3834, An Act Amending Republic Act 9851 'An Act Defining and Penilizing Crimes against Inter-national Humanitarian Law, Genocide and Other Crimes against Humanity, Organizing Jurisdiction, Designating Special Courts, and for Related Purposes', filed 10 August 2016 (IHL Amendment Bill).

as other states in Southeast Asia, the Philippines argued for a broad interpretation of the complementarity principle that is, in particular, sensitive towards developing and conflict-affected nations. Thus, the Philippines' statements at the ASP have suggested the ICC should help states to 'strengthen [their] domestic capability to devise their *own system* of protecting its citizens' and assist with 'the training of judges, prosecutors, the police and the military' (Republic of the Philippines, 2013). Its Kampala statement asked the Conference to review the use of amnesties since 'the conviction of a perpetrator will bring justice to the victims and end impunity, but it will not necessarily usher [in] peace and stability to conflict-affected areas'. Further, in the context of African Union opposition to the ICC in 2013, the Philippines argued that 'justice can be particularly complicated and difficult in countries affected if not devastated by violence', cautioning that 'Rome was not built in one day', but 'began its decay when it failed to be cognizant of the changing needs of the times' (Republic of the Philippines, 2013). At the 2016 ASP, the Philippines' delegate responded to the ICC Prosecutor's indication that she was monitoring drug-related deaths by asking for 'a chance to make complementarity work' (Republic of the Philippines, 2016).

The Philippines government has been more hostile to the Court during President Duterte's administration, even before the ICC preliminary examination (RT, 2016). Duterte has not denied the killings and has even admitted some responsibility (Villamor, 2018a). At times he has presented a more conciliatory attitude towards the ICC: welcoming the examination and asking for a meeting with the ICC Prosecutor, but emphasising that its policy was a 'legitimate police operation' (Villamor, 2018b). The government lodged its notice of withdrawal from the Rome Statute a month later. Duterte's administration has more commonly denigrated the ICC as a European-backed institution, while presenting Duterte as combatting the destabilising impact of drugs – for example: 'Who are you to interfere in the way I would run my country? You know very well that we are being swallowed by drugs' (Pepper, 2018). Still, some former and opposition politicians remain more supportive of the Court (as indicated by the senators' petition in the Supreme Court opposing withdrawal, see Section 3.4.4), and in 2019 two former officials submitted a communication to the ICC Prosecutor concerning Chinese actions in the South China Sea.

Security actors have officially supported accountability initiatives in the past. The Armed Forces of the Philippines have provided international humanitarian law and human rights education programmes at least since 1992 (PCICC, 2008: 34). Several offices consider discipline and ethical issues, including the Office of the Inspector General, Office of Ethical Standards and Public Accountability, and Office of the Judge Advocate General (PCICC, 2008: 33). The 'ICC Task Force' established by Ramos in 1998 included representatives from the Department of Foreign Affairs, Department of Justice, and other government departments and offices, as well as the University of the Philippines. In 1999, the DND and Department of Foreign Affairs were appointed as co-chairs of an International Humanitarian Law 'ad hoc' Committee to manage International Humanitarian Law Day programs 'in collaboration' with the ICRC, Philippine National Red Cross and civil society.[37] The DND declared its support for ratifying the Rome Statute as early as 2001, though in practice officials opposed the idea until shortly before ratification in 2011. At a seminar in 2012, Brigadier General Domingo Tutaan Jr explained that 'our vision is really to have zero reports of IHL violations' and 'join our hands together in ending impunity as far as IHL violations are concerned' (Lozada, 2013: 33).

Security actors and the DND have also publicly suggested that certain international crimes should be prosecuted and expressed support for the IHL Act (Nepomuceno, 2019). In 2018, a Police Regional Officer referred to an NPA landmine attack on police as a 'gross violation' of the IHL Act (Sornito, 2018), while the presidential spokesperson labelled a bombing attack in Lamitan a war crime (Mendez, 2018). These statements suggest some official openness towards prosecuting international crimes – at least when allegedly perpetrated by non-state actors. Section 3.4.4 addresses the enforcement of international criminal laws in more detail, but the military (and police) in the Philippines have not uniformly complied with national laws or their own policies, nor secured accountability for violations of such instruments.

Though positions shift and differ, security actors, authorities, and peace negotiators in the Philippines engage with international criminal justice, including through educational initiatives, monitoring violations, and drafting relevant laws. Yet despite this 'socialisation' of the norm of international criminal justice, official attitudes have been uneven. This is despite significant and often inventive advocacy from Philippine civil society.

---

[37] Executive Order No. 134, Declaring August 12, 1999 and Every 12th Day of August Thereafter as International Humanitarian Law Day, 31 July 1999.

3.3.3   Civil Society

Despite its history of conflict and military dictatorship, 'the Philippines are renowned for the size and the sophistication of their NGO sector' (Bryant, 2005: 61; Encarnacion Tadem, 2009). As elsewhere, however, Philippine civil society has diverse aims and ideological divisions persist (Clarke, 2013). NGOs related to church groups have utilised community networks to document human rights violations, while survivors of political oppression have established NGOs such as SELDA and Karapatan. Political elites have also created NGOs that 'mimic the form and style of regular NGOs' (Bryant, 2005: 68), while Corazón Aquino's endorsement of 'vigilante' groups has been mentioned. A number of individuals have influenced international criminal justice in the Philippines too, crossing between politics, NGO-work, the judiciary, and academia.[38]

This section focuses on advocacy surrounding the Philippines' ratification of the Rome Statute as an example of how civil society in the Philippines promoted international criminal justice. It therefore concentrates on human rights NGOs and especially the PCICC network, alongside the international coalition, CICC – whose regional coordinator during these discussions was from the Philippines. These organisations are not representative of Philippine civil society, but illustrate how some groups have used local initiative to reflect the themes identified in Section 3.2 in their arguments about international criminal mechanisms.

Civil society actors helped to draft domestic international crimes legislation prior to ratification of the Rome Statute. A Philippines-based international organisation representative explained, 'those who were lobbying for the Rome Statute felt that ... if the Philippines would never ratify the Rome Statute at least we would have a domestic law that deals with the same issues'.[39] Civil society moved from framing the proposed legislation as being consistent with the Geneva Conventions and Additional Protocol II[40] (so as not to appear to circumvent executive

---

[38] These include Senators Escudero, Gordon, Legarda, and formerly Defensor Santiago, civil society actors such as Evelyn Serrano (formerly of CICC), Rebecca Lozado (PCICC), Ruben Carranza (International Center for Transitional Justice), current and former Chairs of the Commission on Human Rights, and academic lawyers, such as Judge Raul Pangalangan and former University of the Philippines professor, lawyer, Congress Representative, and former spokesperson for President Duterte, H Harry Roque.

[39] Interview P3.

[40] E.g., Senate Bill No. 2135, Thirteenth Congress of the Republic of the Philippines, Second Regular Session, 26 September 2005 (Senate Bill No. 2135).

ratification processes) (Flores Acuña, 2013), to returning to the Rome Statute model.

International instruments were crucial and international actors provided support, but 'local' actors drove the implementation and ratification process. In particular, PCICC, representing its NGO members, 'pursued the campaign for more than a decade, which included filing a *mandamus* case before the Supreme Court urging it to compel the Executive to transmit the ratification papers to the Senate' (CICC, 2011: 1).

Once the IHL Act was passed, NGOs framed ratification as complementing the Philippines' identity as a human rights respecting state. It was argued that by ratifying the Rome Statute the Philippines would be 'reaffirming its adherence to the rule of law and to justice as a way to lasting peace' (CICC, 2008: 2). PCICC recalled that 'the concept of command responsibility actually derives from the famous Yamashita case', so that now it was simply 'time for us to update our own laws to keep abreast of the highest standards of humanitarian protection' (PCICC, 2009). Indeed, ratifying the Rome Statute would 'put the Philippines in high standing among nations that respect human rights, uphold the rule of law and promote international justice' (PCICC, 2008: 26). These arguments paved the way for the government to ratify the Statute as 'a democracy that champions international law' (Department of Foreign Affairs, 2011).

Civil society actors sometimes conceded that international criminal justice could involve double standards. At a seminar in 2006, Raul Pangalangan (then co-chair of the PCICC), noted that internationalised tribunals like the ECCC were 'custom-tailored' for both United Nations and domestic politics. Indeed, he argued that the ECCC was established 'because the UN did not trust local justice and this is a problem ... not unique to Cambodia' (PICC, 2008: 7–8). To respond to ICC opponents asking, 'Are we shipping off our own countrymen to be tried in The Hague?',[41] advocates took several approaches. They suggested that ratifying the Statute would help to safeguard soldiers deployed overseas and millions of Filipinos working offshore (PCICC, 2008: 24). Witness and victim protection has been a serious issue in the Philippines, so the Rome Statute's victim protection and participation provisions were mentioned (PCICC, 2008: 25). It was also argued that '[u]nder the treaty's

[41] Interview P2.

complementarity principle, the ICC strengthens [a] member state's sovereignty as it recognizes the state's prerogative to try cases using its domestic judicial system and national legislation' (CICC, 2008: 1). The ICC would arguably support the domestic legal system and encourage the professionalisation of the Philippines security sector, while respecting the state's independence (PCICC, 2008: 26).

One argument suggested that the ICC could contribute to securing peace because it could prosecute both state and non-state actors. Pangalangan argued that the ICC would 'de-politicize the prosecution of military abuses and shift these proceedings purely to legal standards' (PCICC, 2008: 6). The Commission for Human Rights echoed this argument (de Lima, 2009).[42] The idea that the 'ICC is created to end impunity and human rights abuses committed by both state and non-state actors' also indicated that it could 'be a deterring factor for further commission of crimes' or prevent criminals finding a 'haven' of impunity in the Philippines (PCICC, 2008: 25), as Japanese perpetrators of sexual slavery had in World War II.

Following ratification, some actors provided training to state and non-state security actors and the judiciary about their legal obligations. Many NGOs have also documented extrajudicial killings, disappearances (commonly known as 'salvaging'), torture, forcible transfers, and evacuations ('hamletting' – where civilians were forced to move to new 'hamlets'), sexual violence, and other acts that could represent the underlying conduct of international crimes. They have publicised such violations in reports, media releases, and submissions to international mechanisms (e.g. Karapatan, 2016). Civil society actors have also submitted communications to the ICC Prosecutor regarding enforced disappearances and extrajudicial killings committed in the Philippines since ratifying the Rome Statute,[43] including under Duterte's presidency (see Section 3.2.5). Recent petitions to the Supreme Court opposing the withdrawal from the Rome Statute were consistent with promoting the Philippines as an esteemed democratic protector of human rights. They claimed that withdrawal 'sends the international community a message that [the

---

[42] Another actor remembered that 'security like[d this argument] a lot because they are always complaining that "you're always talking about our human rights violations". So in this case they are happy: state and non-state', Interview P5.

[43] Anecdotally, in 2014 local and international civil society actors discussed seeking an ICC investigation regarding extrajudicial killings and enforced disappearances (potentially based on the notion of disappearances being continuing crimes).

Philippines] is not a reliable member', could dampen 'foreign investors' confidence in the reliability, predictability and integrity of our democratic institutions', contribute to perceptions of impunity, remove from Filipinos a remedy for human rights violations, and deny rights to participation in governance.[44]

Thus, civil society actors in the Philippines encouraged authorities to adopt the principles of international criminal justice by emphasising: the Rome Statute's consistency with Philippine and international law; the potential to present the Philippines as a human rights protecting state; that the Rome Statute preserves sovereignty and can also protect Filipinos; the possibility for the ICC to encourage peace and stability; and the persistence of legislative and enforcement gaps. However, civil society actors in the Philippines recognise that the Rome Statute is not the only way to respond to international crimes.

3.3.4   Local Adaptation

International, official, and civil society actors have attempted to influence international criminal justice in the Philippines using arguments that draw on themes of sovereignty and development, human rights and democratic principles, and securing internal peace and stability. This section identifies several ways in which actors further challenge any emphasis upon international prosecutions and promote domestic mechanisms.

Improving domestic legal avenues for prosecuting international crimes is consistent with the Rome Statute and the principle of complementarity. Following ratification, the Second National Summit on International Humanitarian Law held in December 2012 identified a need to train investigators and prosecutors, develop standardised data clearinghouses, enhance witness protection, and build the capacity of forensic experts and doctors (Lozada et al., 2013). At the 2015 ASP, PCICC observed that the 'prosecution of crimes ... will be the testament of how justice has consolidated, of whether ... "positive complementarity" is taking root. IHL cases have been filed in the Philippines but prosecutions of such remain very low'. PCICC asked the ICC to provide access to its 'various mechanisms and resources', which regional civil society was 'banking on' to help (PCICC, 2015). Whether or not this was a realistic request, it

---

[44] G.R. No. 239483, 8 June 2018, *SC Petitions*: para. 145.

suggested that the ICC might be most useful if it could facilitate domestic prosecutions.

Yet, civil society actors had pursued the objective of prosecuting violent state conduct within the Philippines for decades (Leary et al., 1984; Angeles, 1994). While PCICC and others engaged with the ICC, many actors recognised the primary role of the domestic system to an extent that minimised the ICC's significance. As one international organisation representative explained, 'I don't think ... ratification of the Rome Statute changes much in terms of the strategy that should be adopted ... because ... what will be utilised here? It would be Republic Act 9851' (the IHL Act).[45] Therefore, some civil society actors focused on improving national judicial processes and employing domestic laws, which faced several challenges (see Section 3.4.4).

NGO representatives have argued that police are unwilling to investigate the military (in a 'command conspiracy' contrasted to 'command responsibility') (Human Rights Online Philippines, 2015) and witnesses face security threats. The Department of Justice has been accused of withdrawing charges against higher-ranking military officers or failing to include international crimes charges filed against lower ranked soldiers (Karapatan, 2015). Anecdotally, prosecutors are less willing to bring charges under the IHL Act because of the need to prove additional elements – prosecuting kidnapping without ransom or murder is sufficiently challenging, even if this would not provide the symbolism of an international crime prosecution. An NGO representative explained that not only are there 'few lawyers who actually know IHL', when asking the Department of Justice about the lack of domestic prosecutions, they say, '"But just file a case, no one's filing", but it's like a chicken and egg! Who will file a case when you have witnesses dying? On the other hand, if we don't file a case ... how can we say [to victims], "We need you to be strong"?'[46] Thus, civil society actors have adjusted their responses to alleged international crimes by focusing on improving domestic institutional processes for witness security and investigations more generally, rather than targeting international crimes prosecutions.

Some justice-focused NGOs have further adapted the concept of international criminal justice by promoting activities not typically addressed by international criminal law. An NGO representative explained that some community stakeholders 'were not really happy with

---

[45] Interview P3.
[46] Interview P5.

a punitive justice' or 'were saying "We supported the Rome Statute because it's the most available . . . but of course we still want to find other ways or other kinds of justice, like transitional justice, restorative justice'.[47] For example, PCICC aims to create awareness for the ICC, build support for the Rome Statute, and promote the integration of ICC principles in the domestic legal system. Yet in 2009 (still prior to ratification), PCICC commenced a project called 'Building Bridges for Peace' to 'foster a change process in areas struggling with social unrest and armed conflict' (PCICC, 2012a: 7). Even though PCICC did not traditionally focus on land issues, communities consulted during the process 'identified land rights as key to peacebuilding' (PCICC, 2012a: 8). A report from the subsequent project hints at the links between justice and land disputes, being titled: 'Laying Justice on the Ground: Moving from Land Disputes to Land Rights' (PCICC, 2014). The first project 'framed its work from a rights perspective, guided by human rights and international humanitarian law standards' (PCICC, 2012a: 7) and the 'Laying Justice' report refers to 'conflict transformation and governance' (PCICC, 2014: 4), rather than international criminal law. The reports published by the Transitional Justice and Reconciliation Commission concerning the Bangsamoro process also emphasise listening methodologies and land dispossession, alongside recommendations for prosecutions.

As another example of an adapted approach towards securing accountability for international crimes, many NGOs appreciate the opportunity to engage with human rights offices and other monitoring mechanisms,[48] as well as forums such as 'community based dialogues' on human rights issues (see Hanns Seidel Foundation Philippines, 2015). These can raise awareness of human rights and violent incidents (which might contribute toward advocacy for prosecutions), but also provide a 'venue for dialogue' and 'collective formation of public proposals' (Hanns Seidel Foundation Philippines, 2015: 16). Community forums underpin a 'top-level policy dialogue' with army and police leaders about the 'major human rights issues, *coming from the ground*'.[49] Similarly, human rights and international humanitarian law training of state actors has become 'more targeted' through using familiar examples, since 'a law is only good when you can apply it practically on the ground'.[50]

---

[47] Interview P5.
[48] Interview P4.
[49] Interview P4, emphasis added.
[50] Interview P3.

However, some actors have become frustrated with the slow impact of these forums, which may even crowd out other priorities. In the human rights field, though in relation to securing accountability for serious violence, one civil society actor saw 'human rights orientation seminars to members of the Armed Forces of the Philippines' and police as 'a waste of time' designed to 'make it appear that they're really doing something' – possibly to secure military aid – whereas instead, 'I'd rather spend my time doing . . . awareness on the ground'.[51] This actor was in favour of the 'education, mobilisation, and organising of peoples', but not as a top-down process or via 'parachuting' in to document violations. Instead, she argued, NGOs must 'invit[e] [individuals] to be human rights defenders themselves'.[52] This approach recognised that the Philippines' legal achievements 'were not really driven by . . . the main officials changing their mindsets . . . it's because of the people who have fought for all these laws'.[53] As Human Rights Watch noted in 2012, '[i]f progress [on cases] has been made, it is often because of the perseverance and courage of family members, rather than aggressive action by police and prosecutors' (Human Rights Watch, 2012b).

Community action may involve local discussion, potentially within *barangay*-level or customary dispute settlement forums, including structures responding to clan conflicts (known as *pangayaw*, *rido*, or by other terms). These might, for example, exile a member of the community who has committed a crime such as murder or rape as a member of a paramilitary group,[54] or more broadly attempt to resolve the conflict (The Asia Foundation, 2005; see Torres III, 2014) and may involve international funding or staff.

Stakeholders have also developed structured forums with international scope. For instance, a group of largely international NGOs organised International Peoples Tribunal (IPT) hearings in Washington, DC in 2015 and Brussels in 2018, following a Permanent Peoples' Tribunal session concerning the Arroyo administration held in 2007. The IPTs found President Duterte guilty of crimes against humanity and forwarded their findings to the ICC Prosecutor, but also to embassies and the United Nations seeking prosecution as well as reparations. Thus, actors used non-legal mechanisms to 'prosecute' human rights violations – adapting some of the language and processes of international crimes trials to serve broader advocacy purposes.

---

[51] Interview P6.
[52] Interview P6.
[53] Interview P6.
[54] Interview P6.

Philippine civil society advocated for the Rome Statute to be ratified by reframing the international criminal justice norm in light of local context. This section has shown that at least some actors interpret international criminal justice as requiring broader changes to the domestic judicial system or NGO strategies informed by community participation. In each case, Philippines-based actors have also drawn on international actors and ideas in a process that is neither driven from the 'inside-out' nor 'outside-in', but involves ongoing engagement and reconstruction.

3.4 Mechanisms for Prosecuting International Crimes in the Philippines

The Philippines legal system provides several avenues to respond to international crimes. The current, 1987, Constitution includes a Bill of Rights and Article II(2) 'adopts the generally accepted principles of international law as part of the law of the land',[55] which seems to refer to customary international law, rather than treaties.[56] Many international criminal and humanitarian law treaties, including the Rome Statute, have been ratified and implemented via domestic legislation. The Philippines also has the capacity to prosecute international crimes under national legislation, although there may be amnesties and immunities. There have been attempts to seek accountability for international crimes through Constitutional and criminal avenues.

3.4.1 International Mechanisms

The ICC has jurisdiction to prosecute crimes committed within the Philippines after Rome Statute ratification on 30 August 2011, subject to the relevant Statute provisions and the withdrawal from the Statute effective March 2019. However, a Bill to facilitate the Philippines' cooperation with the Court was not passed.[57] The ICC Prosecutor is considering alleged extrajudicial killings during the 'war on drugs'

---

[55] Article VII(21), Constitution.

[56] This position is also suggested in G.R. No. 239483, 8 June 2018, *SC Petitions*, which, however, argues that for 'the Rome Statute, the distinction between treaty law and customary international law is erased since the multi-lateral treaty in effect codifies what are ostensibly long-held *jus cogens* principles and *ergo* [sic] *omnes* obligations under customary international law', para. 106, supported also by the *Kuroda* case.

[57] ICC Cooperation Bill, proposed by H. Roque, pending with the Committee on Justice from 17 August 2016, not adopted.

and – depending on the outcome of slow pretrial proceedings – might proceed to investigate and prosecute international crimes (ICC, 2018; Palmer, 2019a). Crimes committed in the Philippines might also be prosecuted under other states' universal jurisdiction legislation, or before an international(ised) tribunal established with or without UN assistance. However, given the lack of concrete proposals to date, such possibilities not addressed here.

3.4.2   Domestic Legislation

There are several options for prosecuting conduct that could be characterised as an international crime under the Philippines domestic legislation. First, some underlying criminal conduct could be prosecuted under the Philippines Revised Penal Code,[58] for example as murder, homicide, illegal detention, slavery, or rape. Second, apart from Executive Order No. 68 to prosecute 'all Japanese accused of war crimes committed in the Philippines', other laws specifically address conduct that might form an international crime. For example, legislation was passed in 2009 to allow the prosecution of torture and other cruel, inhuman, and degrading treatment (Torture Act)[59] and in 2012 the perpetration of enforced or involuntary disappearances was made a crime under the Enforced Disappearances Act.[60] These Acts were passed prior to the Philippines ratifying the Convention Against Torture[61] (in 2012) and the International Convention for the Protection of All Persons from Enforced Disappearance (not yet ratified).[62] Third, the IHL Act incorporated war crimes, genocide, and crimes against humanity into Philippines law before the government ratified the Rome Statute. All of this legislation has prospective operation. This section focuses on the IHL Act, which is of the most direct relevance to international criminal law.

---

[58] Act No. 3815, An Act Revising the Penal Code and Other Penal Laws 1930, 8 December 1930 (Revised Penal Code). This section draws on material in Palmer, 2019a.
[59] Republic Act No. 9745, An Act Penalizing Torture and Other Cruel, Inhuman and Degrading Treatment or Punishment and Prescribing Penalties Therefore, 10 November 2009 (Torture Act).
[60] Republic Act No. 10353, An Act Defining and Penalizing Enforced or Involuntary Disappearance, 21 December 2012 (Enforced Disappearances Act). See also Republic Act No. 11188, An Act Providing for the Special Protection of Children in Situations of Armed Conflict and Providing Penalties for Violations Thereof, 10 January 2019, implementing a range of international treaties and including criminal penalties.
[61] Adopted 10 December 1984, entered into force 26 June 1987.
[62] Adopted 20 December 2006, entered into force 23 December 2010.

The proponents of the bill later adopted as the IHL Act presented it as being consistent with the Constitution's incorporation of 'generally accepted principles of international law' and earlier legislation, as well as an attempt to codify international crimes within the domestic legal system to fully comply with the Philippines' obligations under various treaties and conventions. It would allow the Philippines to keep pace with developments in international criminal law, and more importantly, ensure that those who commit war crimes, genocide, and crimes against humanity are not afforded impunity for their acts.

While one bill allowed for universal jurisdiction,[63] section 17 provides the state with jurisdiction over the crimes addressed by the IHL Act 'regardless of where the crime is committed', where perpetrated by military or civilian persons who are citizens of the Philippines, present in the Philippines, or who are alleged to have committed the crime against a Philippine citizen.[64] This so-called 'reverse complementarity' section provides that authorities in the Philippines can 'dispense with' investigations or prosecutions if an international court such as the ICC is already acting. This provision is to operate in 'the interests of justice' to avoid parallel or duplicate proceedings, while the ICC's own complementarity principle directs that the ICC will not proceed with a case that was or is being investigated or prosecuted elsewhere.[65]

Due to the historic controversy concerning the status of non-state actors in Philippine internal conflicts, section 2(g) of the IHL Act confirms that it 'shall not affect the legal status of the parties to a conflict, nor give an implied recognition of the status of belligerency'. The Act comprehensively adopts the Rome Statute crimes (Flores Acuña, 2013). Most of the definitions in Article 7(2) of the Rome Statute regarding crimes against humanity are provided in section 3 of the IHL Act (Palmer, 2019a)[66] and also apply to war crimes and genocide. There are some minor differences between the crimes provisions in the Rome Statute and IHL Act. For example, the IHL Act's

---

[63] Article 40, Senate Bill No. 2135.

[64] The extension to crimes where the only connection to the Philippines is the victim is not typical under Philippines criminal law, see Article 2, Revised Penal Code.

[65] Article 17, Rome Statute.

[66] While section 3 does not mention 'gender', it defines additional terms such as 'armed conflict', 'military necessity', and 'superior' generally consistently with international law; though compare, e.g., the definition of 'armed conflict' in the IHL Act to Article 1 of Additional Protocol II and Article 8(2)(f), Rome Statute.

crime against humanity of '*arbitrary* deportation or forcible transfer of population' is defined identically to the Rome Statute's 'deportation or forcible transfer',[67] though the different name might suggest an additional requirement of arbitrariness, at least for deportation.[68] However, a change from the grave breach of '*unlawful* deportation' to '*arbitrary* deportation' could represent a lower threshold.[69] These distinctions are unlikely to be crucial in practice, but the offences were considered important due to the practice of forced evacuations known as 'hamletting' in the Philippines and frequency of incidents causing internal displacement.[70] The definition of 'forced pregnancy' in the Act also omits the Rome Statute's qualification that the 'definition shall not in any way be interpreted as affecting national laws relating to pregnancy',[71] of importance given controversies concerning reproductive health policies in the Philippines (see Tanyang, 2015).

Section 4(a) of the IHL Act includes delay in repatriating prisoners of war and other protected persons in an international armed conflict as an additional 'grave breach of the Geneva Conventions' not included in the Rome Statute. Subsection (b) covers the crimes found in common Article 3 of the Geneva Conventions and Article 8(2)(c) of the Rome Statute. Section 4(c) then sets out crimes drawn from Articles 8(2)(b) and (e) of the Rome Statute,[72] without distinction as to whether they were committed in a national or international armed conflict.[73] The ICRC apparently recommended this structure based on the legislation of some European states and Canada.[74] This merge expanded the number of crimes considered relevant in the Philippines, as the country 'deal[s] primarily with non-international armed conflicts'.[75]

---

[67] This discrepancy remained in the IHL Amendment Bill.
[68] In Section 6(d), IHL Act, compare Article 7(1)(d), Rome Statute.
[69] Section 4(a)(6), IHL Act, compare Article 8(2)(a)(vii). The IHL Amendment Bill reversed this discrepancy.
[70] This accords with the suggestion offered by Interview P2 that the latter change would cover a situation such as in Lanao, where 'this displacement happened in such a way that was intentional, but not to the higher standard [of] forcible transfer'.
[71] Section (3)(j), IHL Act, compare Article 7(2)(f), Rome Statute. The IHL Amendment Bill reinserted this qualifier.
[72] With the addition of launching an attack against works containing dangerous forces.
[73] Though section 4(c) IHL Act requires that they be considered 'within the established framework of international law'.
[74] Draft Explanatory Note.
[75] Interview P2. E.g. section 4(c)(6) of the IHL Act is consistent with Article 15 of Additional Protocol II, though it is not included in the Rome Statute. Section 4(c)(7) is drawn from Article 8(2)(b)(v) of the Rome Statute, but here with extension to non-international

Another departure is found in Section 4(c)(24). It retains the Rome Statute's age limit of 15 years for conscription or enlistment into the armed forces, but provides a higher age of 18 for using children in hostilities and 'recruiting' children 'into an armed group other than the national armed forces'.[76] The higher age limit was derived from the Optional Protocol to the Convention on the Rights of the Child on the involvement of children in armed conflict,[77] but a lower age of 15 was considered necessary for state forces 'because the Philippine Military Academy can recruit from high school'.[78]

Section 5 of the IHL Act extends the crime of genocide to acts committed against a 'social or any other similar and permanent group', but otherwise reflects the Rome Statute provision. Similarly, section 6 addresses crimes against humanity and encompasses the crime of persecution on the ground of 'sexual orientation or other grounds that are universally recognized as impermissible in international law',[79] reflecting human rights arguments.

In relation to criminal responsibility, section 8 of the Act is modelled with minor variations on Article 25 of the Rome Statute. Solidifying the legacy of the *Yamashita* case, section 10 provides for superior[80] responsibility. Section 12 adopts the Rome Statute position of allowing a limited defence of superior orders. The Act also includes provisions for witness and victim protection and for a legal representative to present victims' 'views and concerns',[81] whereas victim participation is

---

armed conflict and with the additional wording 'making non-defended localities or demilitarized zones the object of attack', derived from Additional Protocol I.

[76] Compare sections 8(2)(b)(xxvi) (international armed conflict) and 8(2)(e)(vii) (non-international armed conflict), Rome Statute.

[77] Adopted 25 May 2000, entered into force 12 February 2002, ratified 26 August 2003, see Republic Act 1118; Draft Explanatory Note.

[78] Interview P5, though the armed forces requires applicants to be graduates and enlistment is open to male citizens aged 18 to 30 years, Article III, section 27, Commonwealth Act No. 1, An Act to Provide for the National Defense of the Philippines, Penalizing Certain Violations Thereof, Appropriating Funds Therefor, and for Other Purposes, 21 December 1935 (National Defense Act); the Rome Statute does not include 'recruitment' (which is used Article 77(2) of Additional Protocol I), but the ICC has considered conscripting and enlisting to be 'two forms of recruitment': *Prosecutor v. Thomas Lubanga Dyilo*, Case No. ICC-01/04-01/06, Pre-Trial Chamber I, Decision on Confirmation of Charges, 29 January 2007, para. 246.

[79] Section 6(h), IHL Act.

[80] In conjunction with the definition of 'superior' in section 3(r), IHL Act.

[81] Section 13, IHL Act.

not provided for in the general Rules of Criminal Procedure.[82] Further, 'in addition to existing provisions in Philippine law and procedural rules', the Act provides for reparations ordered 'directly against a convicted person'.[83] No 'trust fund' is established under this legislation, though the government could legislate for state-paid reparations, as it did in 2013 in relation to the Marcos regime.[84]

The IHL Act therefore reflects the provisions in the Rome Statute with minor largely progressive differences. Other bills seeking to amend the IHL Act have been submitted since the Rome Statute was ratified.[85] An inter-agency and civil society working group tasked with drafting an amendment to the IHL Act and an ICC Cooperation Bill initially reviewed foreign and model legislation, especially for the cooperation component. However, the process was considered by one participant to be 'a one hundred per cent Filipino endeavour' because 'we have enough ... international criminal law experts that we didn't really need input from the outside'.[86]

The resulting IHL Amendment Bill aimed to bring the IHL Act closer to the Rome Statute.[87] Though some in the working group argued that 'the Rome Statute is one standard, we cannot go lower than that, [but] we can go higher than that',[88] the Bill's explanatory memorandum argued that upon ratification, the Philippines was obligated to adopt the Rome Statute terms.[89] This meant that ratifying the Rome Statute could have indirectly *narrowed* the scope of the Philippines' legislation. For example: the Bill removed two of the IHL Act's additional war crimes;[90] divided the war crimes provisions into those committed in an international or

---

[82] Revised Rules of Criminal Procedure, 1 December 2000, though see Rule 110, section 16 regarding civil actions for recovery in criminal proceedings.

[83] Section 14, IHL Act.

[84] E.g. the Philippines government passed the Republic Act No. 10368, Human Rights Victims Reparation and Recognition Act, 25 February 2013 in relation to crimes committed under Marcos, allocating 10 billion pesos plus interest to approximately 10,000 victims eligible to claim compensation.

[85] E.g. to give 'Philippine authorities the full jurisdiction over suspected or accused persons covered under the said law, regardless of an ongoing investigation or prosecution of another court or international tribunal', Senate Bill No. 1290, Sixteenth Congress of the Republic of the Philippines First Regular Session, 13 August 2015.

[86] Interview P2, though the ICRC had also formed part of the group.

[87] IHL Amendment Bill, 1.

[88] Interview P5.

[89] IHL Amendment Bill, 1.

[90] Those addressing repatriations and attacks against dangerous forces. The introduction to the IHL Amendment Bill suggested that a provision regarding ordering displacement was also to be removed, but it was retained in draft sections 4(c)(xv) (international conflict)

national armed conflict (thereby reducing the number of crimes applicable in the latter, more common, situation in the Philippines); and
excluded a 'social or any other similar stable and permanent group' from
the Act's definition of genocide. In the last case, one actor argued that the
inclusion of other stable groups was 'one of the reasons why our law is
quite good', but 'unfortunately ... their tendency is really to hug as
closely as possible to the Rome Statute',[91] Still, the Bill incorporated the
Rome Statute's Elements of Crimes 'to assist in the application and
interpretation of the crimes',[92] while the crime of persecution based on
sexual orientation remained. The provision on superior responsibility
was kept, because, as one participant explained, 'we're actually very
proud that one of the first command responsibility cases actually
stemmed from the Philippines'.[93] Thus, the Rome Statute can limit the
progressiveness of international crimes laws. On the other hand, these
Bills were not passed into law. Debates concerning how to best legislate
for international crimes in the Philippine context therefore continue.

3.4.3   Amnesties and Immunities

Reflecting tensions between peace and justice, amnesties have been used in
the Philippines for political and other crimes, including for separatist groups
since the 1970s and 1980s, and official security actors (ICRC, 2016b). As an
example, amnesties – or respect for existing amnesties – have been offered as
part of the response to the seemingly 'intractable' conflict in Mindanao
(Jeffery, 2018). Amnesties in the Philippines typically do not cover 'crimes
against chastity, rape, torture, kidnapping for ransom, use and trafficking of
illegal drugs and other crimes for personal ends' (ICRC, 2016; Jeffery, 2018).
The President retains power under the 1987 Constitution to grant pardons
as well as, with Congress' approval, amnesties[94] and the IHL Act does not
exclude their potential operation for crimes against humanity, genocide, or
war crimes. In contrast, the Torture Act and Enforced Disappearances Act
stipulate that perpetrators 'shall not benefit from any special amnesty law or
similar measures'.[95]

---

and 4(d)(viii) (non-international conflict) – compare only Article 8(2)(e)(viii), Rome
Statute.
[91]   Interview P5.
[92]   Section 13, IHL Amendment Bill.
[93]   Interview P2 (the *Yamashita* case).
[94]   Article VII(19), Philippines Constitution.
[95]   Section 16, Torture Act; section 23, Enforced Disappearances Act.

Section 9 of the IHL Act confirms the irrelevance of official capacity *except* for 'the established constitutional immunity from suit of the Philippine President during his/her tenure', or immunities arising from international law.[96] This may have been superseded via the later ratification of the Rome Statute, as it removes immunities as a bar to prosecution at the ICC, although that is only debateable under Philippines law.[97]

Finally, the IHL Act does not clarify that the usual statutory limitation periods (of up to twenty years) do not apply to international crimes, although the Philippines is a party to the Convention on the Non-Applicability of Statutory Limitations to War Crimes and Crimes against Humanity, which should remove the applicability of these limits.[98] Overall, the Philippines has a robust legal framework for prosecuting international crimes that was adapted to reflect some aspects of the domestic context and drafting process. These are arguably more expansive than the Rome Statute in some respects, though immunities and amnesties may still operate.

3.4.4   Enforcement

Despite these laws, Philippine courts have largely failed to convict perpetrators for serious human rights violations that might constitute international crimes (Amnesty International, 2018). In 2008, Alston noted that the 'criminal justice system's failure to obtain convictions and deter future killings should be understood in light of the system's overall structure' (Alston, 2008: para. 45). Today that structure includes a variety of bodies. The Philippine National Police and National Bureau of Investigation investigate crimes in the Philippines, while the IHL Act specifies that the Police, the Department of Justice, and the Commission on Human Rights 'or other concerned law enforcement agencies shall designate prosecutors or investigators' for crimes under the Act.[99] Other

---

[96] Note that the 1987 Constitution does not explicitly provide for Presidential immunity, however the Supreme Court has suggested that such immunity would still apply, see *Maximo V Soliven et al. v. Hon. Ramon P Makasiar*, G.R. No. 82585, Supreme Court, Republic of the Philippines, 14 November 1988; and even that this is 'settled in jurisprudence', *Rodolfo Noel Lozada Jr et al. v. President Gloria Macapagal-Arroyo et al.*, G.R. Nos. 184379-80, Supreme Court, Republic of the Philippines, 24 April 2012.

[97] See G.R. No. 239483, 8 June 2018, *SC Petitions*, paras. 137–9.

[98] Ratified in 1973. If a victim 'surfaces alive', the Enforced Disappearances Act has a limitation period of twenty-five years from their reappearance, see section 22.

[99] Section 18, IHL Act.

bodies monitor the prosecution of alleged international crimes, including the Commission on Human Rights, Ombudsman, national monitoring mechanism, and inter-agency committee. The Commission on Human Rights has been a particularly prominent opponent of alleged extrajudicial killings committed during Duterte's presidency. However, the Commission and its supporters have faced significant opposition, including the imprisonment of a former Chair of the Commission, Leila de Lima, for questionable drug charges and the attempted drastic reduction of its budget (see Palmer, 2019b).

Civil society actors report a number of challenges in bringing international crimes cases. These include security fears, difficulties gathering evidence, and delays. These barriers have affected the investigation and prosecution of incidents occurring before the IHL Act was enacted in December 2009, such as the Maguindanao massacre of 2009, where lawyers for an NGO, Centerlaw, participated as private prosecutors alongside public prosecutors in the criminal case. In 2006, the Melo Commission named General Jovito Palparan as potentially responsible for numerous killings and disappearances,[100] yet he was promoted during Arroyo's administration. In 2007, the families of Sherlyn Cadapan and Karen Empeño, who had been abducted and disappeared, filed a petition for habeas corpus. Despite reports of military interference, in 2011 the Supreme Court ordered the immediate release of the two women and named Palparan as among those apparently responsible.[101] However, the military denied having them in custody and Palparan went into hiding. He was eventually arrested in Manila in 2014. Human Rights Watch observed that it 'took five years . . . for Palparan to be charged but [that he was eventually charged] is really due to the efforts of the victims' families' (Human Rights Watch, 2012a). In September 2018, Palparan was eventually convicted for the kidnapping and illegal detention of Cadapan and Empeño, more than ten years after they disappeared.[102]

Since the IHL Act entered into force, as one civil society representative put it in 2014, 'we have the law, we have IHL Day, of course we have all these treaties signed earlier: Geneva Conventions, Genocide, everything.

---

[100] Palparan himself claimed that 'I did not kill them. I just inspired [the triggermen]' (Human Rights Watch, 2007: 15).

[101] *Rogelio Boac et al. v. Erlinda Cadapan et al.*, G.R. Nos. 184461-62, 184495, 187109, Supreme Court, Republic of the Philippines, 31 May 2011.

[102] *People of the Philippines v. M/Gen Jovito Palparan et al.*, Crim. Case. No. 3905-M-2011 and 3906-M-2011, Regional Trial Court of Bulacan, Republic of the Philippines, 17 September 2018.

But in terms of testing the justice system ... we have one case [at the time] where the current IHL Law is referred to'[103] – the *Bayan Muna* case. In that case in 2011, the Supreme Court rejected an argument that the Philippine-US Non-Surrender Agreement 'defeat[ed] the object and purpose' of the Rome Statute.[104] The Supreme Court refused to find that the IHL Act required the Philippines to surrender suspects to the ICC, because, the Court suggested, there is 'no overwhelming consensus, let alone prevalent practice ... that the prosecution of internationally recognized crimes of genocide, etc. *should be handled by a particular international criminal court*'.[105]

There have been attempts to charge individuals with crimes under the IHL Act. For instance, in 2013, the Department of Justice reportedly issued arrest warrants for MNLF leader Nur Misuari and others related to an attack in Zamboanga, although it appears that the case was stalled for peace talks (Pareño, 2013). The Mamasapano incident of 2015 occurred after the IHL Act was adopted and Rome Statute ratified. Civil society suggested that the case be referred to the ICC. An 'international monitoring team' advised that combatants should be prosecuted, including under the IHL Act, with explicit reference to section 4(c)(7) – attacking undefended localities (International Monitoring Team, 2015). Department of Justice investigators determined that the international crimes provisions would not apply, as there was no 'armed conflict' as defined by the Act (NBI-NPS SIT, 2015)[106] – reflecting how the additional elements of international crimes can seem more challenging for prosecution. Instead, ninety members of the MILF and other separatist groups were charged with 'direct assault with murder' in August

---

[103] Interview P5 was actually referring to *Saturnino C Ocampo v. Ephrem S Abando et al.*, G.R. No. 176830, *Randall B Ecanis v. Thelma Bunyi-Medina et al.*, G.R. No. 185587, *Rafael G Baylosis*, G.R. No. 185636, *Vicente P Ladlad v. Thelma Buni-Medina et al.*, G.R. No. 190005, Supreme Court, Republic of the Philippines, 11 February 2014. Several individuals including Saturnino Ocampo (a politician involved in the Bayan Muna case) unsuccessfully sought the annulment of their indictment and arrest for murder. Leonen J referred to the IHL Act in a separate concurring opinion, arguing that '[s]hould it be shown that there are acts committed in violation of [the IHL Act] ... these acts could not be absorbed in the crime of rebellion'.

[104] *Bayan Muna*.

[105] *Bayan Muna*, emphasis added. Carpio J dissented, finding that '[u]nder no circumstance can a mere executive agreement prevail over a prior or subsequent' inconsistent law.

[106] See also (Board of Inquiry, 2015: 91), which recommended investigating the incident 'to determine criminal and/or administrative liabilities or relevant government officials, the MILF, and other individuals'.

2016 and former President Benigno Aquino and two police officers were charged with usurpation of authority and corruption violations (although these cases were suspended) (Leonen, 2018).

The first conviction under the IHL Act came in March 2019 in relation to the armed conflict surrounding the city of Marawi (Marawi siege), by the Maute-ISIS group in 2017. Junaid Awal was found guilty of rebellion as well as the crime against humanity of rape and other forms of sexual violence, with evidence presented by a minor at the time who was raped and treated as a slave during five months of captivity (Patag, 2019). This case did not involve a perpetrator from official forces (Awal's group was in conflict with Philippines security forces), but does demonstrate a successful prosecution of crimes under the IHL Act, despite the additional elements that needed to be proven.

Constitutional and civil cases have also involved international criminal law issues, such as the *Vinuya* 'comfort women' case mentioned. In a number of cases seeking Constitutional writs of *amparo*, the Supreme Court employed the principle of superior responsibility to establish the respondents' accountability for an individual's disappearance, though not their criminal responsibility.[107] However, following the passage of the IHL Act, it was 'now clear' that enforced disappearances should be understood with reference to that Act. This has meant that 'the petitioner in an *amparo* case has the [additional] burden of proving by substantial evidence the indispensable element of government participation'.[108] It seems that even

---

[107] See with reference to the Rome Statute, *Lourdes D Rubrico et al. v. Gloria Macapagal-Arroyo et al.*, G.R. No. 183871, Supreme Court, Republic of the Philippines, 18 February 2010 and with reference to the IHL Act, separate opinions of Brion J and Carpio Morales J (*Rubrico*); *Cadapan; In the matter of the Petition for the Writ of Amparo and Habeas data in Favor of Noriel H Rodriguez v. Gloria Macapagal-Arroyo et. al.*, G.R. No. 191805, 193160, Supreme Court, Republic of the Philippines, 15 November 2011.

[108] *Navia et al. v. Pardico et al.*, G.R. No. 184467, Supreme Court, Republic of the Philippines, 19 June 2012, with reference to the separate opinion of Brion J in *Rubrico*, ibid. The IHL Act supported findings that situations did not amount to enforced disappearances in *Siegfred B Mison v. Paulino Q Gallegos and Ja Hoon Ku*, G.R. No. 210759, 211403, *Siegfred B Mison v. Ja Hoon Ku*, G.R. No. 211590, Supreme Court, Republic of the Philippines, 23 June 2015; *Julian Yusay Caram v. Marijoy D Segui et al.*, G.R. No. 193652, Supreme Court, Republic of the Philippines, 5 August 2014; *Spouses Rozelle Raymod Martin and Claudine Margaret Santiago v. Tulfo et al.*, G.R. No. 205039, Supreme Court, Republic of the Philippines, 21 October 2015; and from prior to the Act's passage, with reference to the Rome Statute, see *Avelino I Razon et al. v. Mary Jean B Tagitis*, G.R. No. 182498, Supreme Court, Republic of the Philippines, 3 December 2009. This definition was confirmed by section 3(b) of the Enforced Disappearances Act, consistent with the Convention.

before the IHL Act was used to convict any perpetrators, it had some impact on Philippine jurisprudence and public discourse about responding to serious incidents, albeit not necessarily in a progressive manner.

The withdrawal from the Rome Statute highlighted the complex relationship between domestic and international criminal law. Petitioners asked the Supreme Court to determine that this withdrawal was ineffective or void under the Philippines Constitution, which requires Senate concurrence before ratifying treaties.[109] The hearings raised issues concerning the relationship between the executive and judiciary, as well as the implementation of international law in the Philippines. These included whether the Rome Statute text became part of Philippines law upon ratification or as representing customary international law and, if so, whether it would have priority over the earlier IHL Act. Another issue was whether the 'reverse complementarity' provision in the IHL Act and the one-year delay until withdrawal takes effect could allow recourse to the ICC or preserve its proceedings, even if the withdrawal was considered valid. Vigorous questioning from the Bench suggested that this presented standing issues for the petitioners, especially PCICC, since – it was argued – withdrawal would not adversely affect their interests if the ICC case could persist. It was also suggested that if the IHL Act *was* more progressive than the Rome Statute (though the situation is a little more nuanced than that, as described), there could be no standing before the Supreme Court since a domestic remedy would suffice. In other words, there would be no injury to the petitioners to warrant their case.

The proceedings exhibited the Supreme Court's reservations about the ICC and reliance upon foreign law sources (such as South African proceedings concerning Rome Statute withdrawal), strongly emphasising the primacy of domestic institutions in responding to alleged international crimes (Pillai, 2018). Duterte is quoted as saying that police officers who kill during drug operations would be pardoned and promoted (Mogato, 2017). Individuals and institutions promoting investigations have faced considerable challenges (including the detention of Leila de Lima). By June 2019, there had been no convictions for international crimes in relation to the 'war on drugs', though the Philippines National Police claimed that some police had been 'punished' in relation to the 'war on drugs', though without detail (Talabong, 2017). Most notably, in 2018 three police officers were convicted for the murder of

---

[109] *SC Petitions.*

17-year-old Kian Loyd delos Santos, which had been a particularly poignant moment of the 'war on drugs' (Reuters, 2018). Yet, by around the same time, the Department of Justice had reportedly only investigated seventy-six cases of 'murder and homicide cases allegedly related to the government's campaign against drugs' outside of Manila, Quezon City, and Taguig (cities in 'Metropolitan Manila'). Of 1,099 'vigilante killings' in Metropolitan Manila, it was reported that 131 had been solved (Buan et al., 2019).

In summary, the IHL Act largely replicates the provisions of the Rome Statute, although it extends the reach of some crimes. These differences were drawn from international law, but also reflect local context and civil society engagement. Proposed amendments aimed to shift Philippine law back towards the Rome Statute, while in practice the domestic legislation is yet to be systematically enforced and continues to be debated, including within the Philippines courts. The next section considers the extent to which these mechanisms reflect the acceptance, rejection, or adaptation of the norm of international criminal justice.

3.5   Conclusions

The localisation approach argues that 'local actors may offer resistance to new external norms because of doubts about the norms' utility and applicability and fears that the norms might undermine existing beliefs and practices' (Acharya, 2004: 251). As Section 3.2 described, the Philippines has a history of contributing to the development of international criminal law. Further, people's movements have been justified with reference to human rights. Social and economic issues have also contributed to conflict, while internal instability led to an ongoing tension between peace and justice, alongside concerns about the impact of drugs. These 'aspects of the existing normative order' (Acharya, 2004: 251) in the Philippines do not all conflict with the 'normalised' understanding of international criminal justice (which, as discussed in Chapter 1, involves ending impunity via fair international crimes trials, potentially with international involvement). However, there has not been a progression towards internalising the international criminal justice norm over time.

The engagement of some officials with the ICC and human rights law mechanisms, and development and use of domestic international crimes law, does not suggest that international criminal justice has been entirely rejected – even if Duterte has withdrawn the Philippines from the ICC. Yet it is now more than a decade since the Melo Commission and widespread extrajudicial killings and disappearances continue to be reported (Sections 3.2.5 and 3.4.4). The impediments to enforcing international criminal laws in the Philippines are multifaceted and derive from community, military, police, and judicial barriers, including legacies from the Marcos era. In 2014, one actor remarked, 'I think you will meet a lot of persons who will say, "Not much is happening", but I come from a generation where martial law was a reality, so I think a lot is happening for me'.[110]

Temporal developments may be a matter of perspective, but in the Philippines, engagement with international criminal law has not progressed from rejection towards the acceptance of the international criminal justice norm, either. Rather, the situation is complex and involves a range of actors. In the Philippines, responses to international crimes continue to be reconstructed as problems and incidents occur (as for the Mamasapano incident or the 'war on drugs'), laws or mechanisms are adopted or revoked (the IHL Act and Rome Statute), during debates about respecting existing amnesties or avoiding them in future, and in halting cases. This demonstrates that debates about norms reoccur and shift between acceptance, rejection, and other forms of adaptation over *time*, as new legal solutions are proposed, implemented, and enforced through localisation (Zimmermann, 2016).

The diverging positions of the United States, other states, and international organisations, such as the UN, towards events in the Philippines demonstrate how positions towards international criminal justice are not easily divided into *spatial* categories labelled 'international' or 'local'. In the Philippines, rather than international actors persuading states to accept international norms, 'credible local actors' have worked to reconstruct notions of international criminal justice so as to 'supplement' but not 'supplant' the 'existing norm hierarchy' (Acharya, 2004: 251). When early attempts at persuading the government to ratify the Rome Statute failed, civil society actors drafted domestic legislation initially based on pre-existing legal obligations. The IHL Act contributed to constructing a version of 'international criminal justice' that would complement but not replace existing legal institutions.

During the Rome Statute ratification campaign, Philippine and international NGOs and individuals acted as 'norm entrepreneurs', using discourse aimed at 'contextualizing, redefining, and localizing

---

[110] Interview P5.

transnational ideas' of international criminal justice (Acharya, 2012a: 1). In particular, actors reframed ratification as an avenue for securing the Philippines' position as a human rights leader, protecting Filipinos, and providing an independent mechanism capable of pursuing non-state actors. This confirms the challenge involved in classifying particular concepts or arguments as international or local. For instance, 'human rights' hold particular historic importance in the Philippines, despite their 'global' nature. This suggests that it is artificial to conceive of norms as either international or local. Instead, ideas are dynamic and shifting.

However, beyond reframing, some civil society actors have attempted to adapt approaches to international crimes and promote different understandings and meanings of international criminal justice. For example, PCICC's 'Laying Justice on the Ground' project incorporated the principle of 'justice', but complemented local priorities of peace and development. Initiatives involving community-level mobilisation, peoples' tribunals, and 'bottom-up' dialogues do not reject international criminal justice – PCICC in particular remains committed to the ICC. However, some individuals and communities prioritise other issues such as reparations, land reform, social justice, and community-based dialogue (including in *barangay*-level forums). On the other hand, international criminal justice initiatives also supplement existing human rights, rule of law, or conflict transformation activities.

A 'localisation' framework suggests that local actors use their initiative to reframe and reconstruct norms, rather than only rejecting or accepting them. Where such '[b]orrowing and modification ... offer[s] scope for some elements of an existing norm hierarchy to receive wider external recognition through its association with the foreign norm', that is, for these local elements to be 'amplified', this may lead to 'new instruments and practices ... in which local influences remain highly visible' (Acharya, 2004: 251). The creation of new monitoring bodies, often with the participation of civil society, since the late 2000s can be understood as having 'developed from the syncretic normative framework' (Acharya, 2004: 251) contributed to by local civil society, state activities such as the Melo Commission, the Commission on Human Rights, and international attention including from UN processes (such as the Alston report).

The IHL Act is consistent with the process of localisation. It was modelled on the Rome Statute with some additions that could be linked to local engagement and the Philippine's support for international treaties and human rights. Terms relating to recruitment of children, persecution based on sexual orientation, belligerency, the retention of immunities and amnesties, and the combination of international and non-international war crimes related to the Philippine's policies and experiences, even if some wording was derived from international law.[111] The promotion of domestic institutions and laws, including in the few Supreme Court cases that have directly addressed international crimes, also involved localisation. Similarly, ratifying the Rome Statute was suggested as providing an independent arbiter for state and non-state crimes, while providing opportunities for the Philippines to participate in an influential international body, build legitimacy with civil society, and protect Philippine citizens. Yet draft implementation and cooperation legislation was *less* progressive than the existing IHL Act, thus detracting from the norm in some respects.

It is true that United States pressure alongside the Non-Surrender Agreement probably contributed to the delay in ratifying the Rome Statute, whereas trade or aid concerns may have affected the EU initiatives favouring accountability. While the localisation framework takes such influences into account, it emphasises normative concerns rather than geopolitical and material issues and draws attention to the impact of local actors. While many Philippines NGOs would have received foreign donor funding, state and non-state actors promoted the adoption of the IHL Act and Rome Statute ratification in a period where (for example) the United States is unlikely to have encouraged such developments and the laws were not clearly in the Philippine's material interests.

By contrast, the approach to international criminal justice in the Philippines lends itself to constructivist analysis. Norm entrepreneurs have encouraged the socialisation of international norms through dissemination and other advocacy activities. Allegations that international aid was directed towards opposition forces have detracted from NGO's credibility in the past (Section 3.2.3), but 'local' civil society organisations have still attracted international attention towards domestic issues. This international engagement involved features of a 'boomerang' or 'spiral' strategy (Section 2.2, Chapter 2; Jetschke, 1999), but extended well beyond obtaining the support of international actors to pressure the state. Instead, local actors have been instrumental in shaping international criminal justice in the Philippines, including by drafting the IHL Act and via ongoing advocacy.

---

[111] Interviews P2; P3; P5.

This chapter shows that the norm of international criminal justice is not only transmitted in one *direction*: by external actors to receptive locals, but is adapted and applied in divergent ways, including through varied community-derived projects. Further, it seems that attracting the focus of international organisations (for example, Alston's report) has been useful *because* of the history of deploying human rights to challenge non-compliant leaders in the Philippines. Despite the limitations discussed, the localisation framework helps to draw out this insight, as it anticipates that the relatively strong influence of human rights arguments should correspond to the Philippines context (rather than international pressure). Similarly, the challenges in prosecuting human rights violations can be contrasted to the state's willingness to promote an extreme form of accountability for drug-related crimes (extrajudicial killings). Incorporating contextual elements such as insecurity and historic impunity for police abuses of power begins explain this apparent paradox.

This analysis suggests that tensions between a variety of actors and ideas influence international criminal justice in the Philippines. It unsettles assumptions about the evolution of norms over time, the location of influential actors and ideas (space), and how norms are transmitted (direction). Efforts by a range of actors, especially groups like PCICC, contributed to the Philippines' relatively strong support for international criminal justice compared to other states in Southeast Asia (until relatively recently) – through engagement with the ICC and domestic legal developments, although there have been no international crimes mechanisms similar to the ECCC. However, both Cambodia and the Philippines are, or have been, Rome Statute parties. The next chapter considers how a state might engage with international criminal justice from outside the Rome Statute framework, by analysing the approach of one non-party state that has nevertheless adopted international crimes legislation and even prosecuted international crimes: Indonesia.

Engaging with International Criminal Law as a Non-State Party

Indonesia

4.1   Introduction

Indonesia provides a distinct, if challenging, setting to explore the development of mechanisms for prosecuting international crimes.[1] Its national law is 'made up of several legal systems interwoven with each other and operating simultaneously', including customary (*adat*), Islamic (*syariah*), and modifications of the Dutch colonial civil legal tradition (Lindsey & Santosa, 2008: 3). Indonesia's decentralised governance system also means that the actions of the national government cannot be equated with those of regional and local governmental authorities. International crimes are alleged to have occurred in the colonial period, within separatist conflicts (including in relation to Timor-Leste's independence), during 1965 and Suharto's subsequent presidency, and more recently. Indonesia has ratified relatively fewer international human rights and humanitarian law treaties than many states in Southeast Asia and has not ratified the Rome Statute (see Appendix A). However, Indonesia was one of the first states in the region to carry out trials under domestic genocide and crimes against humanity legislation, although all convictions were overturned on appeal.

Given this complexity, this chapter focuses on Indonesia's *national* laws and institutions for prosecuting international crimes committed in Indonesia (as well as in East Timor prior to its independence as Timor-Leste in 2002), although it mentions the internationalised tribunal that operated in Timor-Leste, the Special Panels in the District Court in Dili (Special Panels). Section 4.2 reflects on the history of international criminal law trials in Indonesia. Section 4.3 then analyses statements

---

[1] Note, translations in the footnotes of this chapter are the author's and may not be accurate.

made by representatives of foreign states and international organisations, the Indonesian government, and civil society about approaches to international criminal justice. Sections 4.4 and 4.5 consider how this engagement has resulted in the adoption of laws that reflect some aspects of the norm of international criminal justice, but also amplify other principles and remain the object of debate.

4.2   Historic Engagement with International Criminal Law

This chapter cannot provide in-depth analysis of Indonesia's complex history of internal and external conflicts. Instead, it focuses on national responses to international crimes – especially since World War II – and shows how these raised principles of sovereignty, national unity, military prominence, human rights, and development.

4.2.1   Non-Interference and Selectivity: Dutch Occupation and World War II

During the centuries of Vereenigde Oost-Indische Compagnie (United [Dutch] East India Company, VOC) and Dutch authority, which gradually spread across the thousands of islands that today make up the Republic of Indonesia, administrators engaged in conduct that could be characterised as international crimes (van den Herik, 2012). For example, during a thirty-year conflict in Aceh, '[f]orced labour, torture and sadism were commonplace Dutch tactics' (Vickers, 2013: 11). Japanese troops committed further crimes in the 'Dutch East Indies' during World War II. Then, in the Indonesian independence movement (Revolution) against the Dutch from 1945 to 1949, one estimate is that '[c]ivilian casualties overall exceeded 25,000 and could have been as high as 100,000. Over 7 million people were displaced on Java and Sumatra' (Vickers, 2013: 105). With Indonesia having declared its independence in 1945, at first the 'post-war [Dutch] authorities in the Indies were more concerned with pursuing [Indonesian] collaborators than with arraigning Japanese' (Cribb, 2011: 153; Schouten, 2015).

The Dutch-managed World War II trials in Indonesia applied flexible procedural rules and in at least one case the defendants were convicted as one group (Piccigallo, 1979; Cribb, 2011; Schouten, 2015). Of 1,038 individuals tried, just 7 per cent were found not guilty; a higher conviction rate than those of the Australian, Chinese, and British trials of mid- and low-level perpetrators (Piccigallo, 1979: 174, 184). The proceedings were also selective. Trials in Batavia (now Jakarta) focused on cases involving European victims, though some crimes committed against Indonesians and other Asian nationals were considered elsewhere (Cribb, 2011). Only relatively recently have there been limited attempts by the Dutch government to respond to colonial-era atrocities (van den Herik, 2012). The history of international crimes trials in Indonesia in the first half of the twentieth century is therefore imbued with legacies of selectivity, politicisation, and external interference.

4.2.2   Unity and the Military: Pancasila, 1965, and Santa Cruz

Indonesia's independence was only recognised by the Netherlands in 1949, after a period of armed conflict that embedded the significance of national unity in the context of religious, ethnic, and linguistic diversity. Indonesia's 1945 Constitution was 'a brief document hastily drafted as Indonesia declared its independence' that facilitated the state's control over the populace (Lindsey, 2008: 23). The post-independence laws were influenced by 'an old and continuing debate about the "Indonesian-ness" of law' (Lindsey & Santosa, 2008: 9), while *adat*-based and Islamic legal systems endured.

In this context, President Sukarno developed a new philosophy to guide the new country. The five moral principles of Pancasila include belief in the one and only God, just and civilized humanity,[2] the unity of Indonesia, democracy led by deliberations among representatives, and social justice for all Indonesians. Law No. 8 of 1985 required mass organisations, later extended to cover NGOs, to accept Pancasila as their ideology – though this is no longer required (Hadiwinata, 2002: 94).[3] Pancasila is sometimes considered crucial for Indonesia's stability; as one interviewee explained, 'without state ideology Pancasila we are going to the process of Balkanisation, just like in Jerusalem'.[4]

References to Pancasila can be found in Indonesia's human rights reports.[5] Yet at times Pancasila has been used as part of an 'anti-Western-oriented type of nationalist discourse protecting [the 'ruling elites']

---

[2] The second 'sila' has been described as 'as a commitment either to internationalism or more literally to a just and civilized humanitarianism' (Morfit, 1981: 840).

[3] Article 2, Law No. 8 of 1985, Law on Social Organisations, 17 June 1985.

[4] Interview I11.

[5] E.g. 'Indonesian Constitution and ideology, Pancasila, guarantees the right to freedom of religion and belief as one of the basic and non-derogable human rights': (Indonesia, 2012b: para. 58), see also (Indonesia, 2012a: para. 247).

against Islamic political forces who challenged the secular foundations of the state' (Jetschke, 1999: 137). Thus, Pancasila 'served as a major source of legitimization for Sukarno and later Suharto' (Jetschke, 1999: 137). Public enthusiasm for Pancasila has waned at times – notably in the early post-Suharto years – though it appears to be regaining prominence.[6] Thus Pancasila provides an important set of contested norms that have been linked to Indonesian policy through tumultuous political times, including during Suharto's New Order government.

Although the exact facts are debated, General Suharto seized power following a short-lived coup on 30 September 1965, which was officially linked to a group of Communist Party of Indonesia (PKI) members (Schaefer & Wardaya, 2013). Suharto established a 'Special Military Court' (*Mahmillub*) to try the surviving prisoners accused of being responsible for the alleged PKI plot (Crouch, 2007: 161). With the knowledge of the United States and Australia (Simpson, 2017), perhaps a million alleged communists or sympathisers were killed, transported, or imprisoned by Indonesian authorities or military-supported militias. Many were discriminated against in the decades that followed, including on the basis of family connection (Glasius, 1999; Cribb, 2009; Komnas-HAM, 2012; Schaefer & Wardaya, 2013). In 1967, Sukarno resigned.

The 1965 events provided an important justification for Suharto's New Order regime and re-emphasised the role of Indonesia's military in protecting the nation's unity and stability. In this narrative, annually reinforced on the anniversary of 30 September, the military had not only helped win independence from the Dutch, but also – ostensibly – prevented a communist insurgency, as well as having contained radical Islamic and separatist movements (Jetschke, 2011). Further, under Suharto's *dwifungsi* doctrine, the military held an expansive role across Indonesia's governance system.

The New Order regime restricted or co-opted the activities of Indonesian civil society and perpetrated widespread serious human rights violations and, arguably, international crimes (Hadiwinata, 2002; Schaefer & Wardaya, 2013; Vickers, 2013). However, the Cold War geopolitical environment meant there was little concern from Western powers while Indonesian forces were apparently fighting communism and Islamic extremists, as well as suppressing separatist movements, such as in East Timor (Kiernan, 2008; Robinson, 2010; Jetschke, 2011; Drexler, 2013).

---

[6] Google Trends analysis for 'Pancasila', 2004 to June 2019, www.google.com.au/trends/explore?date=all&q=pancasila.

Yet the Indonesian government was not immune to international influence. By the 1970s and 1980s international human rights organisations,
and eventually states, devoted greater attention towards events within
Indonesia, including the violent 1975 occupation of East Timor (TAPOL,
1975). Campaigns were directed towards the release of political prisoners,
labour rights issues, and human rights and military violations in East
Timor, Irian Jaya,[7] Aceh, and other regions (Amnesty International,
1976: 132). In the context of Indonesia's deteriorating economic situation
and internal power disputes, these civil society campaigns met with some,
albeit limited, success in the early 1990s, particularly when linked to
restrictions, or credible threats of restrictions, to foreign aid. This
included the establishment of a National Commission of Inquiry
(KPN) into the November 1991 'Santa Cruz massacre' in which a
number of protestors were shot in Dili, East Timor (then still occupied
by Indonesia) (Glasius, 1999; Suh, 2012).

The investigations 'did not conform to the appeals of the western
states to identify the perpetrators' (Glasius, 1999: 260). However, after
the KPN investigation, nine low-level soldiers were sentenced to up to
eighteen months' imprisonment on administrative charges (Suh, 2012:
77). The commission also provided a model for establishing a national
human rights institution, *Komisi Nasional Hak Asasi Manusia Republik
Indonesia* (Komnas-HAM), in 1993 and for subsequent reports concerning extrajudicial killings in Liquiçá, East Timor in 1995, and related to
the Freeport mine in (then) Irian Jaya and Nipah dam in East Java. These
investigations were followed by military tribunal proceedings that pronounced light sentences for low-level perpetrators (Suh, 2012: 82–5).
Thus, the New Order period involved the contestation of ideas about
national unity, the role of the military, and accountability for violent
incidents.

4.2.3   *Human Rights, Democracy, and Development:* Reformasi

With interest rates exceeding 75 per cent and a massive devaluation of
Indonesia's currency, growing popular outrage about the economy
during the Asian Crisis of the late 1990s (Lindsey & Santosa, 2008: 12;
Hadiprayitno, 2010: 386) contributed to Suharto's resignation and
replacement by his deputy, Bacharuddin Jusuf Habibie. Legal aid,

---

[7] As Timor-Leste and Papua were known then.

education, and human rights advocacy movements had also played a crucial role in the transition (Wahyuningroem, 2013). As a result, 'human rights' – economic, social, and cultural, as well as civil and political – formed an important language deployed by civil society and political elites during the '*Reformasi*' period.

The legacy of human rights violations involving thousands of individuals and embedded anti-communist narratives provided a complex situation for responding to past atrocities. Given the public dissatisfaction with the former regime, some military actors began to support the process of democratic reform (Crouch, 2010). This required changes that 'would not scare away international investors and aid agencies' and would also avoid further public violence (Vickers, 2013: 223). This led to an emphasis on 'reform' (*Reformasi*), rather than 'revolution' (Vickers, 2013: 223) – to support the principles of progress, national development, and stability.

Given this desire for change, *Reformasi* involved a discourse that contested, to some extent, the principles of sovereignty, national unity, and protecting the military. Instead, Habibie focused on economic reforms, adopted the first National Action Plan for Human Rights for 1998–2003, separated the police from the military, and revoked the law requiring political parties to adhere to Pancasila. In May 1999 Habibie's government allowed a 'popular consultation' on East Timor's independence – a move that the military then sought to undermine (Crouch, 2010). This reform strategy mustered only mixed support. Abdurrahman Wahid (known as Gus Dur) succeeded Habibie as President in October 1999 in the midst of conflict in East Timor.

4.2.4   *International Critique and Responses to Violence in Timor-Leste*

Alarming violence accompanied the popular consultation of August 1999 in which 78.5 per cent of East Timor's population voted against remaining part of Indonesia (Commission for Reception Truth and Reconciliation, 2006). Debate escalated about the appropriate way to respond to alleged international crimes. Following a UN Security Council Resolution demanding that 'those responsible' for this violence be 'brought to justice',[8] UN investigations[9] and Indonesia's own

---

[8] UN SC Resolution 1264 (1999).
[9] See (UN International Commission of Inquiry on East Timor, 2000; United Nations General Assembly, 1999).

Commission on the Human Rights Violations in East Timor (KPP-HAM) acknowledged the commission of international crimes. KPP-HAM identified thirty-three possible perpetrators. A UN Inquiry in 2000 recommended establishing an 'international human rights tribunal', preferably with the participation of East Timorese and Indonesian members.[10] This proposal did not receive an enthusiastic international response, partly because Security Council members lacked the political will to pursue an expensive international court (Reiger & Wierda, 2006), especially given China's possible veto of any resolution and Indonesia's opposition. In line with the norms of sovereignty and non-interference, Indonesia's leaders argued that the best response would be to hold domestic trials, despite UN scepticism.[11] Ultimately both an internationalised structure within Timor-Leste, the Special Panels,[12] and domestic courts established in Indonesia by Law No. 26 of 2000 concerning Human Rights Courts (Law 26/2000) to prosecute 'gross violations of human rights' – defined as crimes against humanity and genocide – were employed, as well as non-criminal responses, some of which incorporated elements of existing community dispute resolution processes (Reiger & Wierda, 2006; Linton, 2008; Harris-Rimmer, 2010a; Kent, 2012; Vieira, 2012).

Yet, a 2005 UN Commission of Experts found that despite KPP-HAM's 'comprehensive, credible and objective' investigation, the Law 26/2000 trials were 'manifestly inadequate' (UN Commission of Experts, 2005: 5). They recommended Indonesia be given six months to initiate appropriate prosecutions, or face the establishment of an international tribunal, although neither event occurred. The Special Panel's performance was also disappointing against normalised standards of international criminal justice given inadequate funding, serious problems with handling sexual violence charges, dissimilar outcomes for different accused without adequate justification, the inability to bring justice to high-level indictees (partly because of Indonesia's lack of cooperation in handing over perpetrators), and generally a failure to adequately protect defence rights. Later in 2005, Indonesia and Timor-Leste established the criticised Commission of Truth and Friendship.

---

[10] UN International Commission of Inquiry on East Timor, 2000: para. 153.
[11] Ibid., para. 113.
[12] See United Nations Transitional Administration for East Timor (UNTAET), Regulation No. 15 of 2000 On The Establishment of Panels with Exclusive Jurisdiction over Serious Criminal Offences, 6 June 2000.

All of these mechanisms featured a lack of in-depth consultation with affected populations (Linton, 2005), were influenced by political priorities (including Timor-Leste's leaders' wish to re-establish relations with Indonesia), and failed to hold higher-level perpetrators criminally accountable (Drexler, 2013). For transitional justice scholar Susan Harris-Rimmer: 'The substantial problem is that the international political process has led to a mixed approach consisting of entrusting the justice process to two national jurisdictions [Indonesia and, after its independence, Timor-Leste], neither of which had the slightest chance of carrying out their mandate for a myriad of reasons, of which most were foreseeable' (Harris-Rimmer, 2010a: 74). Thus, in contrast to Cambodia or the Philippines, two countries' laws and institutions were engaged in prosecuting crimes that occurred in a particular time period within one contested 'space': East Timor. The various reconciliation activities received more positive reactions from some participants, but did not fulfil the demands of those who wished for convictions or other conceptions of 'justice' (Kent, 2004).

Debates about whether or how to apply international norms when responding to historic and contemporary alleged international crimes in Indonesia continued during the presidencies of Megawati Soekarnoputri (Megawati) and Susilo Bambang Yudhoyono. In this period, Komnas-HAM investigations into violence both during and after Suharto's presidency – including in relation to separatist movements or violations by the armed forces in Aceh, Maluku, Central Sulawesi, Tanjung Priok in Jakarta, and Abepura in Papua – led to some prosecutions, including for crimes under Law 26/2000 (ICTJ and KontraS, 2011). However, most of Komnas-HAM's *pro-justicia* reports (special investigations undertaken under Law 26/2000) languished at the Attorney-General's office, which is the only agency empowered to prosecute crimes under that Law. Insufficient resources and training, victim and witness protection issues, interference with the judiciary, prosecutorial ineffectiveness, harassment of court personnel, difficulties securing evidence, and a lack of government cooperation beset the cases that did proceed. Of the minority of cases that led to convictions, all were overturned on appeal (ICTJ and KontraS, 2011). In 2012, President Yudhoyono (whose father-in-law allegedly committed crimes during the 1965 violence) appeared ready to apologise for the violence in 1965 and to ratify the Rome Statute, but neither action eventuated (Pramudatama, 2012). While this period involved increased attention towards prosecuting international criminal conduct, little progress was made in terms of implementing the norm of international criminal justice.

4.2.5   Anti-Communist Rhetoric and Religious and TNI Influence

President Joko Widodo (Jokowi) won elections in 2014, opposed by Prabowo Subianto, who is alleged to have committed serious violations (Tan, 2015). Early hopes that President Jokowi was serious about 'the settlement of' (*penyelesaian*) cases of past human rights violations (*pelanggaran HAM yang masa lalu*) – including in his team's election 'Vision and Mission' priorities (*Nawacita*) (Widodo & Kalla, 2014) – were brought into doubt amid debates about the meanings of justice, reconciliation, development, and national unity. Some steps were taken, such as establishing a Presidential Committee for this purpose, holding a national symposium to discuss the events of 1965, and an effort to reinstate a position at the Attorney-General's office to pursue Law 26/ 2000 prosecutions (though it is not clear whether this remains). Yet even early on, Jokowi appointed controversial members of the military to key roles, including former Special Panels indictee General Wiranto as Security Minister (later, Coordinating Minister for Political, Legal and Security Affairs).[13] In 2016, President Al-Bashir of Sudan, who is the subject of ICC arrest warrants, was able to visit Indonesia without threat of arrest (ELSAM, 2016). In 2018, Wiranto announced the creation of a 'Joint Team to Resolve Cases of Past Human Rights Violations' focused on the 1965 events, but its role and relationship to the Presidential Committee remained obscure. It was accompanied by ongoing anti-communist rhetoric and the banning of books and events about 1965.

As the world's largest Islamic nation, religion also underlies these debates, including because some violations have been perpetrated against Islamic separatist groups (for example, in Aceh), but also because of the growing influence of religious values in Indonesian politics, which are sometimes pitched against human rights (Hamid, 2018).[14] Concerns about a general lack of judicial independence also remain (Human Rights Watch, 2018) and in 2019 the Attorney-General returned to Komnas-HAM files that recommended gross human rights violations be investigated and prosecuted, maintaining that Komnas-HAM had not provided enough information or evidence and proposing that 'the most realistic approach to resolving gross human rights cases in the past is using

---

[13] Though see (Sapiie, 2016); see also regarding the appointment of Ryamizard Ryacudo as Defense Minister (Jakarta Globe, 2014).

[14] E.g. in relation to blasphemy and freedom of speech and religion as in the prosecution of Jakarta's former governor, Basuki Tjahaja Purnama (Ahok).

non-judicial channels'.[15] Indonesia also continues to experience violence involving security officials, including increasing extrajudicial killings in relation to drugs, as well as violations in Papua. Jokowi's focus upon development and infrastructure reform have been associated with human rights violations even likened to the New Order era (Editorial Board Jakarta Post, 2018). He retained his presidency in elections in 2019, opposed again by Prabowo, and protests by Prabowo supporters were violently dispersed. The commission of future international crimes remains a possibility, while debates about establishing new mechanisms are entangled with social and political divisions about resolving *past* violations.

4.2.6   Summary: History

Indonesia has experienced the commission of international crimes, including in relation to separatist and independence-related conflicts (such as in East Timor, Aceh, and Papua), in 1965 and under Suharto's regime, as well as violent incidents involving the armed forces occurring after *Reformasi*. Since World War II, responses to all of these categories of possible international crimes in Indonesia have featured recurring themes of sovereignty, selectivity – including minimal accountability for military perpetrators and inconsistent international responses – and distaste for internationally managed proceedings. There have also been efforts to advance human rights, development, and the restraint of military impunity. There has been no linear progression from ratification of international treaties, to implementation in national law, and enforcement or acceptance of the norm of international criminal justice, nor rejection. Rather, perspectives on international criminal justice have been – and remain – plural and dynamic.

4.3   Local Initiatives and Adaptation

This has been a generally chronological account, so far. However, an analysis of public statements (supplemented by interviews) demonstrates how foreign states and international organisations, Indonesian authorities, and civil society actors have worked to influence perceptions of international criminal justice in Indonesia.

---

[15] '*pendekatan penyelesaian kasus HAM berat masa lalu paling realistis menggunakan jalur non-yudisial*': (Medistiara, 2019).

4.3.1   International States and Organisations

International concepts, international organisations, and other states have played a crucial, if at times unwelcomed, role in Indonesia's development of international criminal mechanisms. Indonesia's Regulation (*Perpu*) 1 of 1999 provided for the prosecution of human rights atrocities under Indonesia's criminal laws. However, the UN Inquiry in 2000 opposed this *Perpu* (UN International Commission of Inquiry on East Timor, 2000: para. 112), which was also rejected by the DPR (Indonesian parliament). Reportedly, a 'strong consideration was fear that the lack of a retroactive clause might fail to satisfy the international community's demand that those responsible for gross violations in East Timor be tried' (International Crisis Group, 2001: 14). Scholars have suggested that the UN investigations of the violence in East Timor and the establishment of the Special Panels influenced Indonesia to pursue its own domestic avenues for prosecutions (e.g. Linton, 2005). Law 26/2000 underwent several rounds of revisions and evolved from having a 'human rights' focus to become modelled quite closely on the Rome Statute, which was negotiated in 1998 but had not yet entered into force (see Section 4.4.2.1) (Suh, 2012: 140).

Yet there was and is no unified international perspective among states or the UN on prosecuting international crimes committed in Indonesia. Despite civil society criticism of Indonesia's occupation after Portugal withdrew from East Timor in 1975, states including the United States and Australia disregarded, or even facilitated, Indonesia's actions (Robinson, 2010). In relation to the independence violence in East Timor in 1999, the UN Inquiry recommended establishing an international tribunal (with UN-appointed judges but including members from both East Timor and Indonesia) (UN International Commission of Inquiry on East Timor, 2000: para. 153). However, some states, including the United States, did not support this approach (International Crisis Group, 2001: 25), while the Security Council welcomed a domestic Indonesian (rather than international) response, if it could be 'swift, comprehensive, effective and transparent legal process, in conformity with international standards of justice and due process of law' (United Nations Security Council, 2000). This projected an understanding of international criminal justice as being ideally speedy, fair, and 'effective'.

Foreign states and the UN have generally been less willing to demand that Indonesia prosecute international crimes outside East Timor. For example, despite well-documented atrocities in the early 2000s in Aceh and international involvement in the peace process, there were no Security Council resolutions focused on the issue. Though the Aceh peace agreement ultimately allowed for trials, the Finnish mediator Martti Ahtisaari did not prioritise accountability issues during the negotiations, as securing stability was the focus (Awaludin, 2009) and human rights abuses 'received relatively little attention from any of the principal actors, including the international community' in subsequent years (Aspinall, 2008: 5).

That said, several states called upon Indonesia to prosecute human rights violations in the Working Group reports for Indonesia's 2008 and 2012 UPR cycles.[16] This was repeated in the 2017 UPR, including in relation to abuses in the past (the United States) and in Papua (Australia) despite those states' historic ambivalence towards human rights violations in Indonesia (UN Human Rights Council, 2017a). Some, especially European, states have engaged in military-to-military exchanges that included international humanitarian law training, human rights programmes, or discussed Rome Statute ratification with the government (e.g. Ministry of Foreign Affairs Indonesia, 2014). These efforts have tended to draw on international norms and mechanisms to encourage accountability for alleged international crimes and human rights violations (though see Topsfield, 2017).

Glasius has found that threats of reduced foreign aid may have influenced Indonesia's domestic human rights policies in the past, including the establishment of KPP-HAM and Law 26/2000 (Glasius, 1999; Linton, 2004). On the other hand, Indonesia rejected a US offer for military aid if it would sign a Bilateral Immunity Agreement (BIA) not to transfer individuals to the ICC, partly because domestic stakeholders purportedly did not want to facilitate perpetrator impunity (Huikuri, 2018: 255). While a large trade agreement may have influenced Indonesia's preference for opposing the ICC's prosecution of Sudan's President Al-Bashir, this position can be explained by Indonesia's support for the principle of state sovereignty. In recent years, as business investment has increased, Indonesia's net receipts of aid have fallen dramatically (World Bank, 2019b). Remaining foreign assistance 'human rights' projects are increasingly focused on institutional corruption and transparency issues, or

---

[16] (UN Human Rights Council, 2008a), e.g. Germany, Brazil in relation to Timor-Leste, Sweden regarding torture; (UN Human Rights Council, 2012a), e.g. Slovenia, Australia, Canada.

discrete issues such as disability rights, rather than explicitly upon accountability for serious violence. This suggests that foreign *aid* is likely to be a declining motivation for Indonesia's leaders to prosecute international crimes, although business investment may still be a relevant factor, with its corresponding focus upon 'good governance'.[17] Clearly, some international instruments (such as the Rome Statute) and actors influenced the development of international criminal law in Indonesia, in part by creating a credible threat of international prosecutions, though states have taken various positions.

4.3.2   *Indonesian Authorities*

Investigating government approaches towards the Rome Statute demonstrates the range of officials' perspectives towards international criminal justice. As discussed shortly, the Habibie administration supported the ICC to some degree, though when Megawati was President, officials focused on amending domestic legislation before acceding to the Rome Statute (Huikuri, 2018). During Yudhoyono's Presidency, two consecutive National Plans of Action on Human Rights incorporated intentions to join the ICC and in 2013 Indonesia's delegation to the UN reiterated the country's 'support to the global efforts to end any form of impunity for crimes against humanity, war crimes and the crime of aggression' (Permanent Mission of the Republic of Indonesia to the United Nations, 2013). However, the level of stated support for international criminal justice has varied within the government and over time.

The military held significant authority during the Suharto regime and military leaders have typically opposed the prosecution of international crimes. For example, it seems that in 2013, following an encouraging visit by Indonesian officials to The Hague, Yudhoyono shifted towards opposing accession to the Rome Statute after meeting with former military generals (Huikuri, 2018: 245). The Defence Minister argued that Indonesia already had sufficient laws to protect human rights, while 'many countries, including major democratic countries' had also not yet ratified

---

[17] E.g. the EU is anecdotally most supportive of human rights initiatives, as both Indonesia and the EU 'recognise that good governance, including respect for human rights, is central to [mutual] ambitions', while projects focus on the environment, economic cooperation, and health and education initiatives, see (European Union, 2015: 2); 'In the meantime [there] is only little support [from donors] for the human rights issues for example, for Indonesia', though with some reframing activists 'can find a way to go to human rights issues through transparency and accountability', Interview I1.

(Aritonang, 2013). The army (*Tentara Nasional Indonesia*, TNI) remains influential under Jokowi's presidency.

Acceding to the Rome Statute would require governmental, including parliamentary, support. While at times some officials have favoured joining the ICC, there has also been political opposition (Aritonang, 2013). Officials at the Ministry of Law and Human Rights and Ministry of Foreign Affairs have supported the ICC, though former Foreign Minister Marty Natalegawa reportedly noted that it 'is no panacea to abolish impunity' (Hermawan, 2009). Some former members of the government play influential roles as academic experts for law reform (such as Professors H. Muladi and Harkristuti Harkrisnowo) and have adopted evolving positions towards ratification and codification of international crimes. As an independent statutory body, Komnas-HAM has linked Rome Statute ratification to the protection of human rights, but lacks direct influence upon ratification decisions. Its recommendations that individuals be prosecuted, or that a court be established to try past crimes (for example, enforced disappearances in 1997 and 1998, consistent with a parliamentary recommendation) have not been implemented by the Attorney-General.

The first National Plan under Jokowi neglected to mention the former priority of accession. Still, in 2014 the government called for 'appropriate measures to hold those responsible accountable' in relation to the downing of Malaysia Airlines flight MH17, although without mentioning the Rome Statute framework (United Nations, 2015). Indonesia has called upon Israel to comply with human rights and international humanitarian law in Palestine (Ministry of Foreign Affairs Indonesia, 2018a). Despite some comments of concern about the commission of international crimes in Myanmar, Indonesia's officials have favoured a cooperative approach, calling upon the Myanmar government to respect human rights in Rakhine State, while funding the construction of hospitals and schools there (Ministry of Foreign Affairs Indonesia, 2017; 2018b).

Thus, Indonesia's officials have different and changing views about international criminal justice, although they have rarely opposed the ICC and its norms as such. Instead, consistent with historic experiences, the government has expressed concerns about the potential for the ICC to politically interfere in domestic affairs, emphasising sovereignty, the potential for selective prosecutions, stability, and national prosecutions. For instance, during the Rome Statute negotiations, as a key member of the Non-Aligned Movement, Indonesia's representatives emphasised that 'first and foremost . . . the Conference . . . must uphold the principle of respecting national sovereignty'.[18] An argument against a 'preference to ICC intervention' was also expressed during the 2010 Kampala ICC Review Conference in relation to the principle of complementarity (Republic of Indonesia, 2010). Officials have suggested that the Rome Statute 'could be misused to encourage the ICC to step in for certain political interests. Therefore, we don't need to rush to ratify it now'.[19] In 2013, during a General Assembly debate on 'The Role of International Criminal Justice in Reconciliation', Indonesia's permanent representative to the UN reiterated that 'the development and improvement of legal institutions and perspective must of course be in conformity to each nation's history, culture, and way of life' (Permanent Mission of the Republic of Indonesia to the United Nations, 2013). Thus, one response to the international criminal justice norm has been to accept its validity, but to propose an approach based on the principles of sovereignty and subsidiarity.

Indonesia's official statements about international criminal justice have also referred to Indonesia's democratic credentials and its progress in responding to 'past violence', including by discussing international criminal law issues alongside human rights achievements. For example, Indonesia's 2012 national UPR report confirmed that 'Indonesia remains committed to work[ing] progressively on' acceding to the Rome Statute (Indonesia, 2012b: para. 20). In terms of 'combating impunity' more generally, that UPR report observed that military courts had tried more than 1,500 cases perpetrated by military officers, 'including human rights violations', and that the government 'continues to promote institutional reforms which will enhance the effectiveness and capacity of security sector institutions in dealing with alleged human rights violations'.[20]

Indeed, turning to Indonesia's domestic international crimes mechanisms, discussions about the 'gross *human rights* violations' that fall under Law 26/2000, which are defined as crimes against humanity or genocide, reveal some overlap and confusion about terminology. For example, in 2013 the Minister of Defence noted that when a group of Indonesian

---

[18] 'Statement by H. E. Mr Muladi, Minister for Justice, Head of Delegation of the Republic of Indonesia, before the Plenipotentiaries Conference of the Establishment of the International Criminal Court, 16 June 1998', in (Muladi 2011: 17).

[19] E.g. the Chair of House Commission I, quoted in Aritonang, 2013.

[20] Ibid., paras. 28–9. The 2017 report included similar statements (with less emphasis upon prosecutions).

Special Forces (*Kopassus*) personnel raided Cebongan prison and killed, extrajudicially, four murder suspects, the 'Human Rights Law' (Law 26/ 2000) did not apply since the incident did not meet the 'criteria' of being widespread, systematic or planned and ordered. He argued this was therefore 'not a human rights violation' (Asril, 2013).[21] Jokowi's election platform included a commitment to the 'equitable settlement of the cases of human rights violations in the past' (Widodo & Kalla, 2014). At that time, this distinguished Jokowi from Prabowo Subianto. The promise appears to have been directed at the incidents identified by Komnas-HAM as 'gross violations of human rights' – in other words, as defined in Law 26/2000 – including the violence of 1965.

Further debates surround the meaning of 'reconciliation' (see Bräuchler, 2009). There is a tension between understandings of reconciliation as involving 'settling' past cases, consistent with the promotion of national unity, and those proposing justice mechanisms or reparations processes. On Human Rights Day in 2015, President Jokowi proposed that '[w]e all must have the courage to embark on reconciliation ... through judicial channels, as well as non-judicial [measures]' (Parlina, 2015). Yet experiences of Truth and Reconciliation Commissions (TRCs) in Indonesia have been problematic. The government has not established the commission mentioned in Article 45 of Law No. 21 of 2000, On Special Autonomy for the Papua Province. The Constitutional Court annulled Law No. 27 of 2004, the first attempt to establish a national TRC (*Komisi Kebenaran dan Rekonsiliasi*, KKR), on the basis that its amnesties provision was inconsistent with Constitutional rights.[22] A regional by-law to establish a TRC regarding conflict in Aceh was not passed until 2013. The Aceh KKR aims to 'strengthen peace', help 'achieve reconciliation', and recommend reparations, though civil society actors suggested that commissioners carefully collect information, including in case it should be used in 'subsequent court proceedings' (AJAR, 2016: 10, 12). The Aceh KKR did not commence operations until October 2016, still with a lack of funding or national legal support, but presented an opportunity

---

[21] The Minister reportedly suggested that this was not a breach of human rights because it is suggested that those are covered by the Law on Human Rights (i.e. Law 26/2000) ('*Ini bukan pelanggaran HAM karena ada saran dikenakan Undang-Undang HAM.*').

[22] *Lembaga Studi dan Advokasi Masyarakat (ELSAM), Komisi untuk Orang Hilang dan Korban Kekerasan (Kontras), Solidaritas Nusa Bangsa (SNB), Inisiatif Masyarakat Partisipatif untuk Transisi Berkeadilan (Imparsial), Lembaga Penelitian Korban Peristiwa 65 (LPKP 65), Raharja Waluya Jati, H. Tjasman Setyo Prawiro*, Case No. 006/PUU-IV/2006, Constitutional Court, Republic of Indonesia, 7 December 2006.

for future official engagement with debates about responding to international crimes.

It seems that the language of 'reconciliation' has received opposition from both those opposed to and promoting judicial responses. Having presented the election 'Vision and Mission' that incorporated resolving human rights abuses, in 2015 the Jokowi government announced the creation of a 'Reconciliation Committee' to respond to past violations (Setiawan, 2016). A national symposium was then held in which survivors and civil society shared testimony about the 1965 violence, but alongside statements from (then) Coordinating Minister for Politics, Law and Human Rights, Luhut Binsar Panjaitan (Luhut), and the military, denying the violence (Wahyuningroem, 2016). Members of the military then organised (with the Defence Minister's support) (Tashandra, 2016), a separate symposium on 'Protecting Pancasila from Threats of the Indonesian Communist Party [PKI] and Other Ideologies', at which participants argued that the reconciliation process 'could open old wounds, disrupt the nation's unity, or even encourage prolonged horizontal conflicts' (The Jakarta Post, 2016). As unfounded rumours circulated about Jokowi's own links to the PKI, it became clear that an apology for the 1965 events would not be forthcoming. As one commentator put it, 'the [national] symposium can only be considered the starting point of a long process towards the nation confronting its past', but 'there is also a real risk that it could be the final chapter' (Wahyuningroem, 2016). On the other hand, the 2018 establishment of the 'Joint Team' suggested that debates will continue, though with a persisting official emphasis on finalising the issue via conflict resolution, rather than judicial procedures. Meanwhile, survivors of many historic violations are growing older. In the 2019 elections, the distinction between the human rights policies of the same presidential candidates, Jokowi and Prabowo, was less obvious than in 2014, though Jokowi did say that he was 'still committed to resolving [the past] human rights issue[s] which will be supported by a fair legal system and good law enforcement', through continued reforms (Jakarta Globe, 2019). In this way, official responses to alleged crimes that happened in the *past* grapple with the present harms experienced by survivors, amid a live domestic political environment and concerns about judicial independence.

In summary, Indonesia's government has supported the notion of international criminal justice, but drawn on the concepts of sovereignty, human rights, and reconciliation in related statements. Prosecuting historic alleged international crimes remains a controversial political topic, as does accountability for contemporary incidents of violence including via the ICC. Official attempts to shape perceptions of international criminal justice correspond to historic debates and are reflected in civil society arguments.

4.3.3   Civil Society

The nature of 'civil society' in Indonesia, as elsewhere, is complex, meaning that some generalisation is involved in discussing civil society strategies (Beittinger-Lee, 2009). That said, Indonesian and internationally based NGOs, legal advocates, academics, and other community leaders and associations have played a significant role in shaping debates about international criminal justice in Indonesia (Farid & Simarmatra, 2004; Herbert, 2008; Beittinger-Lee, 2009). NGOs have taken varied approaches to advocate for international criminal justice, including documenting crimes in detailed reports, drawing on local contexts, and engaging with international actors and state authorities.

Though many civil society actors refer to domestic laws in their advocacy, they are willing to draw on international influence where productive. President Yudhoyono cancelled a visit to the Netherlands in 2010 after a Maluku separatist group asked a court in The Hague to order his arrest (BBC, 2010). Other groups have asked foreign governments to prioritise Rome Statute ratification in their meetings with Indonesia and made submissions to human rights processes such as the UPR and treaty bodies (ICSCICC, 2012). However, local activities have not become less important after international attention was enlisted. Instead, civil society advocacy involves a range of methods, of which recourse to international pressure is just one.

In the years following *Reformasi*, local activists had 'differences of opinion' about how to respond to past crimes, including 'the tension between the model of the truth commission vis-à-vis the model of ... prosecution through the courts'.[23] Survivors' needs are diverse and may even conflict. An NGO representative explained:

> in general we can say that [victims] want justice. But, you know, they have their own interpretation of what justice means ... For the victim[s] of '65 for example, they say that justice for them is ... general rehabilitation ... But ... then for the victim[s] of disappearances in '97 and '98, they say

---

[23] Interview I14.

justice means 'If I found my disappeared loved one'. That's justice. And
not necessarily a human rights court. But for the other[s] ... they said,
justice for us means, 'The perpetrators should be brought to court, to [the]
ad hoc human rights court' for example.[24]

In the early 2000s, NGOs like the Commission for Disappearances and
Victims of Violence (KontraS) and Indonesian Association of Families of
the Disappeared (IKOHI) pressured Komnas-HAM to investigate violence under Suharto, in East Timor, and elsewhere, under Law 26/2000.
Meanwhile, the Institute for Policy Research and Advocacy (ELSAM)
drafted a bill for a TRC and others helped survivors lodge complaints
with police, the Ombudsman, or Komnas-HAM. Both those favouring a
TRC and those seeking prosecutions therefore worked to document and
gather evidence of international crimes. However, most Komnas-HAM
reports remained 'in the desk of the Attorney-General Office',[25] subject
to a disagreement as to what types of evidence are required to pursue
prosecutions and who is responsible for gathering that evidence (see
Herbert, 2008). One interviewee explained how local NGOs realised that
the Attorney-General's sluggishness was 'not because [of] the legal
reason' but was because 'the issue is really [a] political issue'.[26]

The recognition that there were political rather than legal barriers to
seeking justice for international crimes in Indonesia led some NGOs to
adapt their arguments and strategies. For example, when discussing the
main benefits of the Rome Statute with the government, NGOs decided
that: 'because Yudhoyono is very cautio[us] with [his] image, we talk
about the good image'.[27] From 2007, victims groups held weekly Thursday protests in front of the President's palace and on at least one occasion
in 2010 decided to attempt to stay overnight. This strategy was adapted
from a practice of the Mothers of the Plaza de Mayo,[28] but was thought
to have potential because of the President's concern about his reputation
(Suh, 2012).[29] This Thursday 'Action' continues to be held at the same
time and place, demonstrating the survivors' perseverance. More
recently, organisations have compared Jokowi's election 'Vision and
Mission' to the lack of 'real effort ... to address impunity' – to challenge

[24] Interview I2.
[25] Interview I2, see also (ICTJ and Kontras, 2011: 3).
[26] Interview I9.
[27] Interview I2.
[28] An Argentinian association formed by mothers of individuals who disappeared under the
authoritarian regime of the late 1970s and early 1980s.
[29] Interview I2.

the President's domestic political credibility: a failure to live up to election promises (Asian Legal Resource Centre, 2018).

This adaptive approach has also led actors to draw on international and national concepts and legal principles to frame international norms. Particularly during the Yudhoyono administration, some NGOs promoted joining the ICC by emphasising Indonesia's role as a 'champion and beacon of democracy, good governance and human rights in the region' (Sandra & Abidin, 2012).[30] One interviewee explained 'it's a matter of national pride' – since as one of 'the biggest democratic countr[ies] in the world ... we are responsible to the international community, not only [the] Indonesian people'.[31] In 2012, the regional coordinator for the CICC argued that 'Indonesia's membership to (sic) the ICC is consistent with its declaration of strong commitment to human rights and the rule of law' (CICC, 2012). Indonesian actors have also advocated for the prosecution of international crimes committed abroad. An Indonesian former politician and human rights activist, Marzuki Darusman, chaired a UN Independent International Fact-Finding Mission on Myanmar, which recommended that Myanmar's leaders be prosecuted for genocide, crimes against humanity, and war crimes (see Chapter 5).

The Rome Statute campaign also responded to concerns about sovereignty and political interference by emphasising the principles of complementarity and institutional reform. In 2014, CICC argued that: 'The [ICC] is centered on the notion of complementarity — the ICC will not and cannot be involved in cases that Indonesian courts are willing and able to take up' (CICC, 2014). Arguments also incorporated the concept of sovereignty, since, as one former government actor emphasised, 'sovereignty' means 'not only privilege and control... but also responsibility: internally and internationally'.[32]

One reason for pressing for ratification has been that it could provide an 'entry point' ('*pintu masuk*')[33] to develop Indonesia's domestic and international crimes laws. These priorities include accelerating the reform of Indonesia's Law 26/2000, Military Code, Criminal Code, and

---

[30] This language is similar to that used by the Philippines government at its first ASP session as a state party a year earlier (Department of Foreign Affairs, 2011).
[31] Interview I11.
[32] Interview I11.
[33] Interview I10: '*paling penting dengan ratifikasi ICC kami punya pintu masuk untuk reformasi system*' [the most important aspect of ratifying the ICC is that we will have an entry point to reform the system].

Criminal Procedure Code to help to fill the gaps in this legislation (see ICSCICC, 2008; Hukum Online, 2013). This potential is particularly important since civil society advocates are aware that the ICC will not have retrospective jurisdiction over past crimes.[34] Unlike the Law 26/2000 ad hoc courts, the ICC could be portrayed as 'the mechanism for the future not . . . the past', even if it was hoped that joining the Court might encourage a new 'ideology' towards historic violations.[35]

NGOs have also invoked the historically important norm of protecting the military. For example, civil society suggested that the Rome Statute might support the army's peacekeeping activities abroad. Complying with international criminal law, and supporting its enforcement, could 'protect the nation because there is a big consequence if you are not implementing the law' – including potentially barriers to purchasing military equipment.[36] Beyond the ICC debate, one international humanitarian and criminal law trainer has explained to the army that since Law No. 34 of 2004 Concerning the National Army of Indonesia specifies that 'obeying the law' is a measure of professionalism,[37] he is 'just helping [them] to be professional. And they understand it is not my idea, or idea from *bule* [foreigners]. This is from Indonesian law, from the TNI law'.[38] Some have proposed focusing on less controversial violations as an entry point, for instance, those not related to the 1965 events which are complicated by the anti-communist norms promoted by the TNI. These might include the conflict in Aceh or even enforced disappearances in 1997 and 1998, which involved Jokowi's main opponent Prabowo, or incidents which do not accuse highly ranked military officers, such as some incidents in Papua. Yet these contexts are still divisive, so such advocacy can only form part of a careful strategy of 'eating hot porridge',[39] where one must begin by eating around the (slightly) cooler edges before tackling the hot centre.[40]

---

[34] There is an argument that enforced disappearances might be considered a continuing crime that attracts ICC jurisdiction post-ratification – Interview I2.

[35] Interview I9.

[36] Interview I5.

[37] Paragraph D of the preamble refers to the principles of human rights provisions in national law and Indonesia's obligations under international law treaties ('*hak asasi manusia ketentuan hukum nasional, dan ketentuan hukum internasional yang sudah diratifikasi*').

[38] Interview I5.

[39] *Makan bubur panas.*

[40] Interview I2.2.

Finally, drawing on a strategy executed by Komnas Perempuan, Indonesia's National Commission on Violence against Women, ELSAM and an NGO network, Coalition for Justice and Truth Seeking (KKPK), attempted to reframe the debate about past 'human rights' violations as a discussion about existing domestic legal obligations and the social contract of the Indonesian Constitution (Setianti, 2015). Thus, in July 2015 a group of Indonesian civil society actors issued a joint declaration drawing on the Constitution, Laws No. 39 of 1999 (on human rights) and 26/2000, as well as community (including victims') experiences, to argue that the government's reconciliation initiatives for 'past human rights abuses' were 'not in line with the responsibility to actualize the justice for the ... victims' (Dillon et al. 2015). An individual formerly associated with the government has also stressed that Pancasila's five key principles support the idea of state responsibility and respect for the law.[41] Others reference *Reformasi*-era People's Consultative Assembly (MPR) resolutions that, for instance, recommended the establishment of a national truth and reconciliation commission (Fernida, 2014; Dillon et al. 2015).

Thus, some actors use language to 'always try to adapt to the situation in Indonesia. So we mention sometimes the "gross violations of human rights" as mentioned in the law number 26 of 2000 as well as in the law of human rights [39 of] 1999, ... [we are] flexible according to the situation'.[42] For example, if the political environment is such that amending Law 26/2000 might actually erode Komnas-HAM's authority, it might be 'better ... to insist [on] Rome Statute ratification', since 'the risk is that they're going to say no' compared to possibly negotiating a domestic instrument that is 'even worse'.[43] Similar considerations relate to reforming the Criminal Code, as discussed shortly.

Some NGOs have attempted to build 'local credibility' (Acharya, 2004: 251) by engaging with authorities. A strategy of discourse included helping to translate the Rome Statute into Bahasa Indonesia,[44] drafting a Rome Statute accession bill and implementation study (ICSCICC, 2008), responding to misperceptions about the ICC (especially regarding complementarity and non-retroactivity), capacity building and cross-regional seminars, and discussions with parliamentarians (e.g. CICC, 2015). One organisation decided to continue public advocacy and protests about

---

[41] Interview I11.
[42] Interview I7.
[43] Interview I6.
[44] Interview I10.

historic crimes, but also foster dialogue through 'critical engagement' with the government and police. This recognised that 'we cannot just . . . make the press release or just protest . . . we have to meet them'.[45]

However, NGOs who engage government institutions have sometimes felt these closer ties adversely affected their legitimacy with other NGOs.[46] Further, when NGOs discuss international criminal justice with survivor groups and the authorities, their messages can conflict. As one NGO representative recounted, one could be asked by security forces "'What about the case that happened in the past? Will we be tried?" And then when we talk with them we say "No, no, no." But when we talk to victims [we say]: "Yes! They can be prosecuted because disappearances is [a] continuing crime."'[47] Thus, NGO credibility is not always fostered through increased collaboration. Moreover, despite suggestions that Jokowi personally might be open to supporting various responses to past human rights violations, Jokowi's Cabinet included individuals who have been implicated in past violations. Since, at least by 2019, civil society failed to see tangible developments, some felt that the potential value of such collaboration was waning. Although these approaches are creative and derive from local initiative, they all seek to encourage acceptance of international criminal justice, without radically reconstructing it. On the other hand, even with some apparent political will, the persistent influence of certain actors, largely linked to the TNI and supported by some elements of the public, continue to frustrate either national-level judicial or reparative initiatives.

4.3.4   Local Adaptation

Despite these civil society initiatives, not even an official apology for past violence has been forthcoming. One interviewee explained in 2014 that while President Yudhoyono 'did a few things, established mechanisms and made promises . . . When we had to see or assess what real progress has been made, there was none. So in that context . . . we agreed that . . . we cannot wait anymore for the government to do something . . . we should take leadership as citizens, as civil society'.[48]

---

[45] Interview I9.
[46] Interview I9, 'it's very challenging because on the other way, some people who don't really understand what we were thinking, they're "oh" like . . . "police and [this NGO] want to [be] working together" and [so] they [are] thinking that we will reduce our criticism'.
[47] Interview I2.
[48] Interview I14.

At the same time, local NGOs found it increasingly challenging to secure international funding for international criminal justice work (Fernida, 2014: 63). An NGO representative explained that a sense that Indonesia 'is not really a priority country anymore' for transitional justice 'is influencing how [NGOs] ... develop the[ir] strategy[ies] to settle the human rights abuses'.[49] Further, the experience of prosecuting international crimes had not been positive. For instance, not only had the Law 26/2000 trials regarding violence in Tanjung Priok not led to convictions, this also prevented survivors from receiving official reparations and allowed the government to suggest that the matter is now 'considered closed'.[50]

Activists have identified a need to engage with other stakeholders beside state or security actors. It seems that Munir Said Thalib (Munir) – who was later murdered – established the NGO KontraS partly with the model of Argentina's Mothers of the Plaza de Mayo in mind. He and others recognised the symbolic power and endurance of the 'victim' as a political actor.[51] Such NGOs worked hard to increase the knowledge and interest of the public in responding to violence. Yet not all survivors necessarily have the stamina or interest to pursue future-oriented reforms.[52] Moreover, one NGO representative explained: 'There has to be a demand! If there is no demand it's just the fifty, or ... even less ... [activists] ... who continue to say the same thing over and over again because there's nothing more to be said.' She and others advocating for justice realised:

> we couldn't be so focused ... on a very legalistic ... articulation of the problem that this is a crime because of this and it violates, you know, Article this of covenant or convention that ... That kind of approach ... was still important and necessary but ... what we need to do is to ... build a new constituency within the general public.[53]

This shift in target audience, especially towards the 'young generation',[54] required new language.[55] However, this could not just be a 'vernacularisation' aimed at lawmakers internalising the idea of prosecuting international crimes. That norm itself needed to be reimagined.

---

[49] Interview I9.
[50] Interview I2.
[51] See Interview I2.
[52] Interview I9.
[53] Interview I14.
[54] Interview I14.
[55] An NGO representative explained that civil society organisations 'are quite good at translating' [international law terminology] into the language that [is] really understandable for the common people', Interview I1.

One organisation held focus groups and organised events where 'we tr[ied] to invite people who were not the usual suspects'. This helped them to realise 'how huge the gaps are' between existing advocacy strategies based around legal arguments and public interest and understanding.[56] They recognised that in the years following *Reformasi*, 'human rights is so stigmatized in mainstream Indonesia ... as being a Western concept', or even 'a Western conspiracy against the sovereignty' of Indonesia and 'against our culture' that 'we needed to find ... some other language'. It seemed that 'justice' could be achieved through 'a combination of ... measures. Not just legal but also social and ... economic and cultural'. These issues, including the stigma faced by survivors, would not necessarily be resolved 'even if we did have a court'.[57] The network KKPK's initiatives also led to a preference for language about nationality, or '*kebangsaan*'. However, they moved beyond just using different language to describe or frame international criminal law, or transitional justice – instead 'grafting' additional elements onto the familiar international concepts. For instance, 'to emphasize the Indonesian Way [*Jalan Indonesia*] for the settlement of past human rights violations that are based on six pillars': supporting Indonesia's integrity as a nation of law; disclosing and recognising the truth; the dignity and quality of life of victims; education and public dialogue for reconciliation; preventing recurrence through institutional reform; and the active participation of survivors in this process.[58] Moreover, 'creating demand' meant 'meet[ing the public] half way ... particularly for Indonesia where ... one of probably the most powerful modalit[ies] of public discourse is through the arts'.[59] Traditional media including diplomatic briefings, press releases, and opinion pieces remained an important tool, but 'film, social media, an alternative way to reach out to the young[st]ers' were also deployed[60] (Ramadani, 2015), in particular following the success of Joshua Oppenheimer's films *The Act of Killing* (2012) and *The Look of Silence* (2014).

NGOs have also deepened their engagement at the provincial and community level. This has included attempts to adapt religious or other traditional reconciliation practices, including Islamic '*islah*' and '*diyat*'

[56] Interview I14.
[57] Interview I14; and on economic and social demands, Interviews I2, I8.
[58] Translation from (Ovier, 2015).
[59] Interview I14.
[60] Interview I1.

processes and 'peusijuek' in Aceh, though these were controversial (Ehito, 2015). *Adat* laws formed the foundation for reconciliation ceremonies in the absence of prosecutions for violence in Kei, Maluku, in 1999 (Thorburn, 2008: 140). As alluded to, *nahe biti bo'ot* (spreading the large mat) and *lisan* procedures were reconstructed in Timor-Leste to respond to pre-independence violence, alongside community memorial and support work (Kent, 2012; Vieira, 2012). Several local NGOs have worked towards resolving the 1965 violence 'from below' (Wahyuningroem, 2013: 131; Fernida, 2014), recognising that 'reconciliations at the ... grassroots levels are really happening',[61] especially for the 1965 violence. Some offer social assistance for victims, while others provide legal aid to respond to broader human rights violations. In Palu, NGO workers utilised community connections to engage with the municipal government and local religious authorities, organising commemorations and an apology by the Mayor (see Wahyuningroem, 2013), which Komnas-HAM hoped might provide an 'example' for the national government and might be replicated elsewhere, even if it could not 'fulfill the victims' rights such as right to justice through legal accountability' alone (ELSAM, 2017). In East Lampung, civil society actors from national organisations also facilitated discussions between local NGOs and the Mayor to establish memorials for a military massacre of members of an Islamic group in Talangsari in 1989.[62]

These attempts to move beyond translating international norms for local contexts have their limitations and are not entirely 'bottom-up', but draw on multiple influences. Many civil society and government actors have been able to study abroad, incorporate the experiences of other countries like Argentina, or engage with diaspora groups and large international NGOs, as well as subnational provincial communities. For example, the National University of Singapore has developed an online forum for individuals who experienced harms during Suharto's New Order regime to share their stories. In 2012 and 2013, partly inspired by International Center for Transitional Justice initiatives, KKPK organised a 'Year of Truth',[63] which included public survivor testimony in Palu, Solo, Kupang, Takengon, and Jayapura, with additional thematic hearings in Jakarta (Pohlman, 2016). Like Cambodia's Women's Hearings, these aimed to provide 'a space for victim survivors to tell

---

[61] Interview I1.
[62] Interview I2.2.
[63] *Tahun Kebenaran.*

their story'.[64] The International People's Tribunal for 1965 (IPT65) held in The Hague in 2015 drew on the 'positive response from the Indonesian society and media' of the Tokyo Women's Tribunal.[65] Even the strategies in Palu and Lampung now form part of an approach where national civil society actors identify potentially open-minded local officials (mayors); consider what sorts of incidents may have happened in that region; assess the local legal and regulatory framework and social situation (including identifying key influential actors); and then work to facilitate localised discussions and activities about the violence.

Yet these strategies were not applied 'top-down', either. KKPK's report from the Year of Truth was called *Menemukan Kembali Indonesia* (Rediscover Indonesia) (KKPK, 2014). As one interviewee pointed out, 'impunity' remains a key point, but 'the main message is about … the search for Indonesia'.[66] The hearings were supported by social media campaigns (Pohlman, 2016) and the report favours the language of 'violence' rather than technical legal arguments. While its recommendations include familiar affirmations of the importance of justice, they also include suggestions associated with economic, social, and cultural rights. The IPT65 was held in The Hague – the home of the ICC, ICTY, and other international criminal tribunals – with international judges.[67] One activist suggested that the Dutch location would allow Indonesian authorities to argue there was a double standard, saying 'Oh, what are you [the Netherlands] doing with these issues, while you also did unlawful things to Indonesian people' during the colonial period.[68] Apparently the Dutch government shared similar concerns, but holding the IPT in Jakarta presented security dangers (Katjasungkana & Wieringa, 2019). Yet, the IPT65's researchers and prosecutors were predominantly Indonesian and it was organised and attended by diaspora, students, academics, and activists of varied nationalities.

Legal reform and prosecutions have always remained important goals. As one interviewee put it, 'the responsibility is still [with] the government

---

[64] Interview I14.
[65] Interview I1.
[66] Interview I14.
[67] Apparently it was difficult to secure Indonesian judges given the sensitive political nature of the Tribunal.
[68] Interview I1: though she thought that some NGOs and academics had suggested that the Dutch had paid reparations for the Westerling slaughter in Karawang, which could be a positive example for the Indonesian government.

of Indonesia'.[69] These strategies simply recognise the prevailing political realities, including that legal mechanisms are either unlikely to be developed or have proven disappointing. They may even, as Sri Lestari Wahyuningroem argues, aim to 'seduce' the government into taking steps that ultimately lead to justice, since for many '[w]hile these "alternatives" are useful, they are not good enough if they do not lead to the state acknowledging the truth and taking responsibility' (Wahyuningroem, 2013: 135). An example might be calls to strengthen the independence and credibility of Komnas-HAM. In a sense, these adapted initiatives may, like acceding to the Rome Statute, represent attempts to create a *'pintu masuk'* towards justice, however understood. Similarly, organisers of the IPT65 hoped it would open space for public discussion. Indeed, it may have influenced Indonesian officials to propose the 2016 Indonesian symposium as being 'part of the Indonesian way of balancing this human rights discourse' (see Amindoni, 2016; Wahyuningroem, 2016). Responses to 'past human rights violations' are increasingly swamped by the preference that officials have indicated for non-judicial responses (at most), but debate continues.

4.3.5 Summary: Local Initiative and Adaptation

The norm of international criminal justice has not been accepted in Indonesia in any linear manner that can easily be described geographically as 'local' or 'international'. Through various mediums – including protests, public truth-telling proceedings, media, film, and collaborating with authorities – different actors have deployed diverse arguments to support their changing views about prosecuting international crimes: past and future. One approach has been to reframe international norms of human rights and international criminal justice for local use with reference to complementarity, domestic legislation, military professionalism, human rights, national unity, and reconciliation, while also attempting to gain local credibility through building relationships with authorities. Others have reconstructed ideas about international criminal justice as encompassing diverse and locally grounded mechanisms, including through community forums and strategic engagement with local authorities. History suggests that government representatives, international actors, and Indonesia's vibrant civil society, wherever located, will continue to adapt to changing contexts.

---

[69] Interview I9.

4.4   Mechanisms for Prosecuting International Crimes in Indonesia

There are several options for prosecuting international crimes in Indonesia that show aspects of the international norm of international criminal justice, but in which 'local influences remain highly visible' (Acharya, 2004: 251).

4.4.1   International Mechanisms

Indonesia has not yet acceded to the Rome Statute, though it could become subject to the ICC's jurisdiction via a declaration or Security Council referral. Individuals might also be prosecuted by internationalised tribunals or under the universal jurisdiction legislation of other states. The potential for such international trials is unknown and is not addressed here. However, Indonesia has also prosecuted international crimes under domestic legislation and there is legal scope for future prosecutions.

4.4.2   Domestic Legislation

There are several potential avenues for prosecuting international crimes in Indonesian courts. The first is via the provisions in international treaties or conventions that Indonesia has ratified (see Appendix A).[70] However, Indonesia has relied on national legislation to implement its treaty obligations[71] and has ratified few treaties relating to international crimes. Second, Law 26/2000 provides for the prosecution of crimes against humanity and genocide. Third, the civilian Criminal Code, *Kitab Undang-Undang Hukum Pidana* (KUHP, Code) includes 'ordinary' crimes that might be used to prosecute similar conduct and may be updated to include international crimes. Fourth, Indonesia has a Military Disciplinary Code (KUHDT)[72] and Military Criminal Code (KUHPM, Military Code).[73] Law No. 31 of 1997 provides military courts with

---

[70] Article 7(2) of Law No. 39 of 1999 Concerning Human Rights suggests it may incorporate 'international law concerning human rights'; and see Law No. 34 of 2004, section 2(d) regarding the TNI, though see Butt (2014) regarding the uncertainty over whether Indonesia is truly a monist or a dualist system.

[71] E.g. Law No. 5 of 1992 concerning Cultural Objects; Law No. 9 of 2008 on the Use of Chemical Materials and the Prohibition of Chemical Materials as Chemical Weapons.

[72] *Kitab Undang-Undang Hukum Disiplin Tentara*. Law No. 25 of 2014.

[73] *Kitab Undang-Undang Hukum Pidana Militer*. Law No. 39 of 1947.

jurisdiction over crimes committed by soldiers[74] and though Law No. 34 of 2004 suggests that soldiers should submit to the authority of civilian courts for violations of 'general' crimes,[75] in practice they are prosecuted by military courts. Military tribunals have tried soldiers for conduct potentially involving international crimes, though there have been concerns about low sentences and a failure to consider high-level perpetrators, and prosecutions are typically for administrative crimes such as incorrectly obeying orders (Amnesty International, 2013). Attempts to amend these laws have stalled as TNI influence in Indonesia persists. This section focuses on Law 26/2000 and the Criminal Code. These are the only potential avenues for prosecuting core international crimes as such within Indonesia's domestic legal system.

4.4.2.1 Law No. 26 of 2000

Law 26/2000 provides human rights courts with jurisdiction over crimes against humanity and genocide committed in Indonesia or by Indonesian citizens, including abroad (Article 5). The passage of Law 26/2000 through the legislature with unanimous approval would not have been possible without DPR members, the Ministry of Justice,[76] academics, civil society, and lawyers drafting and supporting the Law. Concerns about international views, and civil society work on the draft law, led to the final form of Law 26/2000 being 'closely modeled on the Rome Statute' (Suh, 2012: 12). As discussed in Chapter 1, the Rome Statute represents the primary instrument promoted by the international criminal justice norm, so that this similarity may appear to represent Indonesia's acceptance of this norm. However, there are differences.

First, the draft text for what became Law 26/2000 did not initially include an avenue for retrospective punishment, consistent with the Rome Statute. However, partly as a result of concerns about international (particularly UN) perceptions, the Law was altered to provide for two potential international crimes mechanisms. The first was the establishment of 'Human Rights Courts' in Central Jakarta, Surabaya, Medan, and Makassar,[77] each of which would be a 'special court within the context of

---

[74] Law No. 31 of 1997 Concerning the Trial of the Military.
[75] Article 65(2) of Law No. 34 of 2004; TAP MPR NO VII/2000 Article 3(4).
[76] Now Ministry of Justice and Human Rights.
[77] Article 45, Law 26/2000. Only the Makassar Court was formed – it heard the case regarding Abepura, Papua.

a Court of General Jurisdiction'[78] with prospective jurisdiction. Article 43
(1) then provides for 'ad hoc Human Rights Courts' concerning '[g]ross
violations of human rights occurring prior to the coming into the force of
this Act'.[79] However, Article 28I(1) of Indonesia's Constitution upholds
'the right not to be tried under a law with retrospective effect' as a right
that 'cannot be limited under any circumstances'. Such fair trial principles are arguably promoted by the norm of international criminal
justice.[80] Article 43(1) formed part of a 'compromise' (Herbert, 2008:
467) that was inserted to allow crimes committed during the East Timor
violence and prior to and during the *Reformasi* period to be prosecuted.[81]

The crimes in Law 26/2000, which are termed 'gross violations of
human rights', rather than 'international crimes',[82] also show differences.
Even though Indonesia had ratified the Geneva Conventions (but not its
Additional Protocols),[83] war crimes were excluded from the human
rights courts' jurisdiction. A separate crime of torture was also not
included,[84] even though Indonesia had ratified the Convention Against
Torture in 1998. These omissions were 'no accident' (Linton, 2006: 211)
since the 'missing' crimes are among the most commonly alleged in
Indonesia and war crimes may have been applied to military perpetrators
of violence in East Timor.[85] Article 9 concerning crimes against

---

[78] Articles 2–3, ibid.

[79] Article 43, ibid., makes no reference to Article 15(1) regarding retrospective laws in the
International Covenant on Civil and Political Rights, which was not ratified by Indonesia
until 2006.

[80] See e.g. Article 21(3) Rome Statute; although the principle of 'legality' in international
criminal law has requirements of notice, foreseeability, and accessibility that may allow
the prosecution of crimes not addressed by domestic legislation at the relevant time, e.g.
Prosecutor v. Albilio Jose Osorio Soares, Case No. 01/PID.HAM/AD.Hoc/2002/ph.JKT.-
PST, Human Rights Ad Hoc Court at Central Jakarta, 15 August 2002 (*Soares*); *Prosecutor v. Kaing Guek Eav alias Duch*, Case No. 001/18-07-2007-ECCC/SC, Appeal Judgment,
3 February 2012, paras. 89–91.

[81] The Constitutional Court found that Law No. 15 of 2003, the Anti-Terrorism Law, could
not be applied retroactively to Kadir, the defendant in the 'Bali Bombing' case. *Masykur
Abdul Kadir*, Case No. 013/PUU-I/2003, Constitutional Court, Republic of Indonesia,
23 July 2004. See (Butt & Hansell, 2004).

[82] Article 7, Law 26/2000.

[83] See Law No. 59 of 1958 Concerning the Ratification by the Republic of Indonesia of All
the Geneva Conventions of 12 August 1949 (approving ratification). On the implementation of Indonesia's obligations under the Geneva Conventions, see (Haryomataram,
2001).

[84] Torture is included as a crime against humanity in Article 9(f), Law 26/2000.

[85] The Ad Hoc Human Rights Court for East Timor found that an internal armed conflict
had occurred in East Timor and war crimes might be implemented via Law No. 59 of

humanity also does not include 'other inhumane acts of a similar character intentionally causing great suffering, or serious injury to body or to mental or physical health', which was an important provision for extending the reach of international criminal law at the ICTY and ICTR.[86]

The chapeau of Article 9 on crimes against humanity could be understood in Indonesian as requiring an attack to be 'directly targeted against the civilian population'.[87] This might suggest the accused must personally participate in the particular attack (which could restrict the operation of the provision to relatively lower-level perpetrators), or require a 'direct attack' against '*the*' civilian population such as would arise in armed conflict (Linton, 2006: 213). Otherwise, Law 26/2000 closely replicates the Rome Statute's definitions of crimes against humanity and genocide, although questions have been raised about the interpretation of 'religious group' (*kelompok agama*) in Article 8 in Indonesia, since national law provides that there are only five religions.[88] Still, an explanation attached to the legislation clarified that these crimes are in accordance with the Rome Statute.[89]

The inclusion of the death penalty in Articles 36 and 37 of Law 26/2000 represented a controversial divergence from the Rome Statute, though lower penalties are provided for some crimes.[90] Article 34 affords victims and witnesses limited protection from threats and harassment.[91]

1987, albeit in determining that widespread, systematic attacks had occurred; *Prosecutor v. Tono Suratman*, Case No. 10/Pid. HAM/Ad. Hoc/ 2002/PN. Jkt. Pst, Human Rights Ad Hoc Court at Central Jakarta, Judgment, 13 May 2003.

[86] Linton (2006: 215) also points out that '*penganiayaan*' in some versions of Article 9(h) regarding persecution was interpreted as meaning 'assault' or 'abuse' in the East Timor cases, requiring physical violence, as used in the Criminal Code. See *Adam R Damiri*, Case No. 09/PID.HAM/AD.HOC/2002/PH.JKT/PST, Human Rights Ad Hoc Court at Central Jakarta, Judgment, 31 July 2003.

[87] '*serangan yang meluas atau sistematik yang diketahuinya bahwa serangan tersebut ditujukan secara langsung terhadap penduduk sipil*'.

[88] Interview I13. See also Amnesty International, 2001 regarding other divergences from the Rome Statute and international law.

[89] 'Article by Article' explanation for Article 7, Law 26/2000: https://komisiinformasi.go.id/?p=1793. The Supreme Court apparently also issued a circular letter confirming the relevance of the Rome Statute for interpreting the Law (anecdotal).

[90] E.g. Article 9(c) enslavement; (f) torture; (g) rape and other forms of sexual violence and sexual assault; (h) persecution, and (i) enforced disappearances (Articles 38–40).

[91] See also Government Regulations No. 2 and 3 of 2002; and limited protections, e.g. Article 153(3), in the Law No. 8 of 1981, Code of Criminal Procedure on victim and witness security and protection.

Article 35 also specifies that victims are eligible for compensation, restitution, and rehabilitation if there is a conviction, which was supported by government regulations.[92] The wording differs significantly from Article 75 of the Rome Statute (which addresses reparations) and, consistent with the usual practice in Indonesia's court system, the Law does not provide for victims to participate in proceedings (other than as witnesses) as at the ICC. This suggests that the victims provision was not simply adopted from the international norm. Indeed, because no convictions have been upheld, the attempt to secure reparations for the Tanjung Priok case, for example, resulted only in the '*islah*' (private Islamic) procedure that served to divide victims (Ehito, 2015).

The Law is obscure as to modes of liability, although Article 41 confirms that for attempting, plotting, or assisting with the perpetration of the two relevant crimes, the same sentences will apply as for direct perpetration.[93] Under Article 42 superiors are accountable for their subordinates' actions, although it is unclear whether this extends to crimes that the subordinates 'were committing or *about to commit*', as in the Rome Statute, or just crimes being committed or recently committed.[94] Moreover, the use of '*Komandan militer*' might be interpreted as only extending to lower level commanders – at the field command level or several levels higher – rather than covering generals or higher level policymakers (see Juwana, 2005).

Thus, Indonesia does have a basic legal framework for prosecuting crimes against humanity and genocide via Law 26/2000, although the law is otherwise implemented via the narrower rules of evidence included in Indonesia's Criminal Procedure Code (KUHAP).[95] In reality, despite the potential to develop important international criminal law jurisprudence concerning command responsibility and the interaction of official armed forces and militias, the processes of the Law 26/2000 trials were criticised and none of the few convictions, with short sentences, were upheld on appeal (ICTJ and KontraS, 2011). The Law 26/2000 Courts generally made cursory use of international criminal jurisprudence, mostly in

---

[92] See also Government Regulation No. 3 of 2002; Articles 98–100, Code of Criminal Procedure.

[93] Accused in the Law 26/2000 trials were typically indicted under Article 42, command responsibility, as well as the applicable Article 36–40.

[94] Law 26/2000 uses '*sedang melakukan atau baru saja melakukan*' which suggests only crimes in the process of being committed or just recently committed would be covered.

[95] See Article 10, Law 26/2000.

relation to command responsibility, a novel mode of liability in Indonesia at the time.[96] The Rome Statute was referenced to justify the award of sentences *below* the minimum set by Law 26/2000.[97] International criminal law was also drawn upon to support the retroactive application of the Law.[98] As mentioned, attempts to bring further cases under Law 26/2000 have stalled due to an impasse with the Attorney-General's office. Attempts to amend Law 26/2000, including to resolve this stalemate potentially by affording Komnas-HAM prosecutorial functions,[99] have not progressed, partly due to fears that this process might dilute Komnas-HAM's existing powers.[100]

The application of Law 26/2000 failed to reflect the international norm involving impartial, independent justice, international involvement, or 'ending impunity'. Indeed, the Law 26/2000 prosecutions arguably allowed Indonesia to defend the norms of sovereignty, non-interference, and protecting the military through a legal framework that benefited from its 'association with the foreign norm' (Acharya, 2004: 251), consistent with the idea of 'localisation'. Thus, one former politician explained the development of Law 26/2000 as the convergence of international norms and Indonesia's global identity: we're going to uphold [the] international norm, but supported by the *quality of [the] Indonesian institution itself.* We are going to *demonstrate our accountability to international society* ... Free and active not only to *protect Indonesian institutions* but also to disseminate ... [the] international peace and security of mankind.[101]

4.4.2.2 Criminal Code and Amnesties

As in most countries, Indonesia's Criminal Code includes crimes, such as murder, that could be used to prosecute the underlying conduct involved

---

[96] Though see e.g. *Prosecutor v. Eurico Guterres*, Case No. 04/PID.HAM/AD.HOC/2002/ PH.JKT.PST, Human Rights Ad Hoc Court at Central Jakarta, Judgment, 25 November 2002; a reference to *Prosecutor v. Akayesu*, Case No. ICTR-96, Chamber I, Judgment, 2 September 1998 in *Prosecutor v. Timbul Silaen*, Case No. 02/PID.HAM/AD.Hoc/2002/ PN.JKT.PST, Human Rights Ad Hoc Court at Central Jakarta, Judgment, 15 August 2002.

[97] *Prosecutor v. Letkol Inf. Soedjarwo*, Case No. 08/Pid.HAM/Ad.Hoc/2002/PN.JKT.PST, Ad Hoc Tribunal for East Timor, Judgment, 27 December 2002.

[98] See *Soares*.

[99] Including clear powers for *penyidik* (prosecutorial investigation to gather factual evidence) beyond *penyelidik* (preliminary investigation to identify whether a full investigation should occur), see Article 1, Code of Criminal Procedure.

[100] Interview I6.

[101] Interview I11, emphasis added.

in committing international crimes. The Code extends jurisdiction over crimes committed by civilians (including police) in Indonesia or on an Indonesian ship or plane (Articles 2–3) and in limited circumstances outside Indonesia, including for conduct by Indonesian nationals (Articles 4–5). However, the Criminal Code and the Criminal Procedures Code, which largely reflect colonial-era laws, are badly out of date. Draft new Codes have been under consideration since the *Reformasi* period and successive drafts continue to show considerable differences, as discussions between criminal law experts, the executive government, and parliament continue. The drafting team includes politicians as well as criminal law experts, including international criminal law experts who are highly influential within Indonesian legal academia.

The June 2018 version of the draft Criminal Code[102] included extended jurisdiction ('*Asas Universal*') outside the territory of Indonesia for crimes committed under international law or treaties that are included as crimes in Indonesian law (Article 6). This would be significant since the draft Code has included several international crimes, including (in various drafts) a separate crime of torture, reflecting Indonesia's obligations under the Convention Against Torture (Eddyono et al. 2015).[103] An international crimes section of the draft was placed in a section for 'Special Crimes'[104] alongside terrorism and narcotic crimes, but remains titled 'Serious Crimes against Human Rights'.[105] This title may be necessary to distinguish these international crimes from others in the remainder of the Code, in case including them in the same instrument might 'weaken the gravity' of these 'extraordinary' violations (Eddyono et al. 2015: 12). However, the reference to human rights 'could lead to the misperception that human rights violations consist only of

---

[102] Copies of drafts and explanatory materials are available at Aliansi Nasional Reformasi KUHP, 'R KUHP' (as of 1 June 2019) http://reformasikuhp.org/r-kuhp.
[103] Although the 2018 provision removed 'severe pain' (*rasa sakit yang berat*) from the definition – the Convention refers to 'severe pain or suffering' and as for the use of coercion to obtain a confession, the penalty was reduced and definition altered slightly in the 2018 compared to, for instance, 2015 version.
[104] '*Tindak Pidana Khusus*'.
[105] '*Tindak Pidana Terhadap Hak Asasi Manusia Yang Berat*' or '*Tindak Pidana Berat Terhadap Hak Asasi Manusia*' in some later versions. Law 26/2000 refers to serious or gross violations of (rather than crimes against) human rights, '*pelanggaran hak asasi manusia yang berat*'. There were discussions about the section title during the drafting process, since some 'came with the opinion . . . that the violation of human rights is not only the violations mentioned in the Rome Statute'. Something similar to 'the violation of international law and international peace' was proposed at one stage, Interview I7.

genocide, crimes against humanity, war crimes and even command responsibility' (Agus, 2014), as has occurred with Law 26/2000.

The relationship between the proposed draft Code and existing law has been unclear, including as to how the section on international crimes is intended to interact with Law 26/2000 (Rahmawati, 2018). The draft Code appears to selectively incorporate only some 'core' crimes from Indonesia's 'special' crimes that currently allow investigations by different agencies, such as corruption, narcotics, or international crimes. One former judge suggested that the amendments to the Criminal Code would supersede Law 26/2000, because the aim was for 'codification' where 'there will be no other Code, outside the Code'.[106] Others have explained that the amendments aimed to remove colonial legacies and harmonise relevant national and international instruments (Eddyono et al. 2015).

The draft Code will not have retrospective effect, in contrast to the possibility for 'ad hoc' courts established under Law 26/2000. One official actor thought that the ability to establish such 'ad hoc' courts would at least be retained.[107] Yet Komnas-HAM, in particular, has been concerned that including the international crimes in the Code could undermine its authority under Law 26/2000 – meaning that the whole section should perhaps even be left out of the revisions. The prevailing view appears to be that existing laws and procedures and institutions attached to them – for instance the role of Komnas-HAM and Attorney-General in investigating and prosecuting international crimes – will persist after the Code is adopted, as reflected in Article 624 of the September 2019 draft. This suggests that any cases brought under the international crimes provisions in the new Code would still be investigated pursuant to Law 26/2000. Should Indonesia join the ICC and enact Rome Statute provisions into domestic legislation there could be even greater obscurity as to how or when the different laws apply.

The full list of the Rome Statute's Article 7(2) definitions and Elements of Crimes are not included in the draft Code.[108] This was also the case in Law 26/2000, but unlike that Law, explanatory materials have not suggested that it be interpreted in accordance with the Rome Statute.[109]

---

[106] Interview I13.

[107] Interview I6.

[108] Explanatory materials are likely to include definitions of 'attack', and widespread or systematic attacks, among other terms.

[109] Explanatory materials for one 2018 draft suggested that it included international crimes, including war crimes, that were anticipatory and sourced from the Rome Statute: Indonesia, *Penjelasan atas Rancangan Undang-Undang Republik Indonesia ... Tentang*

The wording of the draft provisions has been slightly different to Law 26/2000, sometimes with the apparent intention of moving closer to the wording of the Rome Statute. For example, draft crimes against humanity provisions in 2019 incorporated a subsection (k) concerning 'other inhumane acts'.[110]

The drafts include the crimes of genocide and crimes against humanity. Drafts had also (unlike Law 26/2000) usually included 'crimes in wartime or armed conflict'[111] and at some stages aggression, apparently at the impetus of an international criminal law expert on the drafting team. The crimes are all punishable with sentences including the death penalty, though lighter penalties have at times been proposed for some underlying crimes (which could be consistent with Law 26/2000).

Despite the potential for the Code to expand upon Law 26/2000 by incorporating war crimes, it will probably capture these crimes in an adapted manner, if at all. The 'draft' crime has applied to 'every person who during a war or armed conflict carries out gross violations against persons or property',[112] that is, apparently during *both* international or non-international armed conflict.[113] Provisions covering the crimes in Article 8(2)(b), (c), and (e) of the Rome Statute were included in a draft Code circulated until 2014,[114] and in 2017,[115] but not in the 2015 draft. By February 2018, the draft included a longer mixed list of underlying crimes than in 2015, but debates continue: the July 2018 draft removed the whole provision, which remained absent in 2019. Additional offences might be included directly into an amendment of Law 26/2000, or within the Military Code to bring these crimes within the jurisdiction of the military courts, which in practice still hear cases involving military

---

Hukum Pidana [Explanation of the Draft Law of Indonesia ... about Criminal law], 2 February 2018, 161.

[110] '*perbuatan tidak manusiawi lainnya yang sama sifatnya yang ditujukan untuk menimbulkan penderitaan yang berat atau luka yang serius pada tubuh atau kesehatan fisik dan mental*'.

[111] *Tindak Pidana dalam Masa Perang atau Konflik Bersenjata.*

[112] '*setiap orang yang pada masa perang atau konflik bersenjata melakukan perbuatan terhadap orang atau harta*'.

[113] Though definitions may still be included. The exception for internal disturbances of Article 8(2)(d), (2)(f), Rome Statute and Article 1(2), Additional Protocol II, included in earlier drafts might have provided the impression that the Code only applies to international armed conflicts.

[114] Copy on file with author, Articles 397–9. The 2008 version may be viewed at Aliansi Nasional Reformasi KUHP Reform, https://kuhpreform.wordpress.com/resources.

[115] Article 402(2), February 2017, http://reformasikuhp.org/r-kuhp.

perpetrators. However, it is unlikely that either law will be amended to include war crimes in the near future (Reza, 2014), though if the Law 26/2000 procedures remain in place, military perpetrators might still be brought before the human rights courts for genocide or crimes against humanity. Attempts to include a draft provision addressing war crimes in the Criminal Code have therefore taken multiple turns as Indonesia's legislature and experts debate the amendments.

The inclusion of a crime against aggression in some, though not all, versions of the draft Code was consistent with Indonesia's position as the Rome Statute was being negotiated in 1998. Similar historic links to the limited scope of the command or superior responsibility provision of Law 26/2000 (Article 42) appear in some versions of the draft Code. A chapeau was introduced that suggested that superior responsibility represents a separate *crime* 'punishable in the same way as Article 400' (on genocide),[116] rather than a mode of liability. The location of this section with the 'offences', rather than among the provisions on criminal liability, attracted criticism (Agus, 2014). The command/superior responsibility provision was apparently removed in the 2018 drafts, though some take the view that the provision in Law 26/2000 could still be drawn upon for future prosecutions. Both the existing and draft Codes do include other relevant provisions for criminal responsibility[117] and a range of 'exclusion, mitigation and enhancement of punishment' provisions that cover similar ground to the Rome Statute.[118]

Earlier drafts of the Code ensured that the normal statutory limitation periods would *not* apply to the international crimes provisions,[119] but this provision appeared to have been removed by 2018, though possibly with the intention of moving its location in the Code.

The potential for a Presidential amnesty under Article 14 of the Constitution also remains. This is consistent with the use of political amnesties in the past to protect national unity, alongside continued discussion about awarding amnesties, including in relation to non-state fighters in the Aceh conflict (Jeffery, 2012). Further, Article 20A(3) of the Constitution provides for parliamentary immunity, though Article 28J

---

[116] 'Dipidana yang sama sebagaimana dimaksud dalam Pasal 400', e.g. in the June 2015 version.
[117] Articles 53–62, 160–1 (incitement to commit a punishable act), Criminal Code.
[118] E.g. Articles 41–52A, Criminal Code.
[119] E.g. in 2015, though Indonesia has not ratified the Convention on the Non-Applicability of Statutory Limitations to War Crimes and Crimes against Humanity.

obliges 'every person' to 'respect the human rights of others'. Thus there is some scope for senior leaders to avoid liability for international crimes under existing and draft legislation.

In relation to victims, unlike Law 26/2000, Indonesia's Criminal Code does not directly refer to victim protection or participation, although compensation may be available via civil proceedings[120] and victims are addressed in Law No. 13 of 2006, Concerning the Protection of the Witnesses and Victims (administered by the Institute for the Protection of Witnesses and Victims, *Lembaga Perlindinguan Saksi dan Korban*, LPSK, under this 'LPSK law'). The LPSK law provides for various protections, rights to medical assistance including psycho-social rehabilitation, and (through a request to the Court by LPSK) compensation for victims of serious human rights violations. LPSK has been under-resourced, but has provided assistance to survivors of violence (ICJT and KontraS, 2011; Lembaga Perlindungan Saksi dan Korban, 2015).

Enforcing an amended Code in the domestic legal system is likely to be challenging and will require resources and political will, as has been evident with Law 26/2000. Conduct that could otherwise have been prosecuted under 'normal' criminal provisions might in future be addressed through the international crimes provisions, which have additional elements to prove. As Linton has argued in relation to prosecuting torture under Law 26/2000, from the perspective of possible perpetrators, 'one can see how the higher threshold crimes are more attractive – the likelihood of conviction is low' (Linton, 2006: 212). Similar difficulties may arise for the draft Code provisions, should they be adopted, since they mostly include additional elements to prove compared to 'ordinary' provisions, while human rights court processes are more complicated to initiate. Some civil society groups (anecdotally) increasingly assess the Criminal Code reform process as potentially leading to greater confusion, rather than increased opportunities to prosecute crimes. They would prefer a process of gradual reform, where each revised section might undergo more extensive and transparent consultation and hopefully be strengthened. Consistent with the localisation framework, laws and institutions for prosecuting crimes in Indonesia typically complement, rather than replace, Indonesia's existing social and legal institutions.

---

[120] Including in combination with criminal proceedings, see Articles 98–100, Code of Criminal Procedure.

4.4.3   Enforcement

Other than the cases brought under Law 26/2000 mentioned in the previous section, there have been other cases relating to conduct that might be considered an international crime prosecuted under other domestic legislation. These demonstrate Indonesia's broader engagement with international criminal justice issues. One case was the trial of Masykur Abdul Kadir and others for their role in carrying out bombings in Bali in 2002. The accused were convicted under Emergency Law No. 12 of 1951, offences in the Code, and Kadir was convicted under terrorism legislation passed after the bombings, in 2003.[121] In Kadir's case, the Constitutional Court found that retrospective laws are prohibited except for gross violations of human rights – that is, crimes against humanity and genocide (Butt & Hansell, 2004: 180). It held that the bombings did not constitute a crime against humanity or genocide, although the minority thought the crimes were so serious that an exception to the principle of non-retrospectivity should apply. The Court's decision – especially that of the minority – demonstrates that national courts may find it challenging to discern the exact parameters of 'international criminal justice' in situations where a plurality of criminal offences might be relevant and the Constitutional framework is invoked.

Civil liability has also been pursued outside[122] and within Indonesia. For example, in 2005, Jakarta Legal Aid Foundation brought a civil suit on behalf of a group of victims from 1965, though it was rejected on technical grounds (ICTJ and KontraS, 2011: 55). The poisoning of KontraS founder Munir on a flight to the Netherlands may not be considered a crime against humanity, but in 2007 Garuda Airlines was found negligent. Two individuals were also jailed as a result of the incident, though the man suspected of ordering the crime, Purwopranjono, was acquitted in 2009 and direct perpetrator Pollycarpus served eight of his fourteen-year sentence.

There are therefore various avenues for responding to past and future international crimes within Indonesia's legal system, including under Law 26/2000 and potentially the Criminal Code, once eventually revised, and (with difficulty) via civil suits. However, convictions for international

---

[121] *Masykur Abdul Kadir*, Case No. 013/PUU-I/2003, Constitutional Court, Republic of Indonesia, 23 July 2004.

[122] E.g. *Todd v. Panjaitan*, Case No. CIV.A. 92-12255-PBS, 1994 WL 827111, United States District Court of Massachusetts, 26 October 1994; *John Doe VIII v. Exxon Mobil Corporation*, Case No. 09-7125, US Court of Appeals, District of Columbia Circuit, 8 July 2011.

crimes have not been upheld and efforts to 'settle' 'past' violations are unlikely to involve prosecutions. In that context, 'the question of why Indonesia would ratify the Rome Statute while it is repeatedly accused of being unwilling and unable to prosecute grave human rights abuses, is a legitimate one' (Huikuri, 2018: 264). In other words, current domestic political debates about responding to 'past' events continue to influence the development of new mechanisms for future violations.

4.5   Conclusions

The Netherlands–operated World War II trials were selective, operated in a colonial context, and failed to establish strong norms in favour of internationally managed prosecutions. Both Sukarno and Suharto elevated the role of the military within society and propounded the principles of Pancasila, while other states exhibited minimal concern about human rights violations during those presidencies. Indonesia also experienced periods of economic deterioration in that time. These events served to embed concerns about Indonesia's sovereignty, development, and the role of the military in ensuring stability.

However, these principles were also contested by international civil society and by groups within Indonesia that advocated for the protection of economic, social, cultural, civil, and political rights alongside demands for truth and justice. By the late 1990s the dominant normative order remained strong, but included aspects that were 'already discredited from within or found inadequate to meet with new and unforeseen challenges' (Acharya, 2004: 251). Yet there has not been linear progress towards a normalised understanding of international criminal justice that seeks impartial, independent international crimes trials via ratification of treaties or implementation of domestic laws. Rather, debates continue, both about prosecuting historic international crimes and legislation that would have prospective effect.

Localisation is said to occur when 'credible local actors' reframe and reconstruct the relevant international and local norms. In Indonesia, international actors, the government, and civil society have deployed arguments that respond to historic concerns about protecting the military, ensuring national stability and unity and, including by emphasising complementarity, the importance of sovereignty and avoiding political interference.

There have been two predominant official responses to alleged serious human rights violations that may amount to international crimes. These are to either avoid the issue, or to investigate and document the incidents, but proceed no further than securing a few low-level prosecutions or promises of 'reconciliation'. Most recently there have been attempts to establish a committee and then team to 'settle' or 'resolve' *past* human rights abuses that may have amounted to international crimes, notably in relation to the 1965 violence. Yet the language of 'settling' itself suggests a reframing of the debate towards resolving past issues via amnesties or contested versions of 'reconciliation', rather than seeking prosecutions or aiming to respond to victims' (albeit diverse) present demands. Some may question the emphasis upon 'past' human rights violations, since survivors' experiences – and continuing crimes such as enforced disappearances – can persist in ways that do not neatly fit that characterisation. These discussions continue.

Civil society actors promoting international criminal justice have documented crimes, presented international criminal justice as aligned with domestic priorities, pursued Rome Statute ratification, and built closer relationships with authorities. Where these attempts were unsuccessful, they adapted their approaches. Some actors have attempted to derive new languages and pursue priorities other than prosecutions. This has involved moving away from considering state authorities as the primary targets of advocacy, towards engaging the general public and youth. Some groups prioritise attempts to secure economic, social, and cultural rights such as social services, or focus on grassroots initiatives or municipal apologies. KKPK's *Menemukan Kembali Indonesia* report and '*kebangsaan*' approach represents an attempt to create a new language of national rediscovery aimed at the Indonesian public, while the Year of Truth and other non-criminal proceedings such as the IPT65 and initiatives in Palu or Lampung have provided alternative spaces for discourse that address, but are not limited to, justice issues. In these ways, actors in diverse locations have adapted the norms surrounding international criminal justice in Indonesia, while also attempting to transform 'local beliefs and practices' (Acharya, 2004: 251).

Indonesia has typically supported the ICC and international criminal justice to the extent that it is not perceived as interfering in domestic politics or peace processes. This approach can be understood as a way to bring wider recognition to the norms of sovereignty, national stability, and non-interference. Indonesia's national laws for prosecuting international crimes were also adapted from the international norm. However, they differ from the Rome Statute in several respects, most notably in the exclusion of war crimes and 'other inhumane acts' in Law 26/2000, and by allowing for retrospective prosecutions. These departures responded to local circumstances as well as international influences.

Still, the Law provides Indonesia with a legal framework concerning international crimes that could in future be enforced or reformed in a progressive manner. Indeed, a draft Criminal Code was, at least initially, closer to the Rome Statute than Law 26/2000 and had the potential to address concerns about the need to synchronise Indonesia's 'human rights' and criminal laws. Yet, the incorporation of international crimes has been sporadic and the drafts fail to include the full spectrum of war crimes. This suggests that the process of localisation will not necessarily lead to the acceptance of international norms over time, although some developments have occurred.

Material concerns do not appear to explain Indonesia's approach to prosecuting international crimes, especially as donor financing has become less relevant, while local initiatives continue to evolve, albeit facing varied challenges. Further, as Indonesia has developed democratic governance structures, liberal frameworks that emphasise domestic politics would interpret Jokowi's inclusion of resolving past human rights violations in his election platform as an indicator of potential change. Yet this would not explain the failure to pursue prosecutions following Jokowi's election on this mandate.

A constructivist framework focused on how the concept of international criminal justice has been adapted by local and international actors may be more suitable for explaining Indonesia's international crimes laws. However, it is difficult to apply *spatial* boundaries to 'local' and 'international' actors. This chapter focuses on national laws, but as the examples of Palu, Lampung, Papua, Aceh make clear, the national government's actions should not be equated with the potentially different actions taking place regionally. Further, laws and institutions in both Indonesia and Timor-Leste responded to crimes perpetrated in East Timor (with Timor-Leste's legislation first adopted under UN administration). Thus, Indonesia's national mechanisms also intersected with international approaches. The main participants in the debate about Indonesian international criminal justice issues include lawmakers, political representatives, military leaders, and NGO activists (including survivors). Some of these actors' views appear to align with government perspectives from time to time, making it difficult to clearly delineate between 'state' and 'non-state' perspectives. Thus, 'local' actors can take opposing positions, including within and across government ministries. Further, many 'locals' are from time to time or normally based offshore in cities like New York, Geneva, Oslo, The Hague, or Sydney – as political exiles, migrants, employees of international organisations, academics, or students. The diversity afforded by multiple and overlapping ethnic (clan), religious, racial, and other groups in Indonesia provides the potential for friction between different perspectives of international criminal justice, but these are not easily classified along local/ international lines.

It is also difficult to distinguish between 'local' and 'international' *norms*. What it means to preserve Indonesia's 'sovereignty', 'human rights', 'reconciliation', and 'national unity' may be contested (see Koskenniemi, 2005), but these norms are also not necessarily 'local', or even always conflicting. Thus, civil society actors refer to Pancasila's emphasis on national unity as an argument *for* prosecutions, just as the government argues for reconciliation (to ensure unity) through *non*-prosecutions. As another example, the *domestic* Law 26/2000 and draft Code adapt the norm of international criminal justice by addressing 'human rights violations' of crimes against humanity and genocide rather than using arguments from domestic or international humanitarian or criminal law. Thus, spatial classifications of ideas can overlap.

Finally, while the situation continues to evolve, rather than a step-by-step process of accepting or rejecting international criminal justice, this concept keeps being reinterpreted and adapted (Zimmermann, 2016). That is, different debates coincide or run in parallel in a 'plural' way. For instance, the government debates new laws with prospective operation (such as the draft Code) at the same time as it explores non-judicial responses to 'past' crimes. Simultaneously, civil society actors advocate for amending domestic laws or ratifying various treaties for future operation. They also ask Komnas-HAM and the Attorney-General to enforce Law 26/2000 for either historic or prospective crimes, while seeking reparations and other non-judicial support for survivors.

Despite these challenges, the localisation approach helped to demonstrate that in Indonesia, domestic international crimes laws and institutions have resulted from frictions between different actors' different arguments. This process has not ceased following the adoption or use of national legislation. Instead, it is ongoing, both in relation to drafting new laws and through attempts to enforce existing laws. Indonesia's mechanisms relating to international criminal justice have not just resulted from norm diffusion by external actors, nor have they solely represented the outcome of 'local' norm entrepreneurs translating or rejecting external norms. Instead, Indonesia's approach to international criminal law presents a continuing interaction of variously located and influenced actors.

Civil society actors are aware of Indonesia's deviation from the mainstream theoretical 'path'. One activist explained that 'we took a wrong turn you know in this journey as a country'.[123] Some are hopeful of redirection, where 'then we go back to the right track and then we can just continue our journey'.[124] Other actors see potential for productivity in this friction: 'We are learning by doing.'[125] How such experiences might be applied in Indonesia's future remains to be seen. However, this chapter suggests that debates by various actors about sovereignty, the military, human rights, and national unity will continue to adapt Indonesia's approaches towards prosecuting international crimes, rather than leading to acceptance (or rejection) of the norm of international criminal justice.

---

[123] Interview I6.
[124] Interview I6.
[125] Interview I5.

5

International Criminal Justice in 'Transition'

Myanmar

5.1 Introduction

In the 2010s, after decades of military rule, internal conflict, and international sanctions, the second largest country in Southeast Asia, the Republic of the Union of Myanmar,[1] was said to be in a process of 'democratic transition' (Cheesman et al., 2012; Rhoads & Wittekind, 2018). There was emerging opportunity to consider how, if at all, to respond to the serious human rights violations of previous decades and to address ongoing violence that persists today. These include allegations of killings, sexual and gender-based violence, forced labour, torture, and the use of child soldiers.[2] Then, in 2017 military operations escalated in Myanmar's Rakhine State, causing an estimated 725,000 individuals including Muslim men, women, and children identifying as Rohingya and Kaman to seek refuge in Bangladesh (Independent International Fact-Finding Mission on Myanmar, 2018). These events have been accompanied by the effects of continuing protracted subnational conflicts, including in Shan and Kachin States and in the South East of Myanmar (Burke et al. 2017). Foreign states and NGOs called for the ICC to take action, as a series of Myanmar government–initiated, NGO, and UN Human Rights Council mechanisms conducted inquiries into the violence.

This chapter explores international criminal justice in a state which has not ratified the Rome Statute (in contrast to the Philippines and Cambodia); established an internationalised tribunal (as in Cambodia) or prosecuted crimes under domestic international crimes legislation

---

[1] Though the legal authority to replace the country name 'Burma' with 'Myanmar' has been contested and many organisations used 'Burma' (e.g. Human Rights Watch) or 'Burma/ Myanmar' (e.g. the Asian Legal Resource Centre), this book adopts UN and now near-uniform practice of using 'Myanmar' and 'Yangon' after 1989, but 'Burma' and 'Rangoon' before then, though there are other historic names for these regions.

[2] E.g. (United Nations High Commissioner for Human Rights, 2015).

(as in Indonesia). This relative lack of mechanisms for prosecuting inter-national crimes, and public statements opposing ICC and UN investigations, suggest that Myanmar's leaders have rejected the norm of international criminal justice and are not 'progressing' towards accepting this norm.

Yet this chapter presents a complex story of ongoing contestation. As in other chapters, Section 5.2 offers a largely chronological account of histor-ical engagement with international criminal law in Myanmar. Section 5.3 analyses the themes that different actors raise when they seek to influence international criminal justice in relation to Myanmar. Section 5.4 then explores Myanmar's laws and institutions for responding to international crimes. Section 5.5 concludes that while Myanmar represents a highly challenging context for encouraging the prosecution of international crimes, there is a dynamic process of engagement with this norm.

5.2   Historic Engagement with International Criminal Law

The task of summarising historic engagement with international criminal law is no less complex in the case of Myanmar than for other countries in Southeast Asia. Contemporary scholarship about Myanmar mostly does 'provide historical context', but often 'with reference to a conventional historical timeline broken into identifiable periods' that emphasises 'isolation and decline' rather than 'interaction and agency' (Rhoads & Wittekind, 2018: 172, 179). This chapter begins with an initially more 'conventional' account, but then emphasises the actions taken by a range of actors within and beyond Myanmar to adapt the norm of international criminal justice. Particular themes have re-emerged in these debates. These include a powerful military; ethnic, racial, and religious co-existence and divisions; ensuring peace, stability, law, and order; seeking independence from foreign countries; and promoting economic and judicial development. Some argue that a 'series of contemporary problems are disrupting attempts to put Myanmar's transition on a linear path to peace and development' (Pierce & Reiger, 2014: 2), or towards securing international criminal justice. These events occur in the context of historic engagement with international criminal law in Myanmar that has never been linear.

5.2.1   Diversity and Nationalism: British and Japanese Occupation

A body of written law based upon authoritative texts known as *dhammathat*, as well as other legal compilations and Buddhist canonical materials, evolved in the area of contemporary Myanmar over centuries, aspects of which share a relationship with principles of international humanitarian law (Harvey et al., 2019). After successive armed conflicts between 'Burman' and British forces during the nineteenth century, eventually the British India Codes displaced most areas of pre-colonial law, at least officially – many such laws, including the Penal Code, technically remain in force (Crouch, 2014b: 33).[3] The British governed Burma as part of British India until 1937 and then as a separate colony until 1948. Colonialism encouraged, in some, the development of 'strong nationalist sentiments' (Taylor, 2008: 224) and mistrust towards foreigners (Egreteau, 2011: 36), while colonial practices including forced evictions, citizenship laws, and administrative structures, contributed to divisions between different groups.

As elsewhere in the region during World War II, to gain local support, the Japanese 'pose[d] as the liberators of the Burmese from the [colonial] oppressor' (Gledhill, 1949: 199) when they invaded in 1942. The Burma Independence Army, which was led by the nationalist figure General Aung San (the father of State Counsellor Aung San Suu Kyi), drew support from Japan, which declared Burma to be independent in 1943. However, Japanese forces committed atrocities there during World War II, including during the construction of the infamous 'Burma-Siam Death Railway' (Totani, 2014). Burmese leaders became disillusioned with what was in practice Japanese occupation (Slim, 1998: 107). General Ne Win, who led the military regime that controlled Burma from 1962 to 1988, later said of the Japanese occupation, 'We learned our lesson . . . So long as we were useful, they were willing to use us. Self-interest was all that mattered.'[4] Occupation by both the British and the Japanese contributed to a cautious approach to foreign intervention.

By 1945, Aung San had aligned with the Allies and the British reoccupied Burma in May 1945. After World War II, British military courts prosecuted Japanese crimes committed in Burma in trials held in Singapore and (then) Rangoon (Piccigallo, 1979; Cribb, 2016). In the first case tried in Rangoon, Ichikawa Seigi and thirteen others were found guilty of massacring 637 civilians in the ethnic Indian community of Kalagon, Burma, in July 1945. Yuma Totani, a historian, suggests that the British authorities took the unusual step of issuing a written judgment to

---

[3] The Penal Code, India Act XLV. 1860 (1 May 1861) (Myanmar Penal Code).
[4] Quoted from Maung Maung (1999). *The 1988 Uprising in Burma*. New Haven, CT: Yale University Southeast Asia Studies, p. 99, in (Taylor, 2007: 62).

'impress' the Burmese 'with the British commitment to justice' in this early period of reoccupation, which embedded the trials with political concerns (Totani, 2014: 140).

Burma achieved independence on 4 January 1948. A 1947 Constitution had established an independent judiciary and bicameral parliament. However, Burma's administrative and judicial systems were badly damaged by the rapid departure of British colonial administrators and World War II. The post-independence government faced significant challenges. Internal armed conflicts continued within ethnically diverse regions including northern Arakan (now Rakhine) State, as well as in ethnic Burman (Bamar) majority areas, as the Communist Party of Burma fought for political influence (Taylor, 2007). Successive Constitutional amendments revoked earlier concessions to ethnic groups (Crouch, 2014b), further contributing to the instability. In this environment, the military greatly increased control over Myanmar's administrative structures.

The early legacies of British administration and World War II therefore included colonial laws, a mistrust of foreign intervention, internal instability, economic crisis, and a powerful military. As internal conflicts worsened, the armed forces managed a 'caretaker government' from 1958–9. The military then seized power in 1962 under the leadership of General Ne Win.

5.2.2   Military Rule and International Sanctions: Ne Win, SLORC, and SPDC

In the 1960s, Myanmar's international profile was elevated by the appointment of U Thant as the third Secretary-General of the United Nations, a position which he held until 1971. This did not indicate that the military government intended to promote engagement with the UN. Rather, General Ne Win's Burma Socialist Programme Party introduced a 'Burmese Way to Socialism'. In 1972 the judiciary was reconstructed as a 'People's Judicial System' and judges were replaced by Party members. Ne Win's regime deployed 'Special Courts', initially to prosecute 'crimes against society and other "important" crimes', but later, crimes determined by the administration at its discretion (Cheesman, 2011: 808). From the 1960s, the armed forces, known as the Tatmadaw, operated a 'Four Cuts Policy' that disrupted insurgency support-lines by targeting civilians (Aung, 2009: 25) and screening ethnic groups for 'foreigners' (MacLean, 2019). By the 1980s, internal conflict and economic mismanagement resulted in the resignation of General Ne Win amidst public protests in the '1988 Uprising' (Holliday, 2011: 55–7). On 18 September 1988 the 'State Law and Order Restoration Council' (SLORC) imposed martial law.

The size and strength of the Tatmadaw expanded after 1988 alongside early economic reforms that encouraged private enterprise, especially via military-owned conglomerates (Selth, 2002; McCarthy, 2019) and investment from China (Steinberg, 2001). SLORC renamed the state Myanmar, stifled internal conflicts, and dismantled or took over the powers of state institutions – shutting the courts until 1989 (and then frequently replacing judges) and effectively closing universities (Zan, 2008). Despite the arrest of opposition leaders including Aung San Suu Kyi, her party, the National League for Democracy (NLD), won elections held in 1990, probably to the surprise of the Tatmadaw. The military may have feared reprisals (including prosecutions) from any new government, though it seems that the NLD were more focused upon diminishing the Tatmadaw's political dominance. SLORC retained power until reorganising as the State Peace and Development Council (SPDC) in 1997, when Myanmar joined ASEAN.

These events were not without contestation, including from within Burma/Myanmar (Hlaing, 2004). Notwithstanding ASEAN's initially 'constructive engagement' with Myanmar alongside Chinese investment, international criticism of the military regime largely increased during the 1990s. The UN Commission on Human Rights appointed a Special Rapporteur to examine 'the situation of human rights in Myanmar' in 1992, who regularly observed serious human rights violations (see Section 5.3.1). The International Labour Organization also reported on forced labour in Myanmar, which probably contributed to the amendment of colonial era laws permitting this practice (Levin, 2011). Civil society campaigns encouraged foreign donors and companies to avoid investing in Myanmar and some countries, including the United States, implemented formal and informal sanctions (Pedersen, 2008; David & Holliday, 2012; Steinberg, 2015). This affected local business activity, reduced foreign trade, and restricted opportunities for receiving overseas aid. In this context, Myanmar was one of few countries that did not participate in the drafting of the Rome Statute in 1998.

In 2003, a violent pro-military attack against Aung San Suu Kyi and NLD supporters that caused numerous deaths drew (unsuccessful) calls for the UN Security Council to refer the situation in Myanmar to the ICC (Htoo, 2003). Myanmar officials announced a 'seven step reform program' and 'Roadmap to Democracy', beginning with Constitutional consultations. Even so, in 2005, former Czech President Havel and South Africa's Bishop Tutu called upon the UN Security Council to 'take action' with regard to Myanmar (Havel & Tutu, 2005: 58). Despite such international attention, when energy price increases accelerated in 2007 (as fuel subsidies were reduced in light of World Bank suggestions), ASEAN members expressed 'revulsion' when the military violently dispersed escalating protests led by civil society actors, including Buddhist monks, in the 'Saffron Revolution' (Eckert, 2007).

In the week following the 'greatest natural disaster in Myanmar's modern history' (International Bar Association's Human Rights Institute, 2012: 20) – Cyclone Nargis – during which the Myanmar government was accused of obstructing humanitarian aid (Ford, 2010), a new Constitution was adopted by a contested referendum and remains in place. While the 2008 Constitution includes a chapter of 'fundamental rights and duties' for citizens,[5] it arguably inadequately protects judicial independence, retains government immunities from prosecution, and provides that military personnel are prosecuted by military courts (Williams, 2014). Importantly, the 2008 Constitution preserves 25 per cent of seats in parliament for the military, meaning that the Tatmadaw can restrict Constitutional amendments. Calls by diaspora groups and foreign states to refer the situation in Myanmar to the ICC persisted (Kubosova, 2008; Nicholson, 2008; Burma Campaign, 2010) and may have alarmed military leaders.[6] Myanmar took the unusual step of sending a delegate to the ICC Assembly of States Parties as an observer (International Criminal Court, 2009).

The NLD boycotted elections in 2010, meaning that the military-associated Union Solidarity and Development Party (USDP) formed government. Many associated the NLD with a commitment to protecting human rights. Yet the *New York Times* suggested that Aung San Suu Kyi did not endorse proposals 'among her supporters overseas' that the military leaders be prosecuted in an international court (Mydans, 2010), though the NLD then 'clarif[ied]' that she had not said that (National League for Democracy, 2010). From the outset, Myanmar's 'transition' from military rule towards more democratic governance involved tensions between local political and military actors, civil society,

---

[5] These limited protections would not apply, for e.g. to those members of Myanmar's Rohingya community who are not considered citizens.
[6] Interview M10.

foreign states, and international organisations, and the issue of prosecuting international crimes.

5.2.3   Institutional Reform, Race, Religion, and Violence: The 'Transition'

In 2011, a notionally civilian government headed by a former General, Thein Sein, was instated. International calls for referral to the ICC slowed. The government undertook significant reforms leading up to elections in 2015. The Myanmar National Human Rights Commission (MNHRC) was established in 2011, the government released many child soldiers and political prisoners, allowed some public commemorations of historic incidents of violence, and there were limited investigations of crimes committed by military personnel (see Section 5.4.4). Foreign states reduced sanctions (though some NGOs warned that this should occur slowly) (Andrews & Smith, 2016) and commended the Thein Sein government for advancing Myanmar towards democracy (e.g. The Irrawaddy, 2014) though many Rohingya were unable to vote or be candidates in the 2015 elections. A Nationwide Ceasefire Agreement was signed by some ethnic armed groups in 2015.[7] Myanmar ratified a range of international human rights and humanitarian law treaties, though not the Additional Protocols to the Geneva Conventions or Rome Statute (see Appendix A).

The NLD won the 2015 elections. Aung San Suu Kyi's close aide, Htin Kyaw, became Myanmar's first civilian elected president in more than fifty years in March 2016 (from 2018 the president was Win Myint), while Aung San Suu Kyi became the head of government in the role of State Counsellor. Among its diverse priorities, the NLD-led government did not immediately pursue the adoption of international crimes legislation for prosecuting past military crimes and international criminal justice was not part of the new government's agenda. In fact, monitors reported ongoing military, police, and government impunity including for sexual violence crimes, land confiscations, the recruitment and use of child soldiers, torture (Lee, 2016). Various 'rule of law' projects commenced during the Thein Sein government continued to be implemented and promoted by Aung San Suu Kyi (see Section 5.3.2), though Myanmar's judicial system has been criticised for its entrenched

---

[7] For example, the Kachin Independence Organization did not sign the agreement.

corruption and lack of independence, especially from the military (Cheesman, 2012), and many in Myanmar viewed laws as existing 'to maintain control and social order' (MyJustice, 2017: 5). Civil society groups and politicians continued to call for the 2008 Constitution to be amended and for the military and MNHRC to be reformed.

The majority of the population in Myanmar is Buddhist and also belongs to the Bamar ethnic group. Issues of race, religion, and citizenship remain divisive and have been associated with military violence and conflict. During Thein Sein and Aung San Suu Kyi's governments, Buddhist nationalist groups such as *Ma Ba Tha* successfully supported four controversial 'race and religion protection laws' that, for example, regulate the marriage of Buddhist women to non-Buddhist men (Walton, 2015). Alongside persistent conflicts in many regions, such as Kachin, Kayin, and Shan States, much of the Muslim population also experienced continuing discrimination and violence. The government continued to deny the existence of a Rohingya ethnic group (UN Human Rights Council, 2016), while over a period of years various groups warned of a potential and unfolding genocide (e.g. Green et al., 2015). The Prosecutor of the ICC launched a preliminary examination into the deportation of the Rohingya people into Bangladesh and asked the Pre-Trial Chamber to authorise an investigation into crimes against humanity of deportation, 'other inhumane acts' and persecution before late 2019.[8] There continued to be calls for the Security Council to refer the situation in Myanmar to the ICC so that the Court might prosecute additional crimes only occurring in Myanmar. The government had established various inquiry mechanisms, but by June 2019 these had not led to prosecutions for international crimes (see Section 5.4). Debates about Constitutional amendments persisted, as preparations began for elections in 2020.

5.2.4   Summary: History

Myanmar has experienced occupation, internal armed conflict, and an authoritarian military regime. Each of these circumstances has been contested and given rise to allegations of international crimes, including from within Myanmar. Immediately following its election in 2015, the

---

[8] *Situation in Bangladesh/Myanmar*, Case No. ICC-01/19, Office of the Prosecutor, 'Request for authorisation of an investigation pursuant to article 15', 4 July 2019 (*Prosecutor's Request*). The Pre-Trial Chamber authorised this investigation in November 2019.

NLD government might have considered establishing domestic mechanisms to investigate and prosecute international crimes of the past, including to aim to prevent future crimes. The challenges in doing so – which include the persistence of military power, a focus on preserving stability, and development constraints – were significant. On the other hand, this is not a story of isolation, rejection, or a 'lack of' activity (see Rhoads & Wittekind, 2018). Rather, actors located in Myanmar and beyond continue to debate international criminal justice in Myanmar.

5.3 Local Initiatives and Adaptation

Drawing on public documents and limited discussions with civil society actors in Myanmar, mostly in 2014 (prior to the NLD forming government), this section shows how different groups of actors have shifted their language and approaches towards international criminal justice. It cannot give an insider or complete account of these debates, which continue to unfold, and focuses on activities surrounding the 2015 election until June 2019, with references to earlier events for context.

5.3.1 International States and Organisations

International organisations and states have addressed the alleged commission of international crimes in Myanmar through monitoring, political and economic pressure, 'constructive engagement', and investment and development assistance, including to encourage the 'rule of law'.

The United Nations Special Rapporteur mandate for Myanmar has been an important source of information about alleged international crimes since 1992. To provide a sense of this critique, in 2006, Special Rapporteur Paulo Sérgio Pinheiro reported that '[s]everal individuals and groups responsible for committing serious violations of human rights, in particular members of the military, have not been prosecuted' (Pinheiro, 2006: 3). Special Rapporteur Tomás Ojea Quintana's 2010 report revealed a 'prevailing culture of impunity', that was 'a necessary consequence of the lack of accountability for grave human rights violations' (Quintana, 2010: 13: para. 13). In 2014 he concluded that 'the pattern of widespread and systematic human rights violations in Rakhine State may constitute crimes against humanity as defined under the Rome Statute' (Quintana, 2014: para. 51). Special Rapporteur Yanghee Lee suggested in 2016 that responding to violations would contribute to Myanmar's stability and 'a sustainable and inclusive peace' (Lee, 2016: para. 60).

By March 2018, she was 'becoming more convinced that the crimes committed following 9 October 2016 and 25 August 2017 bear the hallmarks of genocide and call[ed] in the strongest terms for account-ability' – while warning 'the international community ... must not be beguiled by the proliferating Government committees and commissions' (Lee, 2018). Other UN offices shared these concerns, including the UN High Commissioner for Refugees, Office of the High Commissioner for Human Rights (OHCHR) (especially the High Commissioner for Human Rights, Zeid Ra'ad al-Hussein), and the CEDAW Committee (United Nations, 2017), though the UN office based within Myanmar may have preferred to focus on development as an approach towards protecting human rights (Fisher, 2017).

In 2017, the UN Human Rights Council had established an Independ-ent International Fact-Finding Mission on Myanmar (UNFFM) by reso-lution 34/22. It investigated violations in Kachin, Rakhine, and Shan States and found that 'shocking' violations of international humanitarian law had been committed, many of which 'undoubtedly amount to the gravest crimes under international law' (Independent International Fact-Finding Mission on Myanmar, 2018: paras. 1671–2). The report made extensive recommendations, including that named senior Tatmadaw generals be investigated and prosecuted for genocide, crimes against humanity, and war crimes. It argued that the ICC 'is the most appropri-ate venue' for such trials, or perhaps an 'ad hoc' international tribunal akin to the ICTY or ICTR, given the obstacles to ensuring accountability within Myanmar's courts (paras. 1651, 1654).

To ensure the ongoing collection of evidence, and inspired by the establishment of an International, Impartial and Independent Mechan-ism for Syria in 2016, in October 2018 the UN Human Rights Council also established (in Resolution A/HRC/39/L.22) an:

> ongoing independent mechanism to collect, consolidate, preserve and analyse evidence of the most serious international crimes and violations of international law committed in Myanmar *since 2011*, and to prepare files in order to facilitate and expedite *fair and independent* criminal proceedings, in accordance with international law standards, in national, regional or international courts or tribunals
>
> (UN General Assembly, 2018: para. 22, emphasis added).

This 'Independent Investigative Mechanism for Myanmar', led by a former ECCC prosecutor, will not address alleged crimes committed by the military regime that preceded Thein Sein's presidency. However, it may facilitate prosecutions in courts beyond the ICC, including in other states (or Myanmar) or at the International Court of Justice.[9] It is also mandated to cooperate with any ICC or domestic investigations, reflecting one international approach towards alleged international crimes in Myanmar: to monitor and document violence to support 'independent', 'impartial', and potentially 'international', criminal responses.

Foreign governments and their agencies have contributed to debates about international criminal justice in Myanmar. This has included documenting crimes[10] and the implementation of various sanctions, the impact of which has been debated (Pedersen, 2008; David & Holliday, 2012). Sanctions were eased during Thein Sein's presidency, though reports of human rights violations continued. More recently, the United States, European Union, Australia, and other states implemented targeted sanctions against individuals accused of perpetrating international crimes, stemming from the UNFFM's report.[11]

Some states have also suggested, as Barack Obama did in 2014, that 'the perpetrators of crimes and abuses must be held to account in a credible and transparent manner' (The Irrawaddy, 2014). Explicit calls for justice resurfaced at strategic moments during Myanmar's 'transition', or when reports of violence escalated. For instance, in 2007, the United States and United Kingdom proposed a Security Council resolution calling upon the Myanmar government to cease violations during internal conflicts. The draft resolution was vetoed by China and Russia and opposed by South Africa (three countries including Indonesia abstained) (United Nations Security Council, 2007). Sanctions were broadened in 2008 after Cyclone Nargis and Australia, the European Union, and United Kingdom supported calls for the Security Council to refer the situation in Myanmar to the ICC. After 2011 there was an apparent pause in foreign states' calls for ICC prosecutions, though at Myanmar's UPR in 2015 and alongside the elections, several states noted concerns about accountability for human rights violations (Burma Partnership, 2015).

Violence in Rakhine State and elsewhere in Myanmar in 2017 led to a resurgence in calls for prosecuting international crimes, including genocide. Sweden called for the UN Security Council to refer the

---

[9] *Application of the Convention on the Prevention and Punishment of the Crime of Genocide (The Gambia v. Myanmar), Application instituting proceedings and Request for the indication of provisional measures*, ICJ, 11 November 2019.

[10] E.g. (United States Department of State, 2018: 1).

[11] E.g. (Australian Department of Foreign Affairs and Trade, 2019).

situation in Myanmar to the ICC (United Nations, 2018), as did a group of 132 parliamentarians in ASEAN states (ASEAN Parliamentarians for Human Rights, 2018). Malaysia's Ministry of Foreign Affairs had issued a statement arguing that 'ethnic cleansing' of Rohingya was 'no longer an internal matter' in 2016 (ASEAN-Malaysia National Secretariat, 2016). Later, Malaysian officials argued that generals must be investigated for genocide (Straits Times, 2018). In November 2017 the US Secretary of State Rex Tillerson labelled the violence against the Rohingya 'ethnic cleansing' and called for those 'responsible' to be 'held accountable' (Gramer, 2017). The US House of Representatives resolved that 'all those responsible for these crimes against humanity and genocide should be tracked, sanctioned, arrested, prosecuted, and punished under applicable international criminal statutes and conventions'.[12] The government of Bangladesh assisted the ICC Prosecutor's preliminary examination and facilitated meetings and visits by Court officials. With the support of Bangladesh, the Organisation of Islamic States unanimously adopted a resolution to authorise an action before the International Court of Justice against Myanmar concerning the Rohingya, which was submitted by The Gambia in November 2019. Criminal proceedings based on universal jurisdiction were also proposed in Argentina. Thus, some states and intergovernmental organisations have periodically broadcast concerns about prosecuting historic, and ceasing ongoing, international crimes in Myanmar.

Still, in 2019, apart from the ICC's limited examination of crimes occurring partly in Bangladesh, there was not yet any international criminal tribunal *prosecuting* historic or more recent crimes in Myanmar. Some international actors have not pushed for the prosecution of international crimes committed in Myanmar. Myanmar represents an important locus for Asian regional stability and trade (O'Connell, 2016). Russia and China avoided talks about draft Security Council resolutions and tried to block a briefing by the UNFFM Chair in October 2018 (Nichols, 2018), though Security Council envoys visited Bangladesh and Myanmar in April 2018. Other countries including India and

---

[12] H.Res.1091 – Expressing the sense of the House of Representatives that atrocities committed against the Rohingya by the Burmese military and security forces since August 2017 constitute crimes against humanity and genocide and calling on the Government of Burma to release Burmese journalists Wa Lone and Kyaw Soe Oo sentenced to seven years imprisonment after investigating attacks against civilians by the Burmese military and security forces, and for other purposes, 13 December 2018.

Thailand have also tended to 'prioritize stability over reform' in their diplomatic relationships with Myanmar (Ciorciari, 2009).

Despite a historic preference for 'constructive engagement' with Myanmar, ASEAN leaders had also criticised the Myanmar government's human rights violations and slow reform process (Albar, 2006; Eckert, 2007), though without explicitly encouraging the prosecution of international crimes. A tilt in emphasis was suggested by the Chair's statement at the November 2018 ASEAN Summit, which indicated an expectation that an 'Independent Commission of Enquiry established by the Government of Myanmar [would] seek accountability by carrying out an independent and impartial investigation of the alleged human rights violations and related issues' (ASEAN, 2018: para. 37). This reflected stronger concerns raised by Malaysia and, to a degree, Indonesia (see Chapter 4), particularly concerning violence against Muslims, though these countries have noted the importance of countering terror and ensuring internal stability in Myanmar and Rakhine State (e.g. Nurhayati, 2016).[13] The ASEAN Chair also echoed themes favoured by the Myanmar government (see Section 5.3.2), by expressing 'continued support for Myanmar in its efforts to bring peace, stability, the rule of law, to promote harmony and reconciliation among the various communities, as well as to ensure sustainable and equitable development' (ASEAN, 2018: para. 37).

Other international actors have also responded to alleged human rights violations by promoting Myanmar's economic development, including by encouraging reforms to facilitate foreign investment,[14] sponsoring investment fairs (e.g. Japan), and via capacity building, such as offering human rights training to officials (Kinley & Wilson, 2017). Myanmar historically received relatively low levels of overseas aid compared to other developing countries, but now attracts significant international assistance (World Bank, 2019b), though some funders apparently reduced their support after the escalating violence in Rakhine State. Of most relevance, states fund 'rule of law' and judicial reform initiatives in Myanmar, including 'capacity building' initiatives, such as training seminars and programmes (e.g. USAID, 2019; Prime Minister of Australia et al., 2013).

---

[13] Indonesia and Myanmar held a roundtable about counter-terrorism operations just days before Myanmar's military escalated its engagement in Rakhine State, explicitly on the basis that it was combatting terrorism (State Counsellor Office, 2017b).

[14] E.g. (Embassy of the United States, 2019).

Sometimes this emphasis may reflect a perception that economic and humanitarian assistance could be a pragmatic entry point for engaging with Myanmar communities and civil society in a challenging environment. For example, the government expelled Médecins Sans Frontières personnel from Myanmar in 2014 after they reported treating wounded Rohingya Muslims following an alleged massacre (Weng, 2014). In that context, some international agencies reportedly avoided projects directly addressing serious human rights violations in order to 'maintain relationships' and secure access for other projects (Thomson, 2015: 10). Some academics (and, in conversation, some foreigners based within Yangon) emphasise the complexity of the situation in Rakhine State and express concern that the more condemning approach of those outside Myanmar has encouraged the military to seek to maintain its control over the state (see Pedersen, 2019) or even aligned the NLD with the military, at least in relation to the ICC.

International states, institutions, and individuals have adopted different and shifting stances towards the alleged commission of international crimes in Myanmar. While some have documented incidents and called for international crimes to be prosecuted, potentially even by the ICC, some have prioritised diplomatic relationships and focused on development.

5.3.2   Myanmar Authorities

Individuals within the Myanmar government, military, and public services have differing opinions of the policies pursued by their respective institutions.[15] It is also difficult for an external observer to identify which actors have the most authority over policy in Myanmar at a given time, although the military has retained significant influence since the official end of military rule in 2011 (Farrelly, 2013; McCarthy, 2019). Yet reviewing the statements made by official channels, particularly the President and State Counsellor's Offices, about responding to international crimes reveals some preferred arguments. Myanmar's leaders have tended to emphasise protecting Myanmar's internal stability, avoiding foreign control, encouraging development, and the need for 'evidence' and rule of law, rather than opposing international crimes

---

[15] However, historically '[p]ower in Burma is not merely concentrated within institutions, it is also highly concentrated around a few persons', see (Gravers, 2004: 139). See regarding the army, (Centre for Peace & Conflict Studies (CPCS), 2015).

prosecutions in principle. As in the Philippines, since the ICC turned its attention towards crimes perpetrated in Myanmar, authorities have been increasingly hostile towards the Court, though responses have continued drawing upon those themes.

After 2011, President Thein Sein made 'national unity' his 'top priority' (Ministry of Foreign Affairs Myanmar, 2011). This reflects the history and persistence of subnational conflict, which had entrenched the political dominance of the military (Burke et al., 2017). Thein Sein recalled how the 'Tatmadaw ... saved [Myanmar] several times whenever the country was close to collapse and loss of independence and sovereignty' (Ministry of Foreign Affairs Myanmar, 2011) and later compared the potential for violence in Myanmar to the Middle East and Balkan region (Thein Sein, 2016). The 'overarching goal' of the 2013 final report of a Commission of Inquiry concerning Rakhine State 'was to promote peace and development in the region rather than place the blame on a specific group or community' (Republic of the Union of Myanmar, 2013: i). Government statements, especially surrounding the 2015 elections, promoted 'peace and stability', as well as ethnic and religious harmony (Myanmar President Office, 2015a; 2015b). In order to preserve such stability, the Thein Sein government suggested that reform measures, including 'accountability and responsibility' should be gradual and progressively developed (Ministry of Foreign Affairs Myanmar, 2014: 3).

Similarly, after the 1990s Aung San Suu Kyi and the NLD typically preferred a narrative of reconciliation, peace, and the rule of law. In 2012 Aung San Suu Kyi told an International Bar Association (IBA) delegation that although Myanmar should explore avenues for reconciliation, she opposed criminal trials as these would be 'unacceptable to the military', with which she needed to cooperate (International Bar Association's Human Rights Institute, 2012: 54). Not all NLD members may have agreed, but in those IBA meetings, apparently '[n]o one expressed the view that criminal trials would advance the current reform process' (International Bar Association's Human Rights Institute, 2012: 54). In 2016, Aung San Suu Kyi advised that the NLD would aim to 'ensure national reconciliation, internal peace, the rule of law, amendments to the constitution and keeping the democratic system dynamic' (Associated Press, 2016). This suggested that Myanmar's stability and reform were higher priorities than international crimes prosecutions.

International criminal justice, and transitional justice generally, have not been a prominent feature of the peace process. The 2015 Nationwide Ceasefire Agreement specified that the parties are to '[a]dminster rule of law in ceasefire areas and take action against perpetrators ... in coordination with each other'. In chapter 3(9) on the 'Protection of Civilians' the parties agreed to 'avoid' various criminal acts including sexual violence (The Myanmar Times, 2015). Still, the Agreement did not confirm that military or government perpetrators could be prosecuted[16] and after it was signed the Tatmadaw escalated attacks against non-signatories.

The 'rule of law', which Aung San Suu Kyi has personally championed,[17] has continued to be a prominent principle in official narratives, with one statement about violence in Rakhine State 'reaffirm[ing] that we stand for the rule of law. No one is above the law. Where there is clear evidence, those who breach the law will be brought to justice' (Republic of the Union of Myanmar, 2017). Yet the meaning of 'rule of law' in Myanmar is not straightforward (Cheesman, 2015a). Myanmar's leaders have argued that 'to maintain peace and rule of law ... it is necessary to take legal action against those who violate any existing domestic laws' (Ministry of Foreign Affairs Myanmar, 2014: 3), which has in the past included human rights activists (see Cheesman, 2009; 2015a; 2015b; Crouch, 2019). Terrorism has also been used as a justification for military operations that have led to alleged international crimes. By contrast, international initiatives to investigate or prosecute crimes have been portrayed as having the potential to inflame 'hostility between the different communities' and undermine the government's attempts to 'build stability and find lasting solutions' (State Counsellor Office, 2017a).

Official statements also imply that Myanmar's responses are more in keeping with 'the situation on the ground' (State Counsellor Office, 2017a). Indeed, Myanmar's government has asked international actors to appreciate 'the difficulties and challenges which a young democratic State has to face' and assist Myanmar to overcome them through aid and investment, rather than prosecutions (see Ministry of Foreign Affairs Myanmar, 2014: 3). As Thein Sein advised in 2011, one must 'build roads, railroads and bridges to overcome the natural barriers between regions of national races' (Ministry of Foreign Affairs Myanmar, 2011). There may appear to be a tension between historic misgivings about external intervention and the desire to attract international assistance – for instance from China or the United States. Yet statements arguing that '[i]f our country is not economically strong, it will face underestimation and unfair treatment from other countries' propose that foreign

---

[16] This would require specific legislation, see Sections 5.4.2 and 5.4.3.
[17] E.g. Aung San Suu Kyi chaired the Parliamentary Rule of Law Committee.

investment might increase Myanmar's stability and independence (Ministry of Foreign Affairs Myanmar, 2011). This also reflects experience that unrest has been associated with economic crises, including post fuel subsidies, sanctions, and demonetisation.

As Myanmar increased its engagement in international treaties and other forums, its leaders emphasised the state's progress in reducing and responding to human rights violations. In 2015 Myanmar indicated that it would consider UPR recommendations concerning 'combating impunity' and prosecuting human rights violations, although it did not support acceding to the Rome Statute or bringing military or official perpetrators 'to justice'.[18] Even in the weeks immediately following the upsurge in violence in Rakhine State, Aung San Suu Kyi claimed that Myanmar's 'government has emerged as a body committed to the defence of human rights' (State Counsellor Office, 2017c).

On the other hand, Myanmar's officials have frequently critiqued the application of norm of international criminal justice in Myanmar's case, including by associating it with foreign interference. In the midst of the 2015 elections, Myanmar's leaders argued that 'unfounded allegations [concerning the Rohingya] are interfering in the internal affairs of Myanmar and disturbing [its] peace and tranquility' (Myanmar President Office, 2015c). The government's criticism has been directed towards the UN mechanisms (including the Security Council) and the ICC, rather than completely rejecting the notion of international criminal justice. The government rejected the ICC's 2018 jurisdiction ruling on the basis that Myanmar is not a party to the Rome Statute and denied responsibility for deportations (Republic of the Union of Myanmar, 2018), among other, mostly procedural, concerns.[19] However, the government also claimed that 'Myanmar is both willing and able to investigate any crimes and violations of human rights in its own territory' (Eleven Media Group, 2018) and 'whilst the government is unable to accept this legally dubious intervention by the International Criminal Court, we are fully committed to ensuring accountability where there is concrete evidence of human rights violations committed in Rakhine State' (State Counsellor Office, 2018). It asserted that the 'Government has time and again reiterated its principled position of promoting and

---

[18] Recommendations 143.79, 143.82, 145.28, (UN Human Rights Council, 2015).
[19] *Bangladesh/Myanmar*, Case No. ICC-RoC46(3)-01/18, Pre-Trial Chamber I, Decision on the 'Prosecution's Request for a Ruling on Jurisdiction under Article 19(3) of the Statute', 6 September 2018 (PTC Jurisdiction Decision), fn. 54.

implementing the rule of law, justice and accountability' (Eleven Media Group, 2018).

The government has proposed an understanding of 'accountability' as self-directed (taking responsibility for one's own actions), requiring 'acceptable evidence' (State Counsellor Office, 2017d), and, with a nod to the rule of law, applying 'equally to all. Individuals, organizations, national governments *as well as multilateral organizations*, must be held responsible for the consequences of their words and actions' (State Counsellor Office, 2018, emphasis added). Thus, a series of mechanisms have been established to investigate allegations of human rights violations, with international actors invited to participate in some of the inquiries and commissions (see Section 5.4.4). For example, an Advisory Commission led by Kofi Annan with domestic and international participation, was established to identify 'factors that have resulted in violence, displacement and underdevelopment' (Advisory Commission on Rakhine State, 2017: 12). It focused on development rather than accountability, aiming to 'explain to the international community' that the government was taking some response to reported violence in Rakhine State, with the implication that it might offer a 'shield' from criticism (Zaw, 2017).

Myanmar's officials have also disputed allegations of violations – even when documentation of atrocities, including satellite images, mounted and the ICC began to address the issue (e.g. State Counsellor Office, 2016a). Apart from under-development, the violence is also depicted as resulting from terrorist activity, which 'should not be condoned in any form for any reason' (Aung San Suu Kyi, 2018). Another response has been to propose that the attacks involved international interference (State Counsellor Office, 2017e), whether due to international actors stimulating terrorist activity in the region, or via the circulation of 'fake' news, including via social media, though Tatmadaw soldiers also published inflammatory statements.

Officials have therefore both suggested that Myanmar mechanisms would investigate and prosecute allegations of international crimes – and denied that they even occurred. Arguments presented by Myanmar authorities about international criminal justice under Thein Sein and Aung San Suu Kyi's governments do not defy the *principle* of prosecuting international crimes – in fact, they emphasise the importance of the rule of law, accountability, and evidence. However, they seek to retain government control over investigations, deny culpability, and emphasise longer-term development and stability. In practice, the government has used aspects of the norm of international criminal justice, such as the need for evidence and rule of law, to push back against accusations of criminal activity. This has, in practice, aligned the NLD government with the position of protecting the military from international crimes prosecutions.

5.3.3 Civil Society

Myanmar civil society comprises survivors of human rights violations, lawyers, academics, peace negotiators, and community leaders. Civil society actors may be based in Yangon, in rural areas, or overseas, especially in Thailand – including because many left (or fled) Myanmar (see Prasse-Freeman, 2012). There are Bamar-dominated organisations and ethnic nationality NGOs, though many networks, such as Women's League of Burma, encompass individuals from varied backgrounds (see Falvey, 2010). Some have relied upon international assistance or have responded to the need to fill 'humanitarian gaps created by government restrictions on humanitarian aid' (Fortify Rights, 2018: 9). In areas of Myanmar effectively administered by 'ethnic armed actors' and organisations, or by a mix of official government and ethnic institutions, the division between 'civil society' and 'government' provision of services is difficult to untangle (Jagger, 2016; McCartan & Joliffe, 2016). Ethnic armed actors also have judicial systems that may 'adapt elements of existing justice institutions and practices, including those of the state as well as customary mechanisms, and bring them in line with the organization's interpretation of local cultural norms for regulating civil and criminal practices' (McCartan & Jolliffe, 2016: 2). Moreover, many in Myanmar resolve potentially 'legal' disputes within communities via village administrators (MyJustice, 2017). Religious institutions, including the *sangha* (Buddhist monastic order), have also provided community services, while groups of monks have been involved in activist movements, both against the military regime and opposing minorities (McCarthy, 2015).

Civil society activities have also changed over time, with periods where restrictions on assembly and censorship were more violently enforced (including after 1988 and in 2008), but also opportunities for (relatively) more 'space' for debate (inconsistently, with brief periods in 1988 and after 2011). Those groups that have engaged in debates about prosecuting international crimes have done so in the context of military influence, internal conflict, economic and development considerations (leading to a focus on meeting 'basic needs'), changing levels of international involvement, and prohibitive judicial and other institutional structures. Even focusing on the period leading up to and since the 2015 elections, these experiences have continued to present challenges for civil society to 'borrow and frame' ideas about international criminal justice to establish their 'value' to local officials (Acharya, 2004: 251). Many in Myanmar have not prioritised holding international crimes trials, but this view is not uniform or static (Falvey, 2010). One regional activist observed in 2014 that 'there seems to be an assumption it's not part of our culture to want justice, but then this assumption seems to be more clearly articulated amongst diplomats from the West'.[20] Another based within Myanmar warned that as the political situation stabilises, victims may increasingly demand prosecutions.[21] Others were already articulating this preference, as suggested by the Kachin Peace Network's slogan, 'Justice Guarantees Lasting Peace', which united a range of different organisations. In fact, some argued that 'we need to talk about justice as soon as possible, even now'.[22] Civil society groups with a focus on this topic[23] have pursued multiple approaches that aim to secure 'justice' for international crimes perpetrated in Myanmar. Five are outlined here.

First, some advocate for legal change by engaging with official and opposition figures, revealing experiences of violence or offering 'training' or other collaborative services. This is not a new approach (see Lall, 2016) – in 2007 political prisoners asked individuals to write letters to the SPDC about their experiences of military rule: the Open Heart Letter campaign. Many complaints concerned social and economic rights (Falvey, 2010). However, it has been challenging for many groups to explicitly advocate for prosecuting international crimes, particularly in direct meetings with officials and including for urban organisations. Many have believed that 'if we raise this issue then you will get in trouble',[24] and the government has taken legal action against individuals that pursued cases involving military perpetrators, particularly concerning violence involving ethnic groups and sexual and gender-based violence (see Section 5.4.4). These challenges mean that civil society actors must be 'strategic'.[25] This includes their choice of approaches towards promoting

[20] Interview M1.
[21] 'Most of the peoples are mainly focused on … how to transform, you know how to reform … But to rather speak frankly, we want to take the action to those in the military, [the] higher military officer[s], because … they torture us severely', Interview M8.
[22] Interview M1. See (Falvey, 2010: 261).
[23] Not named here to preserve the anonymity of interviewees.
[24] Interview M10.
[25] Interview M10.

international criminal justice via engagement with officials. Some actors promote military professionalism and compliance with existing domestic instruments, such as the Tatmadaw's Code of Conduct.[26] Others publicise issues through social media (including youth organisations) or hold seminars with community actors including journalists that may report incidents of violence.[27]

This might involve 'framing' discussions that in fact relate to international criminal justice topics ('how do you ... bring to justice ... the person who committed' the crimes)[28] in ways that might be more receptive to officials, but also contest dominant understandings of particular terms. For example, many human rights and peace-oriented groups have responded to the perception that 'the military and ... government ... think that peace is about stability, so for stability they need to trade-off human rights' and 'bring stability at any cost'.[29] As mentioned, the government has compared Myanmar to the Middle East and Balkan region. Similarly, activists suggest that whereas 'rising of nationalism' could 'damage the whole country' as in Bosnia,[30] or government repression may cause groups to 'take up arms' as in the Middle East',[31] justice could 'prevent recurrence' and 'address the harms of the past' to preserve peace.[32]

Stability arguments can be extended to explain broadly that avenues for justice would build trust in institutions[33] and even 'go a long way to demonstrating that an NLD-led government is not another Burman oppressor' (Thomson, 2015: 3). More explicitly, ND-Burma coordinator Han Gyi has argued that as long 'as there is impunity for human rights violations, they will continue ... Without justice there can be no rule of law and no democracy' (ND-Burma, 2017). Attempts generally to promote the rule of law may reflect a perception that, in Myanmar, 'number one, if you're talking about transitional justice, don't say the words

---

[26] Interview M4.

[27] Interviews M6; M8; M10.

[28] Interview M4.

[29] Interview M9.

[30] Interview M10; or use Bosnia as an 'international lesson' for the importance of being receptive to community solutions to conflict, Interview M9.

[31] Interview M6.

[32] Interview M1.

[33] If there is access to a fair court system, 'then the people feel satisfied and ... will not do violence', Interview M6.

transitional justice',[34] or, it follows, prosecutions. In contrast, 'rule of a law is a fairly neutral term' and 'a safe term to use'.[35]

Second, for many years civil society actors within Myanmar have worked with NGOs based across the Thai border, foreign universities such as Columbia and Harvard, United Nations monitors, and foreign states (including their development assistance arms). This is consistent with a 'boomerang' theory of engagement, where international attention is sought to put pressure on the domestic government, as well as to strengthen their own capacities (Keck & Sikkink, 1998). One actor remarked: 'we need the pressure from the international community ... because ... our government neglected ... the local organisation[s]'.[36] Regional groups such as Myanmar-based NGOs 'fight together'[37] with associations such as Forum-Asia, Burma Partnership, Fortify Rights, the Asia Foundation, and Burma Campaign by co-writing reports and delivering seminars within and outside Myanmar. They may issue joint statements that, for example, stress that human rights violations negatively affect the prospects for peace and argue that the government 'should end the endemic culture of impunity' by prosecuting violations and ratifying international treaties (AWDO et al., 2016). Regional forums concerning international criminal justice have been arranged, such as a 'Consultation on the International Criminal Court and the Rule of Law in Burma and Thailand' in 2007, which discussed 'how international mechanisms of justice can be used to bring criminal accountability to the perpetrators of crimes against humanity, war crimes and genocide' (Burma Lawyers' Council, 2007), and other conferences.[38]

NGOs have made submissions to international mechanisms, including the UPR process, sometimes supported by international NGOs, including from Bangladesh and Pakistan (NCJP Media, 2017; Odhikar, 2017). They have called upon the UN Security Council to refer the situation in Myanmar to the ICC so that all crimes, not just those partly committed in Bangladesh, might fall within its jurisdiction. Some have alleged that violence in Kachin, Shan, and Chin states (and elsewhere), as well as

---

[34] Interview M1.

[35] Even if 'for the grown-ups in the room ... they need to be able to say the words "transitional justice" and understand that this is critical'. Interview M1.

[36] Interview M5. Another explained, 'we need to have a strong voice from the civil society and we also need international pressure', Interview M10.

[37] Interview M4; M5.

[38] E.g. a conference on 'The International Conference on Protection and Accountability in Burma', organised by Columbia University, New York, 8–9 February 2019.

gender-based violence perpetrated by military officers, amounts to inter-national crimes (e.g. Women's League of Burma, 2014: 25; Htun, 2018). Civil society actors also submitted information to the ICC Prosecutor[39] and publicly supported the ICC's exercise of jurisdiction concerning Myanmar or encouraged engagement, even if to support the govern-ment's position (Aung, 2018). Civil society engaged with the initial ICC Pre-Trial Chamber proceedings concerning the Court's jurisdiction. One Myanmar-based 'think tank' attempted to provide an *amicus curiae* brief apparently aligned with the government's position – even though the government did not participate in the proceedings.[40] By contrast, a group of 'victims from Tula Toli' believed that international crimes in Rakhine State 'can only be prevented by the involvement of the international community, including this Court'.[41] *Amicus curiae* briefs favouring the ICC's jurisdiction were also offered by a group of NGOs in Bangladesh and other international organisations. Diaspora groups in Australia, the United Kingdom, and across Europe have sought ICC attention at various times and placed pressure upon foreign governments and the ICC to take action. For example, a group of Rohingya refugees and the Kachin National Organization pressured the US Congress to support referral of Myanmar to the ICC and the imposition of sanctions (Burma Task Force, 2018).

Not everyone views engaging with 'international' actors as straightfor-ward. Some have suggested that 'the prioritization of individual agendas over local processes by the INGOs without enough consultation has undermined the role and capacity of local organizations' (Myanmar Civil Society Organizations Forum, 2014). Many observe that international attention, including media coverage, can be fickle. Actors therefore adjust their arguments for international audiences. One strategy discussed in 2014 was to caution that the situation in Rakhine State has ramifications

---

[39] *Bangladesh/Myanmar*, Case No. ICC-RoC46(3)-01/18-1, Office of the Prosecutor, Appli-cation under Regulation 46(3), Prosecution's Request for a Ruling on Jurisdiction under Article 19(3) of the Statute, ICC, 9 April 2018, para. 7.

[40] *Bangladesh/Myanmar*, Case No. ICC-RoC46(3)-01/18, Pre-Trial Chamber I, Decision on the Request of the Thayninga Institute for Strategic Studies for Leave to Submit Amicus Curiae Observations, 10 August 2018 – refusing admission as the request was out of time and did not address the relevant legal issues; (Mratt Kyaw Thu, 2018).

[41] *Bangladesh/Myanmar*, Case No. ICC-RoC46(3)-01/18, Pre-Trial Chamber I, Observa-tions on behalf of victims from Tula Toli, 18 June 2018, para. 12; see also Pre-Trial Chamber I, Submissions on Behalf of the Victims Pursuant to Article 19(3) of the Statute, 30 May 2018.

for ASEAN states and 'will be danger[ous] for regional security, even global security',[42] and 'you don't want Rohingya boat people turning up on your doorstep'.[43] This proved sadly prescient. A regional activist also tried 'to make the argument that transitional justice is essential for investor confidence' and some international actors 'should be interested in ensuring that there's some degree of transitional justice, at least to protect their arses!'[44] International attention and partnership has been a feature of debates about international criminal justice concerning Myanmar.

Third, organisations based within and around Myanmar document and report upon human rights violations and alleged international crimes. ND-Burma was founded in 2004 to document human rights violations and 'prepare for justice and accountability measures in a potential transition' (ND-Burma, 2015: 5). It has thirteen member organisations, typically with addresses in foreign states, but has operations within Myanmar. ND-Burma commenced an 'Unofficial Truth Project' in collaboration with DC-Cam. This was described as a 'truth commission' initiative, rather than targeting international crimes prosecutions, even though Cambodia did not have an official 'truth commission' (International Center for Transitional Justice, 2013). Since then, ND-Burma has documented, and advocated about, the commission of alleged international crimes, including via an investigation that found that victims of human rights violations 'overwhelmingly said they wanted some form of action' and 'many ... asked for justice, but voiced low levels of confidence in the domestic legal system' given that there 'has been no justice for the majority of cases' to date (ND-Burma, 2018: 15–16, though see section 5.3.4). A civil society actor from a different organisation explained that documentation is 'the first step',[45] another considered 'documentation training' to be their 'main subject',[46] and a third observed that, 'if we do not start now, who will start it? When will [they] start it? So ... the first thing is we document everything. Document, document, document.'[47] Statistics and incidents are reported to

[42] Interview M10.
[43] Interview M1. Singapore, Japan, Australia, and the United States were mentioned as countries to whom such arguments were made.
[44] Interview M1.
[45] Interview M6.
[46] Interview M5.
[47] Interview M4.

national and international networks including the UN, media, the MNHRC, and even parliament.[48]

Fourth, there have been limited attempts to respond to violence within Myanmar's judicial system using existing laws, with reference to international standards.[49] Lawyers advocate for the enforcement of military Codes of Conduct, ratified treaties including the Geneva Conventions, and Constitutional or other domestic laws (Cheesman & Kyaw Min San, 2014).[50] At least in the period before the 2015 elections, some anticipated that if international crimes were ever to be prosecuted, it would be 'in Myanmar court[s]. Because [the] International Criminal Court is very expensive and [there is] very little interest by international bod[ies] and up to now we haven't signed this Rome Treaty yet'.[51] Some expected that if there were ever to be prosecutions, this was more likely to occur in Myanmar, but remained cautious about internationalised models like the ECCC. The UNFFM has since concluded that domestic prosecutions are highly unlikely.

Fifth, another theme of civil society advocacy concerning international criminal justice has been to consider the best timing for prosecutions. Khin Ohmar of Progressive Voice agreed with international reports that '[p]atience is not what we need to resolve the deplorable situation of human rights in Myanmar' and the 'international community must urgently send a strong message ... that impunity and destabilization of peace and security will not be tolerated' to avoid further loss of life (Progressive Voice, 2018; see also Khin, 2017). A regional activist advised that 'we often use the Cambodian experience as one that is flawed because it took so long to deliver', which 'perpetuated a kind of impunity in the country'.[52] For one actor, though, in considering 'what is the right time, we need to think about: first 'decreas[ing] the military rule' and then securing an 'independent judiciary' to pursue prosecutions – not only for incidents in 'the present' but also 'in the past, and the future'.[53]

---

[48] Interview M5; M8; M6 – though M10 explained in 2014 that 'we cannot do direct advocacy to the government right now, so what we do is ... advocacy through the media, social media'.

[49] Interview M6.

[50] Interview M6; M2; M4.

[51] Interview M4.

[52] Just as failure to 'prevent recurrence of impunity' has 'led to resurgence of conflict in some areas' in Myanmar, Interview M1.

[53] Interview M6. A peace worker believed that, in terms of 'ancient hatreds', 'we have to accept [the] past, but we cannot bring [the] past to the present'. Interview M9.

Others share this more cautious approach and longer-term horizon: see Section 5.3.4.

Civil society groups, including local actors, have attempted to influence approaches to international criminal justice in Myanmar through various avenues. These include working with international organisations and states (and, where feasible, authorities), framing justice as a precursor for stability or the 'rule of law', documenting violations, and legal advocacy.

5.3.4   Local Adaptation

At least some actors both within and beyond Myanmar draw on local initiative to advocate for international criminal justice for crimes perpetrated in Myanmar. However, the safety of activists or a desire to maintain dialogue, alongside a 'perceived dichotomy of revenge and immediate forgiveness' (Thomson, 2015: 2), have made it challenging to promote this norm, even in an oblique manner. Further, until relatively recently, the ICC was considered unlikely to prosecute crimes in Myanmar, while 'to be able to abolish these kind of crimes in Myanmar, [the] rule of law should be in Myanmar'.[54] Instead, some civil society actors have adapted approaches towards international criminal justice. Many pursue Constitutional and military reform projects, considering that removing military control over the state is the first essential step. Some are disillusioned with the role of foreign actors and have modified their approach accordingly, while others have developed socio-economic projects favouring 'grassroots' consultation.

The previous section described how 'rule of law' language might help to frame international criminal justice ideas in a more domestically acceptable form. Yet, actors might also *use* the idea of international criminal justice to promote a domestic priority: institutional reform. On one hand, recognising equality before the law and building practical capacity would be a critical first step for securing justice for any crimes committed by the military or officials (Pierce & Reiger, 2014). On the other hand, 'if there is no accountability there might be no rule of law'.[55] Here, addressing impunity contributes to the reform process, rather than representing an end in itself. The view that international criminal justice

---

[54] Interview M4.
[55] Interview M9.

should promote institutional reform or the 'rule of law' means that parts of the norm that seem useful for that purpose, such as collecting evidence and attracting judicial reforms, might be welcomed, whereas others might not be prioritised. For instance, some would not actively promote ICC prosecutions while the military retains power, if they think this might be viewed as 'retribution' and risk a backlash counterproductive to their reform aims (see Manley, 2017), even if others see prosecutions as a precursor for reform.

In 2018 'ND-Burma believe[d] the time for justice has arrived'. Yet 'justice' here was defined, in relation to transitional justice, as:

> ensuring access to justice and respect for the rule of law. And it is about rebuilding trust throughout society to bring about reconciliation and lasting peace. Indeed, as our needs assessment shows, victims do not seek retribution. Instead the majority asked for guarantees that human rights violations will not recur, usually through some kind of institutional reform (ND-Burma, 2018: 18).[56]

The prominence of transitional justice, particularly proposals for apologies, reparations, and guarantees of non-repetition, in civil society statements about international crimes in Myanmar does not always just represent a framing device (aimed at securing international criminal justice). Rather, it is pragmatic. While many do want prosecutions, as one regional activist acknowledged, 'I think people understand that it might be easier to get reparations ... and to go after legislative and institutional reforms to prevent, to halt and prevent recurrence of impunity'.[57] Another offered a progression: 'one, the government should say that "Yes we did it". So this is the first step. Even to get that one will [take a] very long long [time]. And then in the future maybe we can establish like [a] monument and also ... like a prayer site or a memorial day'.[58] In particular, research has suggested that some individuals in Myanmar 'just want the military to leave them alone' (Falvey, 2010: 272) or 'enjoy what has already been achieved' (Pierce & Reiger, 2014: 13).[59] Many victim communities also prioritise 'socioeconomic justice'

---

[56] ND-Burma's goals are now presented as including 'to advocate for justice' with a mission to '[a]chieve government recognition, redress and guarantees of non-recurrence for victims of human rights violations', in contrast to the earlier emphasis upon transitional justice mechanisms and accountability measures (ND-Burma, 2019).
[57] Interview M1.
[58] Interview M4.
[59] Or 'get back to normal life', Interview M1.

(Falvey, 2010, 268), including issues such as land reform,[60] health, crime (especially drugs), and other social issues such as gambling.[61] For example, consistent with the Open Heart Letter campaign's emphasis on socio-economic rights, ND-Burma identified remedies for land confiscation and unfair taxation as priority issues in its community discussions, alongside reparation for torture and extrajudicial killings (see Falvey 2010; ND-Burma, 2010; 2015). This reflects intersections between conflict, military rule, dispossession, and development priorities. As Pierce and Reiger (2014: 19) observed from their work in Myanmar, the 'urge to "leave the past behind" is based on a misperception that a before-and-after line can be drawn easily between the previous military regimes and the current reform government. For displaced farmers whose land has been taken, they still do not have their land ... [which] fractured any trust these groups may have once had in the state'. Thus, a 'broadened concept of justice' in Myanmar might build upon the intersections between international criminal justice concerns about ending impunity, transitional justice, and socio-economic priorities (Falvey, 2010: 269; Pierce & Reiger, 2014: 3).

This theme was taken up by the Permanent Peoples' Tribunal on Myanmar, held in Kuala Lumpur in September 2017, which followed an earlier people's tribunal, the International Tribunal on Crimes against Women of Burma, in 2010. The Kuala Lumpur Tribunal attempted to view 'the situation of the Rohingya through a wider lens', including through also addressing complaints of crimes committed against other ethnic groups (Permanent People's Tribunal, 2018). It sought a referral of the situation to the ICC as 'the minimum judicial response', alongside other actions. It also tied the 'tragic situation in Myanmar' to a temporal/spatial position, 'moment in history, not only in this place but in so many other corners of the world' exhibiting the frequent 'failure' 'of international law to protect individuals' (Permanent People's Tribunal, 2018).

While actors within Myanmar have sought out international partners and used international treaties and forums, they have done so opportunistically, sometimes sceptically, and alongside domestic advocacy (though relative to some other countries there have been fewer avenues to engage

---

[60] Interview M6: 'big challenge is probably the Constitutional amendment also the land issue'.

[61] Interview M8: 'gambling is also ... so popular in the rural area[s], ethnic areas', while 'for the rural community [another] difficulty is ... how to cure their disease'.

with government in Myanmar).[62] In 2014, some feared that foreign states have 'come for investment. Their influence, their interest [is] because ... they need some of our country['s] local resources'.[63] One activist felt that 'international governments', naming the United States and European Union,[64] used Aung San Suu Kyi as an 'icon or a logo' for their own aims, rather than being genuinely committed to change.[65] One activist in Yangon reflected that the 'UN has made a lot of damage in Myanmar already from our point of view',[66] while another explained that 'sometimes, I want to blame the international groups' whose primary activities seemed to be meeting famous leaders, 'shooting the video', and then leaving Myanmar.[67] Another local activist thought that the Special Rapporteur's reports had influenced the government, but 'after the transition it is very difficult to bring international [states'] attention [towards] the human rights issues, because the international community, it's enjoying euphoria of change' and this had actually 'empowered' the government to continue violating international law.[68]

These sentiments – expressed prior to the 2015 election – suggested the need for adjusted advocacy strategies. For example, if repeatedly gathering similar groups of people who already 'know that conflict is not good' for conferences is ineffectual, one actor proposed that experience-sharing projects with communities or perpetrators should involve learning from them, 'why [did] they commit the crime[s]?'[69] If international investment is likely to impact upon human rights, then 'it's not just about talking about us and the army and us and the government, there are other stakeholders ... who should be interested in ensuring that there's some degree of transitional justice' and need to be engaged.[70]

---

[62] Interview M4; M9.
[63] Interview M5. A regional actor remarked that 'various states like the US, the European Union, Australia, even Canada, they're all very interested in running in there and grabbing the best of natural resources and grabbing all those opportunities and basically trying to say let's turn a new page on Burma, everything's better now' – while 'Nay Pyi Daw and ASEAN, but Nay Pyi Daw particularly, are gambling on the fact that the rush to natural resources is going to cloud any concerns for justice', Interview M1.
[64] Though another actor mentioned the EU as being on the 'side of the responsibility and accountability', Interview M5.
[65] Interview M4. Similarly: 'the "lady" is the everything ... Ok lots of foreigners, they can take a photo' (but that is all they do), Interview M8.
[66] Interview M4.
[67] Interview M8.
[68] Interview M10: 'Because they know that there will not be that much pressure now'.
[69] Interview M8.
[70] Interview M1.

More recently, if the ICC attention has led the NLD government and the military to share a common opponent and narrative about alleged crimes, a more political approach to public awareness and information-sharing might seem warranted. In this way, the complex impact and sometimes unhelpfulness of international norms, including concerning international criminal justice, might spur community activities and engagement with a wider range of stakeholders than international NGOs, organisations, and states.

Some civil society actors with an interest in international criminal justice have focused on preventing conflict, especially in relation to Muslim and Buddhist violence, through community discourse, genuine listening, and 'grassroots trust building and promoting tolerance' with religious and community leaders.[71] They may also adapt traditional conflict resolution strategies and existing reconciliation initiatives (Leone & Giannini, 2005). Community programmes can create spaces for actors to continue developing their own diverse responses to international crimes. This can reflect the different ways that internal conflicts across Myanmar involve natural resource exploitation, ethnic and religious violence, political ideology, and military authoritarianism (Burke et al., 2017).

However, it is also important to carefully consider the manner in which 'grassroots' responses to violence are implemented. For example, pursuing religion-focused projects in isolation could distract from state responsibility or the influence of rumours spread by outsider 'conflict entrepreneurs'.[72] Some local peace and development initiatives might also exclude marginalised groups, 'like women and children who suffered the most', or be 'manipulated to create more economic opportunities for vested interests'.[73] There are also different types of exposure to the commission of international crimes in central cities in comparison to rural and ethnic-dominated areas, while some suggest that civil society in Yangon is more 'Burmese'.[74] In other words, there is a risk that 'bottom-up' approaches can obscure 'top-down' drivers of both conflict and

---

[71] Interview M10; see Interview M6; M8.

[72] Interview M9.

[73] Interview M1.

[74] In Rakhine State and other areas: e.g. 'Ko Par Gyi, he's a Burman and he used to be Aung San Suu Kyi's bodyguard team, that's why many people give attention to [his death]. But ... like Sumlut Roi Ja [an abducted Kachin woman], there are thousands of Sumlut Roi Ja in the whole country in ethnic areas, but no one cares', Interview M4 (see section 5.4.4).

impunity for criminal actions, or may have limited influence over wider national or international approaches. That said, community discussions and smaller-scale non-justice projects offer an entry point for adapting international criminal justice.

There are international organisations who promote a carefully timed approach to judicial reform that involves close consultation with affected communities, 'rather than push[ing] pre-packaged development pro-grammes' such as a focus upon 'training and preaching on human rights principles', 'which have failed in countries like Cambodia' (Asian Legal Resource Centre, 2016) and Nepal (Falvey, 2010; Pierce & Reiger, 2014; Thomson, 2015; Burke et al. 2017). For example, regional NGO Asia Justice and Rights (AJAR) employed participatory techniques such as collective timelines and mapping to reveal intertwined understandings of justice as involving punishing perpetrators, restoration of property (especially land for those displaced) and a state that would provide 'a decent standard of living and basic human dignity' (AJAR, 2015: 14). Approaches that emphasise local consultation recognise that 'there is no set chronology or order for how things should happen'.[75] One actor discusses how bringing 'bad things from the past to the future is not good ... so for the future what ... would you like to do?'[76] while another suggested that 'sometimes reparations takes precedence of accountability, sometimes the institutional and legal legislation reforms to halt impunity and prevent its recurrence becomes more urgent than all the other considerations, so it's up to people to decide'.[77] Yet 'people' take different views as to when to push for different types of transitional justice measures, including prosecutions, and many are not aware of what options there may be. Many civil society actors therefore favour an interpretation of international criminal justice that would incorporate genuine listening to the priorities and mechanisms proposed by different communities, while recognising the broader context and drivers of conflict.

5.3.5   Summary: Local Initiative and Adaptation

International, official, and civil society actors have sought to influence understandings of international criminal justice in Myanmar through

---

[75] Interview M1.
[76] Interview M8.
[77] Interview M1; M4.

local, regional, and international projects and forums. Many actors do not overtly focus upon securing international criminal justice in Myanmar, but draw on aspects of the norm, as well as transitional justice ideas more broadly, to employ a variety of broader development, rule of law, and local preventative activities. These typically aim to strengthen domestic institutions, community relationships, and consultation. Each of these approaches allows space for new interpretations of international criminal justice in Myanmar.

5.4   Mechanisms for Prosecuting International Crimes in Myanmar

Major economic crises, conflict, systemic change, or domestic political change, are all said to potentially stimulate local actors to adopt or adapt international norms (Acharya, 2004). Each of these events has occurred in Myanmar. Many actors, including within the government, have pursued rule of law and reform projects. However, the continuing power of the military, potential for internal instability, lack of judicial independence, and cynicism about international motivations have all provided reason for some local actors to doubt the 'utility and applicability' of international criminal justice in Myanmar, at least at present (Acharya, 2004: 251). There are mechanisms for addressing crimes in Myanmar, including domestic laws and a series of inquiry commissions, that ostensibly offer steps towards prosecuting international crimes, but 'amplify' stability and development concerns.

5.4.1   International Mechanisms

Myanmar is not a party to the Rome Statute. Myanmar's 2008 Constitution allows the Ministry of Foreign Affairs to conclude and the President to enter into, ratify, or annul treaties. The Pyidaungsu Hluttaw (Union Parliament)[78] approves treaty ratification.[79] Myanmar could accede to the Rome Statute with the support of the NLD, which after

---

[78] Comprising the Pyithu Hluttaw, Lower House, and Amyotha Hluttaw, Upper House.
[79] Unless Parliament confers such authority upon the President, Article 108, Constitution of the Republic of the Union of Myanmar 2008. Article 209 also provides that the President 'may enter into, ratify or annul ... treaties which do not require the approval of the Pyidaungsu Hluttaw'. In the event of disputes about international agreements, the Supreme Court of the Union has original jurisdiction to consider the matter, Article 295, Myanmar Constitution.

the 2015 elections held approximately 60 per cent of seats (Nehru &
Farrell, 2016). If it did, in 2004 Myanmar passed the Mutual Assistance
in Criminal Matters Law (No. 4 of 2004), allowing Myanmar to provide
assistance in criminal proceedings to states parties to an international
convention to which it is a party, or under bilateral agreements. However, given the current level of military influence and government opposition towards the ICC's attention towards the Rohingya, accession to the
Statute is highly unlikely in the near-term.

In September 2018, the ICC Pre-Trial Chamber indicated that the
Court could exercise jurisdiction over deportation and potentially other
crimes, where part of the crime occurred in Bangladesh, which is a state
party to the Rome Statute.[80] In July 2019, the Prosecutor sought the Pre-
Trial Chamber's authorisation that there is a 'reasonable basis to proceed
with an investigation, and that the case appears to fall within the jurisdiction of the Court'.[81] The request focused on crimes against humanity
of deportation, other inhumane acts (violation of the right to return), and
persecution committed against the Rohingya where at least one element
occurred in Bangladesh, in 'waves of violence' in 2016 and 2017. The Pre-
Trial Chamber authorised an investigation in November 2019, to address
crimes within the ICC's jurisdiction that occurred at least in part in
Bangladesh, subsequent to 1 June 2010 (when the Rome Statute entered
into force for Bangladesh).[82] In order for the ICC to investigate or
prosecute crimes only committed on Myanmar territory, either the
Security Council would need to refer a situation in Myanmar to the
ICC, or Myanmar would need to accept the ICC's jurisdiction.[83] Neither
approach is expected in the short term, or would address crimes committed before the Rome Statute entered into force on 1 July 2002. It is
similarly unlikely that the Security Council would establish a tribunal like
the ICTY or ICTR, though this was a recommendation of the UNFFM
and some individuals are exploring the possibility of a General Assembly
established mechanism. Finally, the International Court of Justice is

---

[80] *Bangladesh/Myanmar*, Case No. ICC-RoC46(3)-01/18, Pre-Trial Chamber I, PTC Jurisdiction Decision, 6 September 2018.
[81] Article 15(4) Rome Statute.
[82] *Bangladesh/Myanmar*, Case No. ICC-01/19-27, Pre-Trial Chamber III, Decision Pursuant to Article 15 of the Rome Statute on the Authorisation of an Investigation into the
Situation in the People's Republic of Bangladesh/Republic of the Union of Myanmar,
14 November 2019.
[83] E.g. by confirming the ICC's jurisdiction from 1 July 2002 upon accession or by lodging a
declaration to that effect under Article 12(3) of the Rome Statute.

focused on state responsibility rather than individual criminal prosecutions and so also does not fully satisfy the norm of international criminal justice.

It is possible that other states might prosecute Myanmar defendants under universal jurisdiction laws as has been indicated in Argentina and is planned elsewhere. This would be most likely in relation to the violence against the Rohingya after 2011, potentially supported by evidence gathered by the UNFFM and ongoing Independent Investigative Mechanism for Myanmar established by the UN Human Rights Council in September 2018. International prosecutions will confront political, practical, and legal barriers. As an example, when Aung San Suu Kyi visited Australia in March 2018, lawyers sought her prosecution under Australia's international criminal justice legislation. However, Australia's Attorney-General failed to provide the necessary consent to any prosecution, on the grounds that Aung San Suu Kyi was entitled to immunity as a sitting head of state. It is unclear whether additional international mechanisms for prosecuting crimes in Myanmar (other than the existing ICC proceedings) will be established in future, though it is possible.

5.4.2   Domestic Legislation

Myanmar has not adopted the Rome Statute provisions, or similar, into domestic law or ratified the Additional Protocols, though it is a party to the 1949 Geneva Conventions (since 1992) and the Genocide Convention (since 1956). The British administration passed a Geneva Convention Implementing Act in 1936 to implement the 1929 Geneva Convention on the Wounded and Sick, which would appear to remain in force, though with little authority since it predated Burma's separation from India in 1937 (and the treaty itself was revised by Geneva Convention I in 1949).[84] No implementing legislation seems to have been passed for the four 1949 Conventions, although customary international law should apply. In practice, though, for national courts to prosecute crimes against humanity, genocide, or war crimes as such in Myanmar, Parliament would need to adopt new legislation. Still, individuals could be – and have on occasion been – prosecuted under Myanmar's other legislation.

Myanmar's Penal Code resembles those of Singapore, Malaysia, and Brunei Darussalam, as it replicated the British India Penal Code. It

---

[84] India Act XIV. 1936, Geneva Convention Implementing Act, 27 October 1936.

includes offences of murder, torture, kidnapping, abduction, deportation, slavery, forced labour, forced marriage and prostitution, rape, arson and destroying homes, destruction of property, fouling the water or atmosphere, defiling a place of worship, and sterilisation committed within Myanmar or by a Myanmar citizen.[85] Thus, there is some scope to prosecute crimes committed by civilians that might constitute the underlying conduct of international crimes using Myanmar's domestic criminal laws.

The provisions for modes of liability mirror the other India Code laws by providing for individual and joint commission of and abetting crimes and criminal conspiracy. '[C]oncealing a design to commit an offence' is addressed in sections 119 and 120 and preparation is included within the elements of some crimes (such as section 121: 'prepares by force of arms ... to overthrow' the government). Section 153A also makes it criminal to promote feelings of enmity or hatred between different classes of people within the Union.[86] Similarly, there are exemptions of liability for unsoundness of mind, private defence, involuntary intoxication, and (except for crimes involving the death penalty) duress. Section 76 includes a defence for mistake of fact and good faith belief in justification by law, illustrated by the example that 'A, a soldier, fires on a mob by the order of his superior officer, in conformity with the commands of the law. A has committed no offence'. These provisions remain from the period of British occupation and broadly reflect the scope of the modes of liability in international criminal law.

Chapter VII of the Penal Code sets out specific offences addressing the Army, Navy, and Air Force, such as mutiny and assaults against a superior officer, but does not include war crimes. Further, the Defense Services Act 1959 provides for prosecuting military personnel by court martial for various offences such as murder, culpable homicide, or rape of 'a person not subject to military law' if committed while on active service (very broadly defined), outside of Myanmar, or at a specified frontier post.[87] Similarly, the Myanmar Police Force Maintenance of

---

[85] On jurisdiction, see sections 2–4, Myanmar, Penal Code, India Act XLV. 1860 (1 May 1861) (Myanmar Penal Code), though section 3 suggests that some laws may provide jurisdiction over acts committed outside Myanmar.

[86] This section appears in the Brunei Darussalam Code, but not the Singaporean Code (see Appendix C). It was deleted from the Malaysian Code, although section 298A of the latter covers the use of words or activities to prejudice the 'maintenance of harmony or unity, on the grounds of religion'.

[87] Section 72, Defence Services Act 1959.

Discipline Law 1995 provides for police to be prosecuted by police courts. The 2008 Constitution specifies that the Defence Services have the right to independently administer and adjudicate all affairs of the armed forces.[88] It also confirms that 'Courts Martial' in Myanmar, not the civilian courts, have jurisdiction in respect of all cases involving military personnel and separates them from Myanmar's Supreme Court and Constitutional Tribunal, neither of which abrogates the powers of the Courts Martial (see Articles 293–4, 319, 343). Further, the Constitutional structure ensures that Myanmar's higher courts remain dominated by the military. The combined effect of these provisions is that Myanmar's Courts Martial would ordinarily hear cases for military perpetrators of conduct that may amount to an international crime, which reduces transparency and – in reality – the prospects of convictions.

5.4.3   Amnesties and Immunities

Myanmar's Constitution provides the President with the power to grant a pardon or amnesty, with the latter based on the recommendation of the National Defence and Security Council, thereby affording the military a direct role in providing amnesties.[89] The government has periodically granted political amnesties. However, Article 445 provides that '[n]o proceeding shall be instituted against the [SLORC or SPDC] or any member thereof or any member of the Government, in respect of any act done in the execution of their respective duties'. Some observers interpret this provision as amounting to an immunity for past crimes, although the International Bar Association (IBA) has argued that such a 'narrow interpretation' would involve a 'serious misreading' of the Article (International Bar Association's Human Rights Institute, 2012: 55). In January 2016, Parliament also passed legislation providing the outgoing President with immunity from prosecution for 'any actions' undertaken during his term, 'in accordance with the law' (Aung, 2016; Amnesty International, 2016). Indeed, the political situation in Myanmar and judicial restrictions, including the Constitutional provisions concerning the Courts Martial, suggest little near-term scope for Myanmar courts to allow officials or members of the armed forces to be tried for international crimes.

---

[88] Article 20, Myanmar Constitution.
[89] Article 204, Myanmar Constitution.

5.4.4   Enforcement

Judicial decisions are infrequently reported and reports are difficult to obtain within Myanmar (especially in English). Access to the courts for court monitoring has been extremely limited, particularly for foreigners, and cases that are politically sensitive (including many rape or drugs cases, especially involving military perpetrators) are typically closed. As indicated, many disputes are resolved by village administrators and other mechanisms in Myanmar, including lower-level municipal courts and ethnic armed actor tribunals (MyJustice, 2017). Yet it is still clear that there have been few convictions for conduct that might amount to international crimes in Myanmar. On the other hand, numerous mechanisms have been established to inquire into, advise, or even gather evidence of violence that appear to draw on some of the trappings of the norm of international criminal justice in an attempt to 'enhance the profile and prestige of local actors' (Acharya, 2004: 246).

The Myanmar National Human Rights Commission Law (No. 21 of 2014) improved but did not secure the MNHRC's independence from the government. The MNHRC can visit and inspect the scene of human rights violations and initiate and conduct inquiries, including, under chapter VI, into 'widespread, systematic or entrenched situations or practices that violate human rights'. It may gather documents and evidence, determine that violations have occurred, and recommend that measures be taken, including action by departments or compensation. The MNHRC has received thousands of complaints, the majority of which have related to land disputes (Myanmar Eleven, 2014). It has investigated several high-profile human rights violations and has even recommended the investigation of security forces. As is the case for many National Human Rights Institutions, the MNHRC does not have direct prosecutorial powers. It faces many challenges including a lack of government and public understanding of its role, enduring social and institutional obstacles towards challenging military and police authority, as well as practical limitations including resource constraints and difficulties in securing evidence (Burma Partnership & Equality Myanmar, 2014).

There are several categories of cases that do not constitute international crimes trials or desired outcomes for victims or their families but illustrate how actors have worked within Myanmar's legal system to respond to serious crimes perpetrated by the military. These have not just employed Myanmar's criminal legislation but have involved complaints to government departments and the MNHRC, or attempts to seek Constitutional writs (Crouch, 2014a).[90]

First, as UN Special Rapporteur Yanghee Lee has noted, the government officially has a 'zero-tolerance policy for sexual misconduct' but there 'continues to be a high level of impunity for conflict-related sexual violence perpetrated by State actors and a lack of transparency in military courts' (Lee, 2015: para. 50). Sumlut Roi Ja is one of many women who witnesses claim have been abducted and raped by Tatmadaw soldiers. In this case, the Kachin Women's Association Thailand filed a complaint with the MNHRC and in 2012 Sumlut Roi Ja's family applied to the Supreme Court for a writ of habeas corpus. However, the Supreme Court rejected the petition on the basis that there was insufficient evidence as the military denied detaining Sumlut Roi Ja (FIDH, 2014). There are many examples of investigations not being pursued towards conviction, including the case of two Kachin teachers, Tangbau Hkawn Nan Tsin and Maran Lu Ra, who were alleged to have been raped and murdered by members of the Tatmadaw, but the cases have not been prosecuted (Nyein, 2019). Women's League of Burma has argued that government statistics stating that 'between 2011 and 2015, 31 sexual violence cases involving military perpetrators were transferred to civilian courts' were difficult to verify and, even if correct, the number of violent incidents was much higher (Women's League of Burma & AJAR, 2016).

Second, military perpetrators can be prosecuted before civilian courts, although the circumstances may need to be extraordinary and the process has been arduous. Private Kaung Bo Bo kidnapped and raped a 14-year-old Kachin girl with a mental disability on her way to the market. Initially the military sentenced Private Kaung Bo Bo to one year in prison for leaving his barracks without permission. However, in 2014 and following significant civil society advocacy, he was found guilty of rape and kidnapping by a civilian District Court and sentenced to thirteen years in prison. This case is not indicative of how other incidents have been addressed (Aye Nai, 2011; ND-Burma, 2018). For instance, Brang Shawng complained to the MNHRC after his 14-year-old daughter was killed by indiscriminate gunfire near a school but was convicted of making false accusations against the Myanmar Army (Ja Seng Ing Truth Finding Commission, 2014).

---

[90] E.g. Articles 296, 378, Myanmar Constitution.

Third, prominent individual cases occasionally lead to investigations. In 2014, one of Aung San Suu Kyi's former bodyguards, a journalist known as Ko Par Gyi, was killed while in military custody. President Thein Sein asked the MNHRC (which also received several complaints) to investigate his death. Ko Par Gyi's body was exhumed and an autopsy showed that he had been shot several times. The MNHRC recommended that police investigate the case 'in line with the judicial proceedings' and suggested that 'this case should be tried in a civil court' (likely meaning a 'civilian court') (Myanmar National Human Rights Commission, 2014). However, the case was heard before the Summary General Courts Martial and two lower-ranked soldiers were acquitted. This again showed some opportunities for prosecuting soldiers, yet also that convictions were 'still far from possible' (Asian Human Rights Commission, 2016; Cheesman et al., 2016). Then in 2019 four men, including some with military links, were sentenced (two of them to death) for the murder of Ko Ni, an NLD lawyer who was critical of the military, although the 'alleged mastermind' military officer remained 'at large' in June 2019 (Htun, 2019).

Fourth, military courts do occasionally convict soldiers for their illegal conduct, usually where the incidents were already well publicised. After the deputy commander of the Tatmadaw admitted that soldiers had killed five civilians in Mong Yaw, in 2016 a court martial in Lashio found seven soldiers, including four military officers, guilty of murder and sentenced them to five years of imprisonment with hard labour (Lun Min Mang, 2016). A court martial also convicted six soldiers of the murder of three Kachin civilians and sentenced them to ten years imprisonment with hard labour (Associated Press, 2018). In April 2018 the Tatmadaw reported that seven soldiers had been convicted by court martial for the massacre of ten Rohingya men (which was reported by Reuters) and sentenced to ten years in prison with hard labour, but they were released after serving less than one year.[91] On occasion victims have been offered limited compensation for military violence, which many desire, but the amounts have been small and sometimes accompanied by pressure to cease efforts to secure accountability (Women's League of Burma & AJAR, 2016; ND-Burma, 2018).

Fifth, there have been a range of responses to the violence in Rakhine State, though with a focus on preserving peace and stability and promoting development, rather than prosecuting the alleged international

---

[91] Having served less time than two Reuters journalists who reported on the massacre (Naing & Lewis, 2019).

crimes (see Table 5.1; FIDH, Altsean-Burma & Progressive Voice, 2018; Human Rights Watch, 2018).

When forming the Advisory Commission led by Kofi Annan, Aung San Suu Kyi explained that it would 'consider humanitarian and development issues, access to basic services, the assurance of basic rights, and the security of the people in Rakhine' (Myanmar News Agency, 2016). The aim was therefore not to pursue prosecutions, but to attempt an 'innovative approach to peace building in a country undergoing a challenging national peace and reconciliation process' (Kofi Annan Foundation, 2018: 5). By establishing other inquiry bodies, Aung San Suu Kyi argued that the government 'has adopted short and long term programmes to promote understanding and trust' to foster 'peace and stability' in Rakhine State (State Counsellor Office, 2017e). Government mechanisms suggest that the 'root causes' of violence are developmental, whereas the UNFFM and others characterise the core issue as military impunity (Zaw, 2018).

The publication of the Advisory Commission's report in August 2017 coincided with some of the worst violence against members of the Rohingya. The report 'looks primarily to the future' and focuses on development issues, noting that 'there are no "quick fix" solutions' to the challenges in Rakhine State, though 'finding a path to move forward is an urgent task', since the region represents a development, human rights, and security 'crisis'. The report proclaimed that 'in order to move forward together the past must give way to a renewed vision for a dynamic future' (Advisory Commission on Rakhine State, 2017: 9–10).

Likewise, the government responded to the report by emphasising that 'there are difficulties that cannot be resolved overnight and by Myanmar alone', which would also require capacity building and human rights training (State Counsellor Office, 2017f). This followed earlier arguments that 'time and space are critical for the efforts to bear fruit' (State Counsellor Office, 2016b). A Committee for Implementation of the Recommendations on Rakhine State from the Advisory Commission also favoured a long-term perspective (e.g. Committee for Implementation of Recommendations, 2019).

The mechanisms are not clearly independent (since they usually include military representatives) and though many are 'local' (Myanmar-based) some include international representation, such as the Advisory Board for the Committee for Implementation and the July 2018 'Independent Commission of Enquiry'. They have not led to prominent prosecutions, though Major General Maung Maung Soe, who

Table 5.1 *Myanmar mechanisms concerning violence in Rakhine State since 2012*

Year Established	Name (Investigations in Bold)	Participants	Scope/Recommendations
17 August 2012	**Commission of Inquiry on Sectarian Violence in Rakhine State**	27 national members, Chair Myo Myint	Focused on 'underlying causes of violence', no investigation of human rights violations.
6 February 2014	**Inquiry Commission for Duu-Chee-Yar-Tan incident and related events**	Chair Tha Hla Shwe (all national)	Rejected allegations of police violence and arson.
30 May 2016	Central Committee for the Implementation of Peace, Stability and Development in Rakhine State		Notification No. 23/2016. Development policy: 4 working committees support the Central Committee.
5 September 2016	Advisory Commission on Rakhine State	9 members, Chair Kofi Annan (6 national, 3 international)	Mandate only humanitarian and development issues, made 88 recommendations.
26 October 2016	**State-level Committee**	11 members, Chair Aung Win	Dismissed allegations of human rights violations.
1 December 2016	**Investigation Commission (on violence in Maungdaw)**	13 members, Chair Vice-President U Myint Swe	Investigating military operations. Interim and final reports dismissed allegations of human rights violations.
9 February 2017	**Military Investigation Committee I**	5 members, Chair Aye Win (military)	Rejected allegations of human rights violations. (Found evidence of a minor theft and beating, which were prosecuted.)

Table 5.1 (*cont.*)

Year Established	Name (Investigations in Bold)	Participants	Scope/Recommendations
12 February 2017	**Police Departmental Inquiry** (Ministry of Home Affairs)	5 members, Chair Win Tun (police)	5 police officials to investigate allegations of abuse, no conclusive report, though police filmed beating civilians were sentenced.
13 October 2017	Union Enterprise for Humanitarian Assistance, Resettlement and Development in Rakhine	Chair Aung San Suu Kyi	Order No. 86/2017. Development policy: partnership among the government, people, private sector, local non-governmental organizations and civil society organizations, development partners, UN agencies and international non-governmental organizations.
13 October 2017	**Military Investigation Committee II**	Chair Aye Win (military)	Rejected allegations of human rights violations.
14 December 2017	Advisory Commission Board on Rakhine State	10 members, Chaired by Surakiart Sathirathai (Thailand) (Bill Richardson (US) later resigned)	Development policy. Advise on the implementation of the Kofi Annan-led Advisory Commission's recommendations (not investigating human rights violations).

Date		Members	Notes
30 July 2018	**Independent Commission of Enquiry**	4 members, Chair Rosario Manalo (Philippines), Kenzo Oshima (Japan), 2 nationals.	Possible criminal scope[a] though initial statements indicated a focus on accountability and reconciliation, peace and stability in Rakhine State.[b]
19 March 2019	**Military Investigative Court (III)**	3 members, Chair Myat Kyaw (military)	Responded to the Human Rights Watch, Amnesty International and UNFFM reports and following critique of the October 2017 investigation.

[a] (Independent Commission of Enquiry, 2014a).
[b] (Independent Commission of Enquiry, 2014b).

commanded the forces in Rakhine State and had been named as one of the key individuals responsible for violence against civilians, was dismissed from his position and another commander, Lt General Aung Kyaw Zaw, resigned in 2018. They are among seven individuals who have been the subject of sanctions by the European Union and other states but have not been prosecuted in Myanmar.

There are cases that show that it is possible for military perpetrators of serious crimes against civilians to be prosecuted by Myanmar's Courts Martial and, exceptionally, the civilian courts, but these are limited. The government has promoted responses to alleged international crimes that emphasise long-term stability and development and may still allow for restricted international participation and inquiry. However, these are not intended to lead to trials and the vast majority of cases of serious human rights violations, including alleged international crimes, have not involved prosecutions, with survivors and their families facing a range of risks in pursuing any cases. As the ICC Prosecutor argued, none of these initiatives have amounted (yet) to investigations or prosecutions that would deny the admissibility of an ICC case regarding the Rohingya under Article 17 of the Rome Statute. At this stage the impetus for related trials – as suggested by the UNFFM – 'must come from the international community' (Independent International Fact-Finding Mission on Myanmar, 2018: 1). Yet, for all the Myanmar government's official lack of participation in the ICC proceedings, these events do show that there are actors within Myanmar, including within the government, that are engaging with and attempting to adapt the norm of international criminal justice so as to promote particular arguments and institutions.

5.5   Conclusion

Internal instability, military control, periods of foreign intervention and sanctions, ethnic divisions, and development needs, have created a challenging environment for securing international criminal justice in Myanmar. Foreign states, international organisations, and civil society actors have attempted to influence Myanmar's approach to international criminal justice. The mechanisms for responding to international crimes in Myanmar reflect the prioritisation of stability, military control, development, and an attempt to assuage international criticism. Yet, they do not represent either the 'wholesale acceptance or rejection' of the international criminal justice norm in Myanmar (Acharya, 2004: 239).

To be sure, there has been no linear progression from rejecting the norm of international criminal justice towards acceptance, whether through acceding to the Rome Statute or socialisation by other means. Some might see Myanmar's 'isolation' as an explanation for the apparent rejection of the norm of international criminal justice (a lack of socialisation). Others may consider the Thein Sein and NLD governments to have 'stalled' – showing some signs of traversing a path towards prosecuting international crimes (including ratifying some treaties and initiating legal and institutional reforms), but then failing to 'progress', especially following the extreme violence in Rakhine State in 2016 and 2017. Certainly, government and military denials of wrongdoing and the lack of prosecutions or even charges for criminal conduct are indicative of rejecting that norm. Yet this would not fully capture responses to international crimes in Myanmar and their variation over *time*. Engagement with some countries and international organisations since 2011, and increasingly following the 2015 elections, was accompanied by Myanmar government statements about protecting the 'rule of law' and even the importance of accountability. This 'socialisation' was not associated with any obvious increased willingness to prosecute international crimes, or even the cessation of alleged perpetrations of such crimes. On the other hand, there have been, at times, apparent developments, such as reforms against forced labour, the release of some child soldiers and political prisoners, establishing the MNHRC, allowing some commemorations of past incidents of violence, public investigations occasionally revealing official wrongdoing, and limited prosecutions of military perpetrators.

Civil society actors have undertaken international criminal, human rights and humanitarian law dissemination work domestically, though this has been challenging in some contexts. As a result, NGOs have documented violations and engaged transnational civil society networks, foreign governments, intergovernmental organisations, diaspora, and community groups – often tailoring their arguments for these different audiences. Lawyers have also attempted to respond to serious crimes using Myanmar's existing laws and institutions, including its 2008 Constitution and via military courts. Further, civil society actors have responded to concerns about Myanmar's stability by framing international criminal justice or other transitional justice initiatives as being necessary to foster peace and the 'rule of law'. The relationship between time and justice is understood as related and complicated, because 'without having accountability it will be difficult to stop future violations', but 'it is difficult to ask for [accountability] for past violations'.[92]

These activities sometimes support doubts about the utility of *spatial* distinctions between 'local' and 'international' actors and initiatives, such as where international NGOs fund community reconciliation initiatives or local lawyers pursue the 'rule of law'. On the other hand, certain groups or individuals from Myanmar are more able to access training and consultation opportunities than others – reflected in concerns about the marginal utility of additional seminars for those who already 'know that conflict is not good' (see Section 5.3.3). Different individuals, including within different ethnic groups, may have different or even conflicting understandings of international criminal justice. As anthropologist Patrick Falvey puts it, there is a 'need to take a nuanced view of "the local"' in Myanmar (Falvey, 2010: 266). International criminal justice mechanisms are not designed to take such nuances into account, with the ICC pursuing only crimes partly committed in Bangladesh– consequently focused on relatively recent violence in Rakhine State and particularly against the Rohingya.

According to the localisation theory, 'credible local actors' can highlight links between existing and potential practices that 'make a global norm appear local', including through framing the international norm in more acceptable ways (Acharya, 2004: 251). However, where further adaptation of the norm could provide 'scope for some elements of an existing norm hierarchy to receive wider external recognition through its association with the foreign norm' – that is, for these elements to be 'amplified', this may lead to 'new instruments and practices ... in which local influences remain highly visible' (Acharya, 2004: 251). In Myanmar, the government has established institutions such as the MNHRC and multiple investigative mechanisms that aim to amplify concerns about stability and development, through employing language about accountability, evidence, and the rule of law. Within civil society, some actors have also aimed to reduce some of the barriers to securing international criminal justice through addressing potential investors to respond to Myanmar's development priorities, prioritising rule of law programmes that reform institutions, and encouraging peaceful community relationships and socio-economic rights to secure internal stability. Such projects do not reject international criminal justice 'wholesale', although they may

[92] Interview M10.

avoid 'international criminal justice' terminology or the topic of prosecutions. Many recognise or hope that rule of law and 'grassroots' programs could be precursors for future prosecutions, while others caution that 'top-down' drivers of violence must remain a key focus. Yet, community-developed responses are likely to involve reconstructing ideas about international criminal justice and often have preventative and reform aspects, rather than simply adopting the norm of prosecuting international crimes with international involvement. Such strategies have the potential to generate diverse and dynamic understandings of 'international criminal justice' across Myanmar.

These approaches recognise that international norms do not only flow in one *direction* (from 'international' to 'local'). One activist believes that the military regime formerly 'realised that they couldn't survive' and also changed 'because of global politics and international pressure and domestic pressure and the economic situation'.[93] In other words, there were multiple factors at play. Since then, Myanmar's representatives have not accepted the applicability of the international criminal justice norm in Myanmar due to international pressure or rejected it because of a lack of international influence. Influential states such as China, India, Japan, and most ASEAN states have not argued that Myanmar's leaders should pursue international crimes trials (Section 5.3.1), though others, particularly the EU, have at times – including via targeted sanctions. As described in Section 5.3.2, aspects of civil society have sometimes sought out this international pressure consistent with the 'boomerang' and 'spiral' frameworks (Section 2.2, Chapter 2). Yet, even when international interest in prosecutions waned around the time that the NLD successfully formed government, NGOs in Myanmar documented crimes and pursued domestic legal avenues. They have continued to do so as international calls for prosecutions concerning the Rohingya re-escalated.

Claims that the potential referral of the situation in Myanmar to the ICC alarmed military leaders in 2008–10 (Section 5.2.2) and the response to the ICC's attention in 2018 and 2019 do suggest that the ICC has some impact upon the government, but not to encourage the 'local' acceptance of the international norm. In fact, one consequence may have been to provide a vocabulary concerning evidence and accountability that is used to diminish any wrongdoing, or even to offer an axis for NLD-military alignment. ICC prosecutions are unlikely to address most crimes and it is

---

[93] Interview M10.

unclear how its proceedings might assist activists to work within Myanmar's courts or foster community trust-building (see Sarkin, 2000; Pedersen, 2018; MacLean, 2019), as they seek to establish the preconditions for helpful responses to international crimes – working day-to-day in diverse settings. Some adaptive approaches, including focusing on long-term development as the core response to atrocities, cannot fulfil the norm of international criminal justice alone. Yet, documentation and other transitional justice approaches drawn from meaningful consultation might have the potential to lead, if not to prosecutions, then to productive spheres for debate and engagement between different ideas and actors. These initiatives stem from activities throughout and beyond Myanmar, not only from the transmission of an international norm to that space.

While Myanmar might be placed at the beginning of a spectrum leading from rejection towards the implementation and enforcement of international criminal law, this would not capture the multiple ways in which many different actors are working towards securing justice for international crimes. The localisation framework helps to explain why some scholars view truth commissions or non-criminal transitional justice mechanisms as more likely than trials in Myanmar (e.g. Dukalskis, 2015), since these might better fulfil the stability, development, and other socio-economic priorities (including institutional reform) found in this context. Yet this analysis also presents challenges for localisation, since it reveals a non-progressive picture of engagement with norms, in which actors are not readily categorised as 'local' or 'international', and in which norms can be constructed and promoted in various directions. We can see investigations that deny much serious wrongdoing, but lead to prosecutions of mostly lower-level perpetrators, the promotion of investment and development to resolve past and prevent future violence, a limited role for the ICC (despite the media and political emphasis placed upon its activities), and continued attempts at Constitutional and military reform – alongside diverse community-driven truth-telling, artistic and reconciliation-oriented responses to violence. These may not meet the full requirements of the norm of international criminal justice, but involve ongoing reconstruction of the legal and institutional framework it promotes.

6

Adapting International Criminal Justice in Southeast Asia

6.1 Introduction

This book has explored how states in Southeast Asia, especially Cambodia, the Philippines, Indonesia, and Myanmar, have engaged with the concept of international criminal justice and established laws and institutions to investigate or prosecute international crimes. Drawing on examples, including from the rest of Southeast Asia where relevant and illustrative, we now analyse whether those states have accepted, rejected, or adapted ideas about international criminal justice, and consider what implications that might have in theory and practice.

There has been significant engagement with international criminal law in Southeast Asia. Approaches towards international criminal justice are adapted dynamically over time, across different spaces (not clearly delineated as local/international), and in varying directions (outside-in/inside-out). This has implications for those advocating for international criminal justice in Southeast Asia, including for the development and implementation of relevant legal frameworks.

6.2 Localising International Criminal Justice in Southeast Asia

Various theories, often drawn from the international relations field, have explained how and why states comply with international norms. These include constructivist frameworks that consider how social structures and identities construct ideas about what is appropriate behaviour. Such approaches sometimes suggest a temporal aspect to the diffusion of norms, with states ideally progressing from rejecting an external idea towards accepting it, possibly by ratifying an international treaty and internalising its principles over time. They may also apply spatial divisions to help explain how differently located actors accept (or reject) 'local' or 'international' ideas. Finally, because it has analysed the spread of international ideas across the world – and asked why states might decide to comply with them – much constructivist research has considered how ideas flow in a direction from international actors and organisations towards local recipients.

In the field of international criminal justice, these aspects suggest that states might ideally be socialised towards being included within the international criminal justice 'project' (Section 1.2, Chapter 1) (Mégret, 2014), by ratifying international treaties such as the Rome Statute or (at least) adopting international crimes laws that closely replicate the Statute – and ideally using them to prosecute international crimes, often with international involvement. To some degree, alternative responses to serious and widespread crimes have been 'regarded with suspicion' by international criminal lawyers (Stahn, 2015: 48), although the related area of transitional justice incorporates a wider set of processes addressing international crimes, such as truth commissions, for example. Moreover, a 'local turn' has promoted the integration of community concerns into international criminal justice responses. However, such perspectives have also been critiqued for overly delimiting the global from the local and potentially 'romanticising' the latter (Björkdahl et al., 2016; Kochanski, 2018).

On the other hand, identifying the significance of the 'divide between "inside" and "outside"' 'provides a discursive space' to accommodate power dynamics and the tensions between these spaces – and counters managerial or 'top down' approaches (Stahn, 2015: 47). Acharya's localisation framework and broader 'norm circulation' approach draws attention to how credible local actors reframe and reconstruct ideas in light of local experience – for example by contesting and invoking aspects of sovereignty and stability in relation to international criminal justice (Acharya, 2013). Thus, both international and local norms are modified and converge and ideas might be 'localised', rather than either accepted in the 'normalised' form or completely rejected. In this manner, localisation seeks to challenge external/global/good, internal/local/bad equations (Acharya, 2014: 185), as well as assumptions about the relative influence of local and international actors. The implementation of ideas about international criminal justice reveals the impact of tensions between different ideas and actors.

6.2.1   Time: Dynamic and Non-linear

States in Southeast Asia have not fully accepted the norm of international criminal justice over time, but they have not entirely rejected it, either.

We have focused on Cambodia, Indonesia, the Philippines, and Myanmar, though the UN has not established international tribunals similar to the ICTY or ICTR anywhere in Southeast Asia. Yet some states, including non-parties to the Rome Statute, have established criminal institutions and other transitional justice procedures, adopted domestic legislation addressing international crimes, and/or investigated and prosecuted international crimes within national legal systems.

These initiatives build on a history of engagement with international criminal law in Asia, including via the IMTFE and other post–World War II trials. While states in Southeast Asia are diverse, many share recollections of the politicised nature of international criminal justice, including selective and procedurally challenged World War II war crimes prosecutions and (at least initially) a lack of international, particularly 'Western', interest in prosecuting crimes perpetrated during the Cold War. Since that period, states in Southeast Asia have promoted the use of domestic, rather than external, mechanisms to prosecute international crimes, or for international prosecutions to take place with state consent, with reference to the principle of sovereignty.

Other themes are also evident. Experiences of internal divisions and armed conflict have led stability and the relationship between prosecutions and maintaining peace to be prominent among the case study states. Histories of conflict mean that much of the region hosts powerful militaries, often with the capacity to wield significant political and economic pressure, but also influential religious and other civil society groups that have delivered community services. The Asian Crisis, and, for example, Marcos' and General Ne Win's failed economic strategies, have led many regional states to seek foreign development assistance or investment at times and cite capacity issues as a barrier towards adopting international criminal justice laws, though many states especially in more recent years (such as Malaysia or Singapore) are not reliant upon foreign aid. Principles of human rights and the rule of law are prominent across the region, often included in states' Constitutions and encouraged by development programmes, but are also contested. Discussion of victims' needs and the potential for various types of reparations recur in NGO reports and interviews across Southeast Asia, including in the four states this book has examined in more depth.

Experiences within other regions may have been similar, though this is a question for other comparative research (see Clarke, 2009; Nouwen, 2013; Clark, 2018). However, these themes also vary across Southeast Asia. For example, at a high level, human rights and democracy had greater prominence in discussions about responding to international crimes in the Philippines and Indonesia. In Indonesia, notions of national unity and sovereignty were pronounced, while the rule of law and development issues (including having other priorities) featured in Myanmar and Cambodia. Gender-based violations and race or ethnicity are a common theme of NGO documents concerning Myanmar. All of these issues have been drawn upon (and contested) by various groups, though the prominence of these themes alters for different actors and in response to evolving domestic political circumstances.

Indeed, while states' approaches to international criminal law are embedded in historic experiences, their laws and institutions for prosecuting past and prospective international crimes fail to represent outcomes of 'the linear, progressive time that implicitly underwrites much of the constructivist norms scholarship' (Epstein, 2014: 300).[1] Some states that have 'rejected' the Rome Statute do not necessarily oppose the ICC, or the prosecution of international crimes in principle, but may hold various reasons for not ratifying. Officials from some non-party states, like Indonesia, have still engaged with principles of international criminal justice, such as by participating in the Rome negotiations, attending educational sessions about the Statute, or adopting national international crimes laws. Other states' officials, such as in Lao PDR or Singapore, have also not significantly progressed their engagement with international criminal institutions in recent years, but have not expressed increasing opposition, either. Non-party states can still have laws for prosecuting international crimes or pursue non-judicial responses via official and civil society mechanisms. There may, as in Indonesia, the Philippines, Malaysia, Myanmar, Timor-Leste, and Thailand, be scope for National Human Rights Institutions (or similar bodies) to investigate and document alleged crimes, or for civil society actors to propose alternative transitional justice mechanisms, and for some perpetrators to potentially find accountability within the domestic legal system.

States with domestic international crimes legislation like Cambodia, Indonesia, the Philippines, or Vietnam are not necessarily progressing from a position of rejecting international criminal justice towards acceptance, either. Penal Code provisions and institutional reform projects may

---

[1] In relation to the regional human rights mechanisms in Southeast Asia, Interview R3 commented that 'our ways [are] rather like in a zig zag and [are a] long path'. Similarly, Interview M1 noted that 'ASEAN used to be zig zagging, but zig zagging in a forward manner', whereas now on 'many of these key issues it looks like it's moving backwards'.

be forward focused and non-retrospective, but undermined by persisting power structures or judicial reform issues, and discredited by impunity for past violations. Incorporating principles of peace and stability into notions of international criminal justice may promote the use of amnesties, immunities, and pardons for some perpetrators. International crimes legislation can broaden the terms of the Rome Statute (as in the Philippines and Timor-Leste), but also narrow the potential scope for convicting perpetrators compared to other legislation, by including additional elements to prove. Such legislation may not lead to fairer (or any) trials or prevent human rights violations. The ECCC and Special Panels are internationalised tribunals with limited temporal, personal, and subject-matter jurisdiction, while convictions under Indonesia's Law 26/2000 were overturned. These mechanisms have all been criticised as involving selective prosecutions, restricted resources, and fair trial concerns, despite arguably representing the implementation of international crimes laws. These complexities prevent the identification of sequenced stages of reform towards one normalised ideal and suggest that approaches to international criminal law have multiple temporal dimensions.

Different administrations also take varied positions at different times towards prosecuting different international crimes. Cambodia established the ECCC, was an early party to the Rome Statute, and has been the focus of significant international rule of law development work and advocacy. On the other hand, there have been no convictions for international crimes based on Cambodia's Criminal Code and accountability for contemporary serious human rights violations alleged to amount to international crimes is limited (at best). Decisions can be revisited, or run in parallel, as alternative responses to international crimes are pursued. For example, in 2016, debates about amending Law 26/2000 coincided with proposals to incorporate international crimes into Indonesia's revised Criminal Code (with prospective operation), advocacy for reforming the military Criminal Code, and a national symposium to review past human rights violations. Eight years after first announcing an intention to accede to the Rome Statute, Malaysia's officials did so, then retracted that decision a month later. Myanmar's officials have established inquiries with international involvement to find 'evidence' in Rakhine State, while denying that crimes occurred, refusing to name a 'Rohingya' people and escalating military operations elsewhere. Official positions can also change as domestic political contexts alter – compare the approaches of Benigno Aquino III and Rodrigo Duterte in the Philippines and during Jokowi's presidency in Indonesia – and not change as much as some hoped, as under the NLD government in Myanmar. States and civil society actors also respond (or not) to 'past' crimes – such as under Suharto in Indonesia, DK in Cambodia, or Marcos in the Philippines – while debating different approaches for ongoing or prospective crimes. These experiences lend support to Zimmerman's insight that debates and choices about international and local norms recur as new problems arise (including new incidents of violence), when laws are proposed, as legislation is passed, and again as efforts are made to enforce new instruments (Betts & Orchard, 2014; Zimmermann, 2016).

Does this lack of linear progression mean there will be no 'justice'? Acharya posits that 'over the long term, localization may produce an incremental shift toward fundamental change or norm displacement' as resistance to 'new norms may weaken' (Acharya, 2004: 253). It might be argued that the process of localising international criminal justice in Southeast Asia is not yet sufficiently 'long term' to produce a shift towards acceptance. However, at this stage, processes of localisation are not necessarily positive – or entirely negative – from the perspective of those interested in 'ending impunity'. They simply reflect particular, changing, realities. Rather than norm entrepreneurs socialising states into internalising international norms over time, both before and after international crimes laws are adopted, actors across Southeast Asia (and beyond) debate and reconstruct the norm of international criminal justice in dynamic ways. Still, there is a pattern to this engagement. Debates tend to respond to historic and post-colonial experiences and priorities (including sovereignty, stability and development concerns); diverse international influence; domestic political changes; and changing spaces for and methods of civil society advocacy. None of these is fixed, uncontested, or necessarily likely to encourage states to shift towards accepting international norms over time, especially when operating in combination. Instead, responding to international crimes is a dynamic and continuing debate between various actors and ideas. The practical implications of this observation are taken up in Section 6.4.

6.2.2   Space: Tensions between Different Ideas and Actors

Different actors take diverse and changing positions towards international criminal justice in Southeast Asia. Some have pursued impartial trials that respect the international criminal justice norm, or funded related projects that might lead to such trials, while others have taken little interest, opposed prosecutions, or pursued related aims. There are several points to make about the 'spaces' called 'international' and 'local' in relation to international criminal justice in Southeast Asia, demonstrated at least in relation to Cambodia, Indonesia, the Philippines, and Myanmar, though potentially also in other states.

The first point is that the preferences and arguments of each of these spatial categories is diverse. International actors do play an important, but uneven, role in arguments about prosecuting international crimes. Foreign states and international organisations have monitored and critiqued the commission of international crimes in some states in Southeast Asia and proposed the establishment of 'impartial', 'independent', preferably efficient and international criminal mechanisms. For example, a Group of Experts appointed by the UN, UN agencies, and international NGOs advocated for international control over DK trials. Similarly, the UN arranged the establishment of the Special Panels and it is unlikely that Indonesia would have adopted Law 26/2000 were it not for the international attention directed towards violence in East Timor. The Myanmar UNFFM also recommended independent and impartial, international prosecutions.

Other projects funded by foreign states or international organisations may not directly or overtly seek international crimes prosecutions, but target institutional, including judicial, reform, often employing or training nationals of the countries they are working in. Such initiatives are sometimes termed 'capacity building' and may involve the socialisation of international justice norms related to the principle of complementarity, at least in a general sense (see Bergsmo et al., 2010; Mégret, 2011). For instance, the ICRC has facilitated the drafting of national international crimes legislation (as in the Philippines). Internationally driven projects also respond to 'local' issues through reframing projects that might contribute to international criminal justice with reference to 'rule of law', development, judicial reform, human rights, stability, or other relevant language. The UN and some states also support community-driven reconciliation and justice activities, including in Cambodia (Westoby, 2013; European Union, 2014a; TPO Cambodia, 2015) and Myanmar (European Commission, 2016; USAID, 2019). This may reflect global trends towards 'hybrid' projects that combine local and international input, but which still promote particular international norms.[2]

---

[2] For a discussion concerning hybridity in the peacebuilding space, see (Richmond, 2011). On the relationship between the peacebuilding notion of hybridity and localisation, see (Zimmermann, 2016: 104).

However, states and organisations outside of Southeast Asia have not always promoted the prosecution of international crimes perpetrated within the region. Until the early 2000s there was little international appetite for the Security Council to establish mechanisms similar to the ICTY or ICTR to consider crimes in Cambodia or East Timor. The United States contributed to the establishment of the ECCC, but also asked Southeast Asian states to sign BIAs to agree not to hand over nationals to the ICC.[3] After Myanmar's democratic 'transition' accelerated in 2011, states did not repeat earlier calls for the ICC to prosecute international crimes committed there until violence escalated in 2016–17. China, Russia, and others have periodically demonstrated that they do not promote ICC prosecutions in the region.

Further, regional states' approaches towards international criminal justice are diverse. There has been some interaction among Southeast Asian states on the issue of international criminal justice, often facilitated by CICC or Parliamentarians for Global Action (PGA) (e.g. Acedillo, 2016). However, a regional consensus position on international criminal justice is yet to emerge. In contrast to the public comments made by the African Union, often to oppose the ICC, ASEAN statements regarding the ICC are relatively rare, although in 2003 ASEAN acknowledged the establishment of the ICC as 'a positive development' (ASEAN, 2003). This may be partly due to the ICC's relative lack of attention towards Southeast Asia (especially until 2016), as well as ASEAN's preference for non-interference and for consultative decision-making within the institution. ASEAN bodies such as the ASEAN Intergovernmental Commission on Human Rights (AICHR) may provide forums for promoting international criminal justice in future (see Section 6.4), but in general ASEAN has favoured a 'constructive engagement' approach to the commission of serious violations of human rights and international crimes across the region, rather than directly advocating for prosecutions (see Kapur 2013; Nasu, 2013).

Political leaders and other official actors have also presented varied arguments about prosecuting international crimes within states. Certain senators in the Philippines strongly advocated for the passage of the IHL Act and ratification of the Rome Statute, despite the unwillingness of the

---

[3] Interview R2: 'I think ... [BIAs are] one of the reasons as well that would probably be an obstacle to contribute to accountability'.

executive government under Arroyo. One representative of an international organisation has observed that generally in regional states:

> the military tends to know a lot more about what we're talking about . . .
> and have much more practical reasons for and against [ratifying or
> implementing treaties] . . . the Attorney-Generals chambers tend to be
> very good international lawyers . . . and they . . . come up with good legal
> arguments for and against. The Ministry of Foreign Affairs: . . . It's trying
> to work out which other countries have done different things.[4]

These differences may be exacerbated by rotation within (especially foreign) ministries,[5] a lack of clarity about relative ministerial responsibilities, and political changes – including at the conclusion of armed conflict.

Consistent with the localisation framework, diverse 'civil society' actors
have developed adaptive approaches to responding to international
crimes within Southeast Asia – as demonstrated in the case study states.
In fact, analysing states' approaches to international criminal justice in
isolation would present an incomplete picture. For example, focusing only
on officials' opposition to the Case 003 and 004 trials in Cambodia could
suggest greater 'Cambodian' resistance towards international criminal
justice than is evident from the significant contribution of NGO actors
to the ECCC's victim participation process and outreach. Other non-state
actors might also be considered – such as the NDF and MILF in the
Philippines, which have declared their intention to abide by international
humanitarian law principles. One advantage of the localisation framework
is that it draws attention to these diverse 'local' perspectives as forming
potentially important components of the process of adapting norms.

Of course, civil society comprises heterogeneous actors with different
motivations. In Southeast Asia, there are some Government Organised
Non-Government Organisations (GONGOs) that represent government
interests, but other NGO representatives may also be aligned with political parties or affected by international donor priorities. Some groups
comprise current or former victims and survivors, such as IKOHI in
Indonesia or SELDA in the Philippines, or more formally represent
victims as in the case of Legal Aid of Cambodia, while others may have
a broader human rights advocacy role or operate across borders. Further,
engaging in debates about justice might also construct the identities of
the proponents (Epstein, 2014). For example, NGO actors in Indonesia,

---

[4] Interview R1.
[5] Interview R3.

Philippines, Malaysia, and Thailand have adopted critical engagement strategies.[6] Yet close collaboration can also raise the suspicions of other stakeholders. One regional advocate observed that the relationships she had established within a Southeast Asian state's foreign ministry had 'been quite valuable because I can criticise and my voice had been heard, but some people see this [as meaning that] I'm bought by the governments'.[7] It can also be difficult to balance conflicting messages. Officials may be encouraged to pursue international crimes legislation so as to avoid potential ICC prosecution via the operation of the complementarity principle, while victims are told that supporting such mechanisms would allow official crimes to be punished. Academics and lawyers within the region argue in favour of international criminal justice (ICS-CICC, 2008), but some also suggest reasons for exercising caution in relation to the ICC (Atmasasmita, 2006). Some NGOs prefer transitional justice and truth responses to prosecutions at different times. It is clear that there 'is no unified local. The "local" has many faces' and has many meanings – 'a country, a community, a group, a neighbour and so on' (Stahn, 2015: 46). Equally, there is no unified 'Western', 'international society' or 'global' perspective on prosecuting international crimes in Southeast Asia, though there may appear to be for those monitoring UN or international NGO reports. International states and organisations, authorities, and civil society representatives debate and reconstruct international criminal justice in diverse ways, though often drawing upon principles considered relevant for the particular geographic area.

The second issue that follows is that the divisions *between* 'local' and 'international' groups and actors are porous and even artificial, though sometimes conceptually helpful. Such distinctions recognise that proximity to events and locations, including crime sites or mass graves, can provide specific expertise or points of view (Epstein, 2014; Pohlman, 2015). However, Acharya refers to 'the *divide* between transnational actors who operate across continents and time zones and local actors . . . who are situated within single time zones and marginalized locations' (Acharya, 2012a, emphasis added). In reality, characterising a particular group or individual or action as 'local' or 'global/international' is *subjective*, in the sense that it depends on one's perspective (Merry, 2006; Björkdahl et al., 2016; Buckley-Zistel, 2016; Ullrich, 2016). The focus here on the norm of international criminal justice derived from The Hague has led national

---

[6] Interviews I5; I9; P4; R1; R2.
[7] Interview R3.

authorities and NGOs to be presented as 'local' by comparison. However, just as governments in Indonesia and Myanmar have (to some degree) decentralised authority, NGOs may be far removed from stakeholder communities, especially those in remote areas. KontraS in Indonesia attempts to combat this via internship programmes involving young people from remote locations, while Karapatan and other organisations in the Philippines consult closely with community leaders. Similarly, NGO representatives might consider themselves 'local' (Ullrich, 2016), but be subject to 'international donor imperatives that delimit the power that their own vernacular knowledge forms can have in shaping solutions' (Clarke, 2009: 135), for example, when Cambodian lawyers lost funding to represent ECCC civil parties (Cuddy, 2015). International legal groups produced Article 15 communication inviting the ICC Prosecutor to investigate events in Cambodia 'on behalf of victims' (Global Diligence, 2016) and/or the political opposition. In these circumstances, whether a group or action appears 'local' or 'international' may depend on the observer's perspective.

Partly because of this subjectivity, defining a group or an idea as 'local' is *practically* difficult. Actors often fail to represent particular categories. Judge Raul Pangalangan, the Philippines' nominated ICC judge, has been a member of the government, NGOs, academia, media, and legal profession, sometimes at the same time. European Union experts are seconded to 'local' NGOs to work alongside 'locals' and international expatriates in Cambodia. Cambodian group DC-Cam collaborates with ND-Burma. Indeed, many NGOs cooperate, including through networks and coalitions. Myanmar NGOs operate from the Thailand border. Influential diaspora communities participate in ECCC trials as civil parties, may organise events such as the IPT65, or advocate for the ICC to prosecute crimes in Myanmar. In this way, 'local and global are inherently related to each other rather than mutually exclusive' (Buckley-Zistel, 2016: 25). These arrangements can represent 'transnational advocacy networks' but (as explored shortly) do not always include all 'locals' or 'international' actors and may *not* be 'bound together by shared values, a common discourse, and dense exchanges of information and services' (Keck & Sikkink 1998: 2).

This demonstrates the complexity involved in determining which *ideas* and *practices* are local, as opposed to international (Orford, 1997; Acharya, 2011, 2013; Deitelhoff & Zimmermann, 2016). A spatial awareness cautions that in diverse situations community perspectives of violence and its resolution may (and perhaps often do) differ from the prescriptions offered by the international criminal justice framework.

Yet one activist argued that 'there seems to be this assumption it's not part of our culture to want justice, but then this assumption seems to be more clearly articulated amongst diplomats from the West'.[8] Such a 'Western' perception casts 'local'[9] conceptions of justice in opposition to the international norm.[10] Indeed, the array of legal and traditional rules of engagement and conflict resolution mechanisms in Southeast Asian states might only be grouped together as 'local' when compared to the Rome Statute (see Agus, 1999; Shaw et al., 2010; Linton et al., 2019). The practice of *nahe biti bo'ot* (spreading the large mat) and *lisan* procedures in Timor-Leste are different from the '*islah*' procedure in parts of Indonesia. Various procedures are labelled 'local' for their contrast to the 'non-local' international criminal justice norm. In this way, local and global principles and activities are defined with reference to the other; they are mutually constitutive.

Moreover, apparently 'local' norms may arise from complex sources. For example, many Southeast Asian states have sought to protect their sovereignty from the exercise of ICC jurisdiction. This concern, shared by states in other regions, may be perceived as conflicting with the norm of international criminal justice (Toon, 2004; Kapur, 2013; Findlay, 2014). As Cryer puts it: 'Generally, international criminal law scholars see sovereignty as the enemy' (Cryer, 2005a: 980). Some have responded to this lack of 'fit' through reframing, such as by presenting the principle of complementarity as consistent with state sovereignty (see Kapur, 2013). Similarly, in the Philippines, NGOs suggested that a historic appreciation for protecting human rights would be enhanced by passing international crimes laws and ratifying the Rome Statute. Neither human rights nor sovereignty are only 'local' or (say) 'Western' norms – arguably, that is why they are 'norms' (Acharya, 2011). Yet, the tendency of actors in Indonesia or the Philippines to choose to draw upon these principles is derived from experiences arising within those places. Thus, experiences of international criminal justice found within Southeast Asia demonstrate that categories such as global and local can be useful, but are better viewed as mutually constitutive and dynamic points of perspective, rather than as defined and fixed labels (Buckley-Zistel, 2016).

---

[8] Interview M1.
[9] See (Deitelhoff & Zimmermann), 2014 regarding the problematic nature of the terms 'Western' and 'local'.
[10] E.g. 'different sense of justice that we have in the West': indented quote in Section 2.3.4, Chapter 2, Interview C2.

Importantly, power and material *contexts* intersect with spatial categories. Colonial histories have generated particular experiences of violence and impunity within boundaries of regional states that were defined during occupation (Mahmud, 2007). Historic conflicts and economic conditions in certain places might increase the relative importance of international assistance, for example, as in Cambodia and Timor-Leste, which both became sites for international crimes trials. National laws are adopted by geographically defined states alongside those of their provinces and municipalities, within which different individuals have more or less connection to sites of violence – and where actors' mobility across local, regional, or international scales is uneven. In reality, while it is difficult to define some actors in Southeast Asia as 'local' or 'international', or even 'regional', this does not mean that everyone has access to either characterisation, all the time. Some individuals move between provinces and across the world, as where Indonesian activists invite representatives of the Argentinian NGO Mothers of the Plaza de Mayo to Indonesia, certain Myanmar nationals travel to South Africa to discuss truth and reconciliation options, Cambodian NGO representatives attend the ICC ASP, and activists research and communicate online. In addition, social movements that target the general public (including via social media) play an increasing role in responding to (though also inciting) violence (Pohlman, 2016; see Gready & Robins, 2017). However, even if spatial divisions are social constructs, they can still constrain. This was reflected in a Myanmar activist's complaint that the same 'educated' 'famous . . . CSO leaders', who are already aware that conflict is 'not good' attend meetings and conferences in Asia on that subject.[11] In other words, access to global forums such as the ASP may be relatively restricted for many, even if new institutions such as National Human Rights Institutions, development projects, and online networks provide avenues to create 'new spaces that cut across old barriers' (Buckley-Zistel, 2016: 28).

Identifying these constraints as aspects of power intersecting with socially constructed (generally post-colonial) spaces, rather than (only) consequences of actors being geographically located as either 'local' or 'international', is crucial for at least two reasons. First, it helps to reveal how barriers and opportunities can be compounded across geographic lines. That is, community actors may face restrictions from local, national, and international sources – both past and evolving, even if

---

[11] Interview M8, section 5.3.4.

these also present diverse settings for advocacy. Second, to return to an insight of the localisation framework, recognising that some may find it difficult to move beyond 'local' settings does not suggest that such actors lack agency – or that globalised power divisions are inevitable, evenly spread, or necessary.[12] Yet it also serves as a reminder that local actors disagree, just as international organisations and states do. Softening localisation's spatial divisions allows scope to appreciate other similarities and differences between different actors and groups, including their varying challenges and opportunities – and the ways they seek to change them. This helps to avoid equating a failure to prosecute international crimes with 'local' unwillingness or lack of capacity to support international justice norms without further questioning.

6.2.3   Direction: The Movement of Ideas

Activists and victims' representatives, lawyers, military leaders, journalists, politicians, and other state and non-state actors based – and sometimes moving – around the world engage in debates about international criminal justice. This suggests that ideas flow in multiple directions. On the other hand, we are still discussing the influence of 'norms' – specifically, the norm of international criminal justice (Weber, 2013). This was defined as having particular content related to prosecuting specific 'international' crimes, with an emphasis on international laws and institutions – though different actors reinterpret this idea and may offer alternative approaches towards it. This book therefore analysed states' international crimes legislation with reference to the Rome Statute and focused upon national laws adopted by states, although it also discussed non-state initiatives. As mentioned in Chapter 1, this was because the Rome Statute represents part of the 'normalised' approach to prosecuting international crimes, and therefore offers a useful comparison point for considering states' engagement with that norm.[13] It was also consistent

---

[12] Acharya suggests that the localisation, subsidiarity, and norm circulation concepts are relevant for 'marginalised' and 'less powerful' actors, thus recognising the importance of power. However, Acharya retains a distinction between 'global' and 'local' norms, actors, and 'levels', wherein the 'less powerful' are often the local actors, even if they hold agency, see (Acharya, 2013: 469).

[13] As discussed in Chapter 1, the Statute's provisions do not all represent customary international law. However, it is a focal point for actors seeking to implement international criminal law, especially Rome Statute parties.

with this book's focus on the *laws* and institutions for prosecuting international crimes in Southeast Asia. However, it has consequences.

Defining the 'norm' with reference to 'international' laws may imply that the Rome Statute provides the most important measure against which approaches to international criminal justice are to be judged. This demonstrates how '[l]ocal dimensions are typically considered through a vertical lens, which places the "international" at the centre and uses it as a benchmark against regional, domestic or local responses' (Stahn, 2015: 49). Similarly, some have suggested that the low level of ratifications of the Rome Statute indicates that regional states reject the norm of international criminal justice. In this way, the Statute can dominate debates about responding to international crimes and suggest a 'one-size-fits-all' response to heterogeneous contexts (Linton, 2005: 42). Instead, any analysis of how states and civil societies respond to international crimes should acknowledge the expansive influence of international normative orders. In particular, the focus of international criminal justice research upon the Rome Statute reflects the observation that 'the promotion of the global "fight against impunity" has taken on certain missionary features' (Stahn, 2015: 57). These include the notion that states should implement laws that are consistent with the Rome Statute, even though regional states may have felt that their preferences were not secured during the Rome negotiations (Clarke, 2009; Mégret, 2011).

To the extent that the Rome Statute does dominate legal responses to alleged international crimes in Southeast Asia (for the contrary view more shortly), that emphasis can have practical implications. For instance, prosecuting international crimes may require additional or different evidence compared with proving 'ordinary' criminal offences: crimes against humanity must be widespread or systematic; genocide requires proving specific intent (Cryer, 2005b). This may exacerbate existing witness security and evidentiary challenges in bringing charges within domestic legal systems. States in Southeast Asia have not typically adopted the ICC's Elements of Crimes into domestic legislation or modified their domestic criminal procedures or modes of liability in order to address international crimes. Prosecuting international crimes may therefore be more difficult than pursuing other criminal charges or non-criminal responses, including Constitutional remedies.

An ICC focus could even limit the potential avenues for prosecuting perpetrators of serious or widespread violence more generally. If the ICC is considered the primary institutional regime for responding to atrocities, official actors might argue that the ICC's lack of attention towards a particular incident suggests that international crimes were not committed (Drumbl, 2007; Nouwen & Werner, 2014). If international crimes are not proven or convictions are overturned, whether at the ICC or in domestic courts, perpetrators escape justice, victims might be left without remedy, and violence may continue. A focus on the Rome Statute crimes may indirectly limit the exploration of alternative charges or other responses, including those focused on state or corporate responsibility (Branch, 2010). This may occur even in non-party states through stifling creativity, for example, or because justice advocates focus their resources and attention on joining the ICC to the detriment of other projects. In fact, in states where the ICC is unlikely to have jurisdiction, it is arguably even more important to develop domestic criminal, or alternative, frameworks for responding to 'injustice'. All that said, it is not necessarily the ICC's 'fault' if the Rome Statute provides a focal point for discussions about international criminal law (Stahn, 2015). Yet as Stahn argues, the 'ICC does not directly proscribe how (sic) domestic justice should look like, nor does it have the power to enforce such a vision through regulatory action. But it actively shapes such choices, through narratives, policies and procedures' (Stahn, 2015: 57). In particular, the Rome Statute provides an important and influential model for states' international crimes legislation, even for non-parties.

Turning to the practice in Southeast Asia, civil society representatives, wherever based, have deliberately referred to the Rome Statute when advocating for the prosecution of international crimes committed in the region – and for broader purposes such as the prosecution of gender-based violence (PCICC, 2012b; Waller et al., 2014). As one advocate explained, international instruments can provide a 'torch' by which they seek to guide regional states, including to try and prevent them from adapting norms in undesirable ways.[14] Further, parliamentarians and others drafting legislation find in the Rome Statute a useful model for legislation.[15] Many NGOs rely on international donor funding and use seminars (sometimes with international sponsorship), regional advocacy networks such as Forum-Asia, and UN bodies to draw attention to the commission of international crimes and promote accountability. This

---

[14] Interview R3, e.g. in relation to human rights: 'So we want everywhere [to] have the same treatment, the same understanding . . . so, when we mention about "fire", it means "fire", here, there it's "fire", so that's what we want when we talk about human rights, it means human rights [is] like this, not like that.'

[15] Interview P1.

can resemble a 'boomerang' or 'spiral' approach (regarding Indonesia and the Philippines, see Jetschke, 1999), with national NGOs working with transnational advocacy networks to direct international pressure towards officials in their state, as in relation to the 1999 violence in East Timor, during the Marcos regime, military violence in Myanmar, or via the UPR process.

Civil society actors have also driven legislative and policy changes to encourage the acceptance of the international criminal justice norm from within states, often working with National Human Rights Institutions, international advisors, and political actors. Groups such as DC-Cam and ND-Burma have documented crimes, which represents a core activity for human rights–focused NGOs in the region that is often considered a prerequisite for any form of 'justice'. Across the region National Human Rights Institutions and human rights NGOs document, monitor, and report violations, not only via international processes, but also via public reports, commissions, and social and traditional media. Philippines-based actors drafted and encouraged lawmakers to adopt domestic international crimes legislation in 2009 and ratify the Rome Statute. Due to security challenges in openly advocating for international criminal justice, civil society actors in Myanmar have written complaints, documented violations and brought legal cases, while also working with international organisations and NGOs to publicise reports of international crimes. They have needed to be flexible in carrying out this work. They may face security risks, difficulties securing evidence, a lack of judicial independence, and resource constraints. Moreover, political conditions change, sometimes necessitating a new approach – or opening opportunities, such as the renewed focus on Rome Statute ratification when Benigno Aquino III was elected in the Philippines. One regional advocate likened 'human rights advocacy in this region' to 'trying to keep balance on the greasy log while juggling'.[16]

Being responsive includes efforts to 'borrow and frame' to establish the 'value' of international criminal justice and the Rome Statute 'for local audiences', as anticipated by the localisation framework (Acharya, 2004: 251). The Indonesian Civil Society Coalition for the ICC (ICSICC) argued that the Rome Statute protects Indonesian peacekeeping forces operating on the territory of states parties (ICSCICC, 2012), just as the Philippines Coalition (PCICC) mentioned that the Statute could benefit

---

[16] Interview M1.

Philippine workers living abroad (PCICC, 2008). Similarly, the downing of Malaysia Airlines Flight MH17 over Ukraine led advocates and politicians to to discuss the benefits of Malaysia acceding to the Rome Statute (Kulasegaran, 2015).[17] While officials are prompted to respect their international treaty obligations where relevant,[18] NGO representatives often prefer to refer to Constitutions and provisions under domestic criminal codes to highlight the alignment of the Rome Statute with domestic law. Civil society actors have also stressed the potential for justice to facilitate peace and development (for instance, in Kachin Peace Network's slogan, 'Justice Guarantees Lasting Peace' in Myanmar). These arguments respond to concerns such as sovereignty, politicisation, stability, and development that are often expressed by state and military representatives.

However, actors across the region have also moved beyond reframing notions of international criminal justice (for instance, to encourage ratification of the Rome Statute) towards adapting the concept more fundamentally. This may respond to changing conditions, or to a realisation that ICC-focused or legally oriented strategies are inadequate. It may be insufficient for those promoting international criminal justice to identify persistent barriers – such as sovereignty – and argue against these principles. A regional human rights advocate has found that the principle of 'non-interference can be [a] stumble block, but you just have to go around it because non-interference is here to stay'.[19]

In practice, such approaches may not be promoted, or even perceived by their proponents, as international criminal justice projects, even though they may seek related goals. They may derive from organisations across the region assisting victims of violence to articulate their own priorities. A human rights advocate explained that some 'Thai NGOs like to say, "we need to educate [some] people" – I don't like that because it is not the way we are doing things ... because not only [the public] can learn from us, we also can learn from them ... they actually need to educate us how [to] understand their own problem'.[20] Another regional activist pointed out that for those affected by serious atrocities, although 'we've got to empower them with their knowledge that they are entitled to protection, ... to justice', 'they know best what they want'.[21] Drawing

---

[17] Interview R1.
[18] Interview R1.
[19] Interview R3.
[20] Interview R3.
[21] Interview M1.

on consultations with groups affected by violence, some originally international criminal justice–oriented NGOs, including DC-Cam, PCICC,
and ND-Burma Timor-Leste's Judicial System Monitoring Programme
(JSMP), have broader scopes of advocacy. Communities have suggested
that enforcing existing domestic laws, taxation reform (ND-Burma,
2010), land reform (PCICC, 2012a), reparations (AJAR, 2015), or pursuing other economic and social rights (KKPK, 2014) are priorities. The
varied nature of the projects suggested by communities reflect the diverse
experiences of, and contexts in which, violence has taken place.

These debates involve a variety of perspectives and the outcomes are
evident in laws and mechanisms for responding to international crimes.
Six of the eleven states in Southeast Asia have legislation criminalising
more than one core international crime where committed on their
territories or by their citizens (see Table 1.1, Chapter 1; Appendix C).
These include current or former Rome Statute parties (Cambodia,
Timor-Leste, and the Philippines), but also Indonesia, Vietnam, and
Singapore. Further, all states in Southeast Asia have domestic Criminal
Codes that include crimes such as murder, rape, and slavery that could be
used to prosecute much underlying conduct that might otherwise be
considered an international crime. Thus, if the other judicial, political,
and resource precursors are in place, Southeast Asian states could potentially prosecute perpetrators under national legislation to ensure that they
do not enjoy complete impunity, though 'ordinary' crimes may lack the
symbolic force of war crimes, crimes against humanity, and genocide
trials (Drumbl, 2007).

For Cambodia, Timor-Leste, and the Philippines, the Rome Statute has
served as the model for laws for prosecuting crimes as war crimes, crimes
against humanity, and genocide. This might suggest that, rather than
representing a significant adaptation of the international norm, these
states have accepted the legal framework for international criminal justice represented by the Rome Statute. However, 'local' influences remain
visible. Whether or not the differences are favourable towards the norm
of international criminal justice is not always very clear. For instance, the
Philippines international crimes legislation currently combines international and national war crimes, but was nearly amended to reduce its
differences with the Rome Statute in ways that would have reduced the
scope of these crimes. The ECCC has Cambodian and international
personnel and is described as 'hybrid', 'internationalised', or 'localised',
but while it has secured important convictions and developed international jurisprudence, it is frequently criticised for failing to fulfil

international norms, just as the 1979 People's Revolutionary Tribunal (PRT) was. The point here is not just that the legal content of the norm of international criminal justice matters, but that the particular parts of that content, and their relative importance, are interpreted differently.

In Southeast Asia, some domestic laws also provide an avenue for promoting states' own judicial institutions and for 'amplifying' adapted conceptions of international criminal justice, in which local influences remain evident (Acharya, 2004). Southeast Asian states emphasised the principles of sovereignty and non-interference during the Rome Statute negotiations. Similar concerns were raised within other regions, including by African states, China, and the United States.[22] In some states in Southeast Asia the preservation of sovereignty has involved the promotion of domestic mechanisms and prosecutions. National international crimes prosecutions could reduce international 'interference' and allow states to manage their internal stability and development priorities, for example through jurisdictional limits. Yet, when viewed in the context of the selective World War II trials and histories of colonial occupation, a preference for national proceedings may not seem completely resistant towards the norm of international criminal justice, including in relation to the ICC's complementarity principle. Cambodia secured significant influence over the ECCC, Indonesia enacted Law 26/2000 and prefers to develop an 'Indonesian way' to resolve past human rights abuses (Wahyuningroem, 2016), and the Philippines adopted domestic international crimes legislation before ratifying the Rome Statute. Such national mechanisms do not conflict with every aspect of the norm of international criminal justice. For instance, they may be consistent with existing treaty obligations to prosecute crimes (such as under the Convention Against Torture) and the ICC's complementarity principle, but not reflect international norms concerning the conduct of trials or international involvement. In all cases, international crimes legislation applies alongside other criminal offences and usually requires the application of general criminal modes of liability and existing criminal procedures.

States in Southeast Asia have experienced internal conflicts and in the Philippines, Thailand, Myanmar, and Indonesia these disputes are not completely resolved, while new incidents of violence continue to emerge across the region. Peace and stability have, therefore, also featured in

---

[22] (United Nations, 1998), e.g. United States, 152, 361; Nigeria including regarding the African Union, 111; Mexico, 107; China, 75, 123–4; Pakistan, 78, 127, and including regarding Non-Aligned Movement states, 189; India, 86.

statements about international criminal justice. For instance, officials in the Philippines were interested in how the ICC could contribute to peace by being able to prosecute non-state actors, and IHL Act prosecutions have only been directed against such actors to date. Although armies in the region may incorporate international humanitarian law into their practices, military actors sometimes argue that investigating international crimes could contribute to internal unrest (The Jakarta Post, 2016). In this way, international criminal justice has often been cast as a set of procedures that is appropriate only where it facilitates national stability, supports the prominence of the military, and reinforces existing international and domestic legal commitments.

Some Southeast Asian states have established frameworks for potentially prosecuting international crimes beyond the Rome Statute, including mechanisms such as the ECCC and domestic legislative avenues, though still with a reliance upon international criminal law principles and texts. The ECCC has relatively narrow temporal and personal jurisdiction (as did the PRT), consistent with the interests of the international and Cambodian government negotiators, including to support Cambodia's sovereignty and stability. Similarly, the Special Panels represented the world's first internationalised tribunal, but had narrow jurisdiction, faced procedural complexities, resource limitations, political barriers, and difficulties incorporating community views and preferences, which were contributed to by the UN. Consistent with the significant involvement of international actors and willingness of the government to signal its acceptance of international norms (adaptation), however, the Penal Code in Timor-Leste includes definitions that expand upon the Rome Statute, for example, encompassing additional conduct that could constitute the crime of genocide.[23] Indonesia's Law 26/2000 refers only to genocide and crimes against humanity, excluding more frequently alleged crimes including war crimes and the crime against humanity of 'other inhumane acts'. Many states in Southeast Asia have also deployed amnesties as a measure to resolve conflicts and promote stability. Legislation, including in states parties to the Rome Statute, continues to provide avenues for future amnesties, pardons, and immunities for

---

[23] Article 123, Timor-Leste, Penal Code, Decree-Law No. 19/2009, e.g. 'Widespread confiscation or seizure of property owned by members of the group' and 'Prohibition of members of the group from carrying out certain trade, industrial or professional activities.'

international crimes, amplifying concerns about ensuring peace and stability.

As for the non-party states, they may indicate that they are progressing towards ensuring accountability or already respect consistent norms – albeit through domestic mechanisms. For example, Lao PDR has noted that it is researching the Rome Statute, while Indonesia mentioned its 'efforts to eradicate the practices of impunity', including through training and preventative activities, during its 2012 UPR (Indonesia, 2012b: para. 29). Vietnam's international crimes provisions in its Criminal Code were adopted well before the Rome Statute was negotiated and the provisions are more akin to those applied in Nuremberg and at the IMTFE. In Singapore, alongside an existing grave breaches provision to implement the Geneva Conventions, in 2007 a crime of genocide was incorporated into the Penal Code to implement its obligations under the Genocide Convention.

International criminal law norms propounded from Rome or The Hague therefore have had an important, but not exclusive, influence upon the development of international criminal law within Southeast Asia. Indeed, the ECCC's three trial judgments, the Special Panels' limited convictions, and other domestic proceedings for torture and other crimes under civilian or military criminal laws provide limited examples of criminal accountability for violence that could be charged as international crimes. Further, securing prosecutions (or convictions) under any legislation remains a significant challenge, even though charges of direct assault with murder have been laid in the Philippines, and terrorism in Indonesia, for example. Official investigators and National Human Rights Institutions, where they exist, confront legal, security, and practical barriers when investigating alleged criminal conduct and ensuring that prosecutions are carried out (either appropriately or at all). In Indonesia, the Attorney-General has failed to act on the recommendations for prosecution made by Komnas-HAM and related investigative bodies. Individuals have been charged after submitting complaints about military violence to the MNHRC.[24] It has been difficult to translate investigations by the Commission on Human Rights and other groups such as the Melo Commission into convictions in the Philippines. These organisations have, however, documented and publicised serious violations of human rights and alleged international crimes.

---

[24] E.g. the conviction of Brang Shawng for making false accusations against the Myanmar Army, (Ja Seng Ing Truth Finding Committee, 2014).

Where criminal proceedings are inaccessible or ineffective, constitutional provisions may provide another avenue for responding to international crimes. This has been a particularly active area in the Philippines. However, petitioners for constitutional remedies still face challenges in securing a satisfactory result. Similarly, activists in Myanmar have sought writs of habeas corpus and *mandamus* to respond to cases of arbitrary arrest, detention, or disappearance, but generally without success (Crouch, 2014a).

Finally, some states have developed non-criminal mechanisms for responding to international crimes that adapt notions of international criminal justice in light of domestic concerns, such as the Philippines' monitoring bodies, Myanmar's inquiry mechanisms, or the incorporation of customary dispute resolution practices by the Timor-Leste Commission for Reception, Truth, and Reconciliation and Community Reconciliation Process (CRP) (Kent, 2004, 2012, 2014; Drexler, 2010; Harris-Rimmer, 2010a). Drawing on a contested vocabulary of 'reconciliation', Indonesia organised a national symposium on the 1965 violence, more than ten years after the last international crimes prosecutions under Law 26/2000. Moreover, NGO networks have developed platforms for advocating for prosecutions that also allow victims to share their experiences, including via peoples' courts and public hearings, supported by social media, such as during KKPK's 'Year of Truth' (Wahyuningroem, 2013; Pohlman, 2016), the Cambodian Defenders Project Women's Hearings (Ye, 2014), Kuala Lumpur War Crimes Commission, and the IPT65. These have not necessarily received government support, but represent attempts to adapt to state resistance towards prosecutions and generate new mechanisms for responding to international crimes.

Other actors support community-developed projects that do not overtly promote international criminal justice, but draw on broader reconciliation and transitional justice norms as well as community traditions, often working with international partners. These include Buddhist-inspired reconciliation projects in Cambodia, community-based dialogues in the Philippines, and inter-ethnic forums in Myanmar. Alongside the Special Panels, the CRP in Timor-Leste reconstructed the customary practice of *nahe biti bo'ot* and *lisan* procedures 'anchored in a broad concept of reconciliation' (Kent, 2004; Drexler, 2010; Robins, 2012; Vieira, 2012: 8). To be clear, non-criminal processes do not fulfil the norm of international criminal justice, which requires (at least) genuine investigations of alleged crimes. None of these initiatives met all of their goals, and they should not be romanticised (Harris-Rimmer, 2010b; Drexler, 2013; Kent, 2014).[25] However, they demonstrate that various actors have drawn on varied contexts to adapt their responses to international crimes. Such activities move past seeking a convergence between 'local' and 'international' understandings of international criminal justice. Instead, they generate novel responses to international crimes or produce new spaces for advocacy that reach beyond prosecutions, even if some hope that they may eventually lead to them.

All of the legal mechanisms established to prosecute international crimes in the region have faced allegations that their procedures were politicised, involved selective temporal and personal jurisdiction, procedural inadequacies, witness security issues, and due process concerns. These criticisms are frequently directed to international criminal justice; they were raised historically in relation to the IMTFE and continue to be addressed towards the ICC (Sections 1.2–1.3, Chapter 1). However, they also reflect political debates concerning states' sovereignty, stability, development and justice systems, and victims' demands. Thus, states across the region have implemented mechanisms relating to international crimes that reflect and even amplify considerable domestic, as well as international, priorities. These activities move past rejecting or accepting international criminal justice to generate novel responses to international crimes and produce new spaces for advocacy. They respond to social structures and are drawn from experiences, but also seek to change structures through contesting particular themes and altering activities, languages, and audiences. The Rome Statute and ICC have relevance within Southeast Asia, but only where considered helpful for pursuing responses to alleged international crimes given the domestic context. To focus only (or mainly) on the influence of international actors and instruments upon responses to international crimes, or even according local actors a norm entrepreneurial role, neglects all actors' agency in promoting adapted approaches that, nevertheless, draw on particular aspects of the norm. The norm of international criminal justice is not just understood top-down or bottom-up, but is constantly reconstructed from multiple directions.

---

[25] Customary approaches may be opposed by affected individuals and perpetuate inequalities, including by excluding marginalised groups including women.

6.3 Adjusting for Time, Space, and Direction for International Criminal Justice

The analysis in the previous section has several implications for analysing how states respond to international crimes. First, the norm of international criminal justice will not necessarily be accepted through ratification and socialisation over time. Debates about international criminal justice can generate new laws and institutions, but apparent progress may not persist. Yet, rather than rejecting the international criminal justice norm entirely, different actors also reconstruct responses to international crimes, though not in a linear manner. Thus, resistance is not permanent or comprehensive within states. The 'liberal arrow of progress, then, is at odds with these circular, messy, lived temporalities' (Epstein, 2014: 306).

Second, actors operating within diverse and changing social structures may influence international criminal justice in ways that cut across local and international divisions. Resource constraints, power hierarchies, and the ability to access forums for influencing lawmakers might affect different stakeholders' approaches towards international criminal justice. These structural factors may arise from geographic locations that might be termed 'local' or 'international'. However, they are not confined to spatial categories and may have differential impact. Recognising this complexity avoids characterising the region as an international laggard without appreciating the initiatives for pursuing justice that already exist, as well as barriers and opportunities that may extend across boundaries (Clarke, 2009). Grouping actors as 'local' or 'international' can help to reveal divergent understandings of international norms and highlight the importance of different contexts. However, these constructed spatial placeholders must not mask heterogeneity, the potential for movement across these categorisations, or other axes for tension between different actors (including via power structures and intersectional differences of sex, ethnicity, race, education, etc.). It may be more useful to understand stakeholder's potential influence over international crimes laws by considering their interests, arguments and access to various forums of debate and influence, while also recognising that these elements change.

Third, the mutability of temporal and spatial categorisations suggests that there is scope to investigate how these classifications interact in relation to international criminal law. Arguably 'to isolate the temporal from the spatial dimensions of human existence is problematic' (Valverde, 2015: 9). Instead, we can consider how norms might evolve or be contested in multiple directions (across time and space), by challenging assumptions of external-to-internal norm diffusion. It is beyond the scope of this book to analyse other possible space-time intersections within international criminal law, but two aspects can be raised. One is that, as social constructs, spatial labels such as 'local', 'international', national boundaries, and jurisdictional provisions may be a product of a particular time. That is, what is considered 'local' today is already contested, but may differ again in five or ten years' time. A court's geographic or temporal jurisdiction might also be decided differently at another time and in a different location. Further, the spatial elements of jurisdictions, or decisions about the appropriate location and personnel for 'internationalised' mechanisms, might shape perceptions of time – and transition (Hinton, 2018). It might be argued that international criminal law mechanisms, like penal codes, 'not only secure a spatially defined territory, but also act as a temporal hinge, one that performs the crucial role of *connecting* the past with the future, retribution with prevention' (Valverde, 2015: 12, emphasis added).

A related point concerns how narratives of the 'evolution' of international criminal justice involve accounts of events occurring in particular spaces *and* at certain times.[26] For instance, the dominant norm of international criminal justice might be presented as arising from an accumulation of events progressing from certain spaces and times – from, say, the Treaty of Versailles (or trial of von Hagenbach, or earlier), to Nuremberg and Tokyo from 1945–8, the ICTY's establishment, and Rome in 1998.[27] Likewise, a chronological account told today of Cambodia's progression from ratifying the Rome Statute, to adopting domestic international crimes legislation, to prosecuting international crimes at the ECCC replicates a familiar, linear, socialisation plot promoted since (arguably, at least) the 1998 Rome Conference. This book tells different stories, both in relation to Cambodia and elsewhere in Southeast Asia. For instance, international criminal law could be understood as being 'constituted, not by some inexorable surge towards 'global' justice but by th[e] opposition or movement between the domestic and the international' (Simpson, 2007: 34) and beyond. It therefore invites other 'genres', drawn from alternative perspectives of both space and

---

[26] Told by different observers situated in various spaces at different times.

[27] Whereas the 'history of war crimes law can be comprehended as a series of undulations between recourse to the administration of local justice and grand gestures towards the international rule of law', (Simpson, 2007: 33).

time.[28] These need not only focus on international or state activities. Instead, there is scope to examine how various actors engage state and non-state actors, including the general public, as well as non-state perpetrators of crimes, including corporations (Cloward, 2016).[29]

The fourth implication concerns the direction of influence. The Rome Statute and notions of international criminal justice have affected the way in which some states in Southeast Asia have responded to international crimes. Looking forward, as Stahn has argued, if 'states strengthen domestic systems primarily for the sake of adjudicating specific cases domestically [rather than at the ICC], reform efforts are geared towards ICC priorities rather than long-term domestic interests' (Stahn, 2015: 74). Historic experiences and power structures that encourage the adoption of 'international' mechanisms might restrict the avenues for communities to promote alternative legal and non-legal responses to international crimes.

On the other hand, until the relatively recent attention towards alleged crimes in the Philippines and Myanmar, Southeast Asia could be said to be experiencing the opposite of the ICC's alleged 'Africa bias' (ICC Office of the Prosecutor, 2015), in that the Court had dedicated very little attention to the region. This distance could actually have provided scope for different actors to adapt and develop innovative and context-driven responses to international crimes beyond the Rome Statute. It might also have conveyed the impression that the ICC would make a minimal contribution to civil society goals, whereas promoting international criminal justice requires resources that could be deployed elsewhere.

Structural influences, and perceptions of them, can also change. While economic disadvantage arising out of conflict, occupation or resource depletion may encourage states to seek international aid and investment associated with particular justice paradigms, donor priorities can alter just as states' reliance upon assistance can. Communities, parliamentarians, and other 'local' actors, including the military, have promoted quite different responses to international crimes drawing on arguments related to stability and sovereignty, alongside international states and organisations. The power to shape discourse about international criminal justice

---

[28] Recognising that none of us can 'occupy some God-like place from which to measure or to theorize temporality or spatialization', but that we my appreciate 'the different ways in which the processes and relations that make up the world are temporalized and spatialized', (Valverde, 2015: 32).

[29] Interviews C1; M1 regarding the importance of engaging the business community.

arises from multiple shifting sources. If 'the local and the global engage with each other, rather than one being dominated and imprinted upon the other' (Buckley-Zistel, 2016: 26), the potential influence of a range of actors located in diverse and dynamic positions must be taken into account when analysing international criminal justice. This provides scope to produce a variety of legislative (and non-criminal) models for responding to international crimes. It also raises the question: rather than analysing the transfer of the international criminal justice norm towards receptive states, how does one imagine international criminal law as a dynamic, non-located (yet cognisant of temporal-spatial structures) and multidirectional (plural) phenomenon? Or, removing the focus upon 'international criminal justice', how are ideas about how to respond to serious violence formed through the interaction of various actors across different times and spaces? This involves moving away from either 'local' *or* 'international' perspectives towards shifting viewpoints that anticipate a multiplicity of understandings. None of these perceptions may be spatially bound or stable, but all still arise within social and material structures, while at the same time redefining them (see Ruggie, 1998).

Further, the outcomes of frictional encounters between ideas and actors are multifaceted and may be unpredictable (Björkdahl et al., 2016). This reflects the perception, supported by this book, that on 'balance, the constant interaction between the global and the local creates more plurality rather than greater uniformity' (Menski, 2006: 12; Gready & Robins, 2017). Yet, appreciating this complexity does not suggest that there is no meaningful way of analysing how states (in Southeast Asia) engage with international criminal justice. It is possible to identify some of the key factors that construct adaptive or localised mechanisms, at least in hindsight. As has been observed in relation to the broader democratic reform project in Cambodia, 'the planned outcome of liberal democracy was predictably unfulfilled, while the unpredicted hybridity was entirely natural' (Öjendal & Ou, 2016: 145). In other words, it may be impossible to determine exactly what laws will result from all of this engagement, especially as these processes change, but there is room to consider who is likely to influence them, what arguments they may draw upon, and to identify some of the key dynamics that will affect their operation. For instance, at least in the case study states, experiences of colonial occupation, instability, political interference, human rights advocacy, and development priorities feature in arguments about international criminal justice. Each of these issues has been contested and drawn upon to both reject *and promote* international criminal justice. Elements of these debates can be identified in the resulting laws and institutions, which continue to evolve, without clear or persistent winners or losers (except at individual snapshots of time).

Fifth, this attention to interaction suggests some promise for the normative project of international criminal justice – not because of any inherent progressiveness, but due to the contestation that it can inspire. Tensions between different actors and ideas might stimulate change, or have the potential to be productive, rather than only indicating the rejection of international norms. States and civil society actors have engaged with different ideas to produce diverse responses to international crimes in Southeast Asia, including via the Rome Statute and non-criminal structures. In this regard, it is helpful to refer to Anna Tsing's conception of friction:

> A wheel turns because of its encounter with the surface of the road; spinning in the air it goes nowhere. Rubbing two sticks together produces heat and light; one stick alone is just a stick. As a metaphorical image, friction reminds us that heterogeneous and unequal encounters can lead to new arrangements of culture and power.
>
> (Tsing, 2005: 5)

Localisation draws attention to novel approaches to translating or adapting existing international and local norms. Friction between different ideas and actors might also generate entirely new practices and norms (Björkdahl et al., 2016). To an extent, 'agentic' scholarship addressing norm 'circulation' responds to this insight by considering how norms evolve through feedback loops (Sikkink, 2011a; Acharya, 2013; Zimmermann, 2017). This book also suggests that contestation of particular norms, such as international criminal justice, might have wider implications, such as by encouraging resources to be dedicated towards developing non-judicial mechanisms or human rights offices with mandates that extend beyond investigating international crimes. Examining this potential involves not only analysing those approaches towards international crimes that are not derived from the Rome Statute, but also those that do not target prosecutions at all.

Determining which consequences of such friction might be 'productive' is subjective, however. Stakeholders' own backgrounds and preconceptions inevitably shape their approaches towards analysing responses to violence (Hamati-Ataya, 2012; Nouwen, 2014; Burgis-Kasthala, 2016). For example, this author's international criminal law training as an

Australia-based lawyer led to the focus here upon 'international criminal justice', rather than human rights, transitional justice, or community frames for understanding ideas about prosecuting international crimes. As Chapter 1 revealed, this book has a normative commitment towards opening up sets of opportunities for responding to international criminal justice with input from the widest set of possible participants. By acknowledging our individual normative priorities, politicians, researchers, advocates, and international organisation representatives might become more aware of the possibilities for alternative perspectives, terminologies, and ideas.

Sixth is the question of temporal evolution. While localisation is not static, in the long term it anticipates progression (Acharya, 2004). In Southeast Asia, laws can lie dormant (noting the lack of prosecutions under the Philippines IHL Act until recently, Cambodia's Criminal Code provisions, or Law 26/2000 in more than a decade) and violations of rights and incidents of violence often continue to lack remedy. Apparently 'localised' mechanisms such as the ECCC face challenges, from both domestic and international avenues. Thus, internationalised tribunals or domestic prosecutions, or other localised mechanisms, will not necessarily bring perpetrators of atrocity crimes to justice, break so-called cycles of impunity, or strengthen global justice norms.

On the other hand, concentrating advocacy attention only upon Rome Statute ratification also has limited scope to secure convictions, or ensure future accountability. While localisation processes do not inevitably end impunity, they can contribute to other ends such as developing new legal institutions, encouraging discourse about past events, empowering victims, and promoting political accountability. This may or may not lead to future prosecutions, but involves contestation and engagement within domestic legal systems, even in situations where the ICC is unlikely to act or will provide limited jurisdiction.

The point is that recognising and exploring the options for investigating and prosecuting international crimes beyond the Rome Statute is not the same as rejecting the norm of international criminal justice and promoting impunity (see Tallgren, 2002). Instead, it simply recognises prevailing (and changing) realities and the potential represented by friction between different arguments. In summary, localisation provides a useful device for exploring approaches to different norms, but it is helpful to avoid assumptions of temporal progression or local/global divides, and instead think about how debates around this topic might actually contribute to particular normative goals.

6.4   Adjusting for Time, Space, and Direction in Practice: Beyond the International Criminal Court

This book supports other scholars' analyses of why many states in Southeast Asia are not members of the ICC (Toon, 2004; Findlay, 2010, 2014; Freeland, 2013). Principles of sovereignty, related fears of international interference or selective prosecutions, a preference for domestic proceedings, the influence of other states such as the United States, and the existence of other priorities – including development and threats to stability arising from armed conflict – are all features of the debate about international criminal justice in Southeast Asia, although they may also be relevant beyond the region. For all of these reasons, while some states that have progressed domestic initiatives to join the ICC may accede to the Statute in the medium term depending mainly on domestic political dynamics (see for instance Malaysia's accession then withdrawal from the Rome Statute), it is likely that most states in Southeast Asia will remain outside the ICC framework for some time. It also remains the case that a Security Council or state referral of a situation in Southeast Asia to the ICC Prosecutor is unlikely. China and other states have previously blocked a Security Council resolution concerning military attacks in Myanmar (United Nations, 2007).

Beyond the Rome Statute, most regional states are subject to obligations to adopt legislation to prosecute international crimes arising from the 1949 Geneva Conventions and Genocide Convention. States have established domestic prosecutorial and investigative institutions, adopted international crimes legislation, supported international criminal tribunals outside the region, and contributed to debates about prosecuting contemporary mass violence. Draft legislation in the Philippines and Indonesia would further amend domestic legal approaches to international criminal prosecutions. While the Rome Statute and ICC have been important influences upon the development of international crimes legislation in some states in Southeast Asia, this has not prevented states from adapting various principles and facilitating (or tolerating) limited domestic investigations and non-criminal forums for documenting and publicising international crimes.

This has several implications for those advocating for international criminal justice in the region, and perhaps beyond.[30] We will begin with

---

[30] Some of the suggestions described in this section are mentioned in (Palmer & Sperfeldt, 2016) and I acknowledge and am grateful for Sperfeldt's contribution to some of these ideas.

the more well-accepted or prevalent approaches. First, context and experiences matter, noting the differences across regional States, including the capacity within domestic judicial systems to investigate and prosecute international crimes. Both the Rome Statute's complementarity principle and the challenges for ICC jurisdiction across Southeast Asia suggest that future *prosecutions* of international criminal conduct are more likely to occur within domestic jurisdictions, whether under specific 'international crimes' legislation or ordinary criminal codes, or universal jurisdiction. In order for such crimes to be investigated, let alone for fair trials to be carried out, investigators and judiciaries must be sufficiently independent and have the technical capacities to pursue such prosecutions. This includes ensuring the security of witnesses and overcoming both political barriers to prosecuting influential figures and domestic legal restrictions (such as possible immunities and amnesties). The problems faced by the ECCC, Special Panels and the Law 26/2000 trials demonstrate these challenges. In some jurisdictions, such as Myanmar, and Cambodia and Timor-Leste in the past, recent conflict and resource constraints may exacerbate these issues.

The predominant response to this well-recognised point has been to encourage capacity building, assistance, and other forms of education aimed at institutional reform, including through projects aimed at developing judicial and prosecutorial independence and transparency across the legal system. Another avenue involves 'educating' various stakeholders about international criminal law investigations and prosecutions – for instance, when ECCC lawyers train Cambodian law students and judges, or the Supreme Court of the Philippines Judicial Academy holds a special course on international criminal law.[31] Such initiatives are essential to secure convictions given the additional elements, evidence, and novel modes of liability required to prove the commission of international crimes. International, NGO, or cross-regional assistance in this area could help to prevent a situation where serious violence appears too grave, complicated, or sensitive to be prosecuted under ordinary criminal offences, but the higher threshold of the international crimes provisions seems impossible to meet. Building domestic capacity can involve engaging the ICC's potential for 'positive complementarity', which anticipates the Court taking a broader role in encouraging domestic international crimes prosecutions, but may be

---

[31] See e.g. (Supreme Court of the Philippines Philippine Judicial Academy, 2016).

frustrated by the Court's limited resources and other factors (Burke-White, 2008; Roht-Arriaza, 2013).

However, experience suggests that technical assistance is unlikely to shift state positions towards the ICC or prosecuting international crimes in isolation, *if at all*. In fact, such initiatives have been pursued across the region for many years, with varied success (compare the impact of Rome Statute capacity-building in Lao PDR and Timor-Leste, or consider judicial reforms in Cambodia). To be sure, a degree of misperception about prosecuting international crimes and the ICC likely persists in some quarters. A variety of government departments with rotating staff are involved in lawmaking processes, while the official institutions most interested in seminars (such as National Human Rights Institutions, Ministries of Foreign Affairs, Justice, or Attorney-General's departments) may already be relatively amenable to prosecuting international crimes, whereas opponents, including in the military, can be comparatively harder to access. However, the lengthy engagement within regional states with the issue suggests that a failure to understand the notion of international criminal justice – or for instance the principle of complementarity – is *not* the primary factor restraining states from accepting these norms. Indeed, approaches focused only upon education represent assumptions about the dominance of external influence and domestic incapacity that diminish agency. They may also fail to disrupt persisting political barriers and assume that national authorities represent a 'local' perspective, despite varying levels of decentralisation and representativeness across Southeast Asia.

Second, there is already relevant legislation and a range of actors debating international criminal justice across Southeast Asia. NGOs and networks draw upon 'local' contexts to encourage prosecutions, but often also aim to promote the Rome Statute's underlying aims in broader ways that may not rely upon international criminal law. Existing approaches include documenting and monitoring serious human rights violations and related trials, supporting and complaining to National Human Rights Institutions, and publicising violent incidents via local, national, regional, and international networks including the UPR or social media. Lawyers have brought cases under domestic legislation and contributed to debates about amending relevant laws. Parliamentarians, academics, lawyers, and NGO representatives have ensured that legal analysis is provided to drafting committees and countered arguments from other interest groups seeking less comprehensive criminal jurisdiction. There is therefore potential to use and develop domestic legislation, respond to victims' particular demands, or pursue alternative responses to different past, current, or prospective crimes. The examples offered in this book are not exhaustive, but demonstrate that diverse approaches for promoting international crimes prosecutions already exist in Southeast Asia that look beyond the Rome Statute (Palmer & Sperfeldt, 2016). Those advocating for international crimes prosecutions can learn from and support existing initiatives that already engage with diverse experiences and contexts.

Third, this expertise provides opportunities for cross-regional NGO, parliamentary, judicial, and investigative experience sharing. This may relate to the prosecutions that have occurred, including before the Special Panels, ECCC, and under Law 26/2000, as well as the processes adopted for drafting and enforcing *domestic* legislation such as the Philippine's IHL Act, or how advocacy can best draw on varied traditional and religious processes. International groups such as the Asia-Pacific division of the CICC, Asian International Justice Initiative, Parliamentarians for Global Action, and national networks such as PCICC and ICSICC have already pursued such regional discussions (Linton, 2005). Again, these might not be overtly targeted towards international criminal justice, but allow participants to learn more about other actors' different priorities concerning responding to serious violence (Palmer & Sperfeldt, 2016). AICHR might eventually represent another useful institution for discussions about prosecuting international crimes, although its mandate is limited. Further, militaries across Southeast Asia have often opposed ratifying the Rome Statute or the prosecution of (especially military perpetrators of) alleged international crimes. However, they have also been significant contributors to UN peacekeeping operations and may continue to engage in military-to-military discussions that carefully address accountability issues (see Topsfield, 2017). NGO networks have already recognised that these experiences may encourage militaries to support the enforcement of international humanitarian law principles, including through international crimes mechanisms and notions of command responsibility.

Fourth, while these strategies are often implemented by domestically based or regional NGOs and civil society, foreign states and intergovernmental organisations also play an important role in advocating for prosecuting international crimes in the region (beyond technical assistance or capacity building activities). Arguably few of the laws and institutions for prosecuting international crimes in Southeast Asia would have been adopted in the absence of any international support at all.

Yet, for international states and organisations that continue to promote international criminal justice in the region, context-specific responses that recognise and support the existing initiatives in the region are likely to be more useful (Palmer & Sperfeldt, 2016).

In relation to its role in advocating for international crimes prosecutions, the ICC could further develop its regional consultations with NGOs and official actors to learn about relevant domestic priorities, activities, and concerns. The ICC's former President Judge Sang-Hyun Song was a regular visitor to the region and, after a period of reduced activity, from 2017 the ICC appeared to increase its engagement with Southeast Asia, for instance with the President of the ASP, O-Gon Kwon, also of South Korea, attending seminars in Bangkok, Jakarta, and elsewhere. 'Regional Cooperation Seminars' and other forums can be continued (without expending additional resources), but ideally incorporate a wider variety of civil society ideas and locations, including for those whose access to seminars is limited (perhaps for strategic or security reasons). Their focus should extend beyond only promoting the 'universality' and 'effective implementation of the Rome Statute' (e.g. CICC, 2015; ICC Assembly of States Parties, 2018c), which is sometimes already the case. Structuring these visits as ICC learning exercises would improve the ICC's network and knowledge as it investigates (or considers investigating) alleged international crimes within Southeast Asia in future – for example, in the Philippines or Cambodia. The investigations concerning Myanmar, requiring ICC visits to Bangladesh, and the potential for relatively rapid escalations of violence, as in the Philippines, suggest that future meetings should not be limited to actors based within Rome Statute party states or where potential jurisdiction is more predictable. The shifting physical locations of civil society across borders also means that relevant meetings can be held across the world and online, but should recognise the barriers to travel faced by some. It would also help to build trust with regional actors if the ICC can demonstrate that it incorporates their experiences in ways that are valuable and appropriate to support (amplify) domestic and regional priorities, for instance in strategy documents and ASP outcomes, and by supporting organisations' own activities.

The reasons are plentiful. The ICC faces its own resource and political constraints but will need input from civil society for any investigations in the region or to promote domestic complementarity proceedings, especially as regional official actors are likely to oppose international 'interference'. The Philippines' preference for adopting domestic legislation when ratification remained unpopular, Cambodia's insistence on an internationalised model for the ECCC, and Indonesia's willingness to adopt Law 26/2000 and prosecute perpetrators (even if convictions were overturned) all indicated desires to avoid international political interference, while sustaining international relationships and internal stability. Similar concerns will persist, even if they are contested by civil society. Future ICC investigations in the region may be greeted with wariness and even resistance by ASEAN, though (as in Africa) different states and actors are likely to take different approaches. This is already being demonstrated in the opposition from some authorities in the Philippines and Myanmar and mixed responses from ASEAN states. Thus, prosecutions in Southeast Asia are unlikely to provide an easy method of geographic diversification for the ICC, and witness security and documentation efforts by organisations and activists located within the region and intermediaries will be important, even though political environments will change. The ICC can also draw on the evidence collated by organisations such as the Independent Investigative Mechanism for Myanmar – and encourage national investigators and prosecutors (particularly in states with universal jurisdiction) to do so as well. Speaking generally, resistance to the ICC is likely to continue emphasising domestic legislation, investigations, and adaptation – rather than an overt rejection of the principles of international criminal justice. In that context, sustained civil society education of ICC personnel (wherever they come from) is likely to be a more effective approach in the longer term, particularly if leveraged from existing initiatives.

Yet civil society support for the ICC is likely to remain mixed in Southeast Asia, given other NGO priorities and focuses upon domestic and community-driven responses to violence, as well as sensitivities to the risk of the ICC acting as a type of 'shelter' for perpetrators, excessively raising expectations, or even stimulating a 'backlash' against human rights activism. The ICC has much to learn from civil society based within Southeast Asia (as well as beyond) about how to navigate challenging regional political environments. Indeed, legislators, judiciary and security force members, National Human Rights Institutions, civil society networks, and individual community members including lawyers can all suggest adaptive approaches towards responding to international crimes – beyond only the Rome Statute. These stakeholders might request security, access, resources, expertise, and other assistance in doing so, but international contributions are likely to be most helpful where they are offered in a genuinely consultative and responsive manner with a sustainable and flexible trajectory. This might also involve revisiting the role of CICC in the region, as it provides a potential gateway between the ICC and relevant NGOs in Southeast Asia. However, it should not be presumed that projects – or specific prosecutorial initiatives – lack or have the support of communities without actively integrative and safe (rather than notional or symbolic) dialogue with a wider range of actors. Programmes and offices interested in international criminal justice can continue to support diverse projects that address related aims, such as documentation initiatives and institutional reform – since the process of reconstructing this norm is an ongoing one, during which challenges and opportunities shift and might be shifted.

Fifth, international criminal justice can be developed and reconstructed by civil society actors, including community members. Even when confronted by security and political challenges, NGOs have used 'local initiative' to directly or indirectly contribute to the goals of international criminal justice. These include developing non-criminal public hearings that stimulate public discourse and allow victims to vocalise their experiences and needs, pursuing media campaigns and educational initatives targeting younger generations, and addressing related priorities such as legal aid, social welfare, and land and tax reform. These may reflect the diverse priorities, including socio-economic concerns, of survivors, and the persistent, evolving, and intergenerational nature of harms resulting from the commission of international crimes. Yet political 'space' is required for such events and projects to be developed in safety. Legislation or policing that limits the scope of NGO activities, such as laws passed in Cambodia restricting NGO registrations, or media controls, also inhibit the opportunities for these actors to debate – and reconstruct – notions of international criminal justice. The range of barriers that prevent certain actors from attending seminars, having safe and meaningful engagement with authorities, enjoying satisfactory health, or securely giving evidence, are the same ones that diminish those actors' ability to participate in the norm adaptation, though they may find other routes to participate. Those interested in promoting prosecutorial responses to alleged international crimes might therefore productively pursue a range of non-criminal-justice–focused activities, even to facilitate others' abilities to engage in norm-making.

Finally, local adaptation is not necessarily a progressive or positive process from the perspective of those supporting the norm of international criminal justice. Attempting to meet with authorities and persuade them to take different actions or reform institutions may or may not be more effective for securing convictions. In practice NGOs pursued

244   ADAPTING INTERNATIONAL CRIMINAL JUSTICE

engagement in countries like Indonesia and the Philippines where it was possible and in the absence of other realistic expectations of securing justice. Alternative approaches such as seeking reparations, non-criminal forums, complaints to non-criminal international law bodies (including the International Court of Justice), or institutional reform projects might indirectly contribute to future prosecutions. However, they do not directly ensure that perpetrators of 'the most serious crimes of concern to the international community as a whole'[32] are punished. This should be acknowledged, with scope allowed for different opinions about the ramifications of taking various approaches. Here the tensions and debates in Indonesia between reconciliation and justice approaches are pertinent and might continue to be so, but must occur in a safe and open-minded way. National legislation may expand upon, or limit, the scope of the Rome Statute's crimes, but if not enforced, will not contribute to 'ending impunity'. Domestic investigations and prosecutions are often not pursued, or may not be considered fair or to have sufficiently contributed to post-conflict reconciliation, while reparative aims such as seeking victim assistance may have some, but still uneven, success in meeting survivors' different priorities. These challenges, and possible non-prosecutorial responses to them, can be confronted, even if they generate friction, without necessarily rejecting the norm of international criminal justice. The limited gains of the approaches that have been secured can similarly be appreciated, learned from and developed further. However, the extent to which wider transitional justice projects and victims' movements might actually 'seduce' officials into eventually investigating or prosecuting crimes (see Wahyuningroem, 2013) remains, at least in the states considered, unclear at best (see Gready & Robins, 2017: 964).

The reality is that the core principle that the perpetrators of atrocities ought not to walk free is difficult to publicly reject outright, and state actors or others rarely do so. Instead, it is easier to reject, or perhaps adapt, the aspects of the norm that require specific legal institutional forms, including by denying that crimes occurred on the basis of a lack of evidence (with or without investigations and trials). Still, tensions between different actors may affect the development of laws, institutions, and projects in ways that potentially contribute to some goals associated with international criminal justice, such as the documentation of crimes, monitoring government accountability, or community reconciliation.

---

[32] Preamble, Rome Statute.

Many of these outcomes may have value in and of themselves, including where they are used to contribute to the *other* priorities of those experiencing (and directly responding to) the harms caused by international crimes. This may include the development of novel community reconciliation and reparative projects, legislative reform, domestic trials, and public hearings that draw on diverse influences, even if they were inspired by an apparent 'lack of' international criminal justice. This book calls for an honest appreciation for the multiple and dynamic ways that actors, including within civil society, engage with each other and international criminal law. It views the resulting frictions as a source of opportunity – rather than the rejection or stalling of norm diffusion.

Approaches towards international criminal justice will continue to evolve in Southeast Asian states. However, both linear progression and stagnant resistance towards the ICC, or at least the norms it promotes, are unlikely scenarios. Instead, debates about sovereignty, development, human rights and the rule of law, politicisation and selectivity, and the promotion of peace and stability, are likely to be contested with respect to international criminal justice by actors located within and beyond the region. States may respond to significant events such as the future commission of crimes, new civil society strategies, or ICC action in the region in ways that are not predictable. However, they will probably do so with reference to those themes or other 'local' concerns and vocabularies, with legal responses that reflect the priorities of those who can deploy their arguments effectively.

6.5 Conclusion

This book makes a number of contributions to debates about international criminal law in Southeast Asia, particularly in Cambodia, the Philippines, Indonesia, and Myanmar. These include (i) identifying themes associated with these sates' experiences of international crimes trials since World War II, (ii) providing analysis of the laws and institutions for prosecuting international crimes across Southeast Asia (including of draft legislation in the Philippines and Indonesia), and in doing so, helping to explain the existence and content of international crimes laws and institutions beyond the dominant Rome Statute framework, including within domestic jurisdictions, (iii) evaluating the arguments and strategies employed by various actors, including within civil society, to influence such mechanisms, (iv) exploring the relationship between relevant debates and international crimes laws using a 'localisation' framework and qualitative research methods – and doing so across several case study states, and (v) contesting temporal, spatial, and directional accounts of the diffusion of the norm of international criminal justice in the region.

The laws and institutions for prosecuting international crimes within Southeast Asia reflect the adaptation of the international criminal justice norm by state and non-state actors in various locations. This requires a nuanced approach to examining actors' engagement with international criminal justice that is transparent about its normative aims and learns from how diverse actors already draw on adapted arguments to influence legal responses to violence within and across different times and spaces. It entails a shift in focus beyond the Rome Statute and even beyond international criminal law – towards existing and evolving expertise, mechanisms, debates, and creativity. That shift is crucial as actors throughout and beyond Southeast Asia – including the ICC Prosecutor – continue to debate responses to alleged international crimes in the region. As it is, extrajudicial killings continue in the Philippines, military violence continues in Myanmar, and individuals across the region are forcibly removed from their homes to make way for agricultural and other business interests. There is scope to further adapt 'international criminal justice' to develop a wider range of responses towards investigating prosecuting international crimes as the world continues to change.

Appendix A

Table of Ratifications

Table A.1 Southeast Asia: ratification/accession – International human rights and humanitarian law instruments[1]

	Rome Statute	Genocide Convention	Convention Against Torture (CAT)	OPCAT	Geneva Conventions I-IV	Additional Protocol 1	Additional Protocol 2	Additional Protocol 3	Hague Convention Protn Cultural Property 1954	Optional Protocol to CRoC on Children in Armed Conflict	Non-Applicability of Stat. Limitations on War Crimes and CAH
Brunei Darussalam	No	No	Signed 22/09/15^	No	14/10/91	14/10/91	14/10/91	No	No	17/5/16^	No
Cambodia	11/4/02	14/10/50	15/10/92	30/3/07	8/12/58	14/1/98	14/1/98	No	4/4/62	16/7/04^	No
Indonesia	No	No	28/10/98^	No	30/9/58	No	No	No	10/1/67	24/9/12^	No
Lao People's Democratic Republic	No	8/12/50	26/09/12^	No	29/10/56	18/11/80	18/11/80	No	No	20/9/06^	28/12/84^
Malaysia	No (withdrawn)	20/12/94	No	No	24/8/62	No	No	No	12/12/60	12/4/12^	No
Myanmar	No	14/3/1956^	No	No	25/8/92	No	No	No	10/2/56	Signed 28/9/15	No
The Philippines	No (withdrawn)	7/7/1950^	18/6/86	17/04/12^	6/10/52	30/03/12^	11/12/86	22/8/06	Signed 14/5/54	26/8/03^	15/5/73
Singapore	No	18/8/1995^	No	No	27/4/73	No	No	7/7/08	No	11/12/08^	No
Thailand	Signed 2/10/00	No	2/10/07^	No	29/12/54	No	No	No	2/5/58	27/2/06^	No

Timor-Leste	6/9/02	No	16/4/03	Signed 16/9/05	8/5/03	12/4/05	12/4/05	29/7/11	No	2/8/04^	No
Viet Nam	No	9/6/1981^	5/02/15^	No	28/06/57^	19/10/81	No	No	No	20/12/01^	6/05/83^
Total SEA Ratifications	2	7	7	2	11	6	5	3	5	10	3
Percentage	**18.2%**	**63.6%**	**63.6%**	**18.2%**	**100.0%**	**54.5%**	**45.5%**	**27.3%**	**45.5%**	**90.9%**	**27.3%**
No. parties of 193*	122	151	166	89	196	174	168	76	133	168	55
World %	**63.2%**	**78.2%**	**86.0%**	**46.1%**	**101.6%**	**90.2%**	**87.0%**	**39.4%**	**68.9%**	**87.0%**	

[1] Updated 31 May 2019.

Source: UNTC, ICRC. ^Reservation or declaration.

Table A.2 *Southeast Asia: ratification/accession – International human rights law instruments*[1]

	ICESCR	ICCPR	CEDAW	CRoChild	Enforced Disappearances	Suppression of Apartheid
Brunei Darussalam	No	No	24/5/06^	27/12/95^	No	No
Cambodia	26/5/92	26/5/92	15/10/92	15/10/92	27/6/13	28/7/81
Indonesia	23/02/06^	23/02/06^	13/9/84^	5/9/90	Signed 27/9/10	No
Lao People's Democratic Republic	13/2/07	25/09/09^	14/8/81	8/5/91	Signed 29/9/08	5/10/81
Malaysia	No	No	5/7/95^	17/2/95^	No	No
Myanmar	6/10/2017^	No	22/7/97^	15/7/91	No	No
The Philippines	7/6/74	23/10/86	5/8/81	21/8/90	No	26/1/78
Singapore	No	No	5/10/95^	5/10/95^	No	No
Thailand	5/09/99^	29/10/96^	9/08/85^	27/3/92^	Signed 9/01/12	No
Timor-Leste	16/4/03	18/9/03	16/4/03	16/4/03	No	No
Viet Nam	24/09/82^	24/09/82^	17/02/82^	28/2/90	No	9/6/81
Total	8	7	11	11	1	4
Percentage	**72.7%**	**63.6%**	**100.0%**	**100.0%**	**9.1%**	**36.4%**
No. parties of 193	169	172	189	196	60	109
World %	**87.6%**	**89.1%**	**97.9%**	**101.6%**	**31.1%**	**56.5%**

[1] Updated 31 May 2019.
Source: UNTC. ^Reservation or declaration.

Appendix B

Table of Interviews

Table of formal recorded interviews

Code[1]	Type	Date and Location of Interview
C1	Cambodia civil society	November 2014, Phnom Penh
C2	Cambodia international legal (international)	November 2014, Phnom Penh
C4	Cambodia civil society	November 2014, Phnom Penh
C5	Cambodia civil society	December 2014, Phnom Penh
C6	Cambodia civil society	November 2015, The Hague
I1	International civil society (Indonesia)	October 2014, Jakarta
I2	Indonesia civil society	October 2014, Jakarta
I4	Indonesia civil society	January 2019, Jakarta
I5	Indonesia international legal	October 2014, Jakarta
I6	Indonesia official	October 2014, Jakarta
I7	International civil society (Indonesia) (joint interview)	October 2014, Jakarta
I8	Indonesia official / civil society	October 2014, Jakarta
I9	Indonesia civil society	October 2014, Jakarta
I10	Indonesia civil society	October 2014, Jakarta
I11	Indonesia official / academic	October 2014, Jakarta
I13	Indonesia international legal / academic	October 2014, Jakarta
I14	Indonesia civil society	October 2014, Jakarta
M1	Myanmar civil society	October 2014, Bangkok
M2	International civil society (Myanmar)	November 2014, Yangon
M4	Myanmar civil society	November 2014, Yangon
M5	Myanmar civil society	November 2014, Yangon
M6	Myanmar international legal / civil society	November 2014, Yangon
M8	Myanmar civil society	November 2014, Yangon
M9	Myanmar civil society	November 2014, Yangon
M10	Myanmar civil society	November 2014, Yangon
P2	Philippines international legal	November 2014, Manila

(cont.)

Code[1]	Type	Date and Location of Interview
P3	International civil society (Philippines)	November 2014, Manila
P4	Philippines civil society	November 2014, Manila
P5	Philippines civil society	November 2014, Manila
P6	Philippines civil society	November 2014, Manila
R1	International civil society (regional)	October 2014, Skype
R2	International civil society (regional)	October 2014, Bangkok
R3	Regional civil society	October 2014, Bangkok

[1] Interview codes were also used for some more formal but 'off-the-record' discussions, which are not included in this table. The codes do not proceed in precise order. In total, thirty-three formal recorded interviews were held (included in the table), of forty-eight meetings and countless informal and conference discussions across the region, in Australia, and in The Hague from 2013 until June 2019. Interviews were carried out subject to UNSW Human Research Ethics Requirements, Approval No. HREAP 14084 and, at Griffith University, Reference No. 2018/910.

A copy of the interview protocol for these semi-structured interviews is available upon request.

Appendix C

Selected Legislation Concerning International Criminal Law in Southeast Asia: Domestic Legislation, Bills and Regulations, and Sources[1]

Brunei-Darussalam[2]

Biological Weapons Act, 1975, Cap. 87, Revised 1983, B.L.R.O. 1/1983, Attorney-General's Chambers, www.agc.gov.bn/AGC%20Images/LAWS/ACT_PDF/cap087.pdf

Constitutional Matters I: Constitution of Brunei Darussalam, No. S 97/59, Revised 2011, B.L.R.O 2/2011, Attorney-General's Chambers, www.agc.gov.bn/AGC%20Images/LOB/cons_doc/constitution_i.pdf

Constitutional Matters II: Succession and Regency Proclamation, 1959, Revised 2011, B.L.R.O. 2/2011, Attorney-General's Chambers, www.agc.gov.bn/AGC%20Images/LOB/cons_doc/constitution_ii.pdf

Criminal Procedure Code, 1951, Cap. 7, Revised 1 October 2001, www.agc.gov.bn/AGC%20Images/LOB/PDF/Cap7.pdf

Geneva Conventions Order, 2005, No. S40, 30 May 2005, Order under Article 83(3) Constitution, Attorney-General's Chambers, www.agc.gov.bn/AGC%20Images/LAWS/Gazette_PDF/2005/EN/s040.pdf

Penal Code, 1951, Cap. 22, Revised 1 October 2001, B.L.R.O 3/2001, Attorney-General's Chambers www.agc.gov.bn/AGC%20Images/LOB/PDF/Cap22.pdf

Royal Brunei Armed Forces Act, 1984, Cap. 149, Revised 2018, B.L.R.O 1/2018, Attorney-General's Chambers, www.agc.gov.bn/AGC%20Images/LOB/PDF/Chapter%20149.pdf

Syariah Penal Code Order, 2013, No. S 69, 22 October 2013, Attorney-General's Chambers, www.agc.gov.bn/AGC%20Images/LAWS/Gazette_PDF/2013/EN/S069.pdf

---

[1] This list offers (only) a starting point for researching international criminal law issues in the region, though translations are not all official and websites change frequently. The ICC Legal Tools Database is a helpful resource for further research: www.legal-tools.org.

[2] For further legislation, see Attorney-General's Chambers, 'Laws of Brunei', www.agc.gov.bn/AGC%20Site%20Pages/Laws%20of%20Brunei.aspx 'Text of Orders' www.agc.gov.bn/AGC%20Site%20Pages/Text%20of%20Orders.aspx.

Cambodia

Common Statute on Civil Servants, 1994, Council of Jurists unofficial translation, www.bigpond.com.kh/Council_of_Jurists/Foncpubl/fpl014g.htm

Constitution of the Kingdom of Cambodia, 1993, Refworld 'official translation', www.refworld.org/docid/3ae6b5428.html

Criminal Code of the Kingdom of Cambodia, 2010, translation by Bunleng Cheung, http://sithi.org/admin/upload/law/Criminal_Code_Book_with_cover_Jan_2014.pdf

Criminal Procedure Code of Kingdom of Cambodia, 2007, translation by Bunleng Cheung, www.wipo.int/edocs/lexdocs/laws/en/kh/kh032en.pdf

Decree Law No. 1, Establishment of People's Revolutionary Tribunal at Phnom Penh to Try the Pol Pot – Ieng Sary Clique for the Crime of Genocide, 15 July 1979, Santa Clara Law, http://law.scu.edu/wp-content/uploads/Decree_Law_No._1.pdf

Law on the Establishment of the Extraordinary Chambers in the Courts of Cambodia, amended 27 October 2004, NS/RKM/1004/006, Extraordinary Chambers in the Courts of Cambodia, www.eccc.gov.kh/sites/default/files/legal-documents/KR_Law_as_amended_27_Oct_2004_Eng.pdf

Law on General Statutes for the Military Personnel of the Royal Cambodian Armed Forces, 16 November 1997, CS/RKM/1197/005, International Labour Organisation, www.ilo.org/dyn/natlex/docs/ELECTRONIC/93508/109344/F811412622/KHM93508%20Eng.pdf

Law on the Prohibition of Chemical, Nuclear, Biological and Radiological Weapons, 3 December 2009, ICRC, https://ihl-databases.icrc.org/applic/ihl/ihl-nat.nsf/implementingLaws.xsp?documentId=DCEA072AA8C189C2C1257D890037DE57&action=openDocument&xp_countrySelected=KH&xp_topicSelected=GVAL-992BUP&from=state&SessionID=DYLX2E2BRH

Law on the Protection of Cultural Heritage, 25 January 1996, ICRC, https://ihl-databases.icrc.org/applic/ihl/ihl-nat.nsf/implementingLaws.xsp?documentId=A4BA0BF90C1E0009C1257D890040D033&action=openDocument&xp_countrySelected=KH&xp_topicSelected=GVAL-992BU7&from=state&SessionID=DYLX2E2BRH

Law to Outlaw Democratic Kampuchea Group, 15 July 1994, Extraordinary Chambers in the Courts of Cambodia, unofficial translation, www.eccc.gov.kh/sites/default/files/legal-documents/Law_to_Outlaw_DK_Group_1994.pdf

Indonesia

Constitution of the Republic of Indonesia, 1945 as amended 2002, World Intellectual Property Organization, www.wipo.int/edocs/lexdocs/laws/en/id/id048en.pdf

Kitab Undang-Undang Hukum Pidana [Penal Code of Indonesia], 19 May 1999, UNODC, unofficial translation, www.unodc.org/res/cld/document/ idn/indonesian_penal_code_html/I.1_Criminal_Code.pdf

Kitab Undang-Undang Hukum Pidana Militer [Military Criminal Code], (Indonesian source: www.hukumonline.com/pusatdata/downloadfile/lt52 b2d269c8a6d/parent/lt52b2a19c12d97)

Law No. 59 of 1958 concerning the Ratification by the Republic of Indonesia of All the Geneva Conventions of 12 August 1949, (Indonesian source: www.hukumonline.com/pusatdata/download/lt4ef025a7af2fd/node/lt4ef02 536c82ac)

Law No. 8 of 1981, Code of Criminal Procedure, UNODC, unofficial translation, www.unodc.org/res/cld/document/idn/law_number_8_year_1981_ concerning_the_criminal_procedure_html/I.2_Criminal_Procedure.pdf (Indonesian source: https://peraturan.bpk.go.id/Home/Details/47041/uu-no-8-tahun-1981)

Law No. 8 of 1985, Law on Social Organisations, United States International Grantmaking, (Indonesian source https://peraturan.bpk.go.id/Home/Details/ 46956/uu-no-8-tahun-1985)

Law No. 5 of 1992 concerning Cultural Objects, ICRC, (Indonesian source: https://ihl-databases.icrc.org/applic/ihl/ihl-nat.nsf/0/3116C43FA658290CC 125708C004BD0FA)

Law No. 31 of 1997 concerning the Trial of the Military, Asia-Pacific Centre for Military Law, (Indonesian source http://hukum.unsrat.ac.id/uu/uu_31_ 97.htm)

Law No. 39 of 1999 concerning Human Rights, Refworld, www.refworld.org/ docid/4da2ce862.html

Law No. 21 of 2000 on Special Autonomy for the Papua Province, Refworld, www.refworld.org/docid/46af542e2.html

Law No. 26 of 2000 concerning Human Rights Courts, 23 November 2000, Police and Human Rights Resources, unofficial translation, https:// policehumanrightsresources.org/content/uploads/2019/07/Law-26-2000-Act-on-the-Human-Rights-Courts-2000-Eng.pdf?x39143, (Indonesian source www.dpr.go.id/dokjdih/document/uu/UU_2000_26.pdf)

Law No. 15 of 2003, the Anti Terrorism Law, (Indonesian source https:// peraturan.bpk.go.id/Home/Details/43015/uu-no-15-tahun-2003)

Law No. 34 of 2004 concerning the National Army of Indonesia (Tentara Nasional Indonesia), (Indonesian source www.dpr.go.id/dokblog/doku men/F_20150616_4760.PDF)

Law No. 13 of 2006 concerning the Protection of the Witnesses and Victims, LPSK, www.lpsk.go.id/upload/Buku%20UU%20No%2013%20(English% 20Version).pdf

Law No. 9 of 2008 on the Use of Chemical Materials and the Prohibition of Chemical Materials as Chemical Weapons, ICRC, unofficial translation,

https://ihl-databases.icrc.org/applic/ihl/ihl-nat.nsf/implementingLaws.xsp?
documentId=D217CC78321EB554C12576D9004DDA1C&action=openDo
cument&xp_countrySelected=ID&xp_topicSelected=GVAL-992BUL&from=
state

Law No. 25 of 2014, Kitab Undang-Undang Hukum Disiplin Tentara [Military Discipline Code], (Indonesian source: www.hukumonline.com/pusatdata/downloadfile/lt5461fdb573dbf/parent/lt5461fd7fa5382)

Lao PDR

Constitution of the Lao People's Democratic Republic 2003, No. 25/NA, International Labour Organization, www.ilo.org/wcmsp5/groups/public/@ed_protect/@protrav/@ilo_aids/documents/legaldocument/wcms_117348.pdf (see also The National Assembly of the Lao People's Democratic Republic

Penal Law 2005, No. 12/NA, 9 November 2005, World Intellectual Property Organization, www.wipo.int/edocs/lexdocs/laws/en/la/la006en.pdf

Penal Code 2017, No. 13, 17 May 2017, effective November 2018, Official Gazette, (Lao source: www.laoofficialgazette.gov.la/kcfinder/upload/files/26%E0%BA%AA%E0%BA%9E%E0%BA%8A2018.pdf)

Malaysia

Armed Forces Act, 1972, Act 77, 1 January 2006, International Criminal Court Legal Tools Database, www.legal-tools.org/doc/be5309

Federal Constitution, 1963, 1 January 2006, International Criminal Court Legal Tools Database, www.legal-tools.org/doc/1c0e69

Geneva Conventions Act, 1962, Act 512, 1 January 2006, International Criminal Court Legal Tools Database, www.legal-tools.org/doc/92c1a7

Penal Code, 1976, Act 574, amendments to 1 January 2006, International Criminal Court Legal Tools Database, www.legal-tools.org/doc/e874e1

Myanmar

Constitution of the Republic of the Union of Myanmar, 2008, Burma Library, Ministry of Information www.burmalibrary.org/docs5/Myanmar_Constitution-2008-en.pdf

Defence Services Act, 1959, Burma Library, www.burmalibrary.org/docs19/Defence_Services_Act-ocr-tu-comp.pdf, amended 2010, International Criminal Court Legal Tools Database, https://legal-tools.org/doc/9nzia4

Mutual Assistance in Criminal Matters Law, Law No. 4 of 2004, ILO, unofficial translation, www.ilo.org/dyn/natlex/docs/ELECTRONIC/87409/99603/F1666504333/MMR87409.pdf

Myanmar Police Force Maintenance of Discipline Law, Law No. 4 of 1995, International Criminal Court Legal Tools Database, www.legal-tools.org/doc/beecca/pdf, amended 1997, www.legal-tools.org/doc/559ad8/pdf

Penal Code, 1861, India Act XLV 1860, Myanmar Law Information System, amended 7 January 2016 and 26 March 2019, www.mlis.gov.mm/lsScPop .do?lawordSn=9506, (see also www.legal-tools.org/doc/1a6e18/pdf)

Singapore

Armed Forces Act, Act 7 of 1972, Revised 2000 Singapore Statutes Online, https://sso.agc.gov.sg/Act/SAFA1972

Constitution of the Republic of Singapore, 9 August 1965, S/163, Singapore Statutes Online, https://sso.agc.gov.sg/Act/CONS1963

Enlistment Act, Act 25 of 1970, Revised 2001 Singapore Statutes Online, https://sso.agc.gov.sg/Act/EA1970

Geneva Conventions Act, Act 15 of 1973, Revised 1985, Singapore Statutes Online, https://sso.agc.gov.sg/Act/GCA1973

Hostage-Taking Act, Act 19 of 2010, Revised 2011, Singapore Statutes Online, https://sso.agc.gov.sg/Act/HTA2010

Mutual Assistance in Criminal Matters Act, Act 12 of 2000, Revised 2001, Singapore Statutes Online, https://sso.agc.gov.sg/Act/MACMA2000

Mutual Assistance in Criminal Matters (International Criminal Tribunals) Regulations, GN No. S 368/2001, Revised 2003, Singapore Statutes Online, https://sso.agc.gov.sg/SL/190A-RG1?DocDate=20030131

Penal Code, Ordinance 4 of 1871, Revised 2008, Singapore Statutes Online, https://sso.agc.gov.sg/Act/PC1871

Penal Code (Amendment) Bill No. 38/2007, Singapore Statutes Online, https://sso.agc.gov.sg/Bills-Supp/38-2007/Published/20070918?DocDate=20070918

The Philippines

Administrative Order No. 35, Creating an Inter-Agency Committee on Extra-Legal Killings, Enforced Disappearances, Torture and Other Grave Violations of the Right to Life, Liberty and Security of Persons, 22 November 2012, Official Gazette of the Republic of the Philippines, www.officialgazette.gov .ph/2012/11/22/administrative-order-no-35-s-2012

An Act Defining and Penalizing Crimes against International Humanitarian Law, Genocide and Other Crimes against Humanity, Organizing Jurisdiction, Designating Special Courts, and for Related Purposes, Republic Act No. 9851, 11 December 2009, Official Gazette of the Republic of the Philippines, www.officialgazette.gov.ph/2009/12/11/republic-act-no-9851

An Act Defining and Penalizing Enforced or Involuntary Disappearance, Republic Act No. 10353, 21 December 2012, Official Gazette of the Republic of the Philippines, https://www.officialgazette.gov.ph/2012/12/21/republic-act-no-10353/

An Act Expanding Republic Act No. 9208, Entitled 'An Act to Institute Policies to Eliminate Trafficking in Persons Especially Women and Children, Establishing the Necessary Institutional Mechanisms for the Protection and Support of Trafficking Persons, Providing Penalties for Its Violations and for Other Purposes, Republic Act No. 10364, 6 February 2013, Official Gazette of the Republic of the Philippines, www.officialgazette.gov.ph/2013/02/06/republic-act-no-10364

An Act Penalizing Torture and Other Cruel, Inhuman and Degrading Treatment or Punishment and Prescribing Penalties Therefor, Republic Act No. 9745, 10 November 2009, Official Gazette of the Republic of the Philippines, www.officialgazette.gov.ph/2009/11/10/republic-act-no-9745

An Act Providing for the Functional and Structural Organization of the Office of the Ombudsman, and for Other Purposes, Republic Act No. 6770, 17 November 1989, Office of the Ombudsman, www.ombudsman.gov.ph/docs/republicacts/Republic_Act_No_6770.pdf

An Act to Provide for the National Defense of the Philippines, Penalizing Certain Violations Thereof, Appropriating Funds Therefor, and for Other Purposes, Commonwealth Act No. 1, 21 December 1935, Official Gazette of the Republic of the Philippines, www.officialgazette.gov.ph/1935/12/21/commonwealth-act-no-1

An Act Revising the Penal Code and Other Penal Laws 1930, Act No. 3815, 8 December 1930, Official Gazette of the Republic of the Philippines, www.officialgazette.gov.ph/1930/12/08/act-no-3815-s-1930

Article of War, Commonwealth Act No. 408, Chan Robles, http://laws.chanrobles.com/commonwealthacts/2_commonwealthacts.php?id=74

Executive Order No. 68, Establishing a National War Crimes Office and Prescribing Rules and Regulations Governing the Trial of Accused War Criminals, 29 July 1947, Official Gazette of the Republic of the Philippines, www.officialgazette.gov.ph/1947/07/29/executive-order-no-68

Executive Order No. 163, Declaring the Effectivity of the Creation of the Commission on Human Rights as Provided for in the 1987 Constitution, Providing Guidelines for the Operation Thereof, and for Other Purposes, 5 May 1987, Official Gazette of the Republic of the Philippines, www.officialgazette.gov.ph/1987/05/05/executive-order-no-163-s-1987

Executive Order No. 134, Declaring August 12, 1999 and Every 12th Day of August Thereafter as International Humanitarian Law Day, 31 July 1999, Official Gazette of the Republic of the Philippines, www.officialgazette.gov.ph/1999/07/31/executive-order-no-134-s-1999

House Bill No. 2835, An Act in Compliance by the Republic of the Philippines with Its Obligations under the Rome Statute of the International Criminal Court and for Other Purposes, 10 August 2016

House Bill No. 2834, An Act Amending Republic Act 9851 'An Act Defining and Penalizing Crimes Against International Humanitarian Law, Genocide and Other Crimes Against Humanity, Organizing Jurisdiction, Designating Special Courts, and for Related Purposes', 10 August 2016

Human Rights Victims Reparation and Recognition Act, Republic Act 10368, 25 February 2013, Official Gazette of the Republic of the Philippines, www.officialgazette.gov.ph/2013/02/25/republic-act-no-10368

Memorandum Order No. 259 Requiring Education and Training of Law Enforcement, Police, Military and Prison Personnel, 7 February 1995, Official Gazette of the Republic of the Philippines, www.officialgazette.gov.ph/1995/02/07/memorandum-order-no-259-s-1995

Revised Rules of Criminal Procedure, 1 December 2000, LawPhil, www.lawphil.net/courts/rules/rc_110-127_crim.html

Senate Bill No. 2135, An Act Defining and Penalizing Crimes against International Humanitarian Law and Other Serious International Crimes, Adopting Corresponding Principles of Criminal Responsibility, Applying Universal Jurisdiction, and Designating Special Courts, 26 September 2005

Senate Bill No. 1290, An Act Amending Section 17 of Republic Act No. 9851, 13 August 2015

The 1935 Constitution, Official Gazette of the Republic of the Philippines, www.officialgazette.gov.ph/constitutions/the-1935-constitution

The Constitution of the Republic of the Philippines 1987, Official Gazette of the Republic of the Philippines, www.officialgazette.gov.ph/constitutions/1987-constitution

Thailand

Act for the Enforcement of the Geneva Convention Relative to the Treatment of Prisoners of War of August, 12, 1949, 1955, B.E. 2498, http://thailaws.com/law/t_laws/tlaw0453.pdf

Act on the Organization of the Military Court, 1955, B.E. 2498

Constitution of the Kingdom of Thailand, 2017, International Criminal Court Legal Tools Database, unofficial translation, www.legal-tools.org/doc/f913cc/pdf

Criminal Code of Thailand, 1956, B.E. 2499, Thailand Law Online, www.thailandlawonline.com/laws-in-thailand/thailand-criminal-law-text-translation

Timor-Leste

Constitution of the Democratic Republic of Timor-Leste 2002, International Criminal Court Legal Tools Database, www.legal-tools.org/doc/34f041

Criminal Procedures Code, Decree-Law No. 13/2005, Timor-Leste Government Decree-Laws, http://mj.gov.tl/jornal/lawsTL/RDTL-Law/RDTL-Decree-Laws/Decree-Law%2013-2005.pdf

Penal Code, Decree-Law No. 19/2009, Timor-Leste Government Decree-Laws, http://mj.gov.tl/jornal/lawsTL/RDTL-Law/RDTL-Decree-Laws/Decree%20Law%2019-2009.pdf

United Nations Transitional Administration for East Timor, *Regulation No. 15 of 2000 on the Establishment of Panels with Exclusive Jurisdiction over Serious Criminal Offences*, 6 June 2000, International Criminal Court Legal Tools Database, www.legal-tools.org/doc/c082f8/pdf

United Nations Transitional Administration for East Timor, *Regulation No. 10 of 2001 on the Establishment of a Commission for Reception, Truth and Reconciliation in East Timor*, 13 July 2001, International Criminal Court Legal Tools Database, www.legal-tools.org/doc/afd3d9

Vietnam

Constitution of the Socialist Republic of Vietnam, 1992, Ministry of Justice, https://moj.gov.vn/vbpq/en/lists/vn%20bn%20php%20lut/view_detail.aspx?itemid=10450

Criminal Code, No. 100/2015/QH13, 27 November 2015, amended and supplemented by Law No. 12/2017/QH14. International Criminal Court Legal Tools Database, www.legal-tools.org/doc/8543a1

Criminal Procedure Code, No. 19/2003/QH11, 26 November 2003, International Criminal Court Legal Tools Database, www.legal-tools.org/doc/ba3c4b

Law on Militia and Self-Defence Forces, No. 43/2009/QH12, VBPL, http://vbpl.vn/tw/Pages/vbpqen-toanvan.aspx?ItemID=10485

Law on Organization of the People's Courts, No. 33/2002/QH10, 2 April 2002, International Criminal Court Legal Tools Database, www.legal-tools.org/doc/5349e1/pdf

REFERENCES

Abbott, K. W. (1999). International Relations Theory, International Law, and the Regime Governing Atrocities in Internal Conflicts. *American Journal of International Law*, 93, 361–79.

Acedillo, F. A. (2016). Seminar on Gender Justice and Working Session on the Challenges of the Ratification and Implementation of the Rome Statute by Indonesia: Gender Justice through the Domestic Implementation of Rome Statute Standards – The Philippine Experience, PGA, (26 May 2016) www.pgaction.org/pdf/Rep-Acedillo_remarks-indonesia.pdf.

Acharya, A. (2004). How Ideas Spread: Whose Norms Matter? Norm Localization and Institutional Change in Asian Regionalism. *International Organization*, 58(2), 239–75.

(2011). Norm Subsidiarity and Regional Orders: Sovereignty, Regionalism, and Rule-Making in the Third World. *International Studies Quarterly*, 55(1), 95–123.

(2012a). Local and Transnational Civil Society as Agents of Norm Diffusion, amitavacharya.com/sites/default/files/Local%20and%20Transnational%20Civil%20Society%20as%20Agents%20of%20Norm%20Diffusion.pdf.

(2012b). *The Making of Southeast Asia: International Relations of a Region.* Singapore: Institute of Southeast Asian Studies Publishing.

(2013). The R2P and Norm Diffusion: Towards a Framework of Norm Circulation. *Global Responsibility to Protect*, 5(4), 466–79.

(2014). *Rethinking Power, Institutions and Ideas in World Politics: Whose IR?* Milton Park: Routledge.

Adams, B. (2005). Cambodia's Judiciary: Up to the Task? In J. Ramji & B. Van Schaak, eds., *Bringing the Khmer Rouge to Justice: Prosecuting Mass Violence before the Cambodian Courts*. Liston, NY: Edwin Mellen Press, pp. 127–67.

ADHOC. (2012). Workshop – 10th Anniversary of the Entry into Force of the Rome Statute of the International Criminal Court, (2 July 2012) www.adhoccambodia.org/workshop-%E2%80%93-10th-anniversary-of-the-entry-into-force-of-the-rome-statute-of-the-international-criminal-court.

Advisory Commission on Rakhine State. (2017). Towards a Peaceful, Fair and Prosperous Future for the People of Rakhine: Final Report of the Advisory

Commission on Rakhine State, (August 2017) www.rakhinecommission.org/the-final-report.

Agus, F. (1999). *Traditional Laws of War in Indonesia: Published for 50th Anniversary of Geneva Conventions 1949.* Jakarta: Trisakti University.

(2014). Milestones, Flaws in Draft Penal Code, *The Jakarta Post* (27 March 2014) www.thejakartapost.com/news/2014/03/27/milestones-flaws-draft-penal-code.html.

Ainley, K. (2014). Transitional Justice in Cambodia: The Coincidence of Power and Principle. In R. Jeffery & H. J. Kim, eds., *Transitional Justice in the Asia-Pacific*. New York: Cambridge University Press, pp. 125–56.

Akande, D. & Shah., S. (2010). Immunities of State Officials, International Crimes, and Foreign Domestic Courts. *European Journal of International Law*, 21(4), 815–52.

Albar, S. Y. (2006). It Is Not Possible to Defend Myanmar, *The Wall Street Journal* (24 July 2006) www.wsj.com/articles/SB115369460860014832.

Aliansi Nasional Reformasi KUHP. R KUHP, reformasikuhp.org/r-kuhp.

Alston, P. (2008). Promotion and Protection of all Human Rights, Civil, Political and Cultural Rights, Including the Right to Development: Report of the Special Rapporteur on Extrajudicial, Summary or Arbitrary Executions, UN Doc. A/HRC/8/3/Add.2 (16 April 2008).

(2009). Report of the Special Rapporteur on Extrajudicial, Summary or Arbitrary Executions, Philip Alston, Addendum, Follow-Up to Country Recommendations – Philippines, UN Doc. A/HRC/11/2/Add.8 (29 April 2009).

Amindoni, A. (2016). Indonesia Rejects IPT 1965 Recommendations, *The Jakarta Post* (20 July 2016) www.thejakartapost.com/news/2016/07/20/indonesia-rejects-ipt-1965-recommendations.html.

Amnesty International. (1976). The Amnesty International Annual Report 1975–1976, www.amnesty.org/download/Documents/POL1000011976 ENGLISH.PDF.

(1979). Amnesty International Report 1979, www.amnesty.org/en/documents/pol10/001/1979/en.

(2001). Amnesty International's Comments on the Law on Human Rights Courts (Law No.26/2000), www.refworld.org/pdfid/3c29def1a.pdf.

(2003). Kingdom of Cambodia: Amnesty International's Position and Concerns Regarding the Proposed 'Khmer Rouge' tribunal, (24 April 2003) www.amnesty.org/en/documents/asa23/005/2003/en.

(2013). Indonesia: Military Tribunals Being Used to Shield Human Rights Violators, (19 June 2013) www.amnesty.org/en/latest/news/2013/06/indonesia-kopassus-trial.

(2016). Myanmar: Scrap or Amend New Law that Could Grant Immunity to Former Presidents, (28 January 2016) www.amnesty.org/en/press-releases/

2016/01/myanmar-scrap-or-amend-new-law-that-could-grant-immunity-to-former-presidents.

(2018). Philippines 2017/2018, www.amnesty.org/en/countries/asia-and-the-pacific/philippines/report-philippines.

Anderl, F. (2016). The Myth of the Local. *The Review of International Organizations*, 11(2), 197–218.

Andrews, T. & Smith, M. (2016). This Is Not the Time to Ease Up on Burma, *Fortify Rights* (19 May 2016) https://www.fortifyrights.org/mya-inv-oped-2016-05-19/.

Angeles, L. C. (1994). *The Quest for Justice: Obstacles to the Redress of Human Rights Violations in the Philippines*. Manila: University of the Philippines Press.

Anghie, A. & Chimni, B. S. (2003). Third World Approaches to International Law and Individual Responsibility in Internal Conflicts. *Chinese Journal of International Law*, 2, 77–103.

Anstis, S. (2012). Access to Justice in Cambodia: The Experience of Grassroots Networks in Land Rights Issues, Centre for International Sustainable Development Law, McGill University (June 2012).

Antiporda, J. (2016). Int'l Court Can Look into Drug Killings – CHR, *The Manila Times* (23 August 2016) www.manilatimes.net/intl-court-can-look-into-drug-killings-chr/281635.

Aquino III, B. A. (2011). State of the Nation Address, *Philippine Daily Inquirer* (25 July 2011) newsinfo.inquirer.net/29633/state-of-the-nation-address.

Aritonang, M. S. (2013). Govt Officially Rejects Rome Statute, *The Jakarta Post* (21 May 2013) www.thejakartapost.com/news/2013/05/21/govt-officially-rejects-rome-statute.html.

Arndt, M. (2013). *India's Foreign Policy and Regional Multilateralism*. Basingstoke: Palgrave Macmillan.

Article 2. (2012). Article 2 Special Report: The Philippines' Hollow Human Rights System. *Article 2*, 11(2–3), 25.

ASEAN. (2003). 14th EU-ASEAN Ministerial Meeting Brussels: Joint Co-Chairmen's Statement, (27–28 January 2003) asean.org/?static_post=14th-eu-asean-ministerial-meeting-brussels-27-28-january-2003.

(2018). Chairman's Statement of the 33rd ASEAN Summit, Singapore, (13 November 2018) asean.org/storage/2018/11/33rd_ASEAN_Summit_Chairman_s_Statement_Final.pdf.

ASEAN Parliamentarians for Human Rights. (2018). Myanmar Authorities Must Be Brought before International Criminal Court, Say Southeast Asian Lawmakers, (24 August 2018) aseanmp.org/2018/08/24/mp-statement-rohingya-crisis.

ASEAN-Malaysia National Secretariat. (2016). Rebuttal to the 'Myanmar Times' on the Statement Made by U Zaw Htay, Deputy Director General of the

President's Office, Myanmar, (3 December 2016) www.kln.gov.my/web/
nam_windhoek/news-from-mission/-/blogs/7012601.

AJAR. (2015). Opening the Box: Women's Experiences of War, Peace, and Impunity in Myanmar, (23 September 2015) www.burma partnership.org/wp-con
tent/uploads/2015/09/Opening-the-Box-English.pdf.

(2016). Transitional Justice and the Aceh Truth and Reconciliation Commission, Workshop Report 20–23 September 2016, asia-ajar.org/201611/transi-
tional-justice-aceh-truth-reconciliation-commission.

The Asia Foundation. (2005). Conflict Management Program in the Philippines:
A Semi-Annual Report from The Asia Foundation to the United States
Agency for International Development 01 January 2005–30 June 2005,
pdf.usaid.gov/pdf_docs/Pdacf153.pdf.

Asian Human Rights Commission. (2013). Philippines: 'Licenced' to Torture, Kill
& to Silence the Oppressed, (December 2013) www.humanrights.asia/wp-
content/uploads/2013/07/AHRC-SPR-001-2013-HRRpt-Philippines.pdf.

(2016). Burma/Myanmar: Prosecutor Concludes That Case against Soldiers for
Ko Par Gyi Killing 'Erroneous', (10 April 2016) www.humanrights.asia/
news/ahrc-news/AHRC-STM-046-2016.

Asian Legal Resource Centre. (2016). Burma/Myanmar: International Community
Must Assist in the Re-Eengineering of Justice Institutions, (18 March 2016)
alrc.asia/burmamyanmar-international-community-must-assist-in-the-re-
engineering-of-justice-institutions.

(2018). Indonesia: The Government Cannot Avoid the Ad Hoc Human Rights
Court to Address Past Human Rights Abuses, (28 August 2018) alrc.asia/the-
government-cannot-avoid-the-ad-hoc-human-rights-court-to-address-past-
human-rights-abuses.

Aspinall, E. (2008). Peace without Justice? The Helsinki Peace Process in Aceh.
Centre for Humanitarian Dialogue, www.hdcentre.org/wp-content/uploads/
2016/08/56JusticeAcehfinalrevJUNE08-May-2008.pdf.

Asril, S. (2013). *Priyo: Penyerangan LP Cebongan Kriminal Bukan Pelanggaran
HAM* [Priyo: Cebongan Prison Assault Criminal Not a Human Rights
Violation], *Kompas* (12 April 2013) nasional.kompas.com/read/2013/04/12/
15002171/Priyo.Penyerangan.LP.Cebongan.Kriminal..Bukan.Pelanggaran.HAM.

Associated Press. (2016). Myanmar's Suu Kyi Vows to Amend Junta-Era Constitution,
The Jakarta Post (18 April 2016) https://www.thejakartapost.com/seasia/2016/
04/18/myanmars-suu-kyi-vows-to-amend-junta-era-constitution.html.

(2018). Myanmar Soldiers Jailed for Killing Civilians in Rare Trial, *AP News*
(21 January 2018) apnews.com/7410e80516794e7d99e37a890279f800/Myan
mar-soldiers-jailed-for-killing-civilians-in-rare-trial.

Atmasasmita, R. (2006). *Karakteristik Tindak Pidana Dalam Statuta ICC dan
Dampak Pembentukan Pengadilan Pidana Internasional (ICC) Terhadap
Perkembangan Hukum Pidana* [Characteristics of Criminal Offenses in the

ICC Statute and the Impact of the Establishment of an International Criminal Court (ICC) on the Development of Criminal Law]. *Indonesian Journal of International Law*, 4(1), 61–74.

Aung, M. (2009). *Building the Tatmadaw: Myanmar Armed Forces since 1948*. Singapore: Institute of Southeast Asian Studies.

Aung, N. L. (2018). Legal experts urges Myanmar to Answer ICC Query, *Myanmar Times* (25 June 2018) www.mmtimes.com/news/legal-experts-urges-myanmar-answer-icc-query.html.

Aung, S. Y. (2016). Outgoing Parliament Approves Presidential Protection, Immunity Bill, *The Irrawaddy* (28 January 2016) www.irrawaddy.com/burma/outgoing-parliament-approves-presidential-protection-immunity-bill.html.

Aung San Suu Kyi. (2018). Democratic Transition in Myanmar: Challenges and the Way Forward, (23 August 2018) www.statecounsellor.gov.mm/en/node/2111.

Australian Department of Foreign Affairs and Trade. (2019). Sanctions Regimes: Myanmar, dfat.gov.au/international-relations/security/sanctions/sanctions-regimes/Pages/myanmar.aspx#Financial.

Australian Permanent Mission Geneva. (2012). Universal Periodic Review of the Philippines Statement by Australia, (29 May 2012) geneva.mission.gov.au/gene/Statement330.html.

Awaludin, H. (2009). *Peace in Aceh: Notes on the Peace Process between the Republic of Indonesia and the Aceh Freedom Movement (GAM) in Helsinki* (T. Scott trans). Washington, DC: Centre for Strategic and International Studies.

AWDO et al. (2016). Joint Statement: Five Years of War: A Call for Peace, Justice, and Accountability in Myanmar, (9 June 2016) hrp.law.harvard.edu/press-releases/joint-statement-five-years-of-war-a-call-for-peace-justice-and-accountability-in-myanmar.

Aye Nai. (2014). Burmese Soldier Jailed for Raping Disabled Kachin Girl, *DVB* (12 November 2014) dvb.com.mm/news/burmese-soldier-jailed-for-raping-disabled-kachin-girl-myanmar/45785.

Barton, C. (2006). KR Trial Holds Promise for Court Reform, *The Phnom Penh Post* (10 March 2006) www.phnompenhpost.com/national/kr-trial-holds-promise-court-reform.

BBC. (2010). Indonesia Cancels Netherlands Visit over Arrest Threat, *BBC* (5 October 2010) www.bbc.com/news/world-asia-pacific-11475558.

Becker, E. (1998). *When the War Was Over: Cambodia and the Khmer Rouge Revolution*. New York: Public Affairs.

Bederman, D. J. (2000). Constructivism, Positivism, and Empiricism in International Law. *The Georgetown Law Journal*, 89, 469–99.

Beittinger-Lee, V. (2009). *(Un)Civil Society and Political Change in Indonesia: A Contested Arena*. Milton Park: Routledge.

Bennett, A. & Elman, C. (2007). Case Study Methods in the International Relations Subfield. *Comparative Political Studies*, 40(2), 170–95.

Bennett, L. & Layard, A. (2015). Legal Geography: Becoming Spatial Detectives. *Geography Compass*, 9(7), 406–22.

Bergsmo, M., Bekou, O., & Jones, A. (2010). Complementarity after Kampala: Capacity Building and the ICC's Legal Tools. *Goettingen Journal of International Law*, 2(2), 791–811.

Bernath, J. (2015). 'Complex Political Victims' in the Aftermath of Mass Atrocity: Reflections on the Khmer Rouge Tribunal in Cambodia. *International Journal of Transitional Justice*, 10(1), 46–66.

Betts, A. & Orchard, P. (2014). Introduction: The Normative Institutionalization-Implementation Gap. In A. Betts & P. Orchard, eds., *Implementation and World Politics: How International Norms Change Practice*. Oxford: Oxford University Press, pp. 1–26.

Bhabha, H. K. (1994). *The Location of Culture*. Milton Park: Routledge.

Biron, J. (2017). Full Text of the Complaint before the International Criminal Court (ICC) against Pres. Rodrigo Duterte, *Biron Law* (24 April 2017) www.jamesbiron.com/2017/04/full-text-of-the-complaint-before-the-international-criminal-court-icc-against-pres-rodrigo-duterte.

Björkdahl, A., Höglund, K., Millar, G., van der Lijn, J., & Verkoren, W. (2016). Introduction: Peacebuilding through the Lens of Friction. In A. Björkdahl, K. Höglund, G. Millar, J. van der Lijn, & W. Verkoren, eds., *Peacebuilding and Friction: Global and Local Encounters in Post Conflict-Societies*. Milton Park: Routledge, pp. 1–16.

Blomley, N. K. (1994). *Law, Space and the Geographies of Power*. New York: Guilford Press.

Board of Inquiry. (2015). The Board of Inquiry Mamasapano Report, March 2015, (13 March 2015) www.gov.ph/2015/03/13/boi-mamasapano-report-march-2015.

Boas, G. J. (2012). What's in a Word: The Nature and Meaning of International Criminal Justice. In G. Boas, W. A. Schabas, & M. P. Scharf, eds., *International Criminal Justice: Legitimacy and Coherence*. London: Edward Elgar, pp. 1–24.

Boister, N. & Cryer, R. (2008). *The Tokyo International Military Tribunal – A Reappraisal*. Oxford: Oxford University Press.

Branch, A. (2010). What the ICC Review Conference Can't Fix, *African Arguments* (11 March 2010) africanarguments.org/2010/03/11/what-the-icc-review-conference-can't-fix.

Bräuchler, B. (2009). *Reconciling Indonesia: Grassroots Agency for Peace*. New York: Routledge.

Brinkley, J. (2013). Justice Squandered: Cambodia's Khmer Rouge Tribunal. *World Affairs*, 176(3), 41–8.

Brown, M. & Zasloff, J. J. (1998). *Cambodia Confounds the Peacemakers 1979–1998*. Ithaca, NY: Cornell University Press.

Bryant, R. L. (2005). *Nongovernmental Organisations in Environmental Struggles: Politics and the Making of Moral Capital in the Philippines*. New Haven, CT: Yale University Press.

Buan, L., Talabong, R., & Gavlian, J. (2019). Duterte Gov't Allows 'Drug War' Deaths to Go Unsolved, *Rappler* (14 January 2019) www.rappler.com/news break/in-depth/220595-duterte-government-drug-war-deaths-unsolved.

Buckley-Zistel, S. (2016). Frictional Spaces: Transitional Justice between the Global and the Local. In A. Björkdahl, K. Höglund, G. Millar, J. van der Lijn, & W. Verkoren, eds., *Peacebuilding and Friction: Global and Local Encounters in Post Conflict-Societies*. Milton Park: Routledge, pp. 17–31.

Bureau of Democracy, Human Rights and Labor. (1998). The Philippines Country Report on Human Rights Practices for 1997, (30 January 1998) 1997-2001.state.gov/www/global/human_rights/1997_hrp_report/philippi.html.

(2004). 2003 Country Reports on Human Rights Practices: Philippines, (25 February 2004) 2009-2017.state.gov/j/drl/rls/hrrpt/2003/27786.htm.

Burgis-Kasthala, M. (2016). Scholarship as Dialogue? TWAIL and the Politics of Methodology. *Journal of International Criminal Justice*, 14(4), 921–37.

Burke, A., Williams, N., Barron, P., Jolliffe, K., & Carr, T. (2017). *The Contested Areas of Myanmar Subnational Conflict, Aid, and Development*. The Asia Foundation, asiafoundation.org/publication/contested-areas-myanmar-sub national-conflict-aid-development.

Burke-White, W. W. (2008). Proactive Complementarity: The International Criminal Court and National Courts in the Rome System of International Justice. *Harvard International Law Journal*, 49(1), 53–108.

Burma Campaign UK. (2010). UK Government Supports Burma Regime Referral to International Criminal Court, *Burma Partnership* (25 March 2010) www.burmapartnership.org/2010/03/uk-government-supports-burma-regime-referral-to-international-criminal-court.

Burma Lawyers' Council. (2007). Part C: On Criminal Accountability Issue in Burma and Possible Referral of the UN Security Council to the International Criminal Court. *LawKa PaLaw: Legal Journal on Burma*, 28(32–45), 44.

Burma Partnership. (2015). Joint Statement on Elections from the Embassies of Australia, Canada, Denmark, France, Norway, Japan, Sweden, the United Kingdom, and the United States of America, (15 September 2015) www.burmapartnership.org/wp-content/uploads/2015/09/Emb-RGN-Joint-Statement-on-elections-and-religion-FINAL.pdf.

Burma Partnership & Equality Myanmar. (2014). Burma: All the President's Men, www.burmapartnership.org/wp-content/uploads/2014/09/All-the-Presidents-Men1.pdf.

Burma Task Force. (2018). Hundreds of Rohingya Supporters Stand in Front of Congress and Demand Sanctions on Burma, (27 August 2018) www.burmataskforce.org/news/hundreds-rohingya-supporters-stand-front-congress-and-demand-sanctions-burma.

Butt, S. (2014). The Position of International Law within the Indonesian Legal System. *Emory International Law Review*, 28(1), 1–28.

Butt, S. & Hansell, D. (2004). The Masykur Abdul Kadir Case: Indonesian Constitutional Court Decision No 013/PUU-I/2003. *Asian Law*, 6, 176–96.

Cabico, G. K. (2018). 4 More Communications vs Duterte Filed at ICC – CHR, *The Philippine Star* (4 October 2018) www.philstar.com/headlines/2018/10/04/1857212/4-more-communications-vs-duterte-filed-icc-chr#IWTj4U7RI2lU2RBF.99.

Cambodia. (2013). National Report Submitted in Accordance with Paragraph 5 of the Annex to Human Rights Council Resolution 16/21: Cambodia, UN Doc. A/HRC/WG.6/18/KHM/1 (21 November 2013).

Cambodia Tribunal Monitor. Chronology & Negotiating History, www.cambodiatribunal.org/history/tribunal-background/chronology-negotiating-history.

Cambodian Defenders Project. (2013). Women's Hearing with the Young Genderation (sic): Panel Statement, (24 September 2013) gbvkr.org/wp-content/uploads/2013/11/Women-Hearing-2013-Panel-Statement-EN-final.pdf.

Cambodian Human Rights Action Committee (CHRAC). (2015). CHRAC welcomes the most recent developments in Cases 003 and 004, (5 March 2015) www.adhoccambodia.org/press-release-chrac-welcomes-the-most-recent-developments-in-cases-003-and-004.

Campbell, K. (2014). Reassembling International Justice: The Making of 'the Social' in International Criminal Law and Transitional Justice. *International Journal of Transitional Justice*, 8(1), 53–74.

Capie, D. (2008). Localization as Resistance: The Contested Diffusion of Small Arms Norms in Southeast Asia. *Security Dialogue*, 39(6), 637–58.

Cassese, A. (2008). *International Criminal Law*. Oxford: Oxford University Press.

Central Intelligence Agency. (2019). The World Factbook: Cambodia, (13 November 2019) www.cia.gov/library/publications/the-world-factbook/geos/cb.html.

Centre for Peace & Conflict Studies (CPCS) (2015). Listening to Voices – Perspectives from the Tatmadaw's Rank and File, (July 2015) www.centrepeaceconflictstudies.org/publications/browse/7341-2.

Chandler, D. (2000). Will There Be a Trial for the Khmer Rouge? *Ethics & International Affairs*, 14, 67–82.

    (2008a). *History of Cambodia*. Chiang Mai: Silkworm Books.

    (2008b). Cambodia Deals with Its Past: Collective Memory, Demonisation and Induced Amnesia. *Totalitarian Movements and Political Religions*, 9(2-3), 355–69.

Charlesworth, H. & Larking, E., eds. (2015). *Human Rights and the Universal Periodic Review: Rituals and Ritualism*. Cambridge: Cambridge University Press.

Checkel, J. T. (1998). The Constructivist Turn in International Relations Theory. *World Politics*, 50(2), 324–48.

Cheesman, N. (2009). Thin Rule of Law or Un-Rule of Law in Myanmar? *Pacific Affairs*, 82(4), 597–613.

(2011). How an Authoritarian Regime in Burma Used Special Courts to Defeat Judicial Independence. *Law and Society Review*, 45(4), 801–30.

(2012). Myanmar's Courts and the Sounds Money Makes. In N. Cheesman, M. Skidmore, & T. Wilson, eds., *Myanmar's Transition: Openings, Obstacles and Opportunities*. Singapore: ISEAS Publishing, pp. 231–56.

(2015a). *Opposing the Rule of Law: How Myanmar's Courts Make Law and Order*. Cambridge: Cambridge University Press.

(2015b). That Signifier of Desire, the Rule of Law. *Social Research*, 82(2), 267–90.

Cheesman, N., D'Costa, B. & Haberkorn, T. (2016). Anticipating the Struggle against Everyday Impunity in Myanmar through Accounts from Bangladesh and Thailand. *Asia & the Pacific Policy Studies*, 3(1), 48–61.

Cheesman, N. & Kyaw Min San. (2014). Not Just Defending; Advocating for Law in Myanmar. *Wisconsin International Law Journal*, 31(3), 702–33.

Cheesman, N., Skidmore, M., & Wilson, T. (2012). *Myanmar's Transition: Openings, Obstacles and Opportunities*. Singapore: Institute of Southeast Asian Studies.

Cheunboran, C. (2018). Cambodia-China Relations: What Do Cambodia's Past Strategic Directions Tell Us? In D S. Udom, S. Suon, & S. Bulut, eds., *Cambodia's Foreign Relations in Regional and Global Contexts*. Berlin: Konrad-Adenauer-Stiftung, pp. 227–48.

CHRAC. (2011). CHRAC Expresses Concern over the Emerging Conflict between Co-investigating Judges, (9 December 2011) ckn-media.blogspot.com/2011/12/press-release-on-conflict-between-ecccs.html.

Christensen, M. J. & Kjeldgaard-Pedersen, A. (2018). Competing Perceptions of Hybrid Justice: International v. National in the Extraordinary Chambers in the Courts in Cambodia. *International Criminal Law Review*, 18(1), 127–53.

CICC. (2008). Letter to Her Excellency Gloria Macapagal-Arroyo, Re: Ratification of the Rome Treaty of the International Criminal Court (14 April 2008).

(2011). Philippines, Maldives, Vanuatu: More Asia-Pacific Countries Join Global Fight to End Impunity, *Asia-Pacific Updates*, 8 (December 2011).

(2012). Global Coalition Calls on Indonesia to Join the International Criminal Court, (9 July 2012) archive.iccnow.org/documents/PR_for_Indonesia_July_2012_Final.pdf.

(2014). Jokowi: Act on Promises to Join ICC, (3 December 2014) archive.iccnow.org/documents/CICCPR_CGJ_Indonesia_Dec2014_ENG.pdf.

(2015). Seminar advances ICC prospects for Malaysia, Indonesia, (3 September 2015) ciccglobaljustice.wordpress.com/2015/09/03/seminar-advances-icc-prospects-for-malaysia-indonesia/.

Ciorciari, J. (2009). International Politics and the Mess in Myanmar, *JPRI Working Paper*, 114.

Ciorciari, J. & Heindel, A. (2014). *Hybrid Justice: The Extraordinary Chambers in the Courts of Cambodia (Law, Meaning, and Violence)*. Detroit: University of Michigan Press.

Clarke, G. (2013). *Civil Society in the Philippines: Theoretical, Methodological and Policy Debates*. New York: Routledge.

Clarke, K. M. (2009). *Fictions of Justice: The International Criminal Court and the Challenges of Legal Pluralism in Sub-Saharan Africa*. Cambridge: Cambridge University Press.

Clark, P. (2018). *Distant Justice: The Impact of the International Criminal Court on African Politics*. Cambridge: Cambridge University Press.

Cloward, K. (2016). *When Norms Collide: Local Responses to Activism against Female Genital Mutilation and Early Marriage*. Oxford: Oxford University Press.

Cohen, D., Hyde, M., & Van Tuyl, P. (2015). *A Well-Reasoned Opinion? Critical Analysis of the First Case against the Alleged Senior Leaders of the Khmer Rouge (Case 002/01)*. East-West Center, Asian International Justice Initiative, www.eastwestcenter.org/system/tdf/private/cohen-wellreasoned2015 .pdf?file=1&type=node&id=35372.

Collins, A. (2013). Norm Diffusion and ASEAN's Adoption and Adaption of Global HIV/AIDS Norms. *International Relations of the Asia-Pacific*, 13(3), 369–97.

Commission for Reception Truth and Reconciliation. (2006). Chega! Final Report of the Commission for Reception, Truth and Reconciliation in Timor Leste, www.etan.org/news/2006/cavr.htm.

Committee against Torture. (2010). Consideration of Reports Submitted by States Parties under Article 19 of the Convention: Second Periodic Report of States Parties Due in 1997: Cambodia, UN Doc. CAT/C/KHM/2 (2 February 2010).

Committee for Implementation of Recommendations (2019). Report to the People Submitted by the Committee for Implementation of the Recommendations on Rakhine State, on Its Activities from September to December 2018, *The Global New Light of Myanmar* (8 March 2019) rakhine .unionenterprise.org/index.php/latest-news-en/632-report-to-the-people-submitted-by-the-committee-for-implementation-of-the-recommendations-on-rakhine-state-on-its-activities-from-september-to-december-2018.

Conde, C. H. (2002). World Briefing Asia: Philippines: International Court Questioned, *The New York Times* (6 September 2002) www.nytimes.com/2002/09/06/world/world-briefing-asia-philippines-international-court-questioned .html.

Craven, M., Fitzmaurice, M., & Vogiatzi, M. (2007). *Time, History and International Law*. Leiden: Martinus Nijhoff Publishers.

Cribb, R. (2009). The Indonesian Massacres. In S. Totten & W. S. Parsons, eds., *Century of Genocide*. New York: Routledge, pp. 193–217.

(2011). Avoiding Clemency: The Trial and Transfer of Japanese War Criminals in Indonesia, 1946–1949. *Japanese Studies*, 31(2), 151–70.

(2016). The Burma Trials of Japanese War Criminals, 1946–1949. In K. von Lingen, ed., *War Crimes Trials in the Wake of Decolonization and Cold War in Asia, 1945–1956: Justice in Time of Turmoil*. New York: Palgrave Macmillan, pp. 117–42.

Crothers, L. (2014). Hun Sen Accused of Genocide in ICC Complaint, *The Cambodia Daily* (21 March 2014) www.cambodiadaily.com/archives/hun-sen-accused-of-genocide-in-icc-complaint-54669.

Crouch, H. (2007). *The Army and Politics in Indonesia*. Sheffield: Equinox Publishing.

(2010). *Political Reform in Indonesia after Soeharto*. Singapore: Institute of Southeast Asian Studies.

Crouch, M. (2014a). The Common Law and Constitutional Writs: Prospects for Accountability in Myanmar. In M. Crouch & T. Lindsey, eds., *Law, Society and Transition in Myanmar*. Oxford: Hart Publishing, pp. 141–57.

(2014b). The Layers of Legal Development in Myanmar. In M. Crouch & T. Lindsey, eds., *Law, Society and Transition in Myanmar*. Oxford: Hart Publishing, pp. 33–56.

(2019). Myanmar's Courts in an Era of Semi-Military Rule. In H. P. Lee & M. Pittard, eds., *Asia-Pacific Judiciaries: Independence, Impartiality and Integrity*. Cambridge: Cambridge University Press, pp. 264–83.

Cruvellier, T. (2018). Rithy Panh: Living the Experience of Genocide in Body and Soul, *Justiceinfo.net* (27 November 2018) www.justiceinfo.net/en/justiceinfo-comment-and-debate/in-depth-interviews/39596-rithy-panh-living-the-experience-of-genocide-in-body-and-soul.html.

Cryer, R. (2005a). International Criminal Law vs State Sovereignty: Another Round? *European Journal of International Law*, 16(5), 979–1000.

(2005b). *Prosecuting International Crimes: Selectivity and the International Criminal Law Regime*. Cambridge: Cambridge University Press.

Cuddy, A. (2015). Victim Lawyers Stung by Cuts, *The Phnom Penh Post* (11 May 2015) www.phnompenhpost.com/national/victim-lawyers-stung-cuts.

Curato, N. (2016). Politics of Anxiety, Politics of Hope: Penal Populism and Duterte's Rise to Power. *Journal of Current Southeast Asian Affairs*, 35(3), 91–109.

d'Aspremont, J. (2016). Martti Koskenniemi, the Mainstream, and Self-Reflectivity. *Leiden Journal of International Law*, 29(3), 625–39.

Daqun, L. (2012). Chinese Humanitarian Law and International Humanitarian Law. In C. Stahn & L. van den Herik, eds., *The Diversification and*

Fragmentation of International Criminal Law. Leiden: Martinus Nijhoff Publishers, pp. 349–59.

David, R. & Holliday, I. (2012). International Sanctions or International Justice? Shaping Political Development in Myanmar. *Australian Journal of International Affairs,* 66(2), 121–38.

Davies, M. (2013). ASEAN and Human Rights Norms: Constructivism, Rational Choice, and the Action-Identity Gap. *International Relations of the Asia-Pacific,* 13(2), 207–31.

de Langis, T., Strasser, J., Kim, T., & Taing, S. (2014). *Like Ghost Changes Body: A Study on the Impact of Forced Marriage under the Khmer Rouge Regime.* TPO Cambodia (October 2014) kh.boell.org/sites/default/files/forced_marriage_study_report_tpo_october_2014.pdf.

de Lima, L. M. (2009). Keynote Speech on the Occasion of the Third General Assembly of the Peace Advocates for Truth, Healing and Justice, Bantayog ng mga Bayani, Quezon Avenue, Quezon City, 5 September 2009 (5 September 2009).

de Vos, C. (2015). All Roads Lead to Rome: Implementation and Domestic Politics in Kenya and Uganda. In C. de Vos, S. Kendall, & C. Stahn, eds., *Contested Justice: The Politics and Practice of International Criminal Court Interventions.* Cambridge: Cambridge University Press, pp. 379–407.

deGuzman, M. (2018). The Global-Local Dilemma and the ICC's Legitimacy. In N. Grossman, et al., eds., *Legitimacy and International Courts.* Cambridge: Cambridge University Press, pp. 62–82.

Deitelhoff, N. & Zimmermann, L. (2014). From the Heart of Darkness: Critical Reading and Genuine Listening in Constructivist Norm Research: A Reply to Stephan Engelkamp, Katharina Glaab, and Judith Renner. *World Political Science Review,* 10(1), 17–31.

Department of Foreign Affairs. (2011). Philippines Deposits Instrument of Ratification for Rome Statute of the International Criminal Court (31 August 2011).

Dillon, H. S., et al. (2015). Civil Society Declaration: Demand the Real Justice for Victims of Human Rights Violations in Indonesia (9 July 2015).

Donovan, D. A. (1993). Cambodia: Building a Legal System from Scratch. *The International Lawyer,* 27(2), 445–54.

Dosch, J. (2012). The Role of Civil Society in Cambodia's Peace-Building Process: Have Foreign Donors Made a Difference? *Asian Survey,* 52(6), 1067–88.

Drexler, E., (2010). The Failure of International Justice in East Timor and Indonesia. In A. L. Hinton, ed., *Transitional Justice: Global Mechanisms and Local Realities after Genocide and Mass Violence.* New Brunswick, NJ: Rutgers University Press, pp. 49–66.

(2013). Fatal Knowledges: The Social and Political Legacies of Collaboration and Betrayal in Timor-Leste. *International Journal of Transitional Justice,* 7(1), 74–94.

Drumbl, M. A. (2007). *Atrocity, Punishment, and International Law*. Cambridge: Cambridge University Press.

Dukalskis, A. (2015). Transitional Justice in Burma/Myanmar: Cross-National Patterns and Domestic Context. *Irish Studies in International Affairs*, 26, 1–15.

Ear, S. (2010). Khmer Rouge Tribunal vs. Karmic Justice. *The New York Times* (17 March 2010) www.nytimes.com/2010/03/18/opinion/18iht-edear.html.

ECCC. (2011). ECCC Reaches Out to Buddhist Monks, (10 August 2011) www.eccc.gov.kh/en/articles/eccc-reaches-out-buddhist-monks.

(2014). UN General Assembly Approves US$ 15.5 Million Funding Reserve, (26 May 2014) www.eccc.gov.kh/en/articles/un-general-assembly-approves-us-155-million-funding-reserve.

(2015). The Court Report: December 2015, www.eccc.gov.kh/sites/default/files/publications/The_Court_Report_Dec_2015.pdf.

Eckert, P. (2007). ASEAN Condemns Myanmar Violence, *Reuters* (28 September 2007) uk.reuters.com/article/uk-myanmar-asean-idUKN2736930120070927.

Eddyono, S. W., Djafar, W., & Sumigar, B. R. F. (2016). *Indonesian Penal Code Reform: Challenges in Reforming Criminal System and Protecting Civil Liberties*. ICJR (November 2015) icjr.or.id/data/wp-content/uploads/2016/03/Envisioning-Indonesian-Penal-Code-Reform.pdf.

Egreteau, R. (2011). Burmese Indians in Contemporary Burma: Heritage, Influence, and Perceptions since 1988. *Asian Ethnicity*, 12(1), 33–54.

Ehito, K. (2015). The Struggle for Justice and Reconciliation in Post-Suharto Indonesia. *Southeast Asian Studies*, 4(1), 73–93.

Eleven Media Group. (2018). Myanmar Turns Down ICC's Majority Decision of the Pre-Trial Chamber 1, *The Nation Thailand* (8 September 2018) www.nationmultimedia.com/detail/breakingnews/30354032.

ELSAM. (2016). Receptivity Of Omar Al-Bashir: The Indonesian Government Continuing Impunity, (7 March 2016) elsam.or.id/receptivity-of-omar-al-bashir-the-indonesian-government-continuing-impunity.

(2017). Best Practice from Palu for the Settlement of Past Human Rights Violations, (5 February 2017) elsam.or.id//best-practice-from-palu-for-the-settlement-of-past-human-rights-violations.

Embassy of the United States. (2019). Joint Press Release from the Embassy of the United States and the Embassy of Japan, (20 August 2019) mm.usembassy.gov/joint-press-release-from-the-embassy-of-the-united-states-and-the-embassy-of-japan.

Encarnacion Tadem, T. S. (ed.) (2009). *Localizing and Transnationalizing Contentious Politics: Global Civil Society Movements in the Philippines*. New York: Lexington Books.

Epstein, C. (2011). Who Speaks? Discourse, the Subject and the Study of Identity in International Politics. *European Journal of International Relations*, 17(2), 327–50.

(2014). The Postcolonial Perspective: An Introduction. *International Theory*, 6(2), 294–311.

Etcheson, C. (2004). The Politics of Genocide Justice in Cambodia. In C. P. R. Romano, A. Nollkaemper, & J. K. Kleffner, eds., *Internationalized Criminal Courts and Tribunals: Sierra Leone, East Timor, Kosovo, and Cambodia*. Oxford: Oxford University Press, pp. 181–232.

(2005). *After the Killing Fields: Lessons from the Cambodian Genocide*. Santa Barbara, CA: Praeger.

European Commission, (2016). Reconciliation in Myanmar: Bridging the Divides with Cultural Expression, (March 2014–February 2016) ec.europa .eu/europeaid/projects/reconciliation-myanmar-bridging-divides-cultural-expression_en.

European Union. (2014a). Building Foundations for Justice, (December 2014).

(2014b). Multiannual Indicative Programme 2014–2020 for the European Union's Cooperation with the Kingdom of Cambodia, eeas.europa.eu/sites/ eeas/files/mip-cambodia-2014-2020-en.pdf.

(2015). Blue Book 2015: EU-Indonesian Development Cooperation in 2014, eeas.europa.eu/delegations/indonesia/documents/eu_indonesia/blue_book/ bb2015_en.pdf.

European Union–Philippines Justice Support Programmes (EPJUST I and II). About EPJUST-II, www.epjust2.com/index.php/about-epjust-ii.

Falby, P. (2002). Courting Controversy: Cambodia and the ICC, *The Phnom Penh Post* (11 October 2002) www.phnompenhpost.com/national/courting-con troversy-cambodia-and-icc.

Falvey, P. (2010). Local Transitional Justice Practice in Pretransition Burma. In R. Shaw, L. Waldorf, & P. Hazan, eds., *Localizing Transitional Justice: Interventions and Priorities after Mass Violence*. Palo Alto, CA: Stanford University Press, pp. 253–74.

Farid, H. & Simarmatra, R. (2004). *The Struggle for Truth and Justice: A Survey of Transitional Justice Initiatives throughout Indonesia*. International Center for Transitional Justice (January 2004) ictj.org/sites/default/files/ICTJ-Indo nesia-Survey-Initiative-2004-English.pdf.

Farrelly, N. (2013). Discipline without Democracy: Military Dominance in Post-Colonial Burma. *Australian Journal of International Affairs*, 67(3), 312–26.

Fawthrop, T. & Jarvis, H. (2005). *Getting Away with Genocide? Cambodia's Long Struggle Against the Khmer Rouge*. Sydney: UNSW Press.

Fernida, I. (2014). Calling for Truth about Mass Killings of 1965/6: Civil Society Initiatives in Revealing the Truth of Mass Killings of 1965/6 under the Transitional Justice Framework in Indonesia. PhD Thesis, University of Oslo, www.jus.uio.no/smr/english/about/programmes/indonesia/docs/ thesis-indria-fernida.pdf.

FIDH. (2006a). Implementation of the Rome Statute in Cambodian Law, (March 2006) www.fidh.org/IMG/pdf/cambodge443angformatword.pdf.

(2006b). Civil Society Urges the Cambodian Government to Fully Implement the Statute of the International Criminal Court, (12 May 2006) www.fidh .org/en/region/asia/cambodia/eccc/Civil-Society-Urges-the-Cambodian.

(2014). Burmese Government Urged to Investigate the Enforced Disappearance of Sumlut Roi Ja, (28 October 2014) www.fidh.org/en/region/asia/burma/ 16329-burmese-government-urged-to-investigate-the-enforced-disappear ance-of.

FIDH, Altsean-Burma & Progressive Voice. (2018). Burma/Myanmar's Ongoing Refusal to Pursue Accountability: Time for an ICC Referral, (18 October 2018) altsean.org/reports/ICC_ReferralFactsheetOct2018.pdf.

Findlay, M. (2010). The Challenge for Asian Jurisdictions in the Development of International Criminal Justice. *Sydney Law Review*, 32(2), 215.

(2014). Sign Up or Sign Off – Asia's Reluctant Engagement with the International Criminal Court. *Cambodia Law and Policy Journal*, 1(1), 49–62.

Finnemore, M. (2000). Are Legal Norms Distinctive? *NYU Journal of International Law and Politics*, 32, 699–705.

Finnemore, M. & Sikkink, K. (1998). International Norm Dynamics and Political Change. *International Organization*, 52(4), 887–917.

Fisher, J. (2017). UN Failures on the Rohingya Revealed, *BBC* (28 September 2017) www.bbc.com/news/world-asia-41420973.

Flores Acuña, T. (2013). Definitions of Genocide and Crimes against Humanity: And as Applied in the Philippines RA No. 9851. *The Journal for Social Era Knowledge*, www.synaptiqplus.com/journal-cover-fall-2013/definitions-of-genocide-and-crimes-against-humanity-in-the-philippines-ra-no-9851.

Focarelli, C. (2012). *International Law as a Social Construct: The Struggle for Global Justice*. Oxford: Oxford University Press.

Ford, S. (2010). Is the Failure to Respond Appropriately to a Natural Disaster a Crime against Humanity? The Responsibility to Protect and Individual Criminal Responsibility in the Aftermath of Cyclone Nargis. *Denver Journal of International Law and Policy*, 38(2), 227–77.

Forum-Asia. (2001). Cambodia – 1st ASEAN Country to Ratify International Criminal Court Treaty, (27 November 2001) archive.iccnow.org/docu ments/PRFoumAsiaRatificationCambodia_en.pdf.

Fortify Rights. (2018). 'They Block Everything': Avoidable Deprivations in Humanitarian Aid to Ethnic Civilians Displaced by War in Kachin State, Myanmar, (August 2018) www.fortifyrights.org/downloads/They_Block_ Everything_EN_Fortify_Rights_August_2018.pdf.

Freeland, S. (2013). International Criminal Justice in the Asia-Pacific Region: The Role of the International Criminal Court Treaty Regime. *Journal of International Criminal Justice*, 11(5), 1029–57.

Gaeta, P. (1999). The Defence of Superior Orders: The Statute of International Criminal Court versus Customary International Law. *European Journal of International Law*, 10(1), 172–91.

Gavilan, J. (2017). Additional 'Communication' vs Duterte Filed before Int'l Criminal Court, *Rappler* (6 June 2017) www.rappler.com/nation/172145-supplementary-complaint-duterte-international-criminal-court-drug-killings.

George, A. L. & Bennett, A. (2005). *Case Studies and Theory Development in the Social Sciences*. Boston: MIT Press.

Gidley, R. (2019). *Illiberal Transitional Justice and the Extraordinary Chambers in the Courts of Cambodia*. Basingstoke: Palgrave Macmillan.

Glasius, M. (1999). *Foreign Policy on Human Rights: Its Influence on Indonesia under Soeharto*. Cambridge: Intersentia.

Gledhill, A. (1949). Some Aspects of the Operation of International and Military Law in Burma, 1941–1945. *Modern Law Review*, 12(2), 191–204.

Global Diligence. (2014). Communication under Article 15 of the Rome Statute of the International Criminal Court: The Commission of Crimes against Humanity in Cambodia July 2002 to Present, Executive Summary, (7 October 2014) www.fidh.org/IMG/pdf/executive_summary-2.pdf.

  (2016). Land Grabbers May End Up in The Hague: Global Diligence Welcomes the ICC Prosecutor's New Case Selection Policy, (15 September 2016) www.globaldiligence.com/2016/09/15/land-grabbers-may-end-up-in-the-hague-global-diligence-welcomes-the-icc-prosecutors-new-case-selection-policy.

Global Witness. (2012). Lengthy Jail Sentence for Cambodian Activist Highlights Worsening State Repression amidst Land Grab Crisis, (1 October 2012) www.globalwitness.org/en/archive/lengthy-jail-sentence-cambodian-activist-highlights-worsening-state-repression-amidst-land.

  (2016). Hostile Takeover: How Cambodia's Ruling Family Are Pulling the Strings on the Economy and Amassing Vast Personal Fortunes with Extreme Consequences for the Population, (7 July 2016) www.globalwitness.org/en/reports/hostile-takeover.

Goldstone, R. J. (2011). South-East Asia and International Criminal Law, www.fichl.org/fileadmin/fichl/documents/FICHL_OPS/FICHL_OPS_2_Goldstone_EN.pdf.

Goodale, M. (2006). Ethical Theory as Social Practice. *American Anthropologist*, 108(1), 25–37.

Goodliffe, J., Hawkins, D., Horne, C., & Nielson, D. L. (2012). Dependence Networks and the International Criminal Court. *International Studies Quarterly*, 5(1), 131–47.

Goodman, R. & Jinks, D. (2008). Incomplete Internalization and Compliance with Human Rights Law. *European Journal of International Law*, 19(4), 725–48.

(2013). *Socializing States: Promoting Human Rights through International Law.* Oxford: Oxford University Press.

Gottesman, E. (2003). *Cambodia after the Khmer Rouge: Inside the Politics of Nation Building.* New Haven, CT: Yale University Press.

GRAIN. (2015). Asia's Agrarian Reform in Reverse: Laws Taking Land out of Small Farmers' Hands, (30 April 2015) www.grain.org/article/entries/5195-asia-s-agrarian-reform-in-reverse-laws-taking-land-out-of-small-farmers-hands.

Gramer, R. (2017). Tillerson Finally Brands Myanmar Crisis 'Ethnic Cleansing', *Foreign Policy* (22 November 2017) foreignpolicy.com/2017/11/22/tillerson-finally-brands-myanmar-crisis-ethnic-cleansing-rohingya-muslims-war-crimes-genocide-state-department-asia-refugees.

Gravers, M. (2004). *Nationalism as Political Paranoia in Burma: An Essay on the Historical Practice of Power.* London: Routledge.

Gray, T. (2012). Justice and the Khmer Rouge: Concepts of Just Response to the Crimes of the Democratic Kampuchean Regime in Buddhism and the Extraordinary Chambers in the Courts of Cambodia at the Time of the Khmer Rouge Tribunal. *Working papers in Contemporary Asian Studies*, Lund University.

Gready, P. & Robins, S. (2017). Rethinking Civil Society and Transitional Justice: Lessons from Social Movements and 'New' Civil Society. *International Journal of Human Rights*, 21(7), 956–75.

Green, P., MacManus, T., & de la Cour Venning, A. (2015). *Countdown to Annihilation: Genocide in Myanmar.* International State Crime Initiative (October 2015) statecrime.org/data/2015/10/ISCI-Rohingya-Report-PUBLISHED-VERSION.pdf.

Group of Experts for Cambodia. (1999). Report of the Group of Experts for Cambodia Established Pursuant to General Assembly Resolution 52/135 (18 February 1999) www.legal-tools.org/en/doc/3da509.

Gutman, T. H. (2015). Cambodia, 1979: Trying Khmer Rouge Leaders for Genocide. In K. Sellars, ed., *Trials for International Crimes in Asia*. Cambridge: Cambridge University Press, pp. 167–90.

Hadiprayitno, I. I. (2010). Defensive Enforcement: Human Rights in Indonesia. *Human Rights Review*, 11(3), 373–99.

Hadiwinata, B. S. (2002). *The Politics of NGOs in Indonesia: Developing Democracy and Managing a Movement.* New York: Routledge.

Halliday, S. & Schmidt, P. D. (2009). Introduction: Beyond Methods – Law and Society in Action. In Halliday, S. & Schmidt, P. D., eds., *Conducting Law and Society Research: Reflections on Methods and Practice*. Cambridge: Cambridge University Press, pp. 1–13.

Hamati-Ataya, I. (2012). Reflectivity, Reflexivity, Reflexivism: IR's 'Reflexive Turn' – and Beyond. *European Journal of International Relations*, 19(4), 669–94.

Hamid, S. (2018). Normalising Intolerance: Elections, Religion and Everyday Life in Indonesia. *Centre for Indonesian Law, Islam and Society Policy Paper*, 17, law.unimelb.edu.au/__data/assets/file/0005/2777666/Policy-Paper_Hamid_20180625.pdf.

Hammarberg, T. (2001). How the Khmer Rouge Tribunal Was Agreed: Discussions between the Cambodian Government and the UN, www.d.dccam.org/Tribunal/Analysis/How_Khmer_Rouge_Tribunal.htm.

Hanns Seidel Foundation Philippines. (2015). Community-Based Dialogue Sessions on Human Rights Promotion and Protection between the Philippine Public Security Sector and Civil Society Organizations and Local Communities, (April 2015) southeastasia.hss.de/fileadmin/migration/downloads/150428-Community-based-Dialogue-Sessions-on-Human-Rights-A-Process-Documentation.pdf.

Harris-Rimmer, S. (2010a). *Gender and Transnational Justice: The Women of East Timor*. New York: Routledge.

    (2010b). Women Cut in Half: Refugee Women and the Commission for Reception, Truth-Seeking and Reconciliation in Timor-Leste. *Refugee Survey Quarterly*, 29(2), 85–103.

Hart, F. A. (1980). Yamashita, Nuremberg and Vietnam: Command Responsibility Reappraised. *Naval War College International Law Studies*, 62, 397–414.

Harvey, P. (2019). *Reducing Suffering during Conflict: The Interface between Buddhism and International Humanitarian Law*. Conference Position Paper, 4–6 September 2019, Dambulla, www.icrc.org/en/download/file/89892/exploratory_position_paper_on_buddhism_ihl.pdf.

Haryomataram, G. P. H. (2001). Internal Disturbances and Tensions: Forgotten Conflicts. In T. L. H. McCormack, M. Tilbury, & G. D. Triggs, eds., *A Century of War and Peace: Asia-Pacific Perspectives on the Centenary of the 1899 Hague Peace Conference*. The Hague: Kluwer Law International, pp. 155–66.

Havel, V. & Tutu, D. M. (2005). Threat to the Peace: A Call for the UN Security Council to Act in Burma, (20 September 2005) www.ibiblio.org/obl/docs3/threat.pdf.

Haynes, J. (2014). *Religion in Global Politics*. New York: Routledge.

Heder, S. (1999). The 'Traditions' of Impunity and Victors' Justice in Cambodia, *The Phnom Penh Post* (19 February 1999) www.phnompenhpost.com/national/traditions-impunity-and-victors-justice-cambodia.

    (2011). A Review of the Negotiations Leading to the Establishment of the Personal Jurisdiction of the Extraordinary Chambers in the Courts of Cambodia, (1 August 2011) www.cambodiatribunal.org/sites/default/files/A%20Review%20of%20the%20Negotiations%20Leading%20to%20the%20Establishment%20of%20the%20Personal%20Jurisdiction%20of%20the%20ECCC.pdf.

Herbert, J. (2008). The Legal Framework of Human Rights in Indonesia. In T. Lindsey, ed., *Indonesia: Law and Society*. Sydney: The Federation Press, pp. 456–82.

Herman, J. (2018). Uncooked Rice: Justice and Victimhood at the Extraordinary Chambers in the Courts of Cambodia and Beyond. In V. Druliolle & R. Brett, eds., *The Politics of Victimhood in Post-Conflict Societies*. New York: Springer, pp. 187–209.

Hermawan, A. (2009). ICC Ratification No Panacea to End Impunity: Marty, *The Jakarta Post* (12 June 2009) www.thejakartapost.com/news/2009/06/12/icc-ratification-no-panacea-end-impunity-marty.html.

Hinton, A. L. (2008). Truth, Representation and the Politics of Memory after Genocide. In A. Kent & D. Porter Chandler, eds., *People of Virtue: Reconfiguring Religion, Power and Moral Order in Cambodia*. Copenhagen: Nias Publishing, pp. 62–81.

    (2010). Introduction: Toward an Anthropology of Transitional Justice. In A. L. Hinton, ed., *Transitional Justice: Global Mechanisms and Local Realities after Genocide and Mass Violence*. New Brunswick, NJ: Rutgers University Press, pp. 1–22.

    (2013). Transitional Justice Time: Uncle San, Aunty Yan, and Outreach at the Khmer Rouge Tribunal. In D. Mayersen & A. Pohlman, eds., *Genocide and Mass Atrocities in Asia: Legacies and Prevention*. London: Routledge, pp. 86–98.

    (2018). *The Justice Facade: Trials of Transition in Cambodia*. Oxford: Oxford University Press.

Hlaing, K. Y. (2004). Burma: Civil Society Skirting Regime Rules. In M. Alagappa, ed., *Civil Society and Political Change in Asia: Expanding and Contracting Democratic Space*. Stanford, CA: Stanford University Press, pp. 389–418.

Holliday, I. (2011). *Burma Redux Global Justice and the Quest for Political Reform in Myanmar*. New York: Columbia University Press.

Htoo, A. (2003). The Depayin Massacre: A Crime against Humanity and Its Effect on National Reconciliation, *Article 2* (17 December 2003) alrc.asia/article2/2003/12/the-depayin-massacre-a-crime-against-humanity-and-its-effect-on-national-reconciliation.

Htun, H. (2019). Court Hears Sentencing Appeals for U Ko Ni Murder Conspirators, *The Irrawaddy* (25 June 2019) www.irrawaddy.com/news/burma/court-hears-sentencing-appeals-u-ko-ni-murder-conspirators.html.

Htun, T. (2018). Kachin CSOs Call on UN to Refer Myanmar to International Criminal Tribunal, *Radio Free Asia* (25 April 2018).

Hughes, R. (2008). Dutiful Tourism: Encountering the Cambodian Genocide. *Asia Pacific Viewpoint*, 49(3), 318–30.

    (2015). Ordinary Theatre and Extraordinary Law at the Khmer Rouge Tribunal. *Environment and Planning D: Society and Space*, 33, 714–31.

Hughes, R., Elander, M., Sperfeldt, C., Jarvis, H., Smith, W., Ngyuen, L., & Lobwein, W. (2018). Achievements and Legacies of the Khmer Rouge Trials: Reflections from Inside the Tribunal. *Australian Feminist Law Journal*, 44(2), 303–24.

Huikuri, S. (2018). *The Institutionalization of the International Criminal Court.* New York: Springer.

Hukum Online. (2013). *Pemerintah Masih Takut Meratifikasi Statuta Roma* [Government Still Scared to Ratify the Rome Statute], *Hukum Online* (17 July 2013) www.hukumonline.com/berita/baca/lt51e6c2ca4777c/pemer intah-masih-takut-meratifikasi-statuta-roma.

Human Rights Online Philippines. (2015). PAHRA Disagrees with Chito Gascon's Assessment of the Present Human Rights Situation, (15 October 2015) hronlineph.com/2015/10/15/statement-pahra-disagrees-with-chito-gascons-assessment-of-the-present-human-rights-situation.

Human Rights Watch. (1991). Human Rights Watch World Report 1990: An Annual Review of Developments and the Bush Administrations Policy on Human Rights Wordwide, (January 1991).

   (2003). Serious Flaws: Why the U.N. General Assembly Should Require Changes to the Draft Khmer Rouge Tribunal Agreement (April 2003) www.hrw.org/legacy/backgrounder/asia/cambodia043003-bck.pdf.

   (2007). Scared Silent: Extrajudicial Impunity for Extrajudicial Killings in the Philippines, (June 2007) www.hrw.org/reports/2007/06/27/scared-silent-0.

   (2010). 'They Own the People' The Ampatuans, State-Backed Militias, and Killings in the Southern Philippines, (16 November 2010) www.hrw.org/report/2010/11/16/they-own-people/ampatuans-state-backed-militias-and-killings-southern-philippines.

   (2011). 'No Justice Just Adds to the Pain' Killings, Disappearances, and Impunity in the Philippines, (April 2011) www.hrw.org/node/100305/section/4.

   (2012a). Philippines: Arrest Ex-General Accused of 'Disappearances': Palparan's Prosecution Key to Ending Impunity, (31 January 2012) www.hrw.org/news/2012/01/31/philippines-arrest-ex-general-accused-disappearances.

   (2012b). Philippines: Two Years under Aquino, Abuses Go Unpunished, (27 June 2012) www.hrw.org/news/2012/06/27/philippines-two-years-under-aquino-abuses-go-unpunished.

   (2013). Cambodia: Investigate Killing and Injuries of Election Protesters, (17 September 2013) www.hrw.org/node/119020.

   (2014). Cambodia: Khmer Rouge Convictions 'Too Little, Too Late': Political Interference, Delays, Corruption Make Tribunal a Failure, (8 August 2014) www.hrw.org/news/2014/08/08/cambodia-khmer-rouge-convictions-too-little-too-late.

(2016a). Cambodia: Drop Case against Opposition Leader, (6 September 2016) www.hrw.org/news/2016/09/06/cambodia-drop-case-against-opposition-leader.

(2016b). World Report: Cambodia, www.hrw.org/world-report/2016/country-chapters/cambodia.

(2017). 'License to Kill' Philippine Police Killings in Duterte's War on Drugs, (March 2017) www.hrw.org/sites/default/files/report_pdf/philippines0317_web_1.pdf.

(2018a). Indonesia: Events of 2017 (January 2018) www.hrw.org/world-report/2018/country-chapters/indonesia.

(2018b). Myanmar's Investigative Commissions: A History of Shielding Abusers, (September 2018) www.hrw.org/sites/default/files/supporting_resources/201809myanmar_commissions.pdf.

Hun Sen. (1999). Aide Memoire: An Analysis on Seeking a Formula for Bringing Top KR Leaders to Trial, *Cambodia New Vision* (January 2014) cnv.org.kh/cnv_html_pdf/cnv_14.PDF.

(2000). Address of Samdech Hun Sen to the United Nations General Assembly's Millennium Summit, 8 September 2000, *Cambodia New Vision* (September 2000) cnv.org.kh/cnv_html_pdf/cnv_32.PDF.

(2001). Opening Address at the Cambodia Consultative Group Meeting, Tokyo, 12 June 2001, *Cambodia New Vision* (June 2001) cnv.org.kh/cnv_html_pdf/cnv_41.PDF.

(2002). Address on 'Challenges and Promises of ASEAN Integration: A Cambodian Perspective', *Cambodia New Vision* (March 2002) cnv.org.kh/address-on-challenges-and-promises-of-asean-integration-a-cambodian-perspective.

(2004). The Rectangular Strategy for Growth, Employment, Equity and Efficiency in Cambodia, (July 2004) www.cdc-crdb.gov.kh/cdc/documents/RGC_Rectangular_Strategy_2004.pdf.

(2013). 'Rectangular Strategy' for Growth, Employment, Equity and Efficiency Phase III Of the Royal Government of Cambodia of the Fifth Legislature of the National Assembly, *Cambodia New Vision* (September 2013) cnv.org.kh/wp-content/uploads/2013/10/26sep13_rectangular-strategy_phaseIII.pdf.

Hunt, L. (2016). Cambodia's Ruling Elite One Step Closer to International Court, *The Diplomat* (16 September 2016) thediplomat.com/2016/09/cambodias-ruling-elite-one-step-closer-to-international-court.

Huy, V. (2002). Him Huy Needs Justice. *Searching for the Truth*, 28, 28–9.

Ibon Foundation. (2010). *Oplan Bantay Laya: The US-Arroyo Campaign of Terror and Counterinsurgency in the Philippines*.

ICC. (2003). Transcript, Public Hearing of the Office of the Prosecutor, (17–18 June 2003) www.icc-cpi.int/NR/rdonlyres/74C26DBA-06CB-4F68-AEC4-1FB3AD4AC93E/143739/030714_otp_ph1s1_Billon_Ung_BounHor.pdf.

(2018). ICC Statement on the Philippines' Notice of Withdrawal: State Participation in Rome Statute System Essential to International Rule of Law, (20
March 2018) www.icc-cpi.int/Pages/item.aspx?name=pr1371.

ICC Assembly of States Parties. (2015). Election of a Judge to Fill a Judicial
Vacancy of the International Criminal Court, ICC Doc. ICC-ASP/13/44
(14 April 2015).

(2018a). President of the Assembly of States Parties Regrets Withdrawal from
the Rome Statute by the Philippines, (18 March 2019) www.icc-cpi.int/
Pages/item.aspx?name=pr1443.

(2018b). President of the Assembly of States Parties Responds to Announcement
of Withdrawal from the Rome Statute by the Philippines, ICC Doc. ICC-
ASP-20180316-PR1369 (16 March 2018).

(2018c). Report of the Bureau on the Plan of Action of the Assembly of
States Parties for Achieving Universality and Full Implementation of the
Rome Statute of the International Criminal Court, ICC-ASP/17/32
(23 November 2018) asp.icc-cpi.int/iccdocs/asp_docs/ASP17/ICC-ASP-17-
32-ENG.pdf.

ICC Office of the Prosecutor. (2015). Statement of the Prosecutor of the International Criminal Court, Fatou Bensouda: 'The ICC Is an Independent
Court That Must Be Supported', (24 November 2015) https://www.icc-cpi
.int/Pages/item.aspx?name=otp-stat-24-11-2015.

(2016). Statement of the Prosecutor of the International Criminal Court, Fatou
Bensouda Concerning the Situation in the Republic of the Philippines,
(13 October 2016) www.icc-cpi.int/Pages/item.aspx?name=161013-otp-stat-
php.

(2018). Statement of the Prosecutor of the International Criminal Court, Mrs
Fatou Bensouda, on Opening Preliminary Examinations into the Situations
in the Philippines and in Venezuela, (8 February 2018) www.icc-cpi.int/
Pages/item.aspx?name=180208-otp-stat.

ICRC. (2012). Philippines, Application of IHL by the National Democratic Front
of the Philippines: NDFP Declaration of Undertaking to Apply the Geneva
Conventions of 1949 and Protocol I of 1977, 5 July 1996, (31 January 2012)
casebook.icrc.org/case-study/philippines-application-ihl-national-democratic-
front-philippines#toc-ndfp-declaration-of-undertaking-to-apply-the-geneva-
conventions-of-1949-and-protocol-i-of-1977.

(2016a). Philippines: Practice Relating to Rule 158, Prosecution of War
Crimes, Customary IHL, www.icrc.org/customary-ihl/eng/docs/v2_cou_
ph_rule158.

(2016b). Philippines: Practice Relating to Rule 159: Amnesty, www.icrc.org/
customary-ihl/eng/docs/v2_cou_ph_rule159_sectionb.

ICSCICC. (2008). *Draft Naskah Akademis dan Rancangan Undang-Undang tentang Pengesahan* [Draft Academic Manuscript and Draft Law on the

Ratification of the] Rome Statute of the International Criminal Court 1998, advokasi.elsam.or.id/assets/2015/09/2008_Naskah-Akademik_RUU-ratifikasi-statuta-roma_ICC.pdf.

(2012). Progress Report: Indonesia Efforts to Ratify the 1998 Rome Statute of the International Criminal Court, (November 2012) advokasi.elsam.or.id/assets/2015/09/201211_Progress-Report_Indonesia-effort-to-ratify-1998-Rome-Statute.pdf.

Ileto, R. C. (2007). World War II: Transient and Enduring Legacies for the Philippines. In D. K. W. Hock, ed., *Legacies of World War II in South and East Asia*. Singapore: Institute of Southeast Asian Studies, pp. 74–91.

Imai, K. (2011). Turkey's Norm Diffusion Policies toward the Middle East: Turkey's Role of Norm Entrepreneur and Norm Transmitter. *Turkish Yearbook of International Relations*, 42, 27–60.

Independent Commission of Enquiry. (2014a). Press Release (24 May 2019) www.icoe-myanmar.org/icoe-ps-training.

(2014b). Press Release (31 August 2018) www.icoe-myanmar.org/icoe-pr-rakhinevisit.

Independent International Fact-Finding Mission on Myanmar. (2018) Report of the Detailed Findings of the Independent International Fact-Finding Mission on Myanmar, UN Doc. A/HRC/39/CRP.2 (17 September 2018).

Indonesia. (2012a). Consideration of Reports Submitted by States Parties under Article 40 of the Covenant, Initial Reports of States Parties: Indonesia, UN Doc. CCPR/C/IDN/1 (19 January 2012).

(2012b). National Report Submitted in Accordance with Paragraph 5 of the Annex to Human Rights Council Resolution 16/21, UN Doc. A/HRC/WG.6/13/IDN/1 (7 March 2012).

International Bar Association's Human Rights Institute. (2012). The Rule of Law in Myanmar – Challenges and Prospects, (December 2012) www.ibanet.org/Document/Default.aspx?DocumentUid=DE0EE11D-9878-4685-A20F-9A0AAF6C3F3E.

(2015). Justice versus Corruption: Challenges to the Independence of the Judiciary in Cambodia, (September 2015) www.ibanet.org/Article/Detail.aspx?ArticleUid=fb11e885-5f1d-4c03-9c55-86ff42157ae1.

International Center for Transitional Justice. (2013). DC-Cam to Help Burma Record Rights Abuses, (8 May 2013) www.ictj.org/news/dc-cam-help-burma-record-rights-abuses.

International Center for Transitional Justice (ICTJ) and KontraS. (2011). Derailed: Transitional Justice in Indonesia since the Fall of Soeharto, (March 2011) ictj.org/sites/default/files/ICTJ-Kontras-Indonesia-Derailed-Report-2011-English_0.pdf.

International Criminal Court. (2009). Delegations to the Seventh Session of the Assembly of States Parties to the Rome Statute of the International Criminal

Court, The Hague, 14–22 November 2008, ICC Doc. ICC-ASP/7/INF.1 (8 April 2009) asp.icc-cpi.int/iccdocs/asp_docs/ICC-ASP-7-INF.1.pdf.

International Crisis Group. (2001). Indonesia: Impunity versus Accountability for Gross Human Rights Violations, (2 February 2001) www.crisisgroup.org/asia/south-east-asia/indonesia/indonesia-impunity-versus-accountability.

International Monitoring Team. (2015). Verification and Assessment Report – Ceasefire Violations Mamasapano Incident January 25, 2015, (5 April 2015) peacetalkphilippines.wordpress.com/2015/04/18/verification-and-assessment-report-ceasefire-violations-mamasapano-incident-january-25-2015/.

The Irrawaddy. (2014). Exclusive: The Irrawaddy Interviews US President Barack Obama, *The Irrawaddy* (12 November 2014) www.irrawaddy.org/interview/exclusive-irrawaddy-interviews-us-president-barack-obama.html.

Ja Seng Ing Truth Finding Committee. (2014). Who Killed Ja Seng Ing? (December 2014) www.burmapartnership.org/wp-content/uploads/2014/12/REPORT_Who-Killed-JSI_6.Dec_.14.pdf.

Jagger, S. (2016). Part of the Problem and Part of the Solution? Non-State Armed Groups and Humanitarian Norms in Burma/Myanmar. PhD Thesis, The University of Waikato.

Jakarta Globe. (2014). Human Rights Let-Downs Damp Jokowi's Pledges, *Jakarta Globe* (10 December 2014).

(2019). Jokowi, Prabowo Turn Up Heat in First Debate, Steer Clear of Past Human Rights Cases, *Jakarta Globe* (18 January 2019) jakartaglobe.id/news/jokowi-prabowo-turn-up-heat-in-first-debate-steer-clear-of-past-human-rights-cases.

Jeffery, R. (2012). Amnesty and Accountability: The Price of Peace in Aceh, Indonesia. *The International Journal of Transitional Justice*, 6(1), 60–82.

(2018). Amnesties and Intractable Conflicts: Managed Impunity in the Philippines' Bangsamoro Peace Process. *Journal of Human Rights*, 17(4), 436–52.

Jeffery, R. & Kim, H. J. (2014). Introduction. In R. Jeffery & H. J. Kim, eds., *Transitional Justice in the Asia-Pacific*. Cambridge: Cambridge University Press, pp. 1–31.

Jeffery, R., Kent, L. & Wallis, J. (2017). Reconceiving the Roles of Religious Civil Society Organizations in Transitional Justice: Evidence from the Solomon Islands, Timor-Leste and Bougainville. *International Journal of Transitional Justice*, 11(3), 378–99.

Jetschke, A. (1999). Linking the Unlinkable? International Norms and Nationalism in Indonesia and the Philippines. In S. C. Ropp, K. Sikkink, & T. Risse-Kappen, eds., *The Power of Human Rights: International Norms and Domestic Change*. Cambridge: Cambridge University Press, pp. 134–71.

(2011). *Human Rights and State Security: Indonesia and the Philippines*. Philadelphia: University of Pennsylvania Press.

Juwana, H. (2005). The Concept of Superior Responsibility under International Law as Applied in Indonesia. *Asia-Pacific Yearbook of International Humanitarian Law*, 1, 179–95.

Kapur, A. (2013). Asian Values v. The Paper Tiger: Dismantling the Threat to Asian Values Posed by the International Criminal Court. *Journal of International Criminal Justice*, 11(5), 1059–90.

Karapatan, (2015). Stop Absolving Human Rights Violators, Karapatan Tells DOJ, (12 May 2015) www.karapatan.org/Stop+absolving+human+rights+violators%2C+Karapatan+tells+DOJ.

(2016). 2015 Karapatan Year-End Report on the Human Rights Situation in the Philippines, (13 July 2016) karapatan.org/2015+Human+Rights+Report.

Karnavas, M. (2016). Inducing Case 003 Outcome: US Purse Strings Wielded as a Whip, *The Cambodia Daily* (6 July 2016) www.cambodiadaily.com/opinion/inducing-case-003-outcome-us-purse-strings-wielded-as-a-whip-115088.

Katjasungkana, N. & Wieringa, S. E. (2019). Organisation and Impact of the International People's Tribunal on 1965 Crimes against Humanity in Indonesia. In S. E. Wieringa, J. Melvin, & A. Pohlman, eds., *The International People's Tribunal for 1965 and the Indonesian Genocide*. Milton Park: Routledge.

Keck, M. E. & Sikkink, K. (1998). *Activists beyond Borders: Advocacy Networks in International Politics*. Ithaca, NY: Cornell University Press.

Kendall, S. & Nouwen, S. (2013). Representational Practices at the International Criminal Court: The Gap between Juridified and Abstract Victimhood. *University of Cambridge Faculty of Law Research Paper*, 24/2013.

Kent, A. (2013). Friction and Security at the Khmer Rouge Tribunal. *Journal of Social Issues in Southeast Asia*, 28(2), 299–328.

Kent, L. (2004). *Unfulfilled Expectations: Community Views on CAVR's Community Reconciliation Process*. JSMP, (August 2004).

(2012). *The Dynamics of Transitional Justice: International Models and Local Realities in East Timor*. New York: Routledge.

(2014). Beyond 'Pragmatism versus Principle'. In R. Jeffery & H. J. Kim, eds., *Transitional Justice in the Asia-Pacific*. Cambridge: Cambridge University Press, pp. 157–94.

Keo, B. (2016). *Litigation Lessons from Contesting a Corrupt Land Grab in Cambodia*. Open Society Foundations, (October 2016).

Khin, T. (2017). Only International Pressure Can Save Rohingya Now, *Al Jazeera* (31 August 2017) www.aljazeera.com/indepth/opinion/2017/08/international-pressure-save-rohingya-170830122257236.html.

Kiernan, B. (2003). The Demography of Genocide in Southeast Asia: The Death Tolls in Cambodia, 1975–79, and East Timor, 1975–80. *Critical Asian Studies*, 35(4), 585–97.

(2008). *Genocide and Resistance in Southeast Asia: Justice in Cambodia & East Timor*. New Brunswick: Transaction Publishers.

Kim, H. (2017). Missed Opportunities in the Judicialisation of International Criminal Law? Asian States in the Emergence and Spread of the Rome Statute System to Punish Atrocity Crimes. *Netherlands Quarterly of Human Rights*, 35(4), 246–71.

Kingdom of Cambodia. (1999). Aide-Memoire on Report of the Group of Experts for Cambodia of 18 February 1999, (17 March 1999) www.eccc.gov.kh/sites/default/files/documents/courtdoc/2016-09-20%2022:21/D181_2.16_EN.PDF.

Kinley, D. & Wilson, T. (2017). Engaging a Pariah: Human Rights Training in Burma/Myanmar. *Human Rights Quarterly*, 29(2), 368–402.

KKPK. (2014). *Menemukan Kembali* [Rediscover] Indonesia, asia-ajar.org/2016/02/menemukan-kembali-indonesia.

Klotz, A. (2008). Case Selection. In A. Klotz & D. Prakash, eds., *Qualitative Methods in International Relations: A Pluralist Guide*. Basingstoke: Palgrave Macmillan, pp. 43–58.

Knop, K., Michaels, R., & Riles, A. (2012). From Multiculturalism to Technique: Feminism, Culture, and the Conflict of Laws Style. *Stanford Law Review*, 64, 588–656.

Kochanski, A. (2018). The 'Local Turn' in Transitional Justice: Curb the Enthusiasm. *International Studies Review*, forthcoming, doi 10.1093/isr/viy081.

Koh, H. H. (1997). Why Do Nations Obey International Law? *Yale Law School Legal Scholarship Repository*, 106, 2599–659.

Kofi Annan Foundation. (2018). Advisory Commission on Rakhine State: Lessons Learned Report. www.kofiannanfoundation.org/web/app/uploads/2018/06/180530_Rakine_Lessons-Learned_final.pdf.

Komnas-HAM. (2012). Statement by Komnas-HAM (National Commission for Human Rights) on the Results of Its Investigations into Grave Violation of Human Rights during the Events of 1965–1966 (Unofficial Translation). www.etan.org/action/SaySorry/Komnas%20HAM%201965%20TAPOL%20translation.pdf.

Koskenniemi, M. (2005). From Apology to Utopia: The Structure of International Argument. Cambridge: Cambridge University Press.

(2012). Law, Teleology and International Relations: An Essay in Counterdisciplinarity. *International Relations*, 26(1), 3–34.

Kratochwil, F. V. (2001). How Do Norms Matter? In M. Byers, ed., *The Role of Law in International Politics*. Oxford: Oxford University Press, pp. 35–68.

Kubosova, L. (2008). EU Assembly Seeks Criminal Trial for Burmese Junta, *EU Observer* (23 May 2008) euobserver.com/foreign/26201.

Kulasegaran, M. (2015). Now the Time Than Ever before for Malaysia to Become a Member of International Criminal Court (ICC) and Make Those Who

Shot Down MH17 to Be Accountable, (1 August 2015) ipohbaratvoice
.blogspot.com.au/2015/08/now-time-than-ever-before-for-malaysia.html.

Lao PDR. (2008). Statement by Mrs Viengvone Kittavong, Deputy Director General, Department of Treaties and Law, Ministry of Foreign Affairs, Lao People's Democratic Republic, Assembly of States Parties to the Rome Statuteof the International Criminal Court, 7th Session, General Debate, ICC, (15 November 2008) asp.icc-cpi.int/iccdocs/asp_docs/library/asp/ICC-ASP-ASP7-GenDebe-Lao-ENG.pdf.

Lall, M. (2016). *Understanding Reform in Myanmar: People and Society in the Wake of Military Rule*. London: Hurst & Co Ltd.

Leary, V., Ellis, A. A., & Madlener, K. (1984*). The Philippines: Human Rights after Martial Law: Report of a Mission*. Geneva: International Commission of Jurists.

Lee, Y. (2015). Situation of Human Rights in Myanmar, UN Doc. A/70/412 (6 October 2015).

(2016). Report of the Special Rapporteur on the Situation of Human Rights in Myanmar, Yanghee Lee, UN Doc. A/HRC/31/71 (18 March 2016).

(2018). Statement by Ms. Yanghee Lee, Special Rapporteur on the Situation of Human Rights in Myanmar at the 37th Session of the Human Rights Council, (12 March 2018) www.ohchr.org/en/NewsEvents/Pages/DisplayNews.aspx?NewsID=22806&LangID=E.

Lembaga Perlindungan Saksi dan Korban. (2015). *LPSK Kerjasama Dengan Komnas-HAM Dalam Memenuhi Hak Korban Pelanggaran HAM Berat* [LPSK Collaboration With Komnas-HAM in Fulfilling the Rights of Victims of Serious Human Rights Violations], (11 August 2015) lpsk.go.id/berita/berita_detail/2352.

Leone, F. & Giannini, T. (2005). *Traditions of Conflict Resolution in Burma: 'Respected Insiders', Resource-Based Conflict and Authoritarian Rule*. The Burma Project, Earthrights International Southeast Asia (December 2005) earthrights.org/wp-content/uploads/publications/Traditions-of-Conflict-Resolution.pdf.

Leonen, J. L. (2018). Aquino, et al. Mamasapano Arraignment Halted, *Philippine Daily Inquirer* (9 February 2018) newsinfo.inquirer.net/967543/sc-halts-ombudsman-resolutions-junking-charges-vs-aquino-et-al.

Levin, A. M. (2011) Transitional Justice in Burma: A Survey of Accountability and National Reconciliation Mechanisms after Aung San Suu Kyi's Release. *Human Rights Brief*, 18(2), 21–5.

Leuprecht, P. (2003). Report of the Special Representative of the Secretary-General for Human Rights in Cambodia, Peter Leuprecht, UN Doc. E/CN.4/2004/105 (19 December 2003).

Levitt, P. & Merry, S. (2009). Vernacularization on the Ground: Local Uses of Global Women's Rights in Peru, China, India and the United States. *Global Networks*, 9(4), 441–61.

LICADHO. (2010). New Penal Code a Setback for Freedom of Expression Issues, (9 December 2010) www.licadho-cambodia.org/pressrelease.php?perm=233.

Lindsey, T. & Santosa, M. A. (2008). The Trajectory of Law Reform in Indonesia: A Short Overview of Legal Systems and Change in Indonesia. In T. Lindsey, ed., *Indonesia: Law and Society*. Sydney: The Federation Press, pp. 2–22.

Linton, S. (2005). Putting Things into Perspective: The Realities of Accountability in East Timor, Indonesia and Cambodia. *Maryland Series in Contemporary Asian Studies Series*, 3(182), 1–88.

   (2006). Accounting for Atrocities in Indonesia. *Singapore Year Book of International Law*, 11, 199–241.

   (2008). East Timor and Accountability for Serious Crimes. In M. C. Bassiouni, ed., *International Criminal Law*. Leiden: Koninklijke Brill, pp. 257–82.

   (2010). Post Conflict Justice in Asia. In M. C. Bassiouni, ed., *The Pursuit of International Criminal Justice: A World Study on Conflicts, Victimisation and Post-Conflict Justice*. Cambridge: Intersentia, pp. 515–753.

Lindsey, T. (2008). Constitutional Reform in Indonesia: Muddling towards Democracy. In T. Lindsey, ed., *Indonesia: Law and Society*. Sydney: The Federation Press, pp. 23–47.

Linton, S., McCormack, T. & Sivakumaran, S. (2019). *Asia-Pacific Perspectives on International Humanitarian Law*. Cambridge: Cambridge University Press.

Lindsey, S. & S. Butt. Civil Liability for Criminal Acts at Indonesian Law. law.unimelb.edu.au/data/assets/pdf_file/0009/1546299/CivilLiabilityfor CriminalActsatIndonesianLaw2.pdf.

Lozada, R. D. E. et al. (2013). Itaguyod ang IHL: Sibilyan Pangalagaan – Towards a Philippine Program of Action on Effecting International Humanitarian Law, Proceedings of the Second National Summit on International Humanitarian Law in the Philippines, 11 December 2012, Manila.

Lun Min Mang, (2016). After Guilty Verdict, Families of Killed Mong Yaw Villagers Await Compensation, *The Myanmar Times* (19 September 2016) www.mmtimes.com/national-news/22595-after-guilty-verdict-families-of-killed-mong-yaw-villagers-await-compensation.html.

MacLean, K. (2019). The Rohingya Crisis and the Practices of Erasure. *Journal of Genocide Research*, 21(1), 83–95.

Mahmud, T. (2007). Geography and International Law: Towards a Postcolonial Mapping. *Santa Clara Journal of International Law*, 5(2), 525–62.

Malena, C. & Chhim, K. (2009). *Linking Citizens and the State: An Assessment of Civil Society Contributions to Good Governance in Cambodia*. The World Bank (February 2009) documents.worldbank.org/curated/en/398781468222011480/ Linking-citizens-and-the-state-an-assessment-of-civil-society-contributions-to-good-governance-in-Cambodia.

Manley, S. (2017). Transitional Justice in Myanmar: Fragments of Quieted Voices. *Inter-Asia Cultural Studies*, 18(4), 610–16.

McCartan, B. & Jolliffe, K. (2016). *Ethnic Armed Actors and Justice Provision in Myanmar.* The Asia Foundation, asiafoundation.org/wp-content/uploads/2016/10/Ethnic-Armed-Actors-and-Justice-Provision-in-Myanmar_EN.pdf.

McCarthy, G. (2019). *Military Capitalism in Myanmar: Examining the Origins, Continuities and Evolution of 'Khaki Capital'.* Singapore: ISEAS - Yusof Ishak Institute.

McCarthy, S. (2015). The Limits of Civil Society in Militarised Regimes: Evidence from the Asia-Pacific. *Australian Journal of International Affairs,* 69(6), 711–28.

McCarthy, S. & Un, K. (2015). The Evolution of Rule of Law in Cambodia. *Democratization,* 24(1), 100–18.

McCarthy, T. (1999). Hun Sen: Cambodia's Mr Justice? *Time* (22 March 1999) content.time.com/time/world/article/0,8599,2040423,00.html.

Medistiara, Y. (2019). *Jaksa Agung akan Bicara dengan Komnas HAM soal Kasus HAM Berat* [Attorney-General will Talk to Komnas HAM about the Serious Human Rights Case Issue, *Detik News* (23 January 2019) news.detik.com/berita/d-4397637/jaksa-agung-akan-bicara-dengan-komnas-ham-soal-kasus-ham-berat.

Mégret, F. (2005). In Defense of Hybridity: Towards a Representational Theory of International Criminal Justice. *Cornell International Law Journal,* 38(3), 725–51.

(2011). Too Much of a Good Thing? ICC Implementation and the Uses of Complementarity. In C. Stahn and M. M. El Zeidy, eds., *The International Criminal Court: From Theory to Practice.* Cambridge: Cambridge University Press, pp. 361–90.

(2014). International Criminal Justice: A Critical Research Agenda. In C. Schwöbel, ed., *Critical Approaches to International Criminal Law.* New York: Routledge, pp. 17–53.

(2015). What Sort of Global Justice Is 'International Criminal Justice'? *Journal of International Criminal Justice,* 13(1), 77–96.

Meisenberg, S. M. (2015). Complying with Complementarity? The Cambodian Implementation of the Rome Statute of the International Criminal Court. *Asian Journal of International Law,* 5(1), 123–42.

Melo, J. A. R. et al. (2007). Independent Commission to Address Media and Activist Killings, Created under Administrative Order No. 157 (s. 2006), Report, (22 January 2007) www.humanrights.asia/resources/journals-magazines/article2/0601-2/appendix-ii-the-melo-commission-report.

Mendez, C. (2018). Palace Brands Lamitan Bombing a 'War Crime', *The Philippine Star* (1 August 2018) www.philstar.com/headlines/2018/08/01/1838696/palace-brands-lamitan-bombing-war-crime.

Menski, W. (2006). *Comparative Law in a Global Context: The Legal Systems of Asia and Africa.* Cambridge: Cambridge University Press.

Menzel, J. (2007). Justice Delayed or Too Late for Justice? The Khmer Rouge Tribunal and the Cambodian 'Genocide' 1975–1979. *Journal of Genocide Research*, 9(2), 215–33.

Merry, S. (2006). Transnational Human Rights and Local Activism: Mapping the Middle. *American Anthropologist*, 108(1), 38–51.

Mertha, A. (2014). *Brothers in Arms: Chinese Aid to the Khmer Rouge, 1975–1979*. Ithaca, NY: Cornell University Press.

Michaels, R. (2006). The Functional Method of Comparative Law. In R. Zimmermann & M. Reimann, eds., *The Oxford Handbook of Comparative Law*. Oxford: Oxford University Press, pp. 339–82.

Ministry of Foreign Affairs Myanmar. (2011). President U Thein Sein Delivers Inaugural Address to Pyidaungsu Hluttaw, (30 March 2011) www.burmalibrary.org/docs12/2011-03-30-TS_inaugural_speech_to_Pyi daungsu_Hluttaw.pdf.

(2014). Ms. Yanghee Lee Expresses Her Recognition and Applause for Progress in Sweeping and Far-Reaching Reforms Dramatically Achieved in Land-scape of Political, Economic, Social and Human Rights in Myanmar, (31 July 2014) www.burmalibrary.org/docs19/NLM2014-08-01-red.pdf.

Ministry of Foreign Affairs Indonesia. (2014). Joint Press Release: 5th Indonesia – European Union Human Rights Dialogue, (18 November 2014).

(2017). Construction of Indonesian Hospital in Rakhine State Begins, (20 November 2017) reliefweb.int/report/myanmar/construction-indones ian-hospital-rakhine-state-begins.

(2018a). Indonesia Strongly Condemns Israeli Troops' Attacks on a Demonstra-tion in Gaza, (31 March 2018).

(2018b). Indonesia Continues to Encourage Repatriation Process in Rakhine State (26 September 2018).

Moffett, L. (2015). Elaborating Justice for Victims at the International Criminal Court: Beyond Rhetoric and The Hague. *Journal of International Criminal Justice*, 13(2), 281–311.

Mogato, M. (2017). Philippines War on Drugs and Crime Intensifies, at Least 60 Killed in Three Days, *Reuters* (17 August 2017) www.reuters.com/article/ us-philippines-drugs/philippines-war-on-drugs-and-crime-intensifies-at-least-60-killed-in-three-days-idUSKCN1AX0BO.

Morfit, M. (1981). The Indonesian State Ideology according to the New Order Government. *Asian Survey*, 21(8), 838–51.

Mratt Kyaw Thu. (2018). Thayninga: Building Bridges for the Tatmadaw, *Frontier Myanmar* (19 September 2018) frontiermyanmar.net/en/thayninga-building-bridges-for-the-tatmadaw.

Muladi, H. (2011). *Statuta Roma Tahun 1998 Tentang Mahkamah Pidana Inter-nasional: Dalam Kerangka Hukum Pidana Internasional dan Implikasinya Terhadap Hukum Pidana Nasional* [1998 Rome Statute of the International

Criminal Court On: On the framework of International Criminal Law and Its Implications for National Criminal Law], Trisakti: Alumni Universitas Trisakti.

Myanmar Civil Society Organizations Forum (2014). Civil Societies' Review on Myanmar's Transition Process: Prospects for 2015 and Beyond (17 October 2014) www.asienhaus.de/uploads/tx_news/Statement_-_Myanmar_CSOs_Forum_English.pdf.

Myanmar Eleven. (2014). Land Grabbing Top the List of Rights Violations, *Discovery AEC* (3 September 2014) www.nationmultimedia.com/aec/Land-grabbing-top-the-list-of-rights-violations-30242458.html.

Myanmar National Human Rights Commission. (2014). The Inquiry Report of the Myanmar National Human Rights Commission into the Death of Ko Aung Naing (a) Ko Aung Kyaw Naing (a) Ko Par Gyi, (2 December 2014) www.mnhrc.org.mm/en/2014/12/the-inquiry-report-of-the-myanmar-national-human-rights-commission-into-the-death-of-ko-aung-naing-a-ko-aung-kyaw-naing-a-ko-par-gyi.

Myanmar News Agency. (2016). Establishment of the Advisory Commission on Rakhine State, *The Global New Light of Myanmar* (23 August 2016) www.globalnewlightofmyanmar.com/establishment-of-the-advisory-commission-on-rakhine-state.

Myanmar President Office. (2015a). Joint Statement on Election Issued (17 September 2015).

   (2015b). Undertaking Peace and Stability and Development in Rakhine State in Cooperation with UN (7 November 2015).

   (2015c). Government and People of Myanmar Do Not Recognize the Term 'Rohingya' as It Is an Invented Terminology (8 November 2015) www.globalnewlightofmyanmar.com/government-and-people-of-myanmar-do-not-recognize-the-term-rohingya-as-it-is-an-invented-terminology.

The Myanmar Times. (2015). Extracts from the Nationwide Ceasefire Agreement (15 October 2015) www.mmtimes.com/index.php/national-news/17022-extracts-from-the-nationwide-ceasefire-agreement.html.

Mydans, S. (2010). Myanmar's Leading Dissident Reunites with Youngest Son, *The New York Times* (23 November 2010) www.nytimes.com/2010/11/24/world/asia/24myanmar.html.

MyJustice. (2017). Searching for Justice in the Law: Understanding Access to Justice in Myanmar – Findings from the Myanmar Justice Survey 2017, www.myjusticemyanmar.org/sites/default/files/MJS%20Report_FINAL_online.pdf.

Naing, S. & Lewis, S. (2019). Exclusive: Myanmar Soldiers Jailed for Rohingya Killings Freed after Less than a Year, *Reuters* (27 May 2019) www.reuters.com/article/us-myanmar-rohingya-soldiers-exclusive/exclusive-myanmar-soldiers-jailed-for-rohingya-killings-freed-after-less-than-a-year-idUSKCN1SX007.

Nasu, H. (2013). Revisiting the Principle of Non-Intervention: A Structural
    Principle of International Law or a Political Obstacle to Regional Security
    in Asia? *Asian Journal of International Law*, 3(1), 25–50.
National Democratic Front of the Philippines. (2016). Aim to Win Greater Victor-
    ies in People's War Message of the Central Committee in Celebration of
    the 47th Founding Anniversary of the NPA, (29 March 2016) ndfp.org/aim-
    win-greater-victories-peoples-war-message-central-committee-celebration-
    47th-founding-anniversary-npa/.
National League for Democracy. (2010). Clarification, dated 29 November 2010,
    Burma Partnership (29 November 2010) www.burmapartnership.org/wp-
    content/uploads/2010/12/NY-Times.jpg.
NBI-NPS SIT. (2015). Report of the Joint National Bureau of Investigation –
    National Prosecution Service Special Investigation Team (NBI-NPS SIT) on
    the January 25, 2015 Mamasapano Incident, (March 2015) www.doj.gov.ph/
    files/news/Mamasapano_NBI-NPS_SIT_Report_REDACTED.pdf.
NCJP Media. (2017). From Our Member NCJP, Pakistan – Press Release: Human
    Rights Violations with Rohingya Community in Burma/Myanmar, Forum-
    Asia (10 September 2017) www.forum-asia.org/?p=24801.
ND-Burma. (2010). The Hidden Impact of Burma's Arbitrary & Corrupt Taxation,
    (September   2010)   nd-burma.org/reports/the-hidden-impact-of-burmas-
    arbitrary-a-corrupt-taxation.
    (2015). To Recognize and Repair: Unofficial Truth Projects and the Need for
    Justice in Burma, (8 June 2015) nd-burma.org/reports/to-recognize-and-
    repair.
    (2017). Seeking Justice in Burma: August 2017, (4 September 2017) nd-burma
    .org/august-justice-newsletter.
    (2018). You Cannot Ignore Us: Victims of Human Rights Violations in Burma
    from 1970–2017 Outline their Desires for Justice, (October 2018) nd-burma
    .org/you-cannot-ignore-us-victims-of-human-rights-violations-in-burma-from-
    1970-2017-outline-their-desires-for-justice/.
    (2019). About Us, ND-Burma, nd-burma.org/about-us.
Nehru, V. & Farrell, P. (2016). Myanmar's Post-Election Transition, (8 January 2016)
    carnegieendowment.org/2016/01/08/myanmar-s-post-election-transition/is9j.
Nepomuceno, P. (2019). PH Reiterates Adherence to Rules of War: DND, *Gov.Ph
    Philippines News Agency* (9 September 2019) www.pna.gov.ph/articles/
    1079920.
New Matilda. (2008). How We're Helping the Philippines in Its Dirty War, *New
    Matilda* (12 September 2008) newmatilda.com/2008/09/12/how-were-
    helping-philippines-its-dirty-war.
Nichols, M. (2018). U.N. Security Council Mulls Myanmar Action; Russia,
    China Boycott Talks, *Reuters* (18 December 2018) af.reuters.com/article/
    worldNews/idAFKBN1OG2CH.

Nicholson, B. (2008). Canberra Urged to Uphold Vow to Act on Burma Crimes, *The Age* (2 June 2008) www.theage.com.au/national/canberra-urged-to-uphold-vow-to-act-on-burma-crimes-20080601-2kju.html.

Nouwen, S. (2013). *Complementarity in the Line of Fire: The Catalysing Effect of the International Criminal Court in Uganda and Sudan.* Cambridge: Cambridge University Press.

(2014). 'As You Set Out for Ithaka': Practical, Epistemological, Ethical, and Existential Questions about Socio-Legal Empirical Research in Conflict. *Leiden Journal of International Law*, 27(1), 227–60.

Nouwen, S., & Werner, W. (2014). Monopolizing Global Justice: International Criminal Law as Challenge to Human Diversity. *Journal of International Criminal Justice*, 13(1), 157–76.

Nurhayati, D. (2016). Jokowi Meets Kofi Annan to Discuss Myanmar, *The Jakarta Post* (8 December 2016) www.thejakartapost.com/news/2016/12/08/jokowi-meets-kofi-annan-to-discuss-myanmar.html.

Nyein, N. (2019). Four Years On, Justice Yet to Be Found for Kachin Teachers Raped and Murdered, *The Irrawaddy* (18 January 2019) www.irrawaddy.com/news/burma/four-years-justice-yet-found-kachin-teachers-raped-murdered.html.

O'Connell, K. (2016). Myanmar's Rohingya Genocide Is Aided by Friends in High Places, *Mint Press News* (28 January 2016) www.mintpressnews.com/213161-2/213161.

Odhikar. (2017). From Our Member, Odhikar, Bangladesh – Written Statement Submitted to HRC34: Stop Ethnic Cleansing of the Rohingyas in Burma/Myanmar, Forum-Asia (24 February 2017) www.forum-asia.org/?p=23182.

Office of the Presidential Adviser on the Peace Process. (2014). Switzerland Chairs the Transitional Justice and Reconciliation Commission under the Comprehensive Agreement on the Bangsamoro, (30 September 2014) archive .peace.gov.ph/features/switzerland-chairs-transitional-justice-and-reconciliation-commission-under-comprehensive.

Öjendal, J. & Ou, Y. (2016). The 'Awkward' Success of Peacebuilding in Cambodia – Creative and Incomplete, Unsustainable Yet Resilient, Progressing but Stalling. In A. Björkdahl et al., eds., *Peacebuilding and Friction: Global and Local Encounters in Post Conflict-Societies.* New York: Routledge, pp. 138–54.

Open Society Justice Initiative. (2016). Performance and Perception: The Impact of the Extraordinary Chambers in the Court of Cambodia, (February 2016) www.opensocietyfoundations.org/reports/performance-and-perception-impact-extraordinary-chambers-court-cambodia.

Orford, A. (1997). Locating the International: Military and Monetary Interventions after the Cold War. *Harvard International Law Journal*, 38(2), 443–85.

(2013). On International Legal Method. *London Review of International Law*, 1(1), 166–97.

Ovier, A. (2015). *KKPK Gulirkan Satya Pilar untuk Penyelesaian Kasus HAM Masa Lalu* [KKPK Launches 'Satya Pillar' for Resolving Past Human Rights violation cases], *Berita Satu* (21 August 2015) www.beritasatu.com/nasional/300819-kkpk-gulirkan-satya-pilar-untuk-penyelesaian-kasus-ham-masa-lalu.html.

Palmer, E. (2016). Localizing international criminal accountability in Cambodia. *International Relations of the Asia-Pacific*, 16(1), 97–135.

(2019a). Complementarity and the Implementation of International Criminal Law in the Philippines. *New Zealand Journal of Public International Law*, forthcoming.

(2019b). The Effectiveness of National Human Rights Institutions' Relationships with Civil Society: The Commission on Human Rights in the Philippines. *Australian Journal of Human Rights*, 25(2), 299–316.

Palmer, E. & Sperfeldt, C. (2016). International Criminal Justice and Southeast Asia: Approaches to Ending Impunity for Mass Atrocities. *AsiaPacific Issues*, www.eastwestcenter.org/publications/international-criminal-justice-and-southeast-asia-approaches-ending-impunity-mass.

Pareño, R. (2013). Arrest Warrants Out for Nur, Others, *The Philippine Star* (10 October 2013) www.philstar.com/headlines/2013/10/10/1243489/arrest-warrants-out-nur-others#uKLyGv2tmS1jfG0m.99.

Parlina, I. (2015). Jokowi Vows to Promote Rights, *The Jakarta Post* (12 December 2015) www.thejakartapost.com/news/2015/12/12/jokowi-vows-promote-rights.html.

Patag, K. J. (2019). Maute Member Convicted for Rebellion, Crime against International Humanitarian Law, *The Philippine Star* (15 March 2019) www.philstar.com/headlines/2019/03/15/1901732/maute-member-convicted-rebellion-crime-against-international-humanitarian-law.

Payne, L. A. & Sikkink, K. (2014). Transitional Justice in the Asia-Pacific: Comparative and Theoretical Perspectives. In R. Jeffery & H. J. Kim, eds., *Transitional Justice in the Asia-Pacific*. Cambridge: Cambridge University Press, pp. 33–60.

PCICC. (2008). For Hope & Human Dignity: A Primer on the International Criminal Court for the Security Sector.

(2009). In Search for Justice: Commemorating 60 Years of the Geneva Conventions, (12 August 2009) pcicc.wordpress.com/2009/08/12/in-search-for-justice-commemorating-60-years-of-the-geneva-conventions.

(2012a). Building Bridges for Peace, pcicc.files.wordpress.com/2012/03/bpp2012_8_5x9_final_becky1.pdf.

(2012b). Day of Justice 2012: Women & Human Rights Advocates Talk Gender-Just Reparations for Lubanga Victims, (20 July 2012) pcicc.wordpress.com/2012/07/20/day-of-justice-2012-women-human-rights-advocates-talk-gender-just-reparations-for-lubanga-victims.

(2014). Laying Justice on the Ground: Moving from Land Disputes to Land Rights.

(2015). Breakthrough in Asia-Pacific for Effective Prosecution, (20 November 2015) asp.icc-cpi.int/iccdocs/asp_docs/ASP14/GenDeb/ASP14-GenDeb–NGO-PCICC-ENG.pdf.

Pedersen, M. B. (2008). *Promoting Human Rights in Burma: A Critique of Western Sanctions Policy*. Lanham, MA: Rowman & Littlefield Publishers.

(2019). The ICC, the Rohingya and the Limitations of Retributive Justice. *Australian Journal of International Affairs*, 73(1), 9–15.

Pensky, M. (2008). Amnesty on Trial: Impunity, Accountability, and the Norms of International Law. *Ethics & Global Politics*, 1, 1–40.

Peou, S. (1995). Cambodia after the Cold War: The Search for Security Continues. *Centre of Southeast Asian Studies*, Working Paper No. 96, 1–13.

(2009). The Limits of Collaborative Action on Criminal Justice in East Asia. In S. Peou, ed., *Human Security in East Asia: Challenges for Collaborative Action*. New York: Routledge, pp. 108–24.

Pepper, R. (2018). Philippines' Duterte Tells Personnel Not to Cooperate with Any Investigation into His Bloody War on Drugs, *Business Insider Australia* (2 March 2018) www.businessinsider.com.au/duterte-tells-security-not-to-cooperate-with-war-on-drugs-probe-2018-3.

Permanent Mission of Iceland in Geneva. (2018). Statement of Iceland on the Human Rights Situation in the Philippines, (19 June 2018) www.stjornarradid.is/sendiskrifstofur/fastanefnd-islands-i-genf/raedur/stok-raeda/2018/06/19/Raeda-Islands-um-astand-mannrettindamala-a-Filippseyjum.

Permanent Mission of the Republic of Indonesia to the United Nations. (2013). Statement, H. E. Ambassador Desra Percaya, Permanent Representative, Republic of Indonesia to the United Nations at the United Nations General Assembly Thematic Debate: 'Role of the International Criminal Justice in Reconciliation', (10 April 2013).

Permanent Peoples' Tribunal. (2018). A Call for Justice and Action for Myanmar, (21 September 2018) permanentpeoplestribunal.org/a-call-for-justice-and-action-for-myanmar-september-2017-september-2018-2/?lang=en.

Piccigallo, P. R. (1979). *The Japanese on Trial: Allied War Crimes Operations in the East, 1945–1951*. Dallas: University of Texas Press.

Picker, C. B. (2013). Comparative Legal Cultural Analyses of International Economic Law: A New Methodological Approach. *The Chinese Journal of Comparative Law*, 1(1), 21–48.

Pierce, P. & Reiger, C. (2014). *Navigating Paths to Justice in Myanmar*. International Center for Transitional Justice (June 2014) www.ictj.org/publication/navigating-paths-justice-myanmars-transition.

Pillai, P. (2018). Philippine Withdrawal from the International Criminal Court: 'Much Ado about Nothing' at the Philippine Supreme Court? (Part II), *Opinio*

Juris (18 October 2018) opiniojuris.org/2018/10/18/philippine-withdrawal-from-the-international-criminal-court-much-ado-about-nothing-at-the-philippine-supreme-court-part-ii.

Pinheiro, P. S. (2006). Situation of Human Rights in Myanmar, UN Doc. A/61/369 (21 September 2006).

Pohlman, A. (2015). Telling Stories about Torture in Indonesia: Managing Risk in a Culture of Impunity. *Oral History Forum*, 33, 1–17.

(2016). A Year of Truth and the Possibilities for Reconciliation in Indonesia. *Genocide Studies and Prevention: An International Journal*, 10(1), 60–78.

Ponniah, K. (2014). Complaint Filed at ICC, *The Phnom Penh Post* (8 October 2014) www.phnompenhpost.com/national/complaint-filed-icc.

Pramudatama, R. (2012). SBY to Apologize for Rights Abuses, *The Jakarta Post* (26 April 2012) www.thejakartapost.com/news/2012/04/26/sby-apologize-rights-abuses.html.

Prasse-Freeman, E. (2012). Power, Civil Society, and an Inchoate Politics of the Daily in Burma/Myanmar. *The Journal of Asian Studies*, 71(2), 371–97.

Prévost, A. M. (1992). Race and War Crimes: The 1945 War Crimes Trial of General Tomoyuki Yamashita. *Human Rights Quarterly*, 14(3), 303–38.

Price, R. (2008). Moral Limit and Possibility in World Politics. *International Organizations*, 62(2), 191–220.

Price, R. & Reus-Smit, C. (1998). Dangerous Liaisons? Critical International Theory and Constructivism. *European Journal of International Relations*, 4(3), 259–94.

Prime Minister of Australia, Minister for Foreign Affairs and Minister for Defence. (2013). Australia's Support for Reform in Myanmar, (18 March 2013) reliefweb.int/report/myanmar/australias-support-reform-myanmar.

Progressive Voice. (2018). UN Security Council Must Act Now and Refer the Situation in Myanmar to the International Criminal Court, (25 October 2018) progressivevoicemyanmar.org/wp-content/uploads/2018/10/Final-PR-Oct-25.pdf.

Quintana, T. O. (2010). Progress Report of the Special Rapporteur on the Situation of Human Rights in Myanmar, a Report by the Human Rights Council, UN Doc. A/HRC/13/48 (10 March 2010).

(2014). Report of the Special Rapporteur on the Situation of Human Rights in Myanmar, Tomás Ojea Quintana, UN Doc. A/HRC/25/64 (2 April 2014).

Raab, M. & Poluda, J. (2006). Justice for the Survivors and for Future Generations ADHOC's ECCC/ICC Justice Project December 2006 – March 2010, ADHOC, European Union, ticambodia.org/library/wp-content/files_mf/1437363833ADHOC_KRT_evaluation_RaabPoluda_final003201.pdf.

Rahmawati, M., ed. (2018). *Catatan dan Rekomendasi: Aliansi Nasional Reformasi KUHP Terhadap Rancangan KUHP* [Notes and Recommendations: National Alliance of Criminal Code Reform against Draft Criminal Code],

(28 May 2018) icjr.or.id/data/wp-content/uploads/2018/11/DIM-RKUHP-Baru_Final_30112018.pdf.

Ramadani, R. (2015). Public Discussion: 1965 History in the Nedia, *Arkipel* (27 September 2015) arkipel.org/public-discussion-1965-history-in-the-media.

Ratner, S. R. Abrams, J. S., & Bischoff, J. L. (2009). *Accountability for Human Rights Atrocities in International Law: Beyond the Nuremberg Legacy*. Oxford: Oxford University Press.

Reiger, C. & Wierda, M. (2006). *The Serious Crimes Process in Timor-Leste: In Restrospect*, International Center for Transitional Justice, (March 2006) www.ictj.org/sites/default/files/ICTJ-TimorLeste-Criminal-Process-2006-English.pdf.

Renshaw, C. S. (2014). The Regional Context of Myanmar's Democratic Transition: What Role for ASEAN's New Institutions. In M. Crouch & T. Lindsey, eds., *Law, Society and Transition in Myanmar*. Oxford: Hart Publishing, pp. 359–76.

Republic of Indonesia. (2010). Statement by Mr. Mulya Wirana, Head of Indonesian Delegation to the Review Conference of the Rome Statute, Kampala, 31 Mei – 11 June 2010, asp.icc-cpi.int/iccdocs/asp_docs/RC2010/Statements/ICC-RC-gendeba-Indonesia-ENG.pdf.

Republic of the Philippines. (2010). Review Conference of the Rome Statute of the International Criminal Court, (1 June 2010) archive.iccnow.org/documents/ICC-RC-gendeba-Philippines-ENG.pdf.

(2011). Statement by H. E. Libran N Cabactulan, Permanent Representative, Philippine Mission to the United Nations at the 10th Session of the Assembly of States Parties, (14 December 2011) www.iccnow.org/documents/ICC-ASP10-GenDeba-Philippines-ENG.pdf.

(2012). National Report Submitted in Accordance with Paragraph 5 of the Annex to Human Rights Council Resolution 16/21: Philippines, UN Doc. A/HRC/WG.6/13/PHL/1. (19 March 2012).

(2013). Statement by H. E. Libran N. Cabactulan, Permanent Representative of the Republic of the Philippines to the United Nations, General Debate, 12th session of the Assembly of States Parties, (21 November 2013) asp.icc-cpi.int/iccdocs/asp_docs/ASP12/GenDeba/ICC-ASP12-GenDeba-Philippines-ENG.pdf.

(2014). Statement at the General Debate of the 13th Assembly of States Parties to the Rome Statute of the International Criminal Court, (11 December 2014) www.un.int/philippines/statements_speeches/statement-general-debate-13th-assembly-states-parties-rome-statute-international.

(2015). Statement of the Philippines, General Debate at the 14th Session of the Assembly of States Parties of the Rome Statuteof the International Criminal Court, (19 November 2015) asp.icc-cpi.int/iccdocs/asp_docs/ASP14/GenDeb/ASP14-GenDeb-Phillippines-ENG.pdf.

(2016). Statement of the Philippines, General Debate of the 15th Assembly of States Parties to the Rome Statute of the International Criminal Court, (17 November 2016) asp.icc-cpi.int/iccdocs/asp_docs/ASP15/GenDeba/ICC-ASP15-GenDeba-Philippines-ENG.pdf.

Republic of the Union of Myanmar. (2013). Final Report of Inquiry Commission on Sectarian Violence in Rakhine State, (8 July 2013) www.burmalibrary.org/docs15/Rakhine_Commission_Report-en-red.pdf.

(2017). Statement by His Excellency U Thaung Tun, National Security Advisor to the Union Government of the Republic of the Union of Myanmar at the ARRIA Formula Meeting of the Security Council on the Situation in Myanmar, (13 October 2017) www.statecounsellor.gov.mm/en/node/1091.

(2018). Press Release, (13 April 2018) www.statecounsellor.gov.mm/en/node/1884.

Reuters. (2018). Philippines Police Jailed for Murdering Teenager in Duterte's Drug War, *The Guardian* (29 November 2018) www.theguardian.com/world/2018/nov/29/philippines-police-jailed-for-murdering-teenager-in-dutertes-drug-war.

RT. (2016). Western Court Threats Are Bullsh*t, European Lawyers Stupid: Duterte on Possible Indictment, *RT* (28 November 2016) www.rt.com/news/368468-duterte-court-threats-stupid.

Reza, B. I. (2014). Prevent new Military Discipline Law from Leading to Impunity, *The Jakarta Post* (6 October 2014) www.thejakartapost.com/news/2014/10/06/prevent-new-military-discipline-law-leading-impunity.html.

Rhoads, E. J. & Wittekind, C. T. (2018). Rethinking Land and Property in a 'Transitioning' Myanmar: Representations of Isolation, Neglect, and Natural Decline. *The Journal of Burma Studies*, 22(2), 171–213.

Richmond, O. P. (2011). De-romanticising the Local, De-mystifying the International: Hybridity in Timor Leste and the Solomon Islands. *The Pacific Review*, 24(1), 115–36.

Riles, A. (1995). The View from the International Plane: Perspective and Scale in the Architecture of Colonial International Law. *Law and Critique*, 6(1), 39–54.

Risse, T. (2017). Human Rights in Areas of Limited Statehood: From the Spiral Model to Localization and Translation. In S. Hopgood, J. Snyder, & L. Vinjamuri, eds., *Human Rights Futures*. Cambridge: Cambridge University Press, pp. 135–58.

Risse, T., Ropp S. C., & Sikkink K. eds. (1999). *The Power of Human Rights: International Norms and Domestic Change*. Cambridge: Cambridge University Press.

Risse, T. & Sikkink, K. (1999). The Socialization of International Human Rights Norms into Domestic Practices: Introduction. In T. Risse, S. C. Ropp, & K. Sikkink, eds., *The Power of Human Rights: International*

Norms and Domestic Change. Cambridge: Cambridge University Press, pp. 1–38.

Robins, S. (2012). Challenging the Therapeutic Ethic: A Victim-Centred Evaluation of Transitional Justice Process in Timor-Leste. *International Journal of Transitional Justice*, 6(1), 83–105.

Robinson, G. (2010). *If You Leave Us Here, We Will Die. How Genocide Was Stopped in East Timor.* Princeton, NJ: Princeton University Press.

Roht-Arriaza, N. (2002). Civil Society in Processes of Accountability. In M. Cherif Bassiouni, ed., *Post-Conflict Justice.* Ardsley: Transnational Publishers, pp. 97–114.

(2013). Just a 'Bubble'? Perspectives on the Enforcement of International Criminal Law by National Courts. *Journal of International Criminal Justice,* 11(3), 537–43.

Röling, B. V. A. & Rüter, C. F. (1977). *The Tokyo Judgment: The International Military Tribunal for the Far East (I.M.T.F.E.), 29 April 1946–12 November 1948.* Amsterdam: University Press Amsterdam.

Roux, T. (2014). Judging the Quality of Legal Research: A Qualified Response to the Demand for Greater Methodological Rigour. *Legal Education Review,* 24, 177–204.

Royal Government of Cambodia. (2004). The Khmer Rouge Trial Task Force Indictments and Detention Orders, Ung Choeun, known as Ta Mok, and Kaing Khek Iev, known as Duch, (19 February 2004) www.cambodia.gov.kh/ krt/english/indictments.htm.

Ruggie, J. G. (1998). What Makes the World Hang Together? Neo-utilitarianism and the Social Constructivist Challenge. *International Organization,* 52(4), 855.

Ryan, H. (2015). New Year, Same Problems at ECCC, (9 January 2015) www.ijmonitor.org/2015/01/new-year-same-problems-at-eccc/?utm_source= International+Justice+Monitor&utm_campaign=ffd58c2e08-khmer-rouge& utm_medium=email&utm_term=0_f42ffeffb9-ffd58c2e08-49422597.

Sandra, R. & Abidin, Z. CICC. (2012). Intervention, ICSCICC, (16 November 2012) advokasi.elsam.or.id/assets/2015/09/20121116_Siaran-pers_Intervention-Idonesian-CICC.pdf.

Santos Jr, S. M. (2003). Correspondents' Reports: The Philippines. *Yearbook of International Humanitarian Law,* 6, 561–78.

Sarkin, J. (2000). Dealing with Past Human Rights Abuses: Promoting Reconciliation in a Future Democratic Burma. *Legal Issues on Burma Journal,* 7, www.burmalibrary.org/docs/Legal%20Issues%20on%20Burma%20Journal%207.pdf.

Sapiie, M. A. (2016). Wiranto Vows to Settle Historic Human Rights Abuses, *The Jakarta Post* (15 September 2016) www.thejakartapost.com/news/2016/09/15/wiranto-vows-to-settle-historic-human-rights-abuses.html.

Schabas, W. (2000). *Genocide in International Law: The Crime of Crimes*. Cambridge: Cambridge University Press.

(2001). Problems of International Codification – Were the Atrocities in Cambodia and Kosovo Genocide? *New England Law Review*, 35(2), 287–302.

Schaefer, B. & Wardaya, B. T., eds. (2013). *1965: Indonesia and the World, Indonesia Dan Dunia*. Jakarta: Goethe-Institut and Gramedia Pustaka Utama.

Scheffer, D. (2008). The Extraordinary Chambers in the Courts of Cambodia. In M. C. Bassiouni, ed., *International Criminal Law: International Enforcement*. Leiden: Martinus Nijhoff Publishers, pp. 219–55.

(2012). *All the Missing Souls: A Personal History of the War Crimes Tribunals, Human Rights and Crimes against Humanity*. Princeton, NJ: Princeton University Press, pp. 341–405.

Schiff, B. (2008). *Building the International Criminal Court*. Cambridge: Cambridge University Press.

Schoepfel-Aboukrat, A-S. (2014). The War Court as a Form of State Building: The French Prosecution of Japanese War Crimes at the Saigon and Tokyo Trials. In M. Bergsmo, W. L. Cheah, & P. Yi, eds., *Historical Origins of International Criminal Law: Volume 2*. Torkel Opsahl Academic EPublisher, pp. 119–41.

Schouten, L. (2015). Colonial Justice in the Netherlands Indies War Crimes Trials. In K. Sellars, ed., *Trials for International Crimes in Asia*. Cambridge: Cambridge University Press, pp. 75–99.

Schroeder, M. B. & Tiemessen, A. (2014). Transnational Advocacy and Accountability: From Declarations of Anti-Impunity to Implementing the Rome Statute. In A. Betts & P. Orchard, eds., *Implementation and World Politics: How International Norms Change Practice*. Oxford: Oxford University Press, pp. 50–67.

Schuldt, L. (2015). Southeast Asian Hesitation: ASEAN Countries and the International Criminal Court. *German Law Journal*, 16(1), 75–105.

Schwöbel, C. (2014). Introduction. In C. Schwöbel, ed., *Critical Approaches to International Criminal Law: An Introduction*. New York: Routledge, pp. 1–14.

Selbmann, F. (2016). The 1979 Trial of the People's Revolutionary Tribunal and Implications for ECCC. In S. Meisenberg & I. Stegmiller, eds., *The Extraordinary Chambers in the Courts of Cambodia: Assessing Their Contribution to International Criminal Law*. The Hague: TMC Asser Press, pp. 77–102.

Sellars, K., ed. (2015). *Trials for International Crimes in Asia*. Cambridge: Cambridge University Press.

Selth, A. (2002). *Burma's Armed Forces: Power without Glory*. Manchester: East-Bridge Books.

Setianti, L. (2015). *Konstitusionalisme Penyelesaian Pelanggaran HAM Masa Lalu: Jalan Indonesia Tidak Tunggal* [The Constitutionalism of Resolving Past

Human Rights Violations: There Is Not a Single Way] (21 August 2015), elsam.or.id/konstitusionalisme-penyelesaian-pelanggaran-ham-masa-lalu-jalan-indonesia-tidak-tunggal.

Setiawan, K. (2016). The Politics of Compromise, Inside Indonesia, (27 January 2016) www.insideindonesia.org/the-politics-of-compromise.

Shany, Y. (2013). Seeking Domestic Help: The Role of Domestic Criminal Law in Legitimizing the Work of International Criminal Tribunals. *Journal of International Criminal Justice*, 11, 5–26.

Shaw, R. & Waldorf, L. (2010). Introduction: Localizing Transitional Justice. In R. Shaw, L. Waldorf, & P. Hazan, eds., *Localizing Transitional Justice: Interventions and Priorities after Mass Violence*, Palo Alto, CA: Stanford University Press, pp. 3–36.

Shaw, R., Waldorf, L., & Hazan, P. eds. (2010), *Localizing Transitional Justice: Interventions and Priorities after Mass Violence*. Palo Alto, CA: Stanford University Press.

Sikkink, K. (2011a). Beyond the Justice Cascade: How Agentic Constructivism Could Help Explain Change in International Politics. Paper presented at the Princeton IR Colloquium, 21 November, Princeton University.

(2011b). *The Justice Cascade: How Human Rights Prosecutions Are Changing World Politics*. New York: W. W. Norton & Company.

Sikkink, K. & Kim, H. J. (2013). The Justice Cascade: The Origins and Effectiveness of Prosecutions of Human Rights Violations. *Annual Review of Law and Social Science*, 9(1), 269–85.

Simmons, B. A. & Danner, A. (2010). Credible Commitments and the International Criminal Court. *International Organization*, 64(2), 225–56.

Simpson, B. (2017). U.S. Embassy Tracked Indonesia Mass Murder 1965, (17 October 2017) nsarchive.gwu.edu/briefing-book/indonesia/2017-10-17/indonesia-mass-murder-1965-us-embassy-files.

Simpson, G. (2007). *Law, War & Crime: War Crimes, Trials and the Reinvention of International Law*. Cambridge: Polity Press.

(2014). Linear Law: The History of International Criminal Law. In C. Schwöbel, ed., *Critical Approaches to International Criminal Law: An Introduction*. New York: Routledge, pp. 159–79.

Slaughter, A-M., Tulumello, A. S., & Wood, S. (1998). International Law and International Relations Theory: A New Generation of Interdisciplinary Scholarship. *American Journal of International Law*, 92(3), 367–87.

Slim, W. (1998). The British Reconquest of Burma, 1945. Extract from Field Marshall Sir William Slim, 'Defeat into Victory'. In C. J. Christie, ed., *Southeast Asia in the Twentieth Century: A Reader*. London: I. B. Tauris, pp. 104–9.

Smith, D. (1993). *Texts, Facts, and Femininity: Exploring the Relations of Ruling*. New York: Routledge.

Sok An, (2004). Presentation by Deputy Prime Minister Sok An to the National Assembly on Ratification of the Agreement between Cambodia and the United Nations and Amendments to the 2001 Law Concerning the Establishment of Extraordinary Chambers in the Courts of Cambodia for the Prosecution of Crimes Committed during the Period of Democratic Kampuchea, www.eccc.gov.kh/sites/default/files/legal-documents/Sok_An_Speech_to_NA_on_Ratification_and_Amendments-En.pdf.

Sokchea, M. (2014). ICC Complaint to Lay Shootings at PM's Feet, *The Phnom Penh Post* (7 January 2014) www.phnompenhpost.com/national/icc-complaint-lay-shootings-pm%E2%80%99s-feet.

Sokha, C. & O'Toole, J. (2010). Hun Sen to Ban Ki-moon: Case 002 Last Trial at ECCC, *The Phnom Penh Post* (27 October 2010) www.phnompenhpost.com/national/hun-sen-ban-ki-moon-case-002-last-trial-eccc.

Sokheng, V. (2002). Ranariddh Prefers UN Trial Role, *The Phnom Penh Post* (12 April 2002) www.phnompenhpost.com/national/ranariddh-prefers-un-trial-role.

Song, S-H. (2011). Role of Asian Lawyers in the Emerging System International Criminal Justice, (10 October 2011) www.icc-cpi.int/iccdocs/PIDS/press/WU99/111010ICCPresidentkeynotespeech.pdf.

  (2013). Preventive Potential of the International Criminal Court. *Asian Journal of International Law*, 3(2), 203–13.

  (2016). International Criminal Court-Centred International Criminal Justice and Its Challenges. *Melbourne Journal of International Law*, 17(1), 1–14.

Sornito, I. (2018). NPA Strikes Back, *Panay News* (25 August 2018) www.panaynews.net/npa-strikes-back.

Soumy, P. (2016). CPP 'Not Worried' about International Court's Decision, *The Cambodia Daily* (19 September 2016) www.cambodiadaily.com/news/cpp-not-worried-regarding-international-courts-decision-118149.

Sperfeldt, C. (2012a) Cambodian Civil Society and the Khmer Rouge Tribunal. *International Journal of Transitional Justice*, 6(1), 149–60.

  (2012b). Collective Reparations at the Extraordinary Chambers in the Courts of Cambodia. *International Criminal Law Review*, 12(3), 457–90.

  (2013). From the Margins of Internationalized Criminal Justice: Lessons Learned at the Extraordinary Chambers in the Courts of Cambodia. *Journal of International Criminal Justice*, 11, 1111–37.

  (2014). Broadcasting Justice: Media Outreach at the Khmer Rouge Tribunals, *AsiaPacific Issues*, 115, www.eastwestcenter.org/publications/broadcasting-justice-media-outreach-the-khmer-rouge-trials.

Sperfeldt, C., Hyde M., & Balthazard, M. (2016). *Voices for Reconciliation: Assessing Media Outreach and Survivor Engagement for Case 002 at the Khmer Rouge Trials*. East-West Center, WSD Handa Center for Human Rights & International Justice, www.eastwestcenter.org/publications/voices-reconciliation-assessing-media-outreach-and-survivor-engagement-case-002-the.

Stahn, C. (2015). Justice Civilisatrice? The ICC, Post-Colonial Theory, and Faces of 'the Local'. In C. de Vos, S. Kendall, & C. Stahn, eds., *Contested Justice: The Politics and Practice of International Criminal Court Interventions*. Cambridge: Cambridge University Press, pp. 46–84.

Stahn, C. & van den Herik, L. (2012). 'Fragmentation', Diversification and '3D' Legal Pluralism: International Criminal Law as the Jack-in-the-Box? In C. Stahn & L. van den Herik, eds., *The Diversification and Fragmentation of International Criminal Law*. Leiden: Martinus Nijhoff Publishers, pp. 21–90.

State Counsellor Office. (2016a). Government Refutes Rights Group Report on Rakhine, (17 November 2016) www.statecounsellor.gov.mm/en/node/366.

(2016b). Rakhine Efforts Need Time and Space: State Counsellor, (20 December 2016) www.statecounsellor.gov.mm/en/node/532.

(2017a). State Counsellor: UN Rakhine Probe Would Have Increased Tensions, (13 June 2017) www.statecounsellor.gov.mm/en/node/937.

(2017b). A Roundtable on Counter-Terrorism between Myanmar and Indonesia, (24 August 2017) www.statecounsellor.gov.mm/en/node/1013.

(2017c). Speech delivered by Her Excellency Daw Aung San Suu Kyi, State Counsellor of the Republic of the Union of Myanmar on Government's Efforts with Regard to National Reconciliation and Peace, (19 September 2017) www.statecounsellor.gov.mm/en/node/1028.

(2017d). The State Counsellor Dan Aung San Suu Kyi's Exclusive Interview with Nikkei Asian Review, (22 September 2017) www.statecounsellor.gov.mm/en/node/1035.

(2017e). Ministry of Foreign Affairs Issues a Press Release Regarding OHCHR's Report Titled 'Interviews with Rohingyas Fleeing from Myanmar since 9th October 2016', (8 February 2017) www.statecounsellor.gov.mm/en/node/666.

(2017f). Statement by the Office of the State Counsellor on the Final Report of the Advisory Commission on Rakhine State, (25 August 2017) www.statecounsellor.gov.mm/en/node/998.

(2018). Statement by H. E. U Kyaw Tint Swe Union Minister for the Office of the State Counsellor and Chairman of the Delegation of the Republic of the Union of Myanmar at the General Debate of the 73rd Session of the United Nations General Assembly New York, (28 September 2018) www.statecounsellor.gov.mm/en/node/2155.

Steer, C. (2014). Legal Transplants or Legal Patchworking? The Creation of International Criminal Law as a Pluralistic Body of Law. In E. van Sliedregt & S. Vasiliev, eds., *Pluralism in International Criminal Law*. Oxford: Oxford University Press, pp. 39–67.

Stegmiller, I. (2014). Legal Developments in Civil Party Participation at the Extraordinary Chambers in the Courts of Cambodia. *Leiden Journal of International Law*, 27(2), 465–77.

Steinberg, D. L. (2001). The Burmese Conundrum. In R. H. Taylor, ed., *Burma: Political Economy under Military Rule*. London: C Hurst & Co., pp. 41–69.

Steinberg, D. I. (2015). Myanmar and the United States, Closing and Opening Doors: An Idiosyncratic Analysis. *Social Research*, 82(2), 427–52.

Straits Times. (2018). Myanmar Must Bring Rohingya Genocide Culprits to Justice: Malaysian Minister Saifuddin Abdullah, *Straits Times* (29 August 2018) www.straitstimes.com/asia/se-asia/myanmar-must-bring-rohingya-genocide-culprits-to-justice-malaysian-minister-saifuddin.

Struett, M. J. (2008). *The Politics of Constructing the International Criminal Court: NGOs, Discourse, and Agency*. New York: Palgrave Macmillan.

Studzinsky, S. (2011). Neglected Crimes: The Challenge of Raising Sexual and Gender-Based Crimes before the Extraordinary Chambers in the Courts of Cambodia. In S. Buckley-Zistel & R. Stanley, eds., *Gender in Transitional Justice*. New York: Palgrave Macmillan, pp. 88–112.

Suh, J. (2012). The Politics of Transitional Justice in Post-Suharto Indonesia. PhD Thesis, Ohio State University.

Takemura, H. (2018). The Asian Region and the International Criminal Court. In Y. Nakanishi, ed., *Contemporary Issues in Human Rights Law: Europe and Asia*, pp. 107–25.

Talabong, R. (2017). PNP Says 125 Cops Punished for Drug War-Related offenses, *Rappler* (28 November 2017) www.rappler.com/nation/189788-police-pun ished-pnp-ias-drug-war-sc-ejk.

Tallgren, I. (2002). The Sensibility and Sense of International Criminal Law. *European Journal of International Law*, 13, 561–95.

Tan, N. F. (2015). Prabowo and the Shortcomings of International Justice. *Griffith Journal of Law & Human Dignity*, 3(1), 103–17.

Tanyang, M. (2015). Unravelling the Intersections of Power: The Case of Sexual and Reproductive Freedom in the Philippines. *Women's Studies International Forum*, 53, 63–72.

TAPOL. (1975). East Timor: Indonesian Takeover Means Bloodshed and Terror, *Tapol Bulletin* (October 1975) vuir.vu.edu.au/26422/1/TAPOL12_ compressed.pdf.

Tashandra, N. (2016). *Didukung Ryamizard, Purnawirawan TNI Akan Bentuk Simposium Lawan PKI* [Defence minister backs move by retired TNI officers to hold anti-PKI symposium], *Kompas* (13 May 2016) nasional.kompas.com/read/2016/05/13/15530051/Didukung.Ryamizard .Purnawirawan.TNI.Akan.Bentuk.Simposium.Lawan.PKI.

Taylor, R. H. (2007). The Legacies of World War II for Myanmar. In D. K. W. Hock, ed., *Legacies of World War II in South and East Asia*. Singapore: Institute of Southeast Asian Studies, pp. 60–73.

(2008). Finding the Political in Myanmar, a.k.a. Burma. *Journal of Southeast Asian Studies*, 39(2), 219–37.

Teilee, K. (2010). Cambodian Constitutional Provisions on Treaties: A Story of Constitutional Evolution Beyond Rhetoric (2010). *Cambodian Yearbook on Comparative Legal Studies*, 1, 1–16.

Teitel, R. G. (2000). *Transitional Justice*. Oxford: Oxford University Press.

(2003). Transitional Justice Geneology. *Harvard Human Rights Journal*, 16, 69–94.

Tek, F. & Sperfeldt, C. (2016). Justice and Truth-Seeking for Survivors of Gender-Based Violence under the Khmer Rouge. In P. Tolliday, M. Palme, & D-C. Kim, eds., *Asia-Pacific between Conflict and Reconciliation*. Gottingen, Germany: Vandenhoeck & Ruprecht, pp. 125–38.

The Jakarta Post. (2016). Attempts at Formal Reconciliation 'Will Reopen Old Wounds', *The Jakarta Post* (3 June 2016) www.thejakartapost.com/news/2016/06/03/attempts-at-formal-reconciliation-will-reopen-old-wounds.html.

Thein Sein (2016). President U Thein Sein's State of the Union Address to the Pyidaungsu Hluttaw, *The Global New Light of Myanmar* (29 January 2016) www.globalnewlightofmyanmar.com/president-u-thein-seins-state-of-the-union-address-to-the-pyidaungsu-hluttaw.

Thomson, A. (2015). Opening up Remedies in Myanmar, International Center for Transitional Justice (12 September 2015) www.ictj.org/publication/opening-remedies-myanmar?utm_source=International+Center+for+Transitional+Justice+Newsletter&utm_campaign=c372e4dca7-ICTJ_In_Focus_Issue_52_January_2015&utm_medium=email&utm_term=0_2d90950d4d-c372e4dca7-246000193.

Thorburn, C. (2008). Adat Law, Conflict and Reconciliation: The Kei Islands, Southeast Maluku. In T. Lindsey, ed., *Indonesia: Law and Society*. Sydney: The Federation Press, pp. 115–43.

Titthara, M. (2015). Bandith's behind Bars, *The Phnom Penh Post* (10 August 2015) www.phnompenhpost.com/national/bandiths-behind-bars.

Toon, V. (2004). International Criminal Court: Reservations of Non-State Parties in Southeast Asia. *Contemporary Southeast Asia*, 26(2), 218–32.

Topsfield, J. (2017). Indonesia, Australia Military Co-operation on Hold for 'Technical Reasons', *The Sydney Morning Herald* (4 January 2017) www.smh.com.au/world/indonesia-australia-military-cooperation-on-hold-for-technical-reasons-20170104-gtltai.html.

Torres III, W. M., ed. (2014). Rido: Clan Feuding and Conflict Management in Mindanao, Ateneo de Manila University Press, asiafoundation.org/resources/pdfs/PHridoexcerpt.pdf.

Totani, Y. (2014). *Justice in Asia and the Pacific Region, 1945–1952: Allied War Crimes Prosecutions*. Cambridge: Cambridge University Press.

TPO Cambodia. (2015). Promoting Healing & Reconciliation through Psychosocial Interventions, tpocambodia.org/promoting-healing-and-reconciliation.

Transitional Justice and Reconciliation Commission. (2016). Report of the Transitional Justice and Reconciliation Commission, cdn.viiworksdemo.com/pdf/j7im-report.pdf.

Transitional Justice Research Collaborative. Cambodia, transitionaljusticedata.com/browse/index/Browse.countryid:19.

Tsing, A. L. (2005). *Friction: An Ethnography of Global Connection.* Princeton, NJ: Princeton University Press.

Tusalem, R. F. (2019). Examining the Determinants of Extra-Judicial Killings in the Philippines at the Subnational Level: The Role of Penal Populism and Vertical Accountability. *Human Rights Review,* 20(1), 67 –101.

Ullrich, L. (2016). Beyond the 'Global–Local Divide': Local Intermediaries, Victims and the Justice Contestations of the International Criminal Court. *Journal of International Criminal Justice,* 14(3), 543–68.

United Nations General Assembly. (2018). Resolution adopted by the Human Rights Council on 27 September 2018, Situation of human rights of Rohingya Muslims and other minorities in Myanmar, UN Res. A/HRC/RES/39/2.

UN Commission of Experts. (2005). Summary and Report to the Secretary-General of the Commission of Experts to Review the Prosecution of Serious Violations of Human Rights in Timor-Leste (then East Timor) in 1999, UN Doc. S/2005/458 (15 July 2005, 26 May 2005), Annex I (Summary).

UN Human Rights Council. (2008a). Report of the Working Group on the Universal Periodic Review: Indonesia, UN Doc. A/HRC/8/23 (14 May 2008).

(2008b). Report of the Working Group on the Universal Periodic Review: The Philippines, UN Doc. A/HRC/8/28 (23 May 2008).

(2010). Report of the Working Group on the Universal Periodic Review: Cambodia, UN Doc. A/HRC/13/4 (4 January 2010).

(2012a). Report of the Working Group on the Universal Periodic Review: Indonesia, UN Doc. A/HRC/21/7 (5 July 2012).

(2012b). Report of the Working Group on the Universal Periodic Review: Philippines, UN Doc. A/HRC/21/12 (9 July 2012).

(2015). Report of the Working Group on the Universal Periodic Review: Myanmar, UN Doc. A/HRC/31/13 (23 December 2015).

(2015). Report of the OHCHR Investigation on Sri Lanka (OISL), UN Doc. A/HRC/30/CRP.2 (16 September 2015).

(2016). Report of the Working Group on the Universal Periodic Review: Myanmar, Addendum, Views on Conclusions and/or Recommendations, Voluntary Commitments and Replies Presented by the State under Review, UN Doc A/HRC/31/13/Add.1 (10 March 2016).

(2017a) Report of the Working Group on the Universal Periodic Review: Indonesia, UN Doc. A/HRC/36/7 (14 July 2007).

(2017b). Report of the Working Group on the Universal Periodic Review: Philippines, UN Doc. A/HRC/36/12 (18 July 2017).

(2019). Resolution on the Promotion and Protection of Human rights in the Philippines, UN Doc. A/HRC/41/L.20 (5 July 2019).

UN International Commission of Inquiry on East Timor. (2000). Report of the International Commission of Inquiry on East Timor to the Secretary General, UN Doc. A/54/726, S/2000/59 (31 January 2000).

UN Office of the High Commissioner of Human Rights. (2019). UN Human Rights Experts Call for Independent Probe into Philippines Violations (7 June 2019) www.ohchr.org/EN/NewsEvents/Pages/DisplayNews.aspx?NewsID=24679&LangID=E.

United Nations. (1997). Identical letters dated 23 June 1997 from the Secretary-General addressed to the President of the General Assembly and to the President of the Security Council, UN Doc. A/51/930 S/1997/488 (24 June 1997) www.eccc.gov.kh/sites/default/files/June_21_1997_letters_from_PMs-2.pdf.

(1998). Summary records of the plenary meetings and of the meetings of the Committee of the Whole (Volume II), United Nations Diplomatic Conference of Plenipotentiaries on the Establishment of an International Criminal Court, UN Doc. A/CONF.183/13 (Vol. II), 15 June–17 July 1998, legal.un.org/icc/rome/proceedings/contents.htm.

United Nations General Assembly. (1999). Situation of Human Rights in East Timor, UN Doc. A/54/660 (10 December 1999).

(2002). Statement by UN Legal Counsel Hans Corell: Negotiations between the UN and Cambodia regarding the establishment of the court to try Khmer Rouge leaders, (8 February 2002) www.un.org/press/en/2002/db020802.doc.htm.

(2007). Security Council Fails to Adopt Draft Resolution on Myanmar, Owing to Negative Votes by China, Russian Federation, Press Release SC/8939 (12 January 2007) www.un.org/press/en/2007/sc8939.doc.htm.

(2013). Role and achievements of the Office of the United Nations High Commissioner for Human Rights in assisting the Government and people of Cambodia in the promotion and protection of human rights, UN Doc. A/HRC/24/32 (19 September 2013).

(2015). Security Council Fails to Adopt Resolution on Tribunal for Malaysia Airlines Crash in Ukraine, Amid Calls for Accountability, Justice for Victims, (30 July 2015) un.org.au/2015/07/30/security-council-fails-to-adopt-resolution-on-tribunal-for-malaysia-airlines-crash-in-ukraine-amid-calls-for-accountability-justice-for-victims.

(2017). Myanmar: UN Experts Request Exceptional Report on Situation of Women and Girls from Northern Rakhine State, (28 November 2017) www.ohchr.org/EN/NewsEvents/Pages/DisplayNews.aspx?NewsID=22459&LangID=E.

(2018). Myanmar's Refugee Problem among World's Worst Humanitarian, Human Rights Crises, Secretary-General Says in Briefing to Security Council: SC/13468, (28 August 2018) www.un.org/press/en/2018/sc13469.doc.htm.

United Nations Treaties. (2018). Reference C.N. 138.2018. TREATIES-XVIII.10 (Depositary Notification) Rome Statute of the International Criminal Court, Rome, 17 July 1998, Philippines: Withdrawal, (17 March 2018) treaties.un.org/doc/Publication/CN/2018/CN.138.2018-Eng.pdf.

United Nations General Assembly. (1998). Situation of Human Rights in Cambodia, UN Doc. A/RES/52/135 (27 February 1998).

  (2003). Resolution Adopted by the General Assembly on the Report of the Third Committee, 57/228, Khmer Rouge trials, UN Doc. A/RES/57/228 (27 February 2003).

United Nations High Commissioner for Human Rights. (2015). Summary prepared by the Office of the United Nations High Commissioner for Human Rights in accordance with paragraph 15 (c) of the annex to Human Rights Council resolution 5/1 and paragraph 5 of the annex to Council resolution 16/21: Myanmar, UN Doc. A/HRC/WG.6/23/MMR/3 (28 August 2015).

United Nations Secretary-General. (1993). Report of the Secretary-General Pursuant to Paragraph 2 of Security Council Resolution 808 (1993), UN Doc. S/25704 (3 May 1993).

  (2003). Report of the Secretary-General on Khmer Rouge Trials, UN Doc. A/57/769 (31 March 2003).

United Nations Security Council. (2000). Letter Dated 18 February 2000 from the President of the Security Council to the Secretary-General, UN Doc. S/2000/137 (21 February 2000).

  (2004). Security Council Speakers Support Extension of Timor-Leste Mission for Final Six Months, until 20 May 2005, (15 November 2004) www.un.org/press/en/2004/sc8243.doc.htm.

  (2005). Presidents, Prosecutors of Rwanda, Former Yugoslavia Tribunals Brief Security Council on Progress in Implementing Completion Strategies, (15 December 2005) www.un.org/press/en/2005/sc8586.doc.htm.

  (2007). China and Russia Veto US/UK-backed Security Council Draft Resolution on Myanmar, (12 January 2007) news.un.org/en/story/2007/01/205732-china-and-russia-veto-usuk-backed-security-council-draft-resolution-myanmar.

United States Department of State. (2013). Cambodia 2013 Human Rights Report, 2009–2017.state.gov/documents/organization/220395.pdf.

  (2018). Documentation of Atrocities in Northern Rakhine State, www.state.gov/reports-bureau-of-democracy-human-rights-and-labor/documentation-of-atrocities-in-northern-rakhine-state.

Urs, T. (2007). Imagining Locally-Motivated Accountability for Mass Atrocities: Voices from Cambodia. *International Journal of Human Rights*, 7, 61–99.

USAID. (2019). Democracy, Human Rights, and Rule of Law, (23 August 2019) www.usaid.gov/burma/our-work/democracy-human-rights-and-rule-law.

Valverde, M. (2015). *Chronotopes of Law: Jurisdiction, Scale and Governance*. New York: Routledge.

Van den Herik, L. (2012). Addressing 'Colonial Crimes' through Reparations? Adjudicating Dutch Atrocities Committed in Indonesia. *Journal of International Criminal Justice*, 10(3), 693–705.

Van Sliedregt, E. (2012). *Individual Criminal Responsibility in International Law*. Oxford: Oxford University Press.

Van Sliedregt, E. & Vasiliev, S. (2014). *Pluralism in International Criminal Law*. Oxford: Oxford University Press.

Vickers, A. (2013). *A History of Modern Indonesia*. Cambridge: Cambridge University Press.

Vickery, M. (1984). *Cambodia 1975–1982*. Crows Nest: George Allen and Unwin.

Vieira, L. (2012). The CAVR and the 2006 Displacement Crisis in Timor-Leste: Reflections on Truth-Telling, Dialogue, and Durable Solutions, International Center for Transitional Justice, (July 2012) www.ictj.org/sites/default/files/ICTJ-Brookings-Displacement-Truth-Telling-Timor-Leste-CaseStudy-2012-English.pdf.

Villamor, F. (2018a). Duterte Says, 'My Only Sin Is the Extrajudicial Killings', *The New York Times* (27 September 2018) www.nytimes.com/2018/09/27/world/asia/rodrigo-duterte-philippines-drug-war.html.

(2018b). International Criminal Court Will Investigate Duterte over Drug War, *The New York Times* (8 February 2018) www.nytimes.com/2018/02/08/world/asia/philippines-duterte-hague.html.

Wahyuningroem, A. (2016). Justice Denied?, *Inside Indonesia* (18 July 2016) www.insideindonesia.org/justice-denied.

Wahyuningroem, S. L. (2013). Seducing for Truth and Justice: Civil Society Initiatives for the 1965 Mass Violence in Indonesia. *Journal of Current Southeast Asian Affairs*, 32(3), 115–42.

Waller, E., Palmer, E. & Chappell, L. (2014). Strengthening Gender Justice in the Asia-Pacific through the Rome Statute. *Australian Journal of International Affairs*, 68(3), 356–73.

Walton, M. J. (2015). Monks in Politics, Monks in the World: Buddhist Activism in Contemporary Myanmar. *Social Research*, 82(2), 507–30.

Weber, M. (2013). Between 'Isses' and 'Oughts': IR Constructivism, Critical Theory, and the Challenge of Political Philosophy. *European Journal of International Relations*, 20(2), 516–43.

Wendt, A. (1999). *Social Theory of International Politics*. Cambridge: Cambridge University Press.

Weng, L. (2014). Burmese Govt Reversed MSF Ban Because of 'International Pressure, *The Irrawaddy* (28 July 2014) www.irrawaddy.org/burma/burmese-govt-reversed-msf-ban-international-pressure.html.

Westoby, R. G. (2013). Influencing Official and Unofficial Justice and Reconciliation Discourse in Cambodia: The Role of Local Non-State Actors and Institutions. PhD Thesis, University of Queensland.

White, S. (2014). KRT Trims Budget by Millions, *The Phnom Penh Post* (20 March 2014) www.phnompenhpost.com/national/krt-trims-budget-millions.

Widodo, J & Kalla, J. (2014). *Jalan Perubahan untuk Indonesia yang Berdaulat, Mandiri dan Berkepribadian: Visi Misi, dan Program Aksi* [The Roadmap for an Indonesia that is Sovereign, Independent, and has Personality/Individuality: Vision, Mission, and Programme of Action], (May 2014) kpu.go.id/koleksigambar/VISI_MISI_Jokowi-JK.pdf.

Wiener, A. (2014). *A Theory of Contestation.* New York: Springer.

Williams, D. C. (2014). What's So Bad about Burma's 2008 Constitution? A Guide for the Perplexed. In M. Crouch & T. Lindsey, eds., *Law, Society and Transition in Myanmar.* Portland: Hart Publishing, pp. 117–39.

Williams, P. (2009). The 'Responsibility to Protect', Norm Localisation, and African International Society. *Global Responsibility to Protect*, 1(3), 392–416.

Williams, S. & Palmer, E. (2015). The Extraordinary Chambers in the Courts of Cambodia: Developing the Law on Sexual Violence? *International Criminal Law Review*, 15(3), 452–84.

Women's League of Burma. (2014). Same Impunity, Same Patterns, (January 2014) burmacampaign.org.uk/media/same_impunity_same_patterns.pdf.

Women's League of Burma & AJAR. (2016). Briefing Paper: Access to Justice for Women Survivors of Gender-Based Violence Committed by State Actors in Burma, (24 November 2016) www.womenofburma.org/sites/default/files/2018-06/2016_Nov_VAW_BriefingPaper_Eng.pdf.

Woolaver, H. (2019). From Joining to Leaving: Domestic Law's Role in the International Validity of Treaty Withdrawal. *European Journal of International Law*, 30(1), 73–104.

World Bank. (2019a). Cambodia, data.worldbank.org/country/cambodia.

    (2019b). Net Official Development Assistance and Official Aid Received (Current US$), data.worldbank.org/indicator/DT.ODA.ALLD.CD.

Yam, D. J., Aning, J., & Agoncillo, J. A. (2018). Duterte Wants Maguindanao Massacre Prosecutions 'This Year', *The Philippine Daily Inquirer* (25 August 2018) newsinfo.inquirer.net/1031711/maguindanao-massacre-case-prosecutor-duterte-malacanang-roque.

Ye, B. (2014). Transitional Justice through the Cambodian Women's Hearings. *Cambodia Law and Policy Journal*, 5, 23–38.

Yun, S. & Lipes, J. (2013). Cambodia: Hun Sen Accused of 'Crimes against Humanity', *Radio Free Asia* (3 July 2013) www.rfa.org/english/news/cambodia/complaint-07032013183524.html.

Zan, M. (2008). Legal Education in Burma since the Mid-1960s. *Journal of Burma Studies*, 12(1), 63–107.

Zarakol, A. (2014). What Made the Modern World Hang Together: Socialisation or Stigmatisation? *International Theory*, 6(2), 311–32.

Zaw, H. N. (2017). U Zaw Htay: Kofi Annan Commission Is Govt 'Shield', *The Irrawaddy* (10 July 2017) www.irrawaddy.com/in-person/u-zaw-htay-kofi-annan-commission-govt-shield.html.

Zaw, J. (2018). UN Atrocities Probe Seeks Action against Myanmar, *UCA News* (26 October 2018) www.ucanews.org/news/un-atrocities-probe-seeks-action-against-myanmar/83722.

Zimmermann, L. (2016). Same Same or Different? Norm Diffusion between Resistance, Compliance, and Localization in Post-Conflict States. *International Studies Perspectives*, 17(1), 98–115.

(2017). *Global Norms with a Local Face: Rule-of-Law Promotion and Norm Translation*. Cambridge: Cambridge University Press.

INDEX

For EU product safety concerns, contact us at Calle de José Abascal, 56–1°, 28003 Madrid, Spain or eugpsr@cambridge.org.